UKRAINE AND RUSSIA: REPRESENTATIONS OF THE PAST

SERHII PLOKHY

Ukraine and Russia

Representations of the Past

UNIVERSITY OF TORONTO PRESS
Toronto Buffalo London

Toronto Buffalo London
www.utppublishing.com
Printed in Canada

ISBN 978-0-8020-9327-1

Printed on acid-free paper

Library and Archives Canada Cataloguing in Publication

Plokhy, Serhii, 1957–
Ukraine and Russia: representations of the past/Serhii Plokhii.

Includes bibliographical references and index.
ISBN 978-0-8020-9327-1

1. Ukraine – History – 20th century – Historiography. 2. Ukraine – History – 19th century – Historiography. 3. Nationalism – Ukraine – History – 20th century. 4. Nationalism – Ukraine – History – 19th century. I. Title.

DK508.8.P664 2008 947.7'084 C2007-905355-6

This book has been published with the help of a subvention from the Ukrainian Studies Fund, Inc., New York.

University of Toronto Press acknowledges the financial assistance to its publishing program of the Canada Council for the Arts and the Ontario Arts Council.

University of Toronto Press acknowledges the financial support for its publishing activities of the Government of Canada through the Book Publishing Industry Development Program (BPIDP).

To the memory of
Mykola Kovalsky (1929–2006)

Contents

Part Three: Post-Soviet Debates

Part Four: The Search for a New History

Acknowledgments

This book began with an invitation extended to me in 1993 by Karen Dawisha and Bruce Parrott, the organizers of the Russian Littoral Project supported by the University of Maryland and Johns Hopkins University, to present a paper on the impact of history on Ukrainian foreign policy and Ukrainian-Russian relations. Fascinated with the topic from the very beginning, I actually produced not one but two papers. One concerned the use and misuse of Cossack mythology in the frantic attempts of the late 1980s and early 1990s to secure the territorial integrity of Ukraine, while the other addressed the myth of Sevastopol in Russian historical tradition. Both these papers were subsequently published and now appear as chapters of this volume. Since then I have often returned to issues of Russo-Ukrainian relations and the ways in which they influenced (and were influenced by) the development of Ukrainian and Russian historiography and perceptions of the past. Before I knew it, I had more than a dozen articles, essays, and contributions to discussions linked by the overarching theme of the relations between politics, ideology, and history in Ukrainian historiography and Ukrainian-Russian relations of the period. Hence this book, whose purpose is not only to collect previously published and as yet unpublished contributions to the subject (chapters 1, 2, and 16 fall into the latter category) but also to encourage further research on the Ukrainian-Russian historiographic entanglement and its political and cultural ramifications.

Many people helped me with my original contributions and the preparation and production of the book. Frank E. Sysyn, Zenon E. Kohut, Andreas Kappeler, Oleh S. Ilnytzkyj, and John-Paul Himka made valuable comments on individual essays. Heather Coleman,

Anatolii Boiko, and Maksym Yaremenko shared with me their knowledge of sources and literature on the subject. Hiroaki Kuromiya and Nadieszda Kizenko gave excellent advice on how to improve the first draft of the manuscript. I am grateful to all of them for their help. I also wish to thank my colleague Myroslav Yurkevich for editing 'new' chapters and updates to 'old' ones, as well as for translating a chapter originally published in Ukrainian – as always, he has done a superb job. At the University of Toronto Press, my thanks go to Suzanne Rancourt for her interest in this project and encouragement of my efforts. It was a pleasure to work once again with Miriam Skey and Barbara Porter, who did an excellent job on my previous book. *Unmaking Imperial Russia*, published by the University of Toronto Press in 2005. I am grateful to Oksana Mykhed for compiling the index to this book. I would also like to thank Dr Roman Procyk of the Ukrainian Studies Fund (USA) for helping to secure a subsidy for the publication of this volume. My special thanks go to my wife, Olena. Without her support through all these years, the project would never have come to fruition. I dedicate this book to the memory of Mykola Kovalsky, my professor and dissertation supervisor at the University of Dnipropetrovsk, who was a lifelong student of Russo-Ukrainian relations.

Any errors and shortcomings that may be encountered in this book are my sole responsibility: if I could not get it right the second time around, there is no one to blame but myself. Finally, I wish to express my gratitude to the following publishers for permission to reprint my earlier works in this volume:

Chapter 3
'Ukraine or Little Russia? Revisiting an Early Nineteenth-Century Debate.' *Canadian Slavonic Papers* 48, nos 3–4 (September–December 2006): 260–78.

Chapter 4
'(Mis)understanding the Cossack Icon.' In *Rus' Writ Large: Languages, Histories, Cultures* (=Harvard Ukrainian Studies 28), forthcoming.

Chapter 5
'Between Poland and Russia: The Political Dilemmas of Mykhailo Hrushevsky, 1905–7.' In *Tentorium Honorum: Essays Presented to Frank E. Sysyn on His Sixtieth Birthday.* Edmonton, forthcoming.

Chapter 6
'Renegotiating the Pereiaslav Agreement.' Introduction to Mykhailo Hrushevsky, *History of Ukraine-Rus'*. Vol. 9, bk 2, pt. 1. Edmonton and Toronto, forthcoming.

Chapter 7
'Bourgeois Revolution or Peasant War? Early Soviet Debates on the History of the Khmelnytsky Uprising.' In *Synopsis: A Collection of Essays in Honour of Zenon E. Kohut*, ed. Serhii Plokhy and Frank E. Sysyn, 345–69. Edmonton and Toronto, 2005.

Chapter 8
'Selians'ka Klio: istorychna pam'iat' ta natsional'na identychnist' v Radians'kii Ukraïni.' Introduction to *Dzherela z istoriï Pivdennoï Ukraïny.* Vol. 5, pt. 1, bks 1 and 2, *Memuary ta shchodennyky*, ed. Anatolii Boiko, 12–32. Zaporizhia, 2005.

Chapter 9
'Historical Debates and Territorial Claims: Cossack Mythology in the Russian-Ukrainian Border Dispute.' In *The Legacy of History in Russia and the New States of Eurasia*. The International Politics of Eurasia, vol. 1, ed. S. Frederick Starr, 147–70. Armonk, NY and London, 1994.

Chapter 10
'The City of Glory: Sevastopol in Russian Historical Mythology.' *Journal of Contemporary History* 35, no. 3 (July 2000): 369–83.

Chapter 11
'The Ghosts of Pereyaslav: Russo-Ukrainian Historical Debates in the Post-Soviet Era.' *Europe-Asia Studies* 53, no. 3 (May 2001): 489–505.

Chapter 12
'Remembering Yalta: The Politics of International History.' *The Harriman Review* 15 (2007): 15–26.

Chapter 13
'History of a "Non-historical" Nation: Notes on the Nature and Current Problems of Ukrainian Historiography.' *Slavic Review* 54, no. 3 (fall 1995): 709–16.

Chapter 14
'Imagining Early Modern Ukraine: The "Parallel World" of Natalia Iakovenko.' *Harvard Ukrainian Studies* 25, nos. 3–4 (2005 for 2001): 267–80.

Chapter 15
'Crossing National Boundaries: The Case for the Comparative Study of Cossackdom.' In *Die Geschichte Rußlands im 16. und 17. Jahrhundert aus der Perspektive seiner Regionen*, ed. Andreas Kappeler, 416–30. Wiesbaden, 2004.

Note on Transliteration

In the text of this book, the modified Library of Congress system is used to transliterate Russian, Ukrainian, and Belarusian personal names and toponyms. This system, designed to ease reading by avoiding non-English diacritics and word endings, omits the soft sign (ь) and, in masculine personal names, the final 'й' (thus, for example, Khmelnytsky, not Khmel'nyts'kyi). The same practice is followed in the notes, with the exception of bibliographic references, which are rendered in the full Library of Congress system (ligatures omitted) in order to make possible the accurate reconstruction of the Cyrillic original. The *ALA-LC Romanization Tables* detailing the Library of Congress transliteration of Ukrainian and Russian are available online at www.loc.gov/catdir/cpso/roman.html. Titles of publications issued after 1800 are given in modernized spelling. In bibliographic references to the Russian-language publications of Ukrainian authors, the author's name is transliterated from its Russian form (for example, Mykhailo Hrushevsky appears as Mikhail Grushevskii). Toponyms are usually transliterated from the language of the country in which the designated places are currently located. As a rule, personal names are given in forms characteristic of the cultural tradition to which the given person belonged. If an individual belonged to (or is claimed by) more than one national tradition, alternative spellings are given in parentheses. In this case, as in the use of specific terminology related to the history of the Eastern Slavs and titles of East European officials and institutions, I follow the practice established by the editors of the English translation of Mykhailo Hrushevsky's *History of Ukraine-Rus'*.[1]

The Julian calendar used by the Eastern Slavs until 1918 lagged behind the Gregorian calendar used in the Polish-Lithuanian Commonwealth and Western Europe (by ten days in the sixteenth and seventeenth centuries, eleven days in the eighteenth century, twelve days in the nineteenth, and thirteen days in the twentieth). Dates in this study are generally given according to the Julian calendar; where both styles appear concurrently, the Gregorian-calendar date is given in parentheses, for example, 13 (23) May.

1. The Cossack Hetmanate as Part of Imperial Russia. Zenon E. Kohut, *Russian Centralism and Ukrainian Autonomy: Imperial Absorption of the Hetmanate, 1760s–1830s* (Cambridge, MA: Harvard Ukrainian Research Institute, 1988), xv.

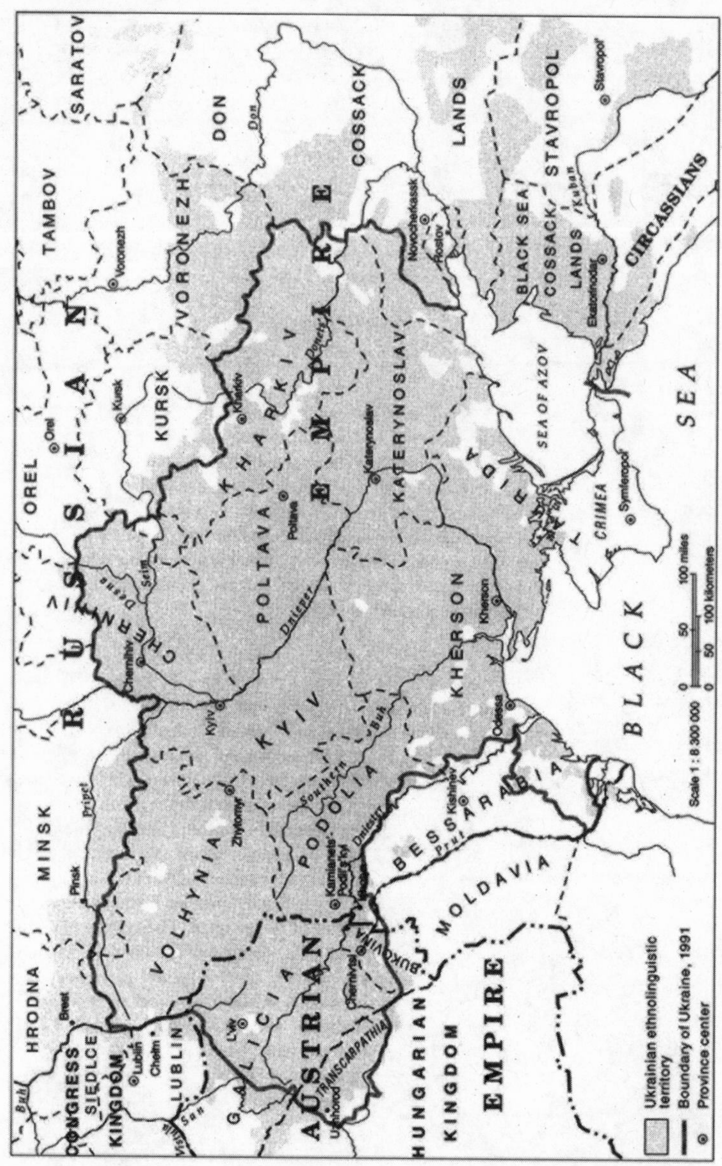

2. Ukrainian Lands in the Nineteenth Century. Zenon E. Kohut, Bohdan Y. Nebesio, and Myroslav Yurkevich, *Historical Dictionary of Ukraine* (Lanham, MD, Toronto, and Oxford: Scarecrow Press, 2005), map 5.

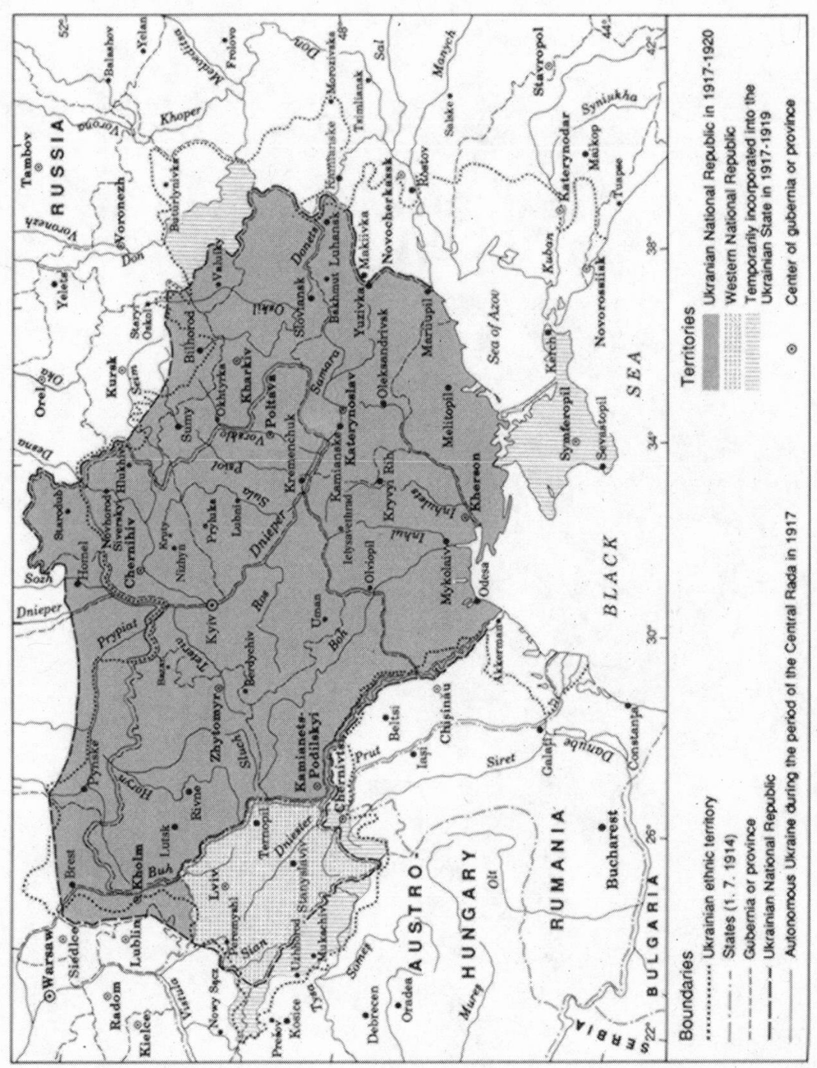

3. Ukraine at the Time of the Revolution of 1917. *Encyclopedia of Ukraine*, ed. Volodymyr Kubijovyč and Danylo Husar Struk, vol. 5 (Toronto: University of Toronto Press, 1993), p. 409.

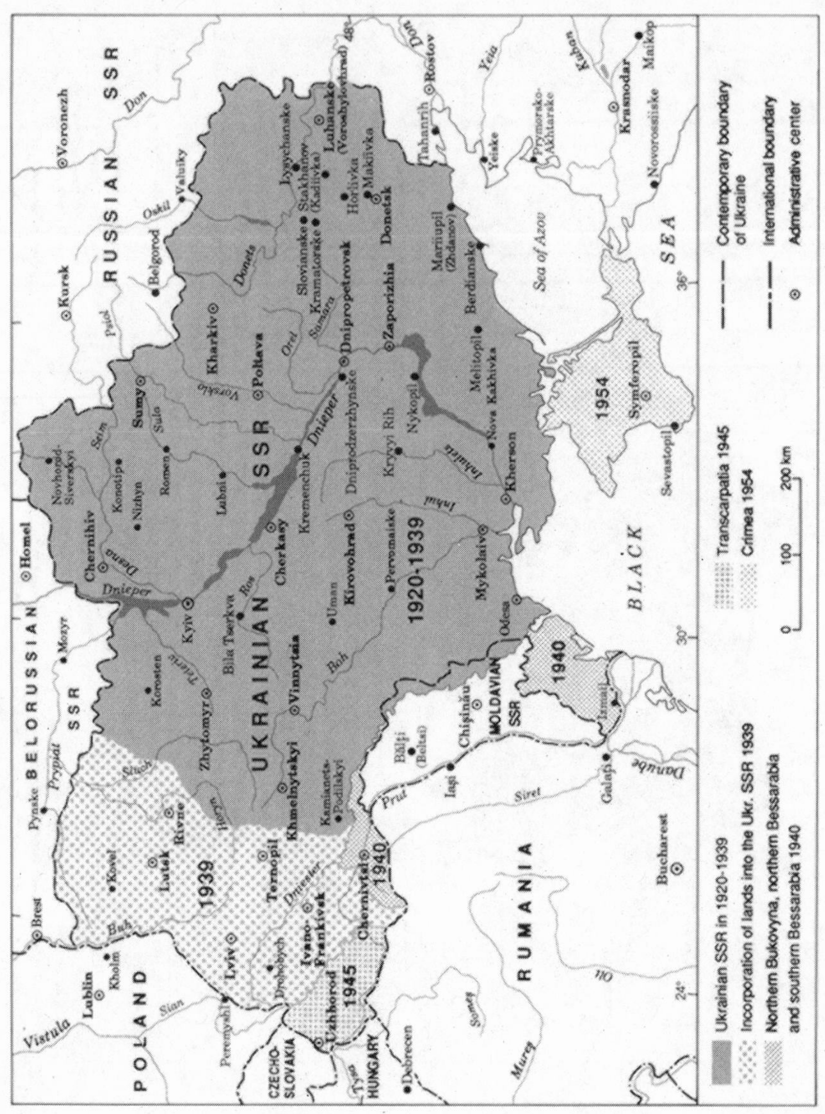

4. Soviet Ukraine. *Encyclopedia of Ukraine*, ed. Volodymyr Kubijovyč and Danylo Husar Struk, vol. 5 (Toronto: University of Toronto Press, 1993), p. 441.

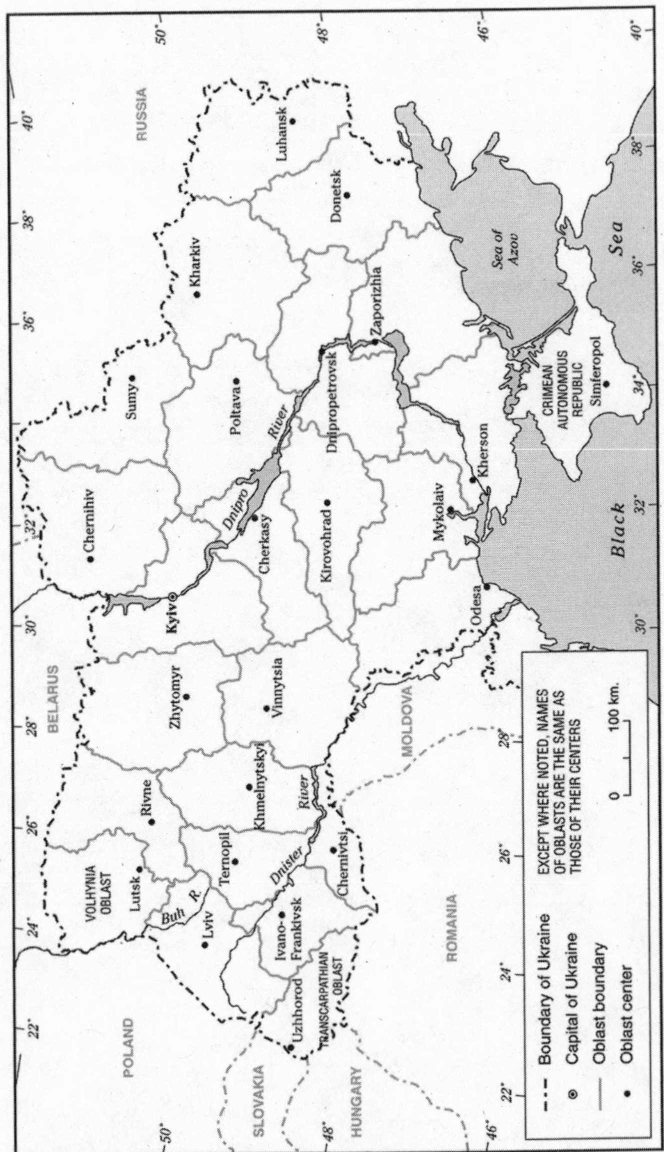

5. Present-Day Ukraine. Zenon E. Kohut, Bohdan Y. Nebesio, and Myroslav Yurkevich, *Historical Dictionary of Ukraine* (Lanham, MD, Toronto, and Oxford: Scarecrow Press, 2005), map 9.

UKRAINE AND RUSSIA

Introduction

Where does Russian history end and Ukrainian history begin? This question, which the dissolution of the Soviet Union placed on the scholarly agenda in the West, has not yet received a satisfactory answer. Should the study of the Russian past begin with the Scythians of the Northern Black Sea region, the Varangian princes who took control of the Dnipro (Dnieper) trade route in the closing centuries of the first millennium, or with the rule of the Kyivan (Kievan) princes who established a major polity, known today as Kyivan Rus', in the first centuries of the second millennium? Generations of historians referred to Kyiv, the capital of Ukraine, as the starting point of the Muscovite dynasty, the Russian state, and, ultimately, the Russian nation. But the historical developments just mentioned have also been claimed by Ukrainian historiography since its inception and are now regarded as integral parts of the history of Ukraine, on whose territory they took place. If these are actually the beginnings of Ukrainian history, when does Russian history start? These questions are fundamental to the formation of modern Russian and Ukrainian national identity and to future relations between these two largest Slavic states and peoples.

This book focuses largely on the development of Ukrainian historiography and its uneasy relations with its Russian counterpart. The separation of Ukrainian history from the Russian narrative was the major challenge faced by Ukrainian historiography in the nineteenth and twentieth centuries. Even after the disintegration of the Soviet Union and the formation of independent Ukraine, Russia remained the largest irritant when it came to modern Ukrainian identity and historiography. The theme of the separation of Ukrainian and Russian imperial and national narratives was at the centre of my book on Mykhailo

Hrushevsky (1866–1934), the Ukrainian historian and statesman who did the most to nationalize the Ukrainian historical narrative and separate it from that of Russia in the late nineteenth and early twentieth centuries.[1] Although some of the essays included in this volume discuss Hrushevsky's contribution to the 'emancipation' of Ukrainian historiography, most of them go far beyond Hrushevsky and his work, both chronologically and historiographically. This book covers more than two and a half centuries of the development of the Ukrainian and Russian historical imagination, ranging from the mid-eighteenth century, when modern national identities began to develop, to the disintegration of the USSR and the search for a new historical identity in independent Ukraine. It considers how the past of these two countries has become entangled in the imagination of modern historians. It also seeks to understand how the two modern nations have dealt and continue to deal with the problems posed by the intertwined but also often conflicting and contradictory accounts of their origins.

The title of this book reflects its focus on the multiple representations of the past in the Ukrainian and Russian historical imaginations, which are viewed as products of encounter, conflict, and negotiation between different political, cultural, and historiographic traditions. This volume is not a comprehensive survey of Ukrainian or Russian historiography, nor is it a systematic account of relations between them. It seeks instead to discuss a number of important tendencies in the development of the two historiographic traditions in their 'contact zone.' In so doing, it focuses on selected topics in the Russo-Ukrainian historiographic encounter.

Individual chapters of the book address the major stages of this encounter, ranging from the vision of common historical origins that arose in the second half of the eighteenth century to the rise of modern national historiographies and debates over the 'nationalization' of the Russian and Ukrainian past in the wake of the disintegration of the Soviet Union. The sixteen essays are grouped in four sections, each with its own historiographic focus and chronological limits.

The Roots of Entanglement

Part 1 of this volume consists of essays that discuss the formation of the common East Slavic historiographic tradition in the eighteenth and nineteenth centuries, as well as the attempts of Ukrainian intellectual elites to secure a place of honour for themselves and their homeland in the emerging grand narrative of the Russian Empire. The opening chapter discusses the role of history in shaping Russian imperial identity – a construct that not only claimed the loyalty of the Ukrainian elites but was formed with their active participation. It analyses the first major debate in Russian imperial historiography, which concerned the alleged invitation to the Varangians (Norsemen) to rule over the people who became known as the Rus' in the closing decades of the first millennium. The chapter explains how different understandings of what constituted the Russian nation produced diverse readings of the Varangian legend in the eighteenth century. Mikhail Lomonosov, who followed in the footsteps of the author of the Kyivan *Synopsis* (1674) – the first printed textbook of 'Russian' history – and considered Russianness an ethnic attribute, treated the Varangians as representatives of a Slavic tribe. Empress Catherine II, on the other hand, regarded the Russian nation as a political and civic entity and thus had no objection to a definition of the Varangians as non-Slavic Normans or Scandinavians. It was this non-ethnic and essentially imperial understanding of Russianness that became dominant in Russian historiography and political thought of the period and later contributed to the ambiguity of the Russian historical and national project.

When it comes to the development of eighteenth-century Ukrainian historical writing and political thought, the imperial idea of all-Russian unity discussed in the opening chapter of the volume played an important role but was not the only source of inspiration. The idea of a distinct Cossack nation of Khazar origin was popular among the Ukrainian elites that supported the revolt of Hetman Ivan Mazepa (1639–1709) against Tsar Peter I in 1708. Their vision of a proud and heroic Cossack nation that concluded the Pereiaslav Agreement (1654) with the tsar during the times of Hetman Bohdan Khmelnytsky (1595–1657) and later was betrayed by the Muscovites found expression in the historical preamble to the constitution of Hetman Pylyp Orlyk, Mazepa's successor in exile. That concept was also reflected in historical works written in the Hetmanate – the Cossack state founded by Khmelnytsky in 1648 and abolished by Catherine II in the 1780s. Among those works are historical chronicles written by the Cossack officers Samiilo Velychko and Hryhorii Hrabianka in the 1720s and 1730s, as well as poems and dramas composed by their contemporaries. The strongest literary manifestation of Cossack pride and assertion of Ukraine's equality with Russia was a poem written by a Cossack secretary, Semen Divovych, in 1762.

That monument of Cossack autonomism is discussed in the second chapter, 'Incorporated Identity,' which explains the historical context of Divovych's 'Conversation between Great Russia and Little Russia' and the political significance of his argument. Divovych, who claimed that Ukraine was no less entitled to use the term *Rossiia* than its northern neighbour, maintained that the two countries were equal in status, linked only by their common loyalty to the tsar. His 'Conversation' was written at a time of high expectations aroused in the Hetmanate by the ascension to the throne of the new empress, Catherine II. Little did Divovych and other representatives of the Ukrainian gentry, who advanced plans for the strengthening of Ukrainian autonomy, know that the rule of Catherine would effectively end the existence of their polity and abolish the autonomous rights of their region. 'Incorporated Identity' follows the interplay of history and politics in the discourse of the Cossack elites as they faced the growing centralization of the imperial state and its encroachment on the Hetmanate's liberties. The leading role in the formation of Ukrainian historical and political identity at that time passed from Cossack officers like Divovych to Ukrainians in imperial service, such as Prince Oleksander Bezborodko, the chancellor of the Russian Empire and co-author of *A Brief Chronicle of Little Russia* (1777), the first book on Ukrainian history to be published after the *Synopsis*. While cherishing memories of their beloved Little Russian homeland, that group of St Petersburg Ukrainians led the way to the complete incorporation of Ukrainian history and identity into the all-Russian imperial construct.

By the turn of the nineteenth century, the tradition of using *Rossiia* to designate both Russia and Ukraine, which had been adopted by the author of the *Synopsis*, was beginning to create problems for those Ukrainian intellectuals who wanted to stress the distinction between the two countries. Their solution was to revive the term 'Ukraine,' which had been widely used in historical writing of the late seventeenth and early eighteenth centuries. By the end of the eighteenth century, it had all but disappeared from use with reference to the territories of the former Hetmanate and was being applied mainly to lands bordering on Russia proper (Sloboda Ukraine). Indeed, some early nineteenth-century writers, such as the anonymous author of the manuscript 'History of the Rus'' – discussed in the chapter entitled 'Ukraine or Little Russia?' – considered the term 'Ukraine' little more than a Polish intrigue. Not unlike Divovych, the anonymous author of the *History* was proud of his homeland's Cossack past but, given the circumstances of the time, invoked it in order to claim a special place for his countrymen in the Russian imperial hierarchy and historical narrative. Ironically, the heroic ethos of the 'History of the Rus'' proved so powerful that the work inspired generations of romantically minded 'awakeners' of the Ukrainian nation. For them the 'History' became the bible of the Ukrainian past, providing rich material (often legendary and inaccurate) for the construction of modern Ukrainian identity.

Among those influenced by the heroic images of the 'History' was Ukraine's greatest poet and 'father' of the modern Ukrainian nation, Taras Shevchenko (1814–61). An accomplished artist employed by the Kyiv Archaeographic Commission, which was in charge of collecting old Ukrainian manuscripts and art works, Shevchenko was especially interested in Cossack-era paintings and iconography. He was in fact the first to describe in considerable detail the magnificent icon of the Holy Protection at the *Pokrova* Church in the town of Pereiaslav, which included a depiction of Tsar Peter I and Cossack officers of the period. The description appeared in one of Shevchenko's novels whose main character was not only an admirer of that icon but also an avid reader of the 'History of the Rus'.' Shevchenko believed that one of the Cossacks depicted in the icon was Hetman Ivan Mazepa – a supposition that would make it virtually impossible to publish or study the work in Soviet times. The essay entitled 'The Missing Mazepa' follows the twists and turns of modern scholarly interpretation of the *Pokrova* icon from Pereiaslav, as well as Cossack iconography in general. It shows how ideological myths created by eighteenth-century imperial elites (Mazepa was anathematized by the Orthodox Church on the orders of Peter I) influenced the development of historical research in a period strongly marked by ideological trends of the modern era.

Between Class and Nation

Part 2 of the book discusses the 'nationalization' of Ukrainian historiography in the late nineteenth and twentieth centuries. If one had to name the single most important historian whose works reversed the historiographic tradition established by the author of the *Synopsis* and separated Ukrainian history from the Russian imperial narrative, that historian would be Mykhailo Hrushevsky. Born to a family from Right-Bank Ukraine and educated at Kyiv University, he made his name as a professor of history at Lviv University in the decades preceding the First World War. He was the first head of the independent Ukrainian state in 1918, led the historical institutes of the Ukrainian Academy of Sciences in the 1920s, and fell victim to Stalin's persecution of Ukrainian culture in the early 1930s.

With his monumental ten-volume *History of Ukraine-Rus'* (1898–1937), Hrushevsky established Ukrainian history as a separate field of research. In so doing, he completed the work begun by the previous generation of Ukrainian historians. One of Hrushevsky's predecessors was Mykola Kostomarov (1817–85), who introduced the theory of two nationalities into the study of Russian and Ukrainian history. According to Kostomarov, the history of the Little Russian (Ukrainian) nationality was characterized by ideas of democracy and freedom, while that of the Great Russian nationality was marked by the dominance of autocratic tendencies. Mykhailo Maksymovych (1804–73) and Hrushevsky's university professor, Volodymyr Antonovych (1834–1908), drew a clear distinction between Polish and Ukrainian history and argued for the Ukrainian identity of the population of Kyiv during the princely era. Following in their footsteps, Hrushevsky not only separated Ukrainian history from Russian but also claimed Kyivan Rus' exclusively for the Ukrainian historical narrative. He thus effectively dismantled the all-Russian historical narrative, depriving it of its traditional beginning. Hrushevsky's historical scheme became the focal point for the Russo-Ukrainian historical debates that continued throughout the twentieth century.

Hrushevsky's role as a political activist during the Revolution of 1905 is discussed in the chapter entitled 'The Historian as Nation Builder.' It highlights his activities as national awakener in the Russian Empire – a function similar to that undertaken by other East European historians of his time. Manoeuvring between the two competing national projects of the period, the Polish and the Russian, Hrushevsky tried to prevent his nation from being used as raw ethnic material for the formation of 'large' Polish and Russian nations. During the Revolution of 1905, he advocated the unity of all democratic forces, including the Ukrainian and Polish national movements and the Russian liberal camp, in the struggle for the 'liberation of Russia,' a term that he used to denote the federalization of the Russian Empire with consequent territorial autonomy for Ukraine. As Hrushevsky's political goals for Ukraine changed from autonomy to independence, so did his interpretation of the Pereiaslav Agreement of 1654, which had brought Ukraine under the 'high hand' of the Muscovite tsar. If Hrushevsky originally believed that the agreement had guaranteed autonomy for the Cossack

Hetmanate, he later decided that at the time of the Russo-Ukrainian deliberations at Pereiaslav Ukraine in fact possessed all the characteristics of an independent polity. As demonstrated in the chapter 'Renegotiating the Pereiaslav Agreement,' Hrushevsky made a strong case for the thesis that the meeting at Pereiaslav produced an agreement resulting from negotiations between the two sides and was not merely a manifestation of popular approval for the idea of bringing Ukraine under tsarist rule, as claimed by Gennadii Karpov and other Russian historians. Not all of Hrushevsky's arguments regarding the Pereiaslav Agreement are equally accepted by Russian and Ukrainian historians today, but his discussion of the subject, the most detailed and thorough one available, continues to influence interpretation of the Pereiaslav Agreement not only in Ukraine and Russia but also in the West.

The development of national projects in twentieth-century Russia and Ukraine coincided with the rise of Marxism, another powerful modern ideology that descended on the Russian Empire in its barbaric Bolshevik incarnation and had a lasting influence on both countries. Soviet reaction to Hrushevsky's works and the Marxist interpretation of the Khmelnytsky Uprising of 1648, which was crucial to Hrushevsky's narrative, is discussed in the chapter 'Bourgeois Revolution or Peasant War?' It considers similarities and differences between the Ukrainian national, Ukrainian Marxist, and Russian Marxist interpretations of events leading up to the Pereiaslav Agreement. Armed with the works of Karl Marx, Friedrich Engels, and Vladimir Lenin, but lacking proper historical training and expertise, the first Soviet specialists in Ukrainian history occupied themselves mainly with the invention of sociological schemes. They also used class-based rhetoric to discredit and dismantle not only the old pan-Russian imperial narrative but also the national narrative of Ukrainian history.

As a result of the Soviet authorities' 'class attack' on national historiography, not only the Ukrainian historical paradigm developed by Hrushevsky and his students but also the narrative created by the founder of Ukrainian Marxist historiography, Matvii Yavorsky, were outlawed as 'bourgeois' interpretations of history. In the conflict between Yavorsky and the leader of the Russian Marxist historians, Mikhail Pokrovsky, the latter emerged victorious, opening the door to Moscow's administrative takeover of Ukrainian Marxist institutions and later to the introduction of a Russocentric narrative of Ukrainian history under the officially approved rubric, 'History of the Peoples of the USSR.' The long-term impact of that narrative on the process of negotiation between Russian and Ukrainian historiography is discussed in the chapters constituting the third part of the book.

While the official Marxist paradigm ruled the 'commanding heights' of Soviet historiography, what was the view of Russian and Ukrainian history from below? This question is posed in the chapter entitled 'The People's History.' It examines how elite visions of history (including that of Hrushevsky) were incorporated into the world view of the peasantry, which had its own alternative version of history based on family legends and personal experiences of ordinary people who survived the turbulent events of the twentieth century. The diaries, memoirs, and family histories analysed in that chapter are often unmarked by official ideology and offer historians unique sources on the formation of historical and national identities in southern Ukraine, one of the most ethnically diverse regions of the present-day Ukrainian state. It would appear that both ethnic Ukrainians and Russians who received their elementary education prior to the First World War were inclined to consider themselves members of one pan-Russian nation – a vision that some of them maintained for the rest of their lives. The Revolution of 1917–20 and the linguistic and cultural Ukrainization of the 1920s challenged that vision, allowing the southern Ukrainian peasantry to construct a distinct Ukrainian identity and integrate their personal and family experience into the history of Ukraine. That process also affected ethnic Russians living in the region, creating the basis for the formation of a Ukrainian political and historical identity that transcended ethnicity. It was largely responsible for the overwhelming popular support of Ukrainian independence in the referendum of December 1991 and, ultimately, for the disintegration of the Soviet Union.

Post-Soviet Debates

The collapse of the Soviet Union and the creation of newly independent states on its ruins was a process that required historical legitimization. The new states also needed historical expertise to settle numerous territorial disputes that arose in the early 1990s. Under these new circumstances, the question of Russia's geographic limits and the boundaries of its historical consciousness took on a clearly political meaning, pregnant with far-reaching international implications. As the Russian public struggled to make sense of support for Ukrainian independence in predominantly Russian-speaking eastern and southern Ukraine, leaders of nationalist parties in the Russian parliament (*Duma*) began to make claims on Ukrainian lands bordering on the Russian Federation. Ukrainian leaders responded with rebuttals and counterclaims. Both sides made liberal use of historical arguments in these disputes. There were particularly heated debates over the Crimean peninsula, which had been transferred from the Russian Federation to Ukraine in 1954, allegedly to mark the three-hundredth anniversary of the 'reunification' of Russia and Ukraine – the official Soviet term for the establishment of a Muscovite protectorate over Cossack Ukraine in the winter and spring of 1654.

In laying their claims to southern and eastern Ukraine, Russian politicians and historians stressed its colonization during the reign of Catherine II, while their Ukrainian counterparts emphasized its rich Cossack history. The chapter 'History and Territory' discusses the development of Cossack mythology in pre-independence Ukraine and its importance for Ukraine's attempts to counter Russian advances in the first years of independence. Research on Cossack history was all but suppressed by the Soviet authorities in the 1970s; a number of scholars working in that field were accused of idealizing the past and dismissed from their positions at the Academy of Sciences. Even the 'History of the Rus'' could not be reprinted prior to 1991, when the advance of perestroika and glasnost effectively removed official restrictions on the publication of works on Cossack history. On the eve of independence, the celebration of the Cossack past became a means of mobilizing Ukrainian historical memory and national identity: not only the national-patriotic forces but also their opponents in the Communist Party of Ukraine jumped on the Cossack bandwagon, organizing marches and public events to mark the five-hundredth anniversary of Ukrainian Cossackdom. Since the Cossacks were the first settlers of the vast steppes of Ukraine, politicians naturally found the newly revived and refurbished Cossack myth a potent weapon in combating Russian claims to eastern and southern Ukraine. Stripped of its traditional anti-Tatar overtones, the new Cossack myth portrayed the Crimean Tatars as neighbours and often allies of the Ukrainian Cossacks, thereby legitimizing the Ukrainian-Crimean Tatar political alliance of the 1990s, which was directed against Russian claims to the Crimean peninsula and the politics of the Russian majority there.

'The City of Glory' analyses the Russian image of the Crimean naval base of Sevastopol as a Russian city *par excellence*. The story begins with the siege of that city during the Crimean War of 1854–6. The dogged resistance mounted by soldiers and sailors of the Russian imperial army and navy against English, French, and Turkish forces turned the defenders of Sevastopol into Russian heroes and the city itself into a symbol of Russian resilience. The myth of Sevastopol that took shape in the second half of the nineteenth century was largely a product of the merging of Russian imperialism and nationalism. The growing self-awareness of Russian society created a need for positive national models; accordingly, the heroism of the multiethnic imperial army and navy was recast as the heroism of Russian soldiers, and defeat in the Crimean War was compensated by this virtual victory of Russian arms. Before the Revolution of 1917, the myth of Sevastopol was rivalled only by that of Port Arthur – the Russian naval base in China lost to the Japanese during the war of 1904–5. It was ignored by the Bolsheviks for most of the 1920s and 1930s, only to be revived during the Second World War as a stimulus to Russian patriotism. It served a similar purpose during the Cold War. Promoted by such luminaries of Soviet historiography as Evgenii Tarle, the myth of Sevastopol was intended to demonstrate the superiority of the Russian military over the armies of Britain, France, and Turkey – former enemies in the Crimean War and now members of the NATO military alliance. The myth took on new life and a somewhat different purpose in the early 1990s, when it was brought out again to question the legitimacy of the transfer of the Crimea to Ukraine in 1954 and to claim Sevastopol as the base of the Russian Black Sea Fleet.

Another historical myth whose origins predate the Soviet era and that is still very much alive in contemporary historical writing is that of the 'reunification' of Ukraine and Russia. As discussed in the chapter 'The Ghosts of Pereiaslav,' particular emphasis on the Pereiaslav Agreement of 1654, which extended a Muscovite protectorate over the Hetmanate, can be traced back to the eighteenth-century Cossack chronicles. In order to preserve the autonomous status of the Hetmanate and their own liberties and privileges, the Cossack elites often referred to the Articles of Bohdan Khmelnytsky, which enshrined the rights granted to the Cossacks by the Muscovite tsar after the Pereiaslav Council. As the tsarist authorities steadily reduced those traditional rights, the Cossack officers continued to insist on the original conditions of 1654, promoting the Pereiaslav Agreement and its architect, Bohdan Khmelnytsky, to almost mythical status. With the nationalization of the Russian and Ukrainian historical narratives in the second half of the nineteenth century, Pereiaslav and Khmelnytsky took on an entirely new meaning in Russian imperial historiography.

The agreement was often praised as the instrument crucial to the 'reunification' of Rus' with Muscovy, and Khmelnytsky was hailed as its pro-Muscovite author.

The latter interpretation regained centre stage when the three-hundredth anniversary of the 'reunification' of Russia and Ukraine was officially celebrated in 1954. The theses issued on that occasion by the Central Committee of the Communist Party of the Soviet Union imposed the Russocentric paradigm of the agreement and the subsequent history of Ukraine on Soviet historiography as a whole. The attempts of some Ukrainian historians to discredit the 'reunification' myth by indicating its non-Marxist and Russocentric characteristics yielded no positive results, and the theses continued to rule supreme until the advent of glasnost. After the disintegration of the USSR, most Ukrainian historians discarded the 'reunification' paradigm, while most of their Russian colleagues continued to insist on it. In Ukraine the term seems to have been permanently discredited by its abuse in Soviet historiography. Even when President Leonid Kuchma tried to please his Russian counterpart, Vladimir Putin, in January 2004 by celebrating the 350th anniversary of the Pereiaslav Agreement, the term 'reunification' was excluded from the presidential decree issued for the occasion. The response of Ukrainian society to this presidential initiative was nevertheless so harshly negative that the celebrations had to be scaled down, to the disappointment of the Russian delegation.

The word 'reunification' also remains highly controversial in Belarusian historiography. There the government of Aliaksandr Lukashenka promotes the use of the term with regard to the Muscovite conquest of Belarusian territories in the mid-seventeenth century, persecuting those historians who refuse to toe the official line. In late 2005 Henadz Sahanovich, the leading Belarusian historian of the early modern era, was dismissed from his position at the Belarusian Academy of Sciences after the publication in Moscow of the minutes of a historiographic discussion in which he questioned the continuing use of the term 'reunification.' The debate continues, claiming new victims and testing not only the professionalism but also the civic courage of participating historians.

Apart from the Pereiaslav Agreement, another area of disagreement between Russian and Ukrainian historians of the post-Soviet era has been the history of the Second World War. There one can see two major fault lines, one going through the historical establishment of Ukraine, dividing the proponents of the national paradigm from those who advocate Soviet-era approaches to the topic, and another separating

Russian and Ukrainian historians and cultural elites. The chapter 'Remembering Yalta' discusses the international controversy caused by the commemoration of the sixtieth anniversary of the Yalta Conference, which brought together the leaders of the anti-Hitler coalition in February 1945. It analyses the position taken on the issue by Russian officialdom and the Russian public, explaining the reasons for the lack of a clearly articulated position on the part of the Ukrainian government and public.

Russia's negative reaction to the attempts of Poland, the Baltic states, and later the United States to indicate the negative consequences of the Yalta agreements for the East European nations occupied by the Red Army gave evidence of growing authoritarian and neo-Stalinist tendencies in the Russian leadership and society. On the other hand, the debate on the decisions of the Yalta Conference and the outcome of the Second World War in Ukraine indicated quite clearly that the country still remains divided by memories of the war, in which western regions of Ukraine became the field of operations of the Ukrainian Insurgent Army, while the population of eastern Ukraine supplied recruits for the Red Army. Ukraine's inability to reach a consensus on the meaning of the Second World War and the consequences of the Yalta Conference, which defined the country's current western border and ensured its membership in the United Nations Organization, demonstrate that the 'search for a usable past' in Ukrainian society is far from over. There is, however, a prevailing negative attitude in Ukraine to the figure of Joseph Stalin and his rule – a marked difference from Russia, where there are clear signs of the return of Stalin's popularity among the elite and the general public alike.

The Search for a New History

While most of the essays in this volume seek to reconstruct, understand, and explain the process of negotiation between (and within) Ukrainian and Russian historiography and society, the essays collected in the last part of the book have a different purpose. They are not meant to follow the debate but to take part in it. With one exception, the chapters in this part of the volume focus on Ukrainian historiography. They discuss the challenges faced by Ukrainian historians after the collapse of the USSR and ways of overcoming the historiographic crisis brought about by the disintegration of the USSR and Russian claims on Ukrainian history.

The chapter entitled 'The History of a Non-Historical Nation' was written in response to Mark von Hagen's influential essay 'Does Ukraine Have a History?' (1995). It considers the problems faced by Ukrainian historiography after the achievement of political independence and suggests the need for a new historiographic discourse and historical myth adequate to the new political circumstances and national expectations. In the last few years, a number of Ukrainian scholars have sought to deal with this challenge by going beyond the limits imposed on the historical profession by the traditional narrative of Ukrainian history. One of the leaders of this 'revisionist' group is Natalia Yakovenko, a specialist in the early modern history of Ukraine and Eastern Europe whose approach to her subject is discussed in the chapter 'Imagining Early Modern Ukraine.' Yakovenko's investigation of the 'parallel world' of opinions, attitudes, perceptions, and stereotypes of the early modern era offers a possible way out of the deadlock between politically motivated historians of Russia and Ukraine in debating seemingly insoluble issues pertaining to their common history.

This certainly applies to the study of Ukrainian Cossackdom, a leading subject of research in traditional Ukrainian historiography. On the one hand, the extreme politicization of research and writing on the history of Ukrainian Cossackdom and Ukrainian-Russian relations of the early modern period has attracted considerable attention to the subject on the part of the scholarly community and the public at large; on the other, it has narrowed the scope of discussion and made a number of important topics unattractive or politically dangerous for historians on both sides of the Ukrainian-Russian divide. The politicization of the field has certainly hindered the comparative study of Ukrainian and Russian Cossackdom – an area of research that promises new and interesting results. Given the considerable attention traditionally paid to the Cossacks in Ukrainian historiography and the relative marginalization of that topic in Russian historiography, Russian historians of Cossackdom might well benefit from consultation with their Ukrainian colleagues. The current status of the field is assessed in the chapter entitled 'Crossing National Boundaries.' It suggests a number of research topics in which a comparative approach to the study of both Cossack communities could be especially productive. It also problematizes the notions of Ukrainian and Russian Cossackdom, pointing to internal tensions and transnational similarities. The chapter discusses the strengths and weaknesses engendered by the dominance of the national paradigm in the study of Cossack history.

The last chapter of the volume, 'Beyond Nationality,' examines alternatives to the national paradigm in Ukrainian historiography and ways in which new approaches can reshape our understanding not only of Ukrainian history but also of the history of Eastern Europe. It looks at the formation of the Ukrainian national paradigm, examines attempts to study Ukraine as a multiethnic and multiconfessional entity, considers approaches to the history of Ukraine as a political, cultural, and civilizational borderland, and finally surveys conceptions of Eastern Europe advanced by proponents of area studies. In so doing, the chapter assesses new prospects for the development of Ukrainian historiography and the integration of the Ukrainian historical narrative into European history.

This volume is the result of more than a decade of research and writing. A number of chapters were written specifically for this book, but the majority began as essays, research papers, articles, and introductions to other volumes. Most of the previously published chapters have been revised and updated for this publication. While these essays are linked together by one overarching theme, they do not (as noted above) present a systematic discussion of the development of Ukrainian historiography or its relations with the Russian historical tradition. Instead, they give an in-depth analysis of a number of 'episodes' that characterize the formation of Ukrainian and, to a lesser degree, Russian national historiography. They also indicate the possible future development of the Ukrainian historiographic tradition. It is the author's hope that this volume will stimulate further research and discussion of the complex development of Ukrainian and Russian historiography and historical identity.

PART ONE

The Roots of Entanglement

1 Empire or Nation?

Vasilii Kliuchevsky, the dean of Russian historiography at the turn of the twentieth century, defined Russian history from the early seventeenth to the mid-nineteenth century as an 'all-Russian' period, in opposition to the earlier age, which he called Great Russian and Muscovite. During the 'all-Russian period,' according to Kliuchevsky, 'the Russian people spreads across the whole flatland from the Baltic and White Seas to the Black Sea, to the Caucasus Mountain range, the Caspian Sea and the Urals, and even penetrates south and east far beyond the Caucasus, the Caspian Sea and the Urals. Politically, almost all parts of the Russian nationality are united under one rule: one after another, Little Russia, White Russia and New Russia join Great Russia, forming the All-Russian Empire.'[1] Kliuchevsky's conception of the empire as essentially a nation-state was more the norm than the exception in European historiography of the period.[2] The roots of that conception are to be found in Russia's encounter with the West in the course of the eighteenth century.

In his groundbreaking study, *National Consciousness in Eighteenth-Century Russia,* Hans Rogger interpreted the development of national identity in the Russian Empire as a process that began under Western influence and in reaction to it. Rogger's discussion of the Russian imperial elites' search for identity in the spheres of politics, customs and morals, historiography, and linguistics laid the foundations for subsequent research on the subject.[3] His view of eighteenth-century Russian identity as a product of interaction between Russia and the West was fully shared by Liah Greenfeld in her *Nationalism: Five Roads to Modernity*[4] and by Vera Tolz in her monograph on the 'invention' of Russia. Tolz also noted the contradiction inherent in the Western-inspired view of the multiethnic Russian empire as a nation-state. 'This idea,' wrote Tolz, 'was articulated by Russian intellectuals in an attempt to apply the West European concept of nation to Russian reality ... Those intellectuals who first formulated it in the late eighteenth century and then developed it more fully in the nineteenth were members of the intellectual elite residing in the two capitals, St. Petersburg and Moscow. This elite was multiethnic, with Ukrainians and Russified Germans playing a particularly important role ... [I]n the course of the nineteenth century, this vision of the entire empire as a Russian nation-state proved to be bluntly at odds with reality.'[5]

This chapter takes the debate over the construction of modern Russian identity one step further, pointing out the existence of two models of Russian identity in the eighteenth-century Russian Empire. One of them, which can be called ethnic or 'nativist,' included in the Russian nation the Slavic imperial elites consisting of Great Russians and Ukrainians from the Hetmanate. The other, which we may call 'civic' or imperial, admitted imperial elites of non-Slavic background to the Russian nation. In my view, competition between these two models of Russian identity was most fully manifested in the realm of historiography, influencing the course of the first public debate in imperial Russia – the controversy over the origins of the Rus' state and the role of the Varangians in it.

Nation and Empire

The reforms of Peter I took the Russian state and its elites an impressive distance along the road to modernization and Westernization. They also sowed the seeds of resentment against the West, and, as Rogger has convincingly shown, created preconditions for the rise of Russian national sentiment and self-assertiveness. Those characteristics of the new Russian spirit first became fully apparent during the rule of the Duchess of Courland, Anna Ioannovna, who was elected to the Russian throne in 1730. The Russian elites particularly resented the influence of the empress's lover and confidant, Ernst Johann Biron (Bühren), on the government of their country. Not surprisingly, the death of Anna was followed by the removal of Biron from power. The subsequent installation of Elizabeth, a daughter of Peter I, on the Russian throne caused an upsurge of patriotic feeling among the 'native' Russian nobility, which led to attacks on foreigners in St Petersburg by guard regiments that supported Elizabeth.[6]

Expressions of support for the empress articulated in terms of anti-Western and Russian patriotic discourse were soon to follow. Representatives of the church hierarchy were especially active: their ranks were swelled by Ukrainian recruits who adopted a new all-Russian identity and felt deep animosity towards Westerners in the Russian service. Archbishop Amvrosii Iushkevych of Novgorod, a native of Ukraine, accused foreigners of discriminating against native Russians and causing the country's decline. He stated in a sermon that foreigners 'spared no means to convict a Russian experienced in the arts, as engineer, as architect, or soldier ... to remove him by exile or execution, simply because he was an engineer or architect, a student of Peter the Great.'[7] Archbishop Amvrosii knew what he was talking about. He was close to one of the Ukrainian 'students of Peter I,' Teofilakt Lopatynsky, who was stripped of his archepiscopal status, imprisoned, and tortured on the orders of Biron. He was released after Biron's exile, sheltered by Amvrosii, and reinstated as an archbishop by Elizabeth. It was claimed that before staging her coup, Elizabeth had visited Lopatynsky, who recognized in her 'the spark of Peter the Great.'[8]

It has long been argued by students of the period that in terms of the presence and influence of foreigners at court, Anna Ioannovna's reign was little different from those of her immediate predecessors or successors on the Russian throne. Why, then, was the change of rulers in 1740–1 accompanied by so much talk about foreigners? Something had clearly changed in Russian society, predisposing it to make the national factor supreme in public discourse. In order to fight foreign influences in the capital, the Russian elites availed themselves of Western instruments – the ideas of nation, the common good, and loyalty to the fatherland. Elizabeth's reign abounded in statements bolstering Russian pride. Her direct descent from Peter I was stressed on numerous occasions, giving a new twist to the interpretation of her father's role in Russian politics and culture. Now Peter was seen not as a Westernizer of Russia but as a protector of Russia against foreign encroachments.[9] It was hoped that the link to Peter and the new anti-Western interpretation of his rule would help Elizabeth overcome the dubious circumstances of her accession to power (a coup d'état, accompanied by the arrest of the child emperor Ivan VI) and mobilize broad support for her.[10] Anti-Western sentiments were further bolstered by wars with the European powers.

The construction of Russian identity took on new characteristics during the reign of Catherine II, the longest-ruling Russian monarch of the eighteenth century. Born Sophia Augusta Frederika Anhalt-Zerbst in Germany, and implicated in the murder of her husband, Emperor Peter III, Catherine also took the throne by means of a coup d'état. Unexpectedly, given her background, but quite logically, given the dominant trends in Russian society of the time, Catherine found support in Russia's growing self-awareness and its acute sense of danger from the West.[11] The manifesto announcing her ascension to the throne read: 'Our Orthodox Church is being menaced by the adoption of foreign rites: our military prestige, raised so high by our victorious army, is being degraded by the conclusion of dishonorable peace. All the respected traditions of our fatherland are being trampled underfoot.'[12] When making her first appearance before the guards who staged the coup, Catherine wore a military uniform dating back to the times of Peter I.[13] Indeed, Catherine followed in the footsteps of Elizabeth, who from the first day of Catherine's arrival in Russia as the bride of Peter III styled her as an admirer of Orthodoxy and Russia in general. A talented student, Catherine played the Russian national card and exploited the existing cult of Peter I to the fullest. On that score she outdid Elizabeth herself, who was, after all, a daughter of Peter I. Catherine II presented herself as Peter's daughter in spirit and a continuator of the emperor's deeds. She often bolstered her own image by invoking the cult of Peter, as in 1782, when she erected a monument to him and inscribed it 'Petro Primo Caterina Secunda.'[14]

At the same time, Catherine's 'official' nationalism was quite different from that of Elizabeth's day. The favouring of 'native' Russians and hatred of foreigners that were so much a part of official discourse in the 1740s and 1750s were replaced in the 1760s with a policy that promoted not the ethnic but the imperial Russian nation. The impressive non-Orthodox churches built on Nevskii prospekt in St Petersburg during Catherine's reign perfectly exemplify the court's toleration of foreign cultures. The government commissioned geographical and ethnographic surveys of the Russian Empire, recognizing if not celebrating its multiethnic character. Andrew Swinton, a British visitor to St Petersburg in 1789, reflected on both features of Russian life in the following note on his voyage to Russia's northern capital: 'In Petersburg there is no need of this compliance: let foreigners be dressed ever so oddly, they will find, in every lane, subjects of the Russian Empire to keep them in countenance. She brings into this ball her various swarms, from the snowy mountains of Kamschatka, to the fertile plains of the Ukraine – a space of 4,000 miles! Siberians, Tongusians, Calmucs, and an endless train of Tatar nations, the Fins, the Cossacs, etc.'[15] On the other hand, the tolerance extended to foreigners and their cultures coexisted in Russian records of the time with a growing sense of Russian pride and superiority manifested even in the writings of Catherine herself. Rejected was the slavish imitation of Western manners, customs, and way of life.[16] The recognition of the empire's multiethnic character was accompanied by a desire to eradicate local particularities in government, law, and custom – a desire clearly apparent in imperial policy towards the Cossack Hetmanate.[17]

Pride in Russia as a state and as the imperial homeland of a variety of ethnic groups was promoted in numerous writings and declarations of the era. The voices of such individuals as Prince Mikhail Shcherbatov, who favoured native Russian rulers, were more the exception than the rule.[18] Anti-Western feeling was directed not against foreigners in Russia but against the Western powers and other enemies of Russia, such as the Catholic Poles. There can be little doubt that the foreign-born empress felt much more comfortable with a discourse exalting the imperial nation than with 'nativist' rhetoric, but Catherine's personal background was only partly responsible for that change in the emphasis of Russian national discourse. Another factor was the penetration into Russia of ideas and vocabulary that advanced the construction of 'civic' or imperial nationalism. These were the ideas of the French *philosophes*, whose works Catherine II admired and with whom she was in constant correspondence. During her reign, special consideration was given to the ideas of the common good and the fatherland, which had first appeared in Russian official discourse in the times of Peter I. Promising young Cossack officers like Oleksander Bezborodko and Petro Zavadovsky were brought to St Petersburg to serve the empire instead of their Little Russian *patria*.

Western ideas embodied in the terms 'citizen,' 'society,' and 'liberty' aroused opposition from Russians who wanted to undo the damage they were inflicting on authoritarian rule. In 1797 Catherine's son and successor, Paul I, sought to obliterate the memory of his mother's rule and curb the penetration of French revolutionary ideas by prohibiting the use of the word 'society,' in print and ordering 'fatherland' to be replaced with 'state' and 'citizens' with 'inhabitants' or 'dwellers.'[19] But it proved impossible to turn back the clock.

Reading Back the Nation: The Expulsion of the Normans

Historical writing was an all-important element in the formation and reformulation of Russian national identity during the rule of both Elizabeth and Catherine II. History, which attracted the attention of

Catherine II in the 1780s, first took on central importance in public debate in the mid-eighteenth century. The autumn of 1749 and the spring of 1750 witnessed the first and longest academic debate on the history of Rus' that ever took place in the Russian Empire. It took twenty-nine sessions of the Conference of the Imperial Academy of Sciences, held between 23 October and 8 March, to reach a conclusion. Polemics dealt with the role played by the Varangians in the early history of Rus' and focused on the origins of the Russian name, state, and nation. The roots of these phenomena were sought in the early history of Kyivan Rus'. The acquisition of Kyiv and Left-Bank Ukraine by the Muscovite tsars in the second half of the seventeenth century encouraged a search for imperial origins in the history of Kyivan Rus'. Although Novgorod featured prominently in debates on the invitation to the Varangians, Kyiv played an important role as the seat of the Rurikid dynasty and the capital of the state. It was particularly significant that the author of the *Synopsis* (1674), which ruled supreme in imperial historiography of the first half of the eighteenth century, placed Kyiv at the centre of the Russian imperial narrative.[20]

The debate itself was provoked by the decision of Gerhard Friedrich Müller, the official historiographer of the Imperial Academy of Sciences, to present a talk based on his dissertation, 'Origines gentis et nominis Russorum,' at a public meeting of the academy. The talk was given initially at a meeting of the Academy Conference on 23 August 1749, where the decision was made to publish it in the academy's two official languages, Latin and Russian. In spite of that decision, two scholars who had attended Müller's lecture, including the all-powerful permanent secretary of the academy, J.D. Schumacher, found certain elements of it 'prejudicial' to Russia and unfit for publication. The president of the academy, Kyrylo Rozumovsky (Kirill Razumovsky), a native of the Hetmanate and brother of Empress Elizabeth's husband, Oleksii Rozumovsky (Aleksei Razumovsky), decided to postpone the public meeting of the academy that was to feature the reading of Müller's dissertation.[21] Its text was forwarded for appraisal to a group of scholars that, aside from the German members of the academy, included two native Russians, Mikhail Lomonosov and Vasilii Trediakovsky.[22] That was the starting point of the debate that lasted until March 1750. Its outcome was unfavourable to Müller, who was accused of denigrating Russia and its people by denying their ancient origins. His assertion that the Varangians of the Primary Chronicle were in fact Scandinavians who had given the name Rus' to the region and its population caused particular offence. Müller's dissertation was banned, he was demoted in academic rank, and his salary was halved.[23]

What factors contributed to this outcome, and what was their relation to the construction of Russian national identity? To answer these questions, a number of relevant contexts must be considered. One of them is the internal politics of the academy. J.D. Schumacher and Petr Krekshin, the two employees of the academy who raised the issue of Müller's 'political unreliability,' were in fact his personal enemies and rivals. Müller had numerous conflicts with Schumacher on issues pertaining to the administration of the academy, while Krekshin could not forgive Müller a negative review of his work on the genealogy of the Rus' princes written in 1747. Lomonosov, the author of a number of negative assessments of Müller's dissertation, also held grudges against him. In 1744, Müller had prevented the publication of Lomonosov's textbook of rhetoric. It is important to note that the attack on Müller was led by the permanent secretary of the academy (Schumacher), an amateur historian (Krekshin), and a professor of chemistry (Lomonosov), while such recognized specialists in the humanities as Vasilii Tatishchev and Vasilii Trediakovsky were reluctant to take an active part in the campaign orchestrated by Schumacher, indicating that there was more academic politics than pure scholarship in the controversy over Müller's dissertation.

Another important context that helps explain the course of events and illuminates their broader significance is the nationalist sentiment that marked the age of Elizabeth and the negative attitude of the Russian public to the West in general and to Westerners in their midst in particular. Schumacher and Krekshin's accusations that Müller had assaulted the dignity of the Russian nation fell on fertile ground. They were addressed ultimately to Kyrylo Rozumovsky, the first 'Russian' to be appointed president of the academy (in 1746) after the consecutive rule of four German presidents. Rozumovsky and his former tutor and honorary member of the academy, G.N. Teplov, were trying to establish the court's control over that institution, composed mostly of foreigners whose loyalty to Russia was presumed to be questionable.[24] In the eyes of the public, the academy was failing to carry out one of its basic tasks, that of training 'Russians,' and continuing to employ mostly foreigners. In the early 1740s, a number of prominent members of the academy left Russia for the West, taking with them the results of their work, whose publication in the West was regarded as undermining Russian interests. Schumacher, suspected of having a hand in Western publications unfavourable to Russia, was even arrested by the authorities but soon released and reinstated in the academy. In 1744, the authorities reacted to criticism by imposing severe restrictions on the use of the academy's library, archives, and research materials. Guards were posted at academy buildings, indicating official distrust. In 1748, Müller, whose task was the writing of a 'general history of Russia,' was placed under house arrest on suspicion of having sent documents on the history of the academy abroad. His working papers were confiscated, and two Russians, Lomonosov and Trediakovsky, were assigned to study his archive. The report compiled by Lomonosov found Müller innocent but left certain doubts about his true intentions.[25]

Thus the historiographic discussion concerning Müller's dissertation took place in a charged atmosphere of suspected espionage and a search for traitors among the academy's foreign members. But what exactly was so harmful to Russian pride in Müller's dissertation? Here one must consider yet another context of the debate – the historiographic one. This debate, later known as the 'Varangian controversy,' correctly identified the principal bone of contention – the role of the Varangians in founding the Russian state and nation. Those scholars who considered that role all-important and regarded the Varangians as Normans (Scandinavians) became known as Normanists, while their opponents, who either dismissed the leading role of the Varangians in early Rus' history or considered them Slavs, were dubbed anti-Normanists. In his thesis, Müller presented the main elements of what came to be known as the 'Norman theory.' He claimed that the Slavs had not settled the Dnipro region until the times of the Byzantine emperor Justinian and thus did not possess the glorious ancient history attributed to them by Rus' chroniclers and early modern historians. He also maintained that the Varangians in general and Rurik in particular were of Scandinavian stock. They had conquered the Slavs and given the name 'Rus'' to their dynasty and state.

This was not the first time that such ideas had been expressed in public. Back in 1732, in his introduction to an excerpt from the Primary Chronicle, Müller had identified the Varangians as Normans who came mainly from Norway. In his introduction Müller developed ideas first put forward by his predecessor in the academy, Gottlieb-Siegfried Bayer, who published a number of important essays on early Rus' history, including 'De Varagis' (1729), and 'Origines russicae' (1736), claiming that the Varangians were Scandinavians or 'Normans.' But times were changing. As noted above, the rule of Elizabeth saw rising xenophobia, particularly against foreigners in the Russian service. Moreover, the war with Sweden in 1741–2 reminded Russians of the long Northern War of the early eighteenth century, making the very thought that the Russians could have been conquered and given their name, dynasty, and state by the Scandinavians insupportable to the Russian elites.[26]

Lomonosov was probably not far wrong when he stated that the presentation of Müller's views at a public meeting of the academy would turn the Russian public not only against Müller but also against the academy itself. It was Lomonosov, then an amateur historian, who presented an alternative Russian view of the origins of Rus' in his numerous memoranda on Müller's dissertation. The factual basis for his critique was provided by the Kyivan *Synopsis*, whose focus on the origins of the nation had finally found appreciation in Russia. Defenders of Russian historical pride had little choice but to turn to that source, whose treatment of the Varangians as Slavs and concept of a 'Slavo-Rossian nation' offered a rebuttal to the views advanced by the early Normanists. Consequently, Lomonosov urged the academy to adopt the *Synopsis* as the standard text on Russian history. In his repudiation of Müller, Lomonosov rejected his opponent's alleged presentation of the Slavic record as a history of defeats and expulsions from the territories they had originally settled. Lomonosov claimed that the Slavs, whose name he derived from the word 'glory' (*slava*), and whom he traced back to the ancient Roxolani, had settled the Dnipro basin long before the times of Emperor Justinian. He also maintained that the Varangians were Slavs, as was Rurik and his dynasty, and that the latter had not conquered the local Slavs but had been invited to Novgorod. Lomonosov's views on the origins of Rus' were shared to various degrees and with different reservations by the members of the commission struck to investigate the Müller case. They served as the basis for Rozumovsky's report, which reprimanded Müller and called his dissertation 'prejudicial.'[27]

The outcome of the Müller debate marked a major change in Russian historiography. The treatment of Rurik and his dynasty as Slavs flew in the face of the long tradition of Rus', Muscovite, and Russian historiography, which considered the foreign origins of the Rurikids a positive factor, not a negative one. In the past, the foreign origins of the dynasty had not only helped Kyivan princes differentiate clearly between the Rurikid clan and the boyar elites but also allowed Ivan the Terrible to consider himself a German and trace his origins back to Emperor

Augustus. As late as the first decades of the eighteenth century, the Russian historian Aleksei Mankiev, the author of *Iadro rossiiskoi istorii* (The Kernel of Russian History), continued to regard Augustus as Ivan's ancestor.[28] Now all that was rejected, mainly because of the endless confrontation with the West, punctuated by wars with Sweden, Prussia, and France, and the backlash against powerful foreigners in the St Petersburg administration. Given this new outlook, the concept of the nation emerged in Russian historiography as no less important than the concept of the dynasty, and both were considered quintessentially Russian.

Lomonosov's historiographic revolution was a sign of things to come in nineteenth-century Russian historiography, but the potential of the new paradigm was less obvious to contemporaries. The debate became a turning point at which Russian historiography failed to turn. Catherine II adopted a different approach to the writing of Russian history. One might assume that the German-born empress was not displeased by a theory that claimed Germanic ancestry for the first rulers of Rus'. In any case, over Lomonosov's protests, the new empress appointed another German, A.N. von Schlözer, as historiographer of the academy – a position theoretically reserved for 'native Russians.' As it turned out, Schlözer was an ardent supporter of the Norman theory.

Reading Back the Empire: The Return of the Normans

Müller's and Lomonosov's interpretations of Russian history, as shaped by the debate of 1749–50, represented fundamentally opposing views of the Russian past. Müller, applying the latest achievements of Western scholarship in the criticism of historical texts, allegedly denied Russia its 'proper' place in history, while Lomonosov, relying on outdated compilations like the Kyivan *Synopsis*, presumably restored Russian history to the glory it was thought to deserve. The historians of Catherine's age appear to have regarded this as a false dichotomy and sought to combine scholarship with love of the fatherland without detriment to either. The first attempts to chart an independent course between 'Normanism' and 'nativism' may be seen in the writings of Russia's foremost historian of the first half of the eighteenth century, Vasilii Tatishchev. His political outlook was formed in the era of Peter I, and his historical views were developed in the 1730s, during the rule of Anna Ioannovna. Tatishchev began work on his *Istoriia Rossiiskaia* (Russian History) in 1729, submitted the first draft of the manuscript ten years later, and continued working on it until his death in 1750. The publication of the mammoth history, which was largely a compendium of Rus' and Muscovite chronicles, did not begin until the late 1760s, but the work was known in manuscript to Müller and Lomonosov and influenced the field long before its appearance in print. In his views on Rus' history, Tatishchev was closer to the Normanists than to their opponents, and during the Varangian debate he refused to condemn Müller, whom he deeply respected as a scholar. Indeed, around the time of the debate, he was busy translating into Russian the 'Normanist' articles of Bayer, which he included as chapters of his history of Russia.[29]

At the same time, Tatishchev was by no means lacking in Russian patriotism. He began his historical research with the goal of paying tribute to Peter I and his accomplishments. He criticized Western historians for denying Russia its ancient past and resolved to cleanse Russian history of Polish 'lies and legends.' How did Tatishchev manage to combine his patriotism with his 'Normanism'? First of all, he rejected the theory that the Varangians had conquered the Novgorodian Slavs, asserting that they had been invited to Novgorod by the legendary Slavic ruler Gostomysl. This ruler, unknown to chroniclers prior to the fifteenth century, was most probably an invention of a fifteenth-century Novgorodian chronicler who tried to counter the aggression of the Muscovite Rurikids with legends about Novgorod's pre-Rurikid past. Now the Gostomysl legend was used to counter the perceived German threat. By adopting it, Tatishchev not only implicitly rejected the view that the Slavs had been conquered but also suggested that the Kyivan state had been established by the Slavs long before the arrival of the Varangians. He also traced the non-Slavic Rus'/Varangians not to Sweden or Norway, as did the Normanists of the time, but to the politically more acceptable Finland. The population of the Rus' realm, according to Tatishchev, consisted of autochthonous Slavs, whose name he derived from the word 'glory' and whom he traced back to the Scythians, and migrant Rus'/Varangians, whose ancestors he located among the Sarmatians dwelling in Finland.[30] This view of the old Rus' nation as a conglomerate of peoples of various ethnic backgrounds contradicted Lomonosov's thesis of the Slavic origins of the Rus' nation. At the same time, it was much more in accord with the sources and the latest achievements of historical scholarship; moreover, it had the advantage of being politically correct in a multinational empire ruled for most of the eighteenth century by foreign-born tsars and tsarinas. It comes as no surprise that the Tatishchev scheme found numerous followers at the court of Catherine II, not least the empress herself.

While the writings of Bayer and Müller contained only a potential threat to Russian national pride, historical works produced by foreigners and published in the second half of the eighteenth century turned that threat into reality, ironically proving Lomonosov right on the issue of the political danger posed by foreign dominance of imperial historiography. Once von Schlözer, the new official historiographer of the academy, left the Russian Empire for Germany in 1767, he was free of Russian censorship. While his works on Russian history published abroad laid the foundations for Russian historical scholarship, in St Petersburg they were regarded as offensive to Russian pride. Schlözer slighted his Russian colleagues, who, in his opinion, knew little but their chronicles and did not read foreign-language sources or historical works. He also denied Russia its glorious legendary past, stating in that regard: 'May patriots not be incensed, but their history does not go back to the Tower of Babel.' He also stressed the savagery of Russian life before the arrival of the Varangians, claiming that the latter, whom he considered to be of Germanic descent, had civilized Russia. Schlözer's views on Russian history were echoed by another foreigner in the Russian service, the French physician Nicolas-Gabriel LeClerc. His six-volume *Physical, Moral, Civil, and Political History of Ancient and Modern Russia* appeared in France between 1783 and 1794. LeClerc extended Schlözer's thesis about the primitivism and barbarism of the Russians to the times of Peter I, who, in his opinion, was the first ruler to introduce civilization in Russia. In many ways LeClerc's view of Russian history reflected the main postulates of Western Enlightenment historiography, whose writers took a dim view of the pre-Enlightenment past of their own countries. Needless to say, the 'enlightened' foreigners saw much less civilization and much more barbarism in Russia than in the West and reacted accordingly. For the Russian elites, who generally discovered the concept of the fatherland and became interested in its history only in the Age of Enlightenment, Western 'revisionism' of the historical foundations of their patriotism was hardly acceptable.[31]

Few people were more upset by the Western attack on the Russian past than Catherine II. Existing Russian historiography did not satisfy her. The history of Russia written and published in the early 1770s by Prince Mikhail Shcherbatov was no match for Western writings. Shcherbatov, a much more sophisticated historian than Lomonosov (he endorsed Tatishchev's stand on Normanism), was not only suspected of having helped LeClerc produce his blasphemous attack on the

Russian past but was also considered by the empress to be a boring writer (for good reason). Besides, Shcherbatov's work on Russian history progressed too slowly. The publication of Tatishchev's history had just begun, but his work was even less readable than Shcherbatov's. Thus, on being presented with Tatishchev's multivolume work, the empress set out to write a history of Russia herself. It was serialized in one of the Russian journals beginning in 1783. Her closest collaborators also sought to enlist the services of a 'full-time' historian to rebut LeClerc's allegations. Such a historian was found in the person of Major-General Ivan Boltin, a subordinate of the empress's closest collaborator, Prince Grigorii Potemkin. Boltin indeed turned out to be a saviour of Russian historical pride. In 1788, five years after the appearance of the first volume of LeClerc's history, he produced a two-volume critique of the Frenchman's work. Ideologically, Boltin was very much under Catherine's influence. His study demonstrated the growing maturity of Russian imperial historiography and its considerable progress since the times of the Lomonosov-Müller debate. Boltin managed to turn Enlightenment ideas against the enlightened critics of Russian barbarism. On the one hand, he insisted on the universality of historical laws and claimed that the Russian nation was like any other in Europe, since the major developments in Russian history had their parallels in the West. On the other hand, indicating the importance of climate in human history, he insisted on the peculiarity of the Russian national character and customs. For the first time, the defence of Russian pride was formulated in a language common to all of Europe – that of scholarship and enlightenment.[32]

What about the accursed question of Rus' origins? Here Tatishchev's interpretation of the past served as a guiding light to both Catherine II and Boltin. Tatishchev's acceptance of the non-Slavic Germanic origins of the Varangians was balanced by his insistence on the multiethnic character of the original Rus'/Russian nation. Following in Tatishchev's footsteps, the empress believed that the Varangians were related to the Novgorodian ruler Gostomysl and thus were not invaders but lawful rulers of Novgorod. The invitation to the Varangians had been extended by the Rus', Slavs, and Chud. According to Catherine, the Rus' constituted the autochthonous population of the region, which merged with the Slavs and later with the Varangians, eventually forming one people. Boltin presented a slightly different picture of early Rus' nation-building. According to him, Rus' was the name of a Sarmatian (Finno-Ugric) tribe, part of which merged with the Varangians to form a people known as the Varangian Rus'. The Rus' were eventually conquered by the Slavs, whose language and letters were adopted by the whole realm. Boltin nevertheless believed that the Rus' (Finno-Ugric) and Slavic languages coexisted for a long time. He wrote in that regard: 'Both the Rus' and the Slavs understood, just as today in Olonets all Russians can speak Karelian and all Karelians can speak Russian.' Boltin confused the issue somewhat with this example, creating the impression that the Rus' language had developed into the Karelian of his own day, while the language he originally called 'Slavic' had turned into 'Russian.' More importantly, Boltin's interpretation showed that he was prepared to read the eighteenth-century ethnolinguistic situation back into the past.[33]

The Russian intellectual elite celebrated the multiethnic character of the empire. That motif was quite prominent in the panegyrics written to praise the colonization of southern Ukraine by Prince Grigorii Potemkin, the governor-general of New Russia – the province carved out of the Hetmanate and Zaporozhian and Tatar lands. The author of one of those texts, V.P. Petrov, who was a student of Mikhail Lomonosov's, stressed the multiethnic character of the project and declared the loyalty of the new subjects to the empress:

All Kherson has bestirred itself
One sees no end to it ...
The Moldavian, the Armenian,
The Indian and the Hellene
Or the black Ethiopian
Whatever the sky beneath which
He came into the world
Catherine is the mother of all.

Praising Potemkin for his achievements in settling southern Ukraine with foreigners, Petrov wrote, addressing the governor general,

May you be known as the foster father
Of tribes from the whole world,
Plants from foreign countries
Are moving north.
Transform alien peoples
Into Russians.[34]

According to Petrov, the settlers who accepted Catherine as their sovereign were also embarking on the path of political Russification. The Little Russians, whose territories were appropriated by the empire along with their history, did not count for much in this context, since they were considered no less Russian than their counterparts in Russia proper. They and their history were fully incorporated into the all-Russian narrative and identity, comprising both the narrow Slavic and 'nativist' models and the broader 'civic' or imperial ones.

2 Incorporated Identity

In the course of the eighteenth century, as a result of successful wars with its western and southern neighbors, the Russian Empire was increasingly becoming a multiethnic and multicultural polity. The dramatic expansion of its territory brought millions of new subjects under the rule of St Petersburg and greatly changed the ethnic balance of the population. If at the time of Peter I ethnic Russians constituted roughly 70 per cent of the entire population of the state, by the time of the third partition of Poland they had been reduced to little more than 50 per cent, with ethnic Ukrainians increasing from 13 to 22 per cent and Belarusians constituting 8 per cent of the population of the empire in 1795.[1]

Ukrainians emerged as the most active builders of the imperial ideology, institutions, and state apparatus, but they were also among the principal victims of the new imperial project. When it comes to dominant trends in philosophy and scholarship, the Age of Enlightenment was first and foremost an age of reason. Whether they governed small principalities or multiethnic empires, eighteenth-century rulers attempted to turn their realms into well-ordered states. The ideas of cameralism, which, like the vision of the well-ordered state, were products of post-1648 development, set rulers of Central and Eastern Europe on the road of cooperation with existing social estates, cities, and regions, which jealously guarded their rights and privileges and were in no hurry to sacrifice them for the greater glory of advancing absolutism. The Russian Empire, a self-styled 'European state,' was no exception to that general rule. The ideas of the well-ordered state and cameralism came to Russia from Germany, and, unsurprisingly, it was westward-looking Kyivan intellectuals who helped prepare the empire for the acceptance of the new political culture. 'Its philosophical underpinning,' writes Marc Raeff, 'was natural law and neo-stoicism, its intellectual foundation the rationalism of seventeenth-century natural philosophy, and its institutional implementation was to be found in the policies of absolute monarchies and territorial sovereignties. The rhetoric, logic and neo-scholastic metaphysics taught at the Kyivan Academy served as indispensable mental preparation for the reception of the intellectual presuppositions of European political culture, while information on institutional practices was provided by foreign residents and Russian envoys abroad.'[2]

Throughout the eighteenth century, the alumni of the Kyivan Academy continued to transmit Western ideas and play an important part in the affairs of state and church – roles they had assumed under Peter I. Between 1754 and 1768 alone, more than three hundred students and alumni of the Kyivan Academy moved to Russia. The Latin that they learned at the academy prepared them well for classes in medicine. Thus, in the eighteenth century there were twice as many Ukrainian doctors in the empire as Russian ones. In the last two decades of the century, more than one third of the students at the St Petersburg teachers' college came from Ukraine.[3] By some estimates, Ukrainians accounted for half the non-noble intelligentsia in the eighteenth-century Russian Empire.[4]

The peak of Ukrainian influence in the empire occurred during the rule of Elizabeth, when Oleksii Rozumovsky, the son of a rank-and-file Cossack from the Hetmanate, became the empress's husband. At that time, all Russian eparchies except one were administered by Kyivans.[5] And the office of hetman, abolished under Anna Ioannovna, was restored, with Oleksii's younger brother, Kyrylo Rozumovsky, assuming the new position. Despite the spectacular achievements of Ukrainians in the imperial capital, the administrative, economic, and military decline of the Hetmanate in the second half of the eighteenth century undermined the Cossack elite's power base and its ability to weather unfavourable turns of imperial policy. Such a turn came with the enthronement of Catherine II. In her pursuit of enlightened forms of government and rationalization of the empire's administrative and economic system, she resolved to abolish Cossack autonomy and the traditional rights and privileges of the Cossack institutions.[6] In 1763, the office of hetman was abolished once and for all. In 1775, the imperial authorities liquidated the Zaporozhian Host in the lower Dnipro region. That Cossack polity had outlived its usefulness to the empire after the decisive victories over the Crimean Tatars and Ottomans in the first

Russo-Turkish War (1768–74), while its lands were needed for the imperial province of New Russia, which was to be settled by foreign colonists. The Cossack Hetmanate became history in 1782: its administrative structure was replaced with imperial provincial administrations.[7]

What was the impact, if any, of these developments on the self-awareness of the Cossack elites of the Hetmanate? Did they manage to preserve their unique political, social, and cultural identity despite the incorporation of their homeland into the empire, or did they modify it to fit new circumstances, or even abandon it altogether? This chapter sketches the development of Ukrainian identity in the second half of the eighteenth century, paying special attention to the role of history in the political and literary discourse of the period.

The Dialogue That Never Happened

Although it seems incredible in retrospect, Catherine's rule began on a positive note for the Hetmanate. Hetman Kyrylo Rozumovsky was among those who helped the German-born empress ascend the Russian throne. Thus the enthronement of Catherine II emboldened the Hetmanate's elites, making them believe that the time was ripe to build on what they had achieved during the rule of Elizabeth and extend the Hetmanate's rights and privileges in the Russian Empire. The tactic chosen to achieve that goal was quite traditional – a demand for the restoration of the rights promised by Moscow to Hetman Bohdan Khmelnytsky in 1654.

The spirit and expectations of the time are well reflected in a long poem by Semen Divovych, a secretary at the hetman's chancellery in Hlukhiv. In the words of Andreas Kappeler, Divovych's work was 'the swan song of the autonomous Hetmanate.'[8] Entitled 'A Conversation between Great Russia and Little Russia,' the poem was completed on 21 September 1762, less than three months after Catherine's accession. It offered a historical excursus on Ukrainian-Polish and Ukrainian-Russian relations, based predominantly on the anonymous 'Brief Description of Little Russia' (1734).[9] The poem's historical narrative, which stressed the glorious deeds of the Cossacks and their loyalty to the Russian emperors, was the basis for the assertion of two main points. The first was that Great and Little Russia constituted two equal parts of a single state linked by their loyalty to the common sovereign. Secondly, Divovych demanded the equalization of Little Russian ranks with those of Great Russia. Since the Hetmanate's ranks did not correspond to the imperial system, which was based on Peter I's Table of Ranks, Little Russians found themselves at a disadvantage vis-à-vis their Russian counterparts. While the first of Divovych's arguments bolstered the cause of Ukrainian autonomy, the second advocated the integration of the Hetmanate's elites into imperial society and the Russian imperial system in general. The author of the 'Conversation' and his readers apparently saw no contradiction between the two arguments, since both were intended to raise the status of the Hetmanate and its elites in the Russian Empire.

Divovych resolved the disagreement on these issues between Great and Little Russia in favour of the latter. Impressed by the tale of the Cossacks' heroic deeds and their loyalty to the tsars, illustrated inter alia by Rozumovsky's role in Catherine's ascension to the throne, Great Russia accepts the Little Russian 'truth.' She says to Little Russia:

> Enough – I now accept your truth;
> I believe it all; I respect you and acknowledge your valour;
> Hence I shall adjust your ranks to the measure
> And will never renounce friendship with you.
> We shall live in unprecedented harmony from now on
> And both serve faithfully in one state.[10]

In making his argument in favour of Little Russian distinctiveness and equality with Great Russia, Divovych touched upon a number of important issues pertaining to eighteenth-century Ukrainian identity. First of all, the text of the poem indicates that the author did not think in terms of a common Russo-Ukrainian history or identity but recognized only the state and its ruler as common or 'all-Russian.' Beyond that, his world was clearly divided into two parts, Little Russian and Great Russian. For him, even the imperial ranks were 'Great Russian,' not 'imperial.' Little Russia, which Divovych alternatively calls 'Ukraine,' had an origin and history different from those of Great Russia. It began with the legendary period of Khazar dominance and then came under the rule of Polish kings (among whom Stefan Batory won the author's special praise for his organization of the Cossacks) and Russian tsars. Crucial for Divovych (and, apparently, for his contemporaries) was the confusing issue of the Little Russians' and Great Russians' exclusive claims to the name 'Russia.' In the 'Conversation,' Divovych asserted his compatriots' right to call their land 'Russia,' simultaneously stressing the differences between the two countries:

GREAT RUSSIA: Do you know with whom you are speaking, or have you forgotten?
I am Russia, after all: why do you ignore me? …
LITTLE RUSSIA: I know that you are Russia; that is my name as well.
Why do you intimidate me? I myself am trying to put on a brave face.
I did not submit to you but to your sovereign,
Under whose auspices you were born of your ancestors.
Do not think that you yourself are my master,
But your sovereign and mine is our common ruler.
And the difference between us is in our given names:
You are great, I am little; we live in neighbouring lands.[11]

The 'Conversation' impresses one as the strongest manifestation of Ukrainian political and historical distinctiveness since the times of Hetman Ivan Mazepa, and it comes as little surprise that Divovych reinforced his argument with a number of themes taken from the discourse of Mazepa's days. Among them were the Khazar myth, which established the separate ethnic origins of the Cossacks; the idea of Ukraine's voluntary submission to the rule of the Russian monarchs; the cult of Bohdan Khmelnytsky as the guarantor of Little Russian rights and freedoms; and, last but not least, the idea of the Little Russian nation as collective possessor of rights granted by the Polish kings and Russian tsars.[12] Of course, given prevailing circumstances, Divovych put as much distance as possible between himself and Hetman Mazepa's legacy. He stressed that Mazepa alone, not Little Russia as a whole, had committed treason in 1708 and pointed out that the Great Russians had had quite a few traitors of their own, thereby dismissing the accusation that the Ukrainian hetmans and Ukrainians in general were unreliable subjects. Declaring himself a loyal subject of the tsars, Divovych nevertheless indicated his preference for a republican form of government: in the 'Conversation,' Little Russia notes that Great Russia does not rule it in a republican manner.

Was Divovych alone in expressing such dangerous views? It appears not. Catherine's ascension to the throne, followed by her ukase of May 1763, which reinstated chamberlains' courts in Ukraine and proclaimed that the Hetmanate should be administered according to 'Little Russian rights,' aroused great expectations among the elite of the Hetmanate. It emboldened the participants in the Hlukhiv general officers' council of September 1763, which was convened at the invitation of Hetman Rozumovsky to initiate reforms in the Hetmanate. The council approved a judicial reform restoring the court system according to the provisions of the Lithuanian Statute, thereby distancing it from the imperial model. The participants in the council also petitioned Catherine II for a broad range of reforms, including the establishment of a Ukrainian Diet. If implemented, these reforms would have strengthened Ukrainian autonomy and widened the gap between Ukraine and Russia in political, legal, and economic terms. The texts of a speech delivered at the council and of a petition to the empress on behalf of 'the hetman, the nobility, the Little Russian Host and nation' give a good idea of how Divovych's poetic vision was translated into the language of political, legal, and economic demands.[13]

The speech in question was modelled on Polish political speeches of the era, which lamented the decline of the fatherland and looked to the glorious past for inspiration. For the author of the Hlukhiv speech, such a 'golden age' was the era of Bohdan Khmelnytsky, when Ukraine had been assured of the recognition of its rights and privileges by the Russian tsars. The speaker's praise for the rights granted to the 'Rus' nation' under the Commonwealth ('of which the above-mentioned republic should boast even today to the whole world') and his statement that Little Russia's troubles had begun with its transfer to the rule of the Russian tsars found certain parallels in declarations made by Hetmans Ivan Mazepa and Pylyp Orlyk concerning their breaches with Muscovy. The difference, however, was that the Hlukhiv speaker pointed a finger not at the Russian rulers but at the Little Russian elites: in the spirit of the Enlightenment, he accused them of acting selfishly and neglecting the common good. The anonymous author of the speech saw the source of the problem in the growing preponderance of the Cossack Host over the nobility and called for a return to the judicial system and privileges of the Khmelnytsky era, probably unaware (or disregarding the fact) that in those days the Host had indeed ruled supreme. In the name of past Cossack glory, he called for reform, starting with the drafting of a Little Russian law code and the translation of the laws 'into our language.' He also suggested a number of measures to improve the status of the rank-and-file Cossacks vis-à-vis the peasants, reclaim Ukrainian lands appropriated by the empire, promote commerce, restore the privileges of the clergy, enserf the peasantry, and develop education in the Hetmanate.[14]

Most of these proposals (with the notable exception of the one to codify and translate the Little Russian laws) were included in the petition submitted to the empress. It asked Catherine II to confirm the privileges granted to the Little Russian hetman, the estates, and the 'whole nation' by Lithuanian princes, Polish kings, and Russian tsars. It also asked for the continued election of hetmans, the creation of a Little Russian Diet (General Council), reform of the court system according to the provisions of the Lithuanian Statute, recognition of Little Russian ranks, and confirmation and amplification of the rights of Cossack officers, rank-and-file Cossacks, and burghers. The reform of the tax system suggested by the authors of the petition was intended to equalize Ukraine with the Polish-Lithuanian Commonwealth in its trade with the rest of the empire.[15] The satisfaction of the Hlukhiv council's demands would effectively have established a distinctive political, social, and economic system in the Hetmanate, differentiating it from the rest of the empire and helping to materialize Divovych's vision of Little and Great Russia as countries united by little more than allegiance to their joint ruler.[16]

At the same time, the program of the Hlukhiv council was more modest than the vision advanced by Divovych. The authors of the Hlukhiv speech and petition had to be much more careful in formulating their views than did a Ukrainian officeholder writing to his peers. Thus, for example, they made no mention of the Khazar origins of the Cossacks, which established Ukraine's distinct, non-Rus' origins. While the author of the Hlukhiv speech maintained that the Rus' nation had become associated with the Commonwealth partly of its own free will and partly as a result of conquest, the authors of the petition cleared their ancestors of any suspicion of disloyalty towards St Petersburg, claiming that the 'Little Russian nation' had been separated from Russia by Lithuania and Poland. It is quite apparent that they tried to present their case within the context not only of Ukrainian but also of Russian historical mythology. Thus Bohdan Khmelnytsky was said to have brought Little Russia under the tsar's rule and helped to liberate the Grand Principality of Smolensk from the Poles. Nor did the Hlukhiv authors overlook the potential of the imperial myth of Peter I, which they used to bolster the Hetmanate's demand for traditional Little Russian rights. The preamble to the petition referred to Peter's decree of November 1708, which claimed that no other people had such privileges as the Little Russian nation. For all these concessions to the imperial narrative, the Hlukhiv authors clearly indicated their descent from and loyalty to the 'Little Russian nation' (in whose ranks they included everyone except the peasants), which was the possessor of rights and privileges accumulated over the centuries. And it was the Little Russian fatherland, not the Russian Empire, that commanded their primary loyalty. From that perspective, little had changed in Ukraine since the turn of the eighteenth century.

The Incorporation of the Hetmanate

In late 1763 and early 1764, obviously misreading signals coming from St Petersburg, Rozumovsky augmented the Hlukhiv petition with his own request for the establishment of a hereditary hetmancy – a project that aroused controversy in Ukraine itself. It was rejected by the local Orthodox hierarchy and supported only by a fairly limited number of the hetman's clients. His enemies at court made the most of this project, potentially threatening to the imperial power, in order to discredit Rozumovsky in the eyes of the empress. Even his allies, such as his former tutor and assistant Grigorii Teplov, changed sides as soon as Rozumovsky fell out of favour. As a result, Rozumovsky was summoned to St Petersburg and forced to resign from the hetmancy, with no new hetman elected or appointed in his stead. Another blow to Rozumovsky's standing at court came from a direction that he could hardly have expected. The ghost of Hetman Ivan Mazepa entered the higher realms of Russian politics when Vasyl Myrovych, the son of one of Mazepa's supporters, made an abortive attempt to liberate Tsar Ivan VI, imprisoned since the enthronement of Elizabeth in 1741, and install him as tsar. The tsar-prisoner was killed by the guards, and Myrovych was investigated and executed, but not before he testified that Rozumovsky had encouraged his act. The charge was groundless and did not stick, but a shadow of suspicion fell on Rozumovsky and Ukrainians in general.[17]

While the timing of Catherine's decision to abolish the office of hetman might be attributed to bad luck, such a decision would probably have been made sooner or later in any event. Even as Rozumovsky formulated a plan for the extension of Ukrainian autonomy and cherished his dynastic dreams, Catherine began the realization of her own plan for strengthening central control over the imperial periphery and introducing a number of programs to promote her vision of a well-regulated state. In December 1763, Catherine signed a decree that rationalized the imperial bureaucratic system and doubled the number of government officials. Even earlier, she interfered directly in Ukrainian affairs by issuing a decree to put an end to the Hetmanate's appropriation of imperial lands. Measures were taken to prepare a new census of

Little Russia. The reason behind the new policies emerges from Catherine's letter of 1764 to Prince A.A. Viazemsky: 'Little Russia, Livonia, and Finland are provinces which are governed by confirmed privileges and it would be improper to violate them by abolishing them all at once. However, to call them foreign and to deal with them on that basis is more than a mistake; it would be sheer stupidity. These provinces as well as Smolensk should be Russified in the easiest way possible, so that they should cease looking like wolves to the forest. The approach is easy if wise men are chosen as governors of the provinces. When the hetmans are gone from Little Russia every effort should be made to eradicate from memory the period and the hetmans, let alone promote anyone to that office.'[18]

The empress clearly regarded the autonomous territories as a nuisance that she was obliged to tolerate but whose privileges she was determined to abolish. What she meant by 'Russification' was a series of political, administrative, and judicial reforms. At stake were the region's rights and privileges, as well as its historical identity. The historical argument appeared in Grigorii Teplov's memorandum of June 1763, which laid the groundwork for the removal of Rozumovsky. Entitled 'A Note on the Disorders in Little Russia,' the memorandum asserted that 'Little Russia, not only the land but the very people, are Russian from ancient times, and consequently belong under Your Majesty's suzerainty as the possessor of the all-Russian state.'[19] Teplov thus invoked the idea of the Kyivan origins of the Russian nation and state, which was well entrenched in Russian political and historical thought, and turned it against the Ukrainian elites. He considered Little Russian privileges a remnant of the Polish era and saw them as an obstacle to the development of the Hetmanate and the empire as a whole. By this logic, 'Russification' meant cleansing the region of Polish-era rights and privileges.

Instead of an extension of traditional rights, the Little Russians were confronted with a drastic reduction of their privileges, beginning with Rozumovsky's forced resignation and the abolition of the hetmancy. It was the Russian governor-general, not the Ukrainian hetman, who became the top official in the Hetmanate. After the abolition of the hetmancy by Catherine II, the gentry of the Hetmanate continued its fight for ancient Cossack rights and privileges. At the Legislative Commission in Moscow, the cause of the Hetmanate's gentry was championed by a St Petersburg Ukrainian, Hryhorii Poletyka, who criticized the historical role of the Ukrainian hetmans but insisted on the preservation of the gentry's traditional rights and privileges and advocated the creation of a Little Russian Diet. Catherine II dissolved the Legislative Commission in 1768, not only ending her brief flirtation with parliamentarism but also denying the Ukrainian gentry a tribune for the defence of its prerogatives.[20]

The liquidation of the hetmancy and the establishment of the Little Russian College as the Hetmanate's ruling body was only the first step towards the abolition of the Hetmanate and its institutions. That process culminated in 1782 with the extension to the Hetmanate of the imperial system of provincial administration: it was divided into the provinces (*namestnichestva*) of Kyiv, Chernihiv, and Novhorod-Siverskyi. Catherine had finally fashioned an administrative structure applicable not only to the core regions of the empire but also to the Little Russian 'wolves looking to the forest.' It was an important milestone in her creation of a well-ordered unitary state: the centre gained full administrative and economic control of the Hetmanate, while its inhabitants could take full advantage of the empress's enlightened policies.

The incorporation of the Hetmanate into the Russian Empire was accompanied by the integration of the Ukrainian gentry into the Russian nobility. As Andreas Kappeler has shown, such elite co-option was standard practice in Moscow's and, later, St Petersburg's establishment of control over new territories. Ukraine was no exception to the rule. In the Ukrainian case, however, the standard exchange of regional autonomy for estate rights encountered a serious problem. The ratio of gentry to the population of Ukraine was at least twice as great as in Russia proper. That ratio was greater still in the lands of the partitioned Commonwealth. Consequently, in the last decade of the eighteenth century, the imperial authorities rescinded the recognition of the noble status of thousands of the Hetmanate's gentry. The former Cossack officers would now have to supply proof of their noble status. Not all those recognized as nobles between 1782 and 1785 retained their status, as the two lowest Ukrainian ranks were excluded from consideration. A much larger section of the Ukrainian gentry was threatened with a similar fate, which resulted in the spread of oppositionist sentiment among the Ukrainian elites of the period.[21]

Towards an All-Russian Identity

In the second half of the eighteenth century, the political decline of the Hetmanate was accompanied by a brain drain from the Cossack lands and a gradual decline of the Hetmanate's educational institutions. The opening of Moscow University and the Cadet Corps during that period intensified the exodus of Ukrainian youth to Russia. In order to get a good education, they now had to move north, joining the earlier waves of Ukrainian emigrants – a circle that Isabelle de Madariaga has called 'a veritable Ukrainian mafia.' Interesting in that regard is an observation on the educational situation in Little Russia by Opanas Shafonsky, an alumnus of the Kyivan Academy and the Universities of Halle and Leiden, a medical doctor, and author of a topographic description of Chernihiv province. 'Forty years or so ago,' wrote Shafonsky in 1786, 'when Little Russians looked for service nowhere but in Little Russia itself, the children of the gentry and of the most respected members of the community used to study Russian at home and then enter the Latin schools ... Now, because of the continuing absence of adequate gymnasia and universities [in Ukraine], gentry with sufficient means keep foreigners as teachers, but the others send their children to schools in Moscow, St. Petersburg and other places or to the various cadet corps, and some even send them abroad, so that already in the Little Russian schools it is practically only the sons of priests and other clerical children who study.'[22] The Ukrainian gentry's demands for institutions of higher learning, including universities, which we encounter in petitions to the government starting with the Hlukhiv council of 1763, fell on deaf ears in the capital. Not until 1820 was the first college-level school established in Nizhyn with funds left by Prince Oleksander Bezborodko, by far the most successful Ukrainian migrant to St Petersburg.

Bezborodko was the son of a prominent Cossack officer who served as general chancellor and general judge of the Hetmanate. He began his career as head of the chancellery of the governor-general of Little Russia, Petr Rumiantsev. Bezborodko distinguished himself by carrying out the most controversial orders of his superior, thereby provoking the animosity of his peers. In 1775, Rumiantsev recommended Bezborodko, then colonel of Kyiv and fresh from the Russo-Turkish War, to Catherine II as a person 'devoid of local sentiments.' Bezborodko was to have a spectacular career in St Petersburg, becoming secretary to the empress and advancing to a number of important posts in the Russian Foreign Office. Eventually he was appointed imperial chancellor. Bezborodko did much to attract young men from the Hetmanate to the imperial service, working diligently to help his countrymen adjust to life in the northern capital and advance their careers. Among his most famous protégés was his nephew Viktor Kochubei, a member of the inner circle of Emperor Alexander I during the early years of his rule and chairman of the Imperial Council under Nicholas I. Bezborodko encouraged his numerous relatives and clients to enter the cadet corps and then the imperial service, which, as he pointed out, promised career advancement and material remuneration. On the other hand, despite his spectacular successes in the capital, Bezborodko remained intimately attached to his homeland. When he died in 1799, the Russian dignitary Fedor Rastopchin wrote: 'Russia will be proud of him, but he did not love her as a son loves his mother.'[23]

A person 'devoid of local sentiment' or a son lacking in love for Russia – who was Bezborodko when it comes to his national identity? Most likely he considered himself 'all-Russian' in the imperial sense of that word. A clear indication that he viewed Little Russians as part of the larger Russian nation comes from the instruction of the gentry of the Chernihiv regiment to the Legislative Commission (1767). The document was heavily edited by Bezborodko on Rumiantsev's orders. The first paragraph of the instruction read: 'that as equal to equal, free to free, true and principal member of the Rus' nation since ancient times, we may be joined to its original body, united by one law.'[24] If anything, this formula echoed the traditional Ruthenian interpretation of the Union of Lublin (1569), which maintained that the Ruthenians had joined the Kingdom of Poland as equals. It also strongly recalled the *Synopsis*-style treatment of Ukrainians as part of a larger Russian entity, with the Russian state treated as a continuation of the Rurikids' Kyivan Rus'. The instruction can also be seen as foreshadowing the later claim of Ukrainian primogeniture in the larger Russian nation. Such a reading of Rus' history is particularly apparent in the anonymous 'History of the Rus',' a historical pamphlet written at the turn of the nineteenth century. The concept of the Little Russian nation as part of a larger Russian entity was also present in Bezborodko's St Petersburg writings.[25] Bezborodko was a strong believer in the benefits of good government and despised the traditionalism, irrationality, and confusion of the administrative and judicial system of the Hetmanate. He thought that its interests and those of its elites were best served by imperial institutions and laws. Bezborodko was a sincere promoter and enforcer of the Enlightenment, with its cult of reason.

He was also deeply interested in the history of his homeland and even contributed to Vasyl Ruban's *Brief Chronicle of Little Russia*, covering the history of the Hetmanate from 1734 to 1776. His account of the

Hetmanate's history was completely loyal to the empire and full of praise for the Russian rulers of Ukraine, with lists of Cossack officeholders and their achievements.[26] Bezborodko was proud of his work, as he sent a copy of the book to his father. 'I present it to you,' wrote the younger Bezborodko, 'In all fairness it belongs to you, for you have proven in many instances your love for that country, Our Beloved Fatherland, on behalf of which sincere efforts will always be made so as to preserve from oblivion the events and circumstances that indicate the fame and glory of our ancestors.'[27] It was Little Russia, not the Russian Empire, that Bezborodko called the beloved fatherland, and it was its history that he revered. But he did not want to revive that tradition and objected to the restoration of Cossack detachments: in his opinion, they might give rise to a 'nation in arms' and disturb peace and tranquillity in the region, whose inhabitants remembered the times of Khmelnytsky and were known for their devotion to Cossack ways.[28] Bezborodko conducted research on the history of Ukraine and stressed the heroic deeds of its people in order to present his homeland to a larger imperial audience in the best possible light, ostensibly as an equal partner of the Great Russians. In so doing, he wanted to facilitate its integration into the empire, not to make a case for the restoration of the Hetmanate.

The same task was carried out in St Petersburg by a number of Ukrainian writers who came to St Petersburg in the wake of their more powerful predecessors. Vasyl Ruban, the publisher of the *Brief Chronicle of Little Russia* (1777), co-authored by Bezborodko, was one of them. Before turning to the publication of books on Little Russia, he tried his hand at journalism, establishing a number of short-lived journals: *Ni to ni se* (Neither This Nor That), *Trudoliubivyi muravei* (The Industrious Ant), and *Starina i novizna* (The Old and the New). In 1773 he published *Brief Geographical, Political and Historical Notes on Little Russia*, a work dedicated to Petr Rumiantsev that introduced Ukraine to readers in the empire in the same manner as published descriptions of its other territories. In 1777 Ruban issued a revised edition of the *Notes* under the title *A Description of the Little Russian Land*. Judging by his publications, Ruban considered Little Russia to be a Russian land that had originally belonged to all-Russian rulers. In his article of 1770 entitled 'Historical Information Taken from Polish Writers and Belonging to Russian History about Russian Provinces and Cities Once under Polish Rule and Then Recovered by the Russians,' Ruban included, along with information about Livonia and Smolensk, data on 'the principalities of Kyiv,

Siver, and Chernihiv,' as well as on the Zaporozhian Cossacks.[29] Another prominent Ukrainian, Fedir Tumansky, edited the St Petersburg *Russkii magazin* (Russian Magazine), in which he published a good deal of material on Ukrainian history.[30] Tumansky's publications show that his concept of fatherland clearly extended across the boundaries of the Hetmanate to encompass the whole empire. He wrote in one of his articles: 'I think that the general history of our Fatherland will hardly attain the necessary completeness if the histories of the parts (*udelov*) of this extensive empire long remain unknown.'[31] Tumansky was a strong proponent of Russianness in opposition to the West and Western values. He certainly was one of the 'sons of Little Russia' whose activities lend some credibility to Liah Greenfeld's estimate that 'as much as 50 percent of this first mass of Russian nationalists were Ukrainians.'[32]

While Ukrainian intellectuals in St Petersburg and Moscow were successfully taking on a new imperial identity, one constituent of which was their non-exclusive Little Russian identity, what was happening in Ukraine itself? There are indications that not all Cossack officeholders were prepared to follow Bezborodko in his pursuit of Enlightenment ideals and imperial identity. As late as 1791, a group drawn from the Hetmanate's gentry sent one of their own, Vasyl Kapnist, to Berlin to negotiate with the Prussian authorities for support of an anti-Russian revolt in the former Hetmanate in the event of a Russo-Prussian war.[33] The negotiations yielded no results, and it is not clear whether the conspirators could have mustered enough support for another Mazepa-style attempt to free Ukraine from Russian control.

Generally speaking, there is good reason to believe that in the final decades of the eighteenth century the 'Russification' of the Ukrainian elites that was taking place in the imperial capitals was also being replicated in the Hetmanate. The most prominent political figures of the Hetmanate were now making their careers in the capitals, as were Ukrainian intellectuals. The journals and books that they published in St Petersburg and Moscow often relied on subscriptions and sales in Ukraine. While the concepts of the Little Russian nation and fatherland remained prominent in the political and historical discourse of the epoch, they no longer delineated the exclusivist identity of the Hetmanate's elites of the earlier period. This change in the structure and character of the national identity of the Hetmanate elites was reflected in the historical works of the period. By the turn of the nineteenth century, after the Hetmanate, its institutions and military forces had been fully incorporated into the empire, Ukraine began to witness an upsurge of historical writing. The thirst for historical knowledge was felt above all by the Ukrainian gentry, which was involved in a lengthy struggle for admission to the exclusive (and privileged) estate of the Russian nobility. The demand for historical data proving the nobiliary status of their forefathers fuelled the boom in research and writing on the history of Ukrainian ranks and the glorious deeds of those who had held them. That boom produced one of the most mysterious monuments of Ukrainian historiography, 'History of the Rus',' which has been regarded both as a strong statement of all-Russian identity and as the first work of Ukrainian national historiography. Like the Little Russian identity that it articulated, 'History' appears to have been capable of performing both functions.

3 Ukraine or Little Russia?

Few factors are as crucial to the formation of modern national identities as the creation and dissemination of common historical myths that explain the origins of a given ethnic or national group and provide it with a sense of common belonging.[1] The late eighteenth and early nineteenth centuries were a period of mass production of national myths, given the high demand for them on the burgeoning European market of ideas. Historical writing was successfully taken over by national projects and turned into a vehicle for the popularization of national mythologies at a time when history was just beginning to establish itself as a scholarly discipline.[2] A short cut to the production of elaborate mythologies that 'proved' the ancient origins of modern nations and provided them with respectable pasts was the forging of ancient documents and literary and historical works allegedly lost at some time and now 'rediscovered' to the astonishment and approval of a grateful public. More often than not, the authors of such 'rediscovered' treasures were in pursuit of literary success and/or money. They did not suspect that they were fulfilling a social demand, serving as agents of history, or acting as builders of as yet non-existent modern nations.[3]

James Macpherson (1736–96), a Scottish poet little known in his own right, produced the best-known literary mystification of the era. In the 1760s he published what he claimed to be English translations of poems by a third-century bard named Ossian. These were in fact old Irish ballads of Scottish origin that Macpherson turned into 'old Scottish epics,' contributing in the process to the formation of modern Scottish identity. Although the translations were shown to be forgeries soon after Macpherson's death, his poems appealed to the reading public far beyond Scotland and contributed to the rise of literary romanticism and national movements all over Europe.[4] Soon after the appearance of the first Russian translation of 'Ossian,' lovers of literature in the Russian Empire discovered, to their surprise and delight, that they had their own Ossian. His name was Boian, and he was a character in the *Igor Tale*, purportedly a twelfth-century epic poem once lost and now happily rediscovered, proving that the Russians had an ancient and glorious literary tradition of their own.[5] The *Tale* described a campaign against the Polovtsians by a twelfth-century prince of Novhorod-Siverskyi, a town that was fully incorporated into the Russian Empire only a few decades before the publication of the newly 'rediscovered' text in 1800. Apparently the publishers and readers of the *Tale* saw nothing unusual in the fact that their national literature had its beginnings in one of the centres of the Ukrainian Hetmanate, a Cossack state created in the mid-seventeenth century and fully absorbed by the Russian Empire in the 1780s. But the inhabitants of Novhorod-Siverskyi and the surrounding area were less than satisfied with the kind of historical mythology produced in imperial capitals. Indeed, they were on the hunt for their own ancient manuscripts that would help them make sense of their less distant Cossack past. Not surprisingly, they found one.

The manuscript, entitled 'History of the Rus',' began to circulate in the Novhorod-Siverskyi region in the mid-1820s. It traced the history of the local Cossacks, known as the Rus', to the era of the Kyivan princes, and from them, via the history of Slavic settlement in Eastern Europe, all the way back to biblical times. As an exercise in mystification, it was a much less ambitious undertaking then either Ossian or the *Igor Tale*. The introduction to the 'History of the Rus'' claimed that the manuscript had been produced by generations of monks working at the Orthodox monastery in Mahilioŭ and completed in 1769 – a mere fifty-six years before we encounter the first clear evidence of the existence of the work. The anonymous author covered his tracks by claiming that the work had passed through the hands of two highly respected and, by now, safely dead individuals, the Orthodox archbishop of Mahilioŭ, Heorhii Konysky (1717–95), and the best-known Ukrainian delegate to Catherine II's Constitutional Assembly of 1767–8, Hryhorii Poletyka (1723/25–84). Konysky had allegedly given the manuscript to Poletyka, leading readers to assume that it was finally 'rediscovered' in Poletyka's library and thus became available to the public. The 'History' was an unqualified success, copied and recopied again and again before it finally saw print in 1846.[6] By that time it had shaped the views of scores of professional and amateur historians, as well as Russian and Ukrainian authors, including Aleksandr Pushkin, Nikolai Gogol, and Taras Shevchenko, about the Ukrainian past. Romantic authors of the era were excited by the discovery of an 'ancient' manuscript that went beyond the dry facts presented in the Rus' chronicles. It narrated the heroic deeds of the Cossacks in terms that fired the imagination of the literary public. While the fascination of Russian literary figures with the 'History of the Rus'' turned out to be short-lived, it had a spectacular career in Ukrainian historiography and literature, shaping generations of Ukrainian patriots both directly and through the medium of Taras Shevchenko's works.[7]

Like all influential mystifications, the 'History of the Rus'' has inspired a voluminous literature. The most contested question discussed by students of the work has been the identity of its author. The first possible author considered (and rejected) was Archbishop Konysky. A more serious candidate emerged in the person of Hryhorii Poletyka, who has been regarded as either the author or a co-author (together with his son, Vasyl Poletyka [1765–1845]). Another high-profile candidate was Catherine II's chancellor and a native of the Hetmanate, Prince Oleksander Bezborodko (1747–99). Other candidates have been mentioned in the literature, but only the Poletykas and Bezborodko have had a steady following among historians. Opinions on the time of the work's appearance often depend on a given scholar's favoured candidate for authorship. Those supporting the authorship of Poletyka or Bezborodko stick to the eighteenth century. Others, who favour the authorship of Vasyl Poletyka or believe that the manuscript was created in the circle of Nikolai Repnin, the military governor of Little Russia in the years 1816–34, prefer the first two decades of the nineteenth century. The only point relating to the origins of the manuscript on which historians tend to agree is the unknown author's close association with the Novhorod-Siverskyi region of northeastern Ukraine – a hypothesis advanced by one of the most devoted students of the 'History,' Oleksander Ohloblyn.[8]

The name of the author and the time and place of the creation of the 'History of the Rus'' are not the only questions debated by scholars. The political and cultural identity of the unknown author, whose work contributed immensely to the process of Ukrainian nation building, remains as obscure today as it was a century and a half ago. The ability of every new generation of students to find in the text ideas consonant with its own seems to explain both the lasting success of the work and the lack of a comprehensive study on the identity of its author. The first generation of Ukrainian national awakeners influenced by the 'History' included such luminaries of the national movement as Mykola Kostomarov and Panteleimon Kulish, who had a love-hate relationship with the work. On the one hand, they were inspired by the heroic and colourful images of the Ukrainian past presented by the unknown author; on the other, they regarded the 'History' as the product of separatist thinking and nobiliary conservatism, which their populism led them to reject. Mykhailo Drahomanov, by far the most influential Ukrainian political thinker of the nineteenth century, took it upon himself to defend the unknown author against populist attacks. He saw in the author an early promoter of all that the Ukrainian movement was striving for in the last decades of the nineteenth century: Ukrainian autonomy, constitutionalism, and the federal restructuring of the Russian Empire. Instead of treating him as a separatist, Drahomanov saw in the author of the 'History' a person who shared the liberal and democratic views of the Russian and Ukrainian Decembrists. Oleksander Hrushevsky, whose brother Mykhailo wrote the first history of Ukraine as a nation, regarded the 'History of the Rus'' as an account of a people as opposed to the chronicle of a province – an approach consonant with the one later adopted by Mykhailo Hrushevsky. Two adherents of the statist school in twentieth-century Ukrainian historiography, Dmytro Doroshenko and Oleksander Ohloblyn, considered the unknown author a forerunner who allegedly paid special attention to the history of the Ukrainian state.[9]

Not surprisingly, the revival of the Ukrainian national movement in the USSR in the late 1980s and the emergence of independent Ukraine in 1991 cast the political and cultural views of the author of the 'History of the Rus'' in a new light. As the advance of Russification in the Soviet Union threatened the very existence of the Ukrainian nation, some students of the 'History' came to see its author as a defender of Ukrainian identity. 'The individual who wrote it,' asserted the Ukrainian author and historian Valerii Shevchuk in 1991, 'truly burned with great love for his unfortunate and enslaved land. Thus, at a time when everything Ukrainian was being barbarously destroyed, he managed the feat of casting this passionate pamphlet – a historical remembrance – before the eyes of his foolish and indifferent countrymen, who were scrambling, as Taras Shevchenko wrote, for "tin buttons," who "knew all the ins and outs"; who were grasping for estates and jumping out of their skin to obtain Russian noble rank by any and all means; who had even forgotten their mother tongue.'[10] It would appear that quite a few studies dealing with the 'History of the Rus'' published in Ukraine in the 1990s and early 2000s adopted Shevchuk's patriotic interpretation of the work and the goals that its author set himself.[11]

Clearly, the 'History of the Rus'' played a major role in the formation of Ukrainian national identity, but the questions that remain unanswered are whether and to what degree that role corresponded to the aspirations of the unknown author of the 'History' and what his political and ethnocultural identity actually was. The present chapter intends to contribute to the discussion of these questions by taking a closer look at the polemic, largely neglected in historiography, between the author of the 'History' and an unnamed opponent concerning the use of the terms 'Ukraine' and 'Little Russia.' In modern political discourse, the first term is closely associated with the idea of Ukrainian distinctiveness and independence, while the second indicates a belief in the existence of one indivisible Russian culture and nation, of which the Ukrainian people and culture are considered mere branches.[12] Did these terms have the same meaning when the 'History' made its appearance, and, if so, what does that tell us about its author's political and ethnocultural program?

The passage of the 'History of the Rus'' that seems most important to our discussion appears in the introduction to the work. It reads as follows: '[I]t must be said with regret that certain absurdities and calumnies have unfortunately been introduced into Little Russian chronicles themselves by their creators, native-born Rus'ians, who have carelessly followed the shameless and malicious Polish and Lithuanian fabulists. Thus, for example, in one textbook vignette, some new land by the Dnieper, here called Ukraine, is brought onto the stage from Ancient Rus' or present-day Little Russia, and in it Polish kings establish new settlements and organize Ukrainian Cossacks; and until then the land was allegedly empty and uninhabited, and there were no Cossacks in Rus'. But it is apparent that the gentleman writer of such a timid little story has never been anywhere except his school, and in the land that he calls Ukraine he has not seen Rus' towns, the oldest ones – or at least much older than his Polish kings, namely: Cherkassy, Krylov, Mishurin, and old Kodak on the Dnieper River, Chigirin on the Tiasmin, Uman on the Ros, Ladyzhin and Chagarlyk on the Bug, Mogilev, Rashkov, and Dubossary on the Dniester, Kamennyi Zaton and Belozersk at the head of the [Dnieper] Estuary. Of these towns, some have been provincial and regional Rus' towns for many centuries. But for him all this is a desert, and he consigns to nothingness and oblivion the Rus' princes who sailed their great flotillas onto the Black Sea from the Dnieper River, that is, from those very lands, and made war on Greece, Sinope, Trabzon, and Constantinople itself with armies from those regions, just as someone hands back Little Russia itself from Polish possession without resistance and voluntarily, and the thirty-four bloody battles that it required, with Rus' armies opposing the Poles and their kings and the levy en masse, are of insufficient merit that this nation and its chieftains be rendered due justice for their exploits and heroism.'[13]

What should we make of this statement? Andrei Storozhenko, who was the first to focus attention on this particular passage of the 'History' in 1918, treats it as a manifestation of the anonymous author's discontent with the efforts of the Polish authors Jan Potocki and Tadeusz Czacki to treat the Ukrainians as a people separate from the Russians – theories that in Storozhenko's opinion laid the historical foundations for the modern Ukrainian movement.[14] While such a possibility cannot be ruled out, in the above extract the author of the 'History of the Rus'' does not argue either against Potocki's theory linking Ukrainian origins with those of the Polianians, Derevlianians, Tivertsians, and Siverianians or against Czacki's theory that the Ukrainians were descended from a tribe called 'Ukr.' Instead, he rejects the notion that credits Polish kings with the establishment of Cossackdom and the settlement of the Dnipro region even as it neglects the Rus' origins of the Cossacks, ignores their long and determined struggle for union with Russia, and undermines the claim of the Rus' nation to its glorious history. It should also be noted that the anonymous author's protest was provoked not by Polish (and Lithuanian) writings per se but by the adoption of the views set forth in those writings by the authors of 'Little Russian chronicles.' Identifying the writer whose work provoked this polemical outburst on the part of the author of the 'History of the Rus'' is an important step towards understanding the nature of the debate and, among other things, can help establish the time frame within which the famous 'History' was written. I shall therefore begin my discussion with an attempt to identify the author and title of the work that provoked the polemic – an approach overlooked or deemed impossible of realization by all students of the 'History' known to me.

The author of the 'History of the Rus'' left some useful clues on where to seek the object of his attack. The mysterious author must have been a professor or teacher in some kind of school, and his allegedly pro-Polish views were apparently set forth in a textbook or other pedagogical work. The teacher-historian Tadeusz Czacki (1765–1813), mentioned by Storozhenko, might well be considered a candidate for the role. In 1804–5 he was the founder (and subsequently a professor) of the Volhynian gymnasium, which later became the Kremianets Lyceum, a springboard of the Polish national revival in the early nineteenth century. He was also a historian and a rather prolific author. But Czacki, a prominent Polish educator, is not known for having written textbooks dealing with 'Little Russian' history. His views on Ukrainian origins were most fully expressed in his article 'On the Name of Ukraine and the Origin of the Cossacks,' first published in a Warsaw periodical in the autumn of 1801, before the founding of the Volhynian gymnasium. Besides, the 'History of the Rus'' is silent about the tribe of 'Ukr,' the hallmark of Czacki's theory. More importantly, Czacki can by no means be considered a 'native Rus'ian,' as was the mysterious author of the textbook, according to the 'History.'[15] Tadeusz Czacki should therefore be eliminated as a possible addressee of the polemical statement quoted above.

In searching for the author of the textbook among professors/teachers of East Slavic origin, it makes sense to begin with schools in northeastern Ukraine, where most scholars believe the 'History of the Rus'' to have been written. The town of Novohorod-Siverskyi, on which the author of the 'History' focuses attention, had its own school from 1789, but none of the teachers at the secular school or (from 1805) the gymnasium is known for having published anything on the history of Ukraine.[16] Still, we know of a published historian who was then employed in neighbouring Chernihiv, which had emerged in the late eighteenth century as not only the administrative but also the intellectual centre of the region. One of the leading historians there was Mikhail Markov (1760–1819), a Great Russian by origin who served as a prosecutor in Novhorod-Siverskyi. In 1799 Markov moved to Chernihiv, where he was appointed director of schools in the Little Russian gubernia, and from 1805 he served as director of the Chernihiv gymnasium. He published a number of works on the history of Chernihiv and vicinity, and in 1816–17 he contributed to the periodical *Ukrainskii vestnik* (Ukrainian Herald), discussing the origins of Rus' history.[17] The problem with Markov's possible authorship of the textbook that so upset the author of the 'History of the Rus'' is that although he contributed to publications dealing with education, he never wrote anything approaching a history textbook, and his eight-page essay ambitiously titled 'An Introduction to Little Russian History' (1817) advanced no further than the period of Kyivan Rus'. On top of that, while Markov contributed to *Ukrainskii vestnik* (so titled because it appeared in Kharkiv, the capital of the Sloboda Ukraine gubernia), he avoided Ukrainian terminology in his writings and can hardly be suspected of Polonophilism or Ukrainophilism in the senses implied by Storozhenko.

The school and gymnasium next closest to Novhorod-Siverskyi with a published historian on its staff was in Kyiv. The historian in question was Maksym Berlynsky (1764–1848), who lived long enough to chair the organizing committee for the establishment of Kyiv University. Having been born in the vicinity of Putyvl into the family of an Orthodox priest, Berlynsky could certainly be considered a 'native Rus'ian,' a term that could be applied by the anonymous author of the 'History of the Rus'' to Great Russians and Ukrainians alike. He was appointed a teacher at the recently opened secular school (later gymnasium) in Kyiv in 1788, after graduating from the Kyiv Mohyla Academy and training for two years at the teachers' college in St Petersburg. Berlynsky taught at the Kyiv gymnasium until his retirement in 1834, thereby meeting another qualification – that of a lifelong teacher who had never been anywhere except his school, as specified by the author of the 'History.' But probably the most important of his formal qualifications is that his many works on 'native' history included a textbook, *Kratkaia rossiiskaia istoriia dlia upotrebleniia iunoshestvu* (Short History of Russia for the Use of Young People, 1800).[18]

Even more interesting in this connection is that the textbook included an essay on Ukrainian history entitled 'Primechanie o Malorossii' (Note on Little Russia). It was inserted into a basically Great Russian historical narrative, in the section dealing with the rule of Tsar Aleksei Mikhailovich, and covered the history of Ukraine from the Mongol invasion to the Truce of Andrusovo (1667). Subsequent Ukrainian history was treated within the context of imperial Russia.[19] Thus Berlynsky perfectly matches the image of the mysterious opponent invoked by the author of the 'History of the Rus'' in the introduction to that work. But does Berlynsky's textbook indeed use 'Ukrainian' terminology and include pro-Polish passages, as suggested by the anonymous author? The very first sentence of Berlynsky's 'Note on Little Russia' gives a positive answer to this question, since it implies that the original name of that land was indeed Ukraine. It reads: 'Ukraine received its name of Little Russia after its union with Russia.' According to Berlynsky, King Sigismund I of Poland, 'seeing that the Ukrainians engaged in military pursuits, who were known as Cossacks, were accomplishing very brave and valiant exploits ... gave them permission to occupy places above and below the town of Kiev and, in 1506, gave them their first leader with the title of hetman, a certain Liaskoronsky [Lanckoroński], to whom he granted the towns of Chigirin and Cherkassy as possessions.' King Stefan Batory, for his part, 'confirmed the Ukrainians' previous privileges in 1576 and gave them new ones; hence the empty lands between the Dnieper, Bar, and Kiev were soon settled by them.'[20] Thus the author of the 'Note on Little Russia' was indeed 'guilty as charged' by the author of 'History of the Rus'' when it comes to the origins of the name Ukraine, the Polish kings' organization of the Cossack Host, and the settlement of the steppe borderlands.

What might this finding mean for our discussion? First, it appears that Berlynsky was indeed the target of the author of the 'History of the Rus'.' It also indicates that the 'History' could not have been written prior to 1800, the year in which Berlynsky's textbook was published. Nor could it have been written later than the first decade of the nineteenth century; otherwise the critique of the textbook would have lost its significance to the anonymous author and appeal to the reader. This finding is supported by Oleksander Ohloblyn's research, which places the creation of the original manuscript of the 'History of the Rus'' between 1802 and 1805, and George Y. Shevelov's hypothesis that final changes to the text may have been made in 1808–9.[21] It gives us much better grounds than any previously available to place the monument into a particular time frame and political context. Last but not least, an analysis of Berlynsky's textbook and his other writings can offer a better understanding of the historical and ideological message of the 'History' and the nature of the 'Ukraine vs. Little Russia' debate initiated by its anonymous author.

A reading of Berlynsky's *Short History of Russia* indicates that he hardly deserved the harsh treatment meted out to him by the author of the 'History.' Berlynsky was by no means systematic in his use of the terms 'Ukraine' and 'Ukrainians,' which he considered interchangeable with 'Little Russia' and 'Little Russians.' The textbook also shows that he was far from being a Polonophile: for example, he noted with regret that the Time of Troubles did not allow Little Russia to unite with Russia ('our fatherland') in the early seventeenth century. Berlynsky condemned the Poles for their persecution of Ukrainians on the eve of the Khmelnytsky Uprising (1648), allegedly against the wishes of King Władysław IV. He even wrote in that regard: 'That was the main reason for the civil war! What the crown affirmed, the Polish nation rejected. And that discord united all the Little Russians against the republic.'[22] Although Berlynsky did not produce colourful descriptions of the Cossack wars with the Polish-Lithuanian Commonwealth prior to the Khmelnytsky Uprising, as did the author of the 'History of the Rus',' he noted that Khmelnytsky 'was not the first to take up arms against the Poles, for at various times in the course of fifty years his predecessors had done so, but always in vain.'[23] In general, Berlynsky produced a brief but quite accurate description of the period, especially as compared with the one offered by the author of the 'History of the Rus'.' The latter clearly resorted to simplifying and vilifying the arguments of his opponent. But were his suspicions regarding Berlynsky's Polish leanings completely groundless?

Berlynsky did not identify his sources, leaving us no direct evidence of possible influences on his work. He certainly could not have taken his lead from the above-mentioned article by Tadeusz Czacki on the origins of Ukraine and the Cossacks, for it was published a year later than his own textbook. But this does not mean that he lacked access to other works by Polish authors or had no direct contact with Polish historians. We have no indication that Berlynsky was close to Polish intellectuals or alleged 'Polonophiles' in the Russian Empire around 1800, but there is plenty of such evidence pertaining to the later period. The secular school in Kyiv where Berlynsky taught, which later became a gymnasium, belonged to the Vilnius educational district; from 1803 it was headed by the close confidant of Emperor Alexander I and ardent Polish patriot Adam Czartoryski. Not surprisingly, it was to him that Berlynsky sent the manuscript of his new work, entitled 'A History of Little Russia' (1803), requesting permission and financial assistance to publish the book. Czartoryski was quite supportive of Berlynsky's initiative. In a memorandum on the issue he pointed out that there was no published history of Little Russia, he endorsed the publication of Berlynsky's manuscript, and he noted that it would have 'a great bearing on general Russian history as well.' Also supportive of the project was Czartoryski's superior at the time, the minister of education, Petro Zavadovsky, to whom the memorandum was addressed. A native of the Hetmanate and a former lover of Catherine II, Zavadovsky began his education at a Jesuit seminary in Orsha and was known for his good relations with Tadeusz Czacki and general sympathy towards the Poles. Acting on Czartoryski's endorsement, he allocated 500 rubles for Berlynsky's 'History,' but that was insufficient to cover the costs of publication, and it never appeared in print.[24]

Excerpts from the book were eventually published by another reputed Ukrainian 'Polonophile,' Vasyl Anastasevych, who was a secretary to Czartoryski during his years as head of the Vilnius educational district (1803–17) and a close acquaintance of Czacki and the Polish ethnographer Zorian Dołęga Chodakowski (Adam Czarnocki). In 1811, Anastasevych published the first excerpt in his journal *Ulei* (Beehive), where it appeared several issues after the Russian translation of Tadeusz Czacki's famous article on the origins of Ukraine and Cossackdom. It seems that Anastasevych then took possession of the manuscript, for he published the last known excerpt of the book as late as 1844.[25] Berlynsky's close contacts with 'Polonophiles' among the Ukrainian bureaucrats and intellectuals may well have been known to broader circles in the former Hetmanate. An episode that may have revealed such contacts was the controversy of 1805 over the language of instruction in the Kyiv gymnasium, whose director insisted on Russian, while Minister Zavadovsky, who, given his background and education, considered Russian and Polish mutually intelligible, favoured the latter.[26] We do not know whether Berlynsky took a position on the issue, but if he did so, he may well have supported Zavadovsky, who (as noted above) sought to promote the publication of his history. There were certainly other occasions for former Cossack officeholders of northeastern Ukraine to learn of Berlynsky's contacts and possible sympathies, which must have been at odds with the traditional anti-Polish sentiments of the region's elites. The author of the 'History of the Rus'' may well have read back into Berlynsky's textbook what he knew about the author otherwise.

The irony of the situation is that Ukrainian terminology may have entered Berlynsky's textbook and his 'History of the City of Kyiv,' a work written in the late eighteenth century, not from Polish but from Ukrainian writings. One of the last eighteenth-century Cossack chroniclers, Petro Symonovsky, the author of 'Kratkoe opisanie o kazatskom malorossiiskom narode' (Brief Description of the Cossack Little Russian Nation), was Berlynsky's supervisor and mentor during his first years at the Kyiv school.[27] The major Cossack chronicles of the early eighteenth century, including that of Hryhorii Hrabianka – an important source for Cossack historiography of the later period – were full of references to 'Ukraine,' used interchangeably with 'Little Russia,' as in Berlynsky's textbook.[28] At the turn of the nineteenth century, Berlynsky was by no means the only Ukrainian author prepared to make a connection between Stefan Batory, the Cossacks, and the name of Ukraine. Similar views were expressed by his contemporary Yakiv Markovych, who published his *Notes on Little Russia* (1798), a historical, geographical, and ethnographic description of his homeland. But Markovych never wrote anything remotely resembling a textbook or taught in any 'school' in Russia or Ukraine, which excludes him as a possible object of attack by the author of the 'History of the Rus'.'[29]

Even the unknown author of the 'History of the Rus',' who objected to Ukrainian terminology as a sign of Polish intrigue, was unable to keep the term 'Ukraine' out of his own work. It penetrated the narrative despite the author's intentions, proclaimed in the programmatic statement included in his introduction. He was overcome by his sources – apocryphal eighteenth-century letters, foreign histories, and Russian official documents of the late seventeenth and early eighteenth centuries, which were full of Ukrainian terminology. For example, in an apocryphal letter of May 1648 from Bohdan Khmelnytsky, the term 'Little Russian Ukraine' appears four times in a variety of combinations, and there is a reference to 'all Ukraine.'[30] The anonymous author also writes of Ukraine when referring to Voltaire's comment on the Ukrainian expedition of Charles XII of Sweden in 1708–9.[31] There are at least two references in the text of the 'History' to the 'Ukrainian line,' the group of Russian forts built by the imperial government to protect Ukrainian and Russian territories from Tatar incursions.[32] Under the influence of his sources, the anonymous author often uses 'Ukraine' with reference to the Right Bank of the Dnipro – the territory that he defines as Rus', not Ukraine, in his introduction.[33] In the main text of his work, the anonymous author also writes about 'Ukrainian peoples' and 'Christians of Ukrainian faith (*veroispovedaniia*).'[34] Whatever his ideological postulates, the author of the 'History of the Rus'' was unable to divest himself entirely of the tradition established by earlier Ukrainian authors, for whom the term 'Ukraine' had no negative connotations and entailed no suggestion of Polish intrigue.

The hostility shown by the author of the 'History of the Rus'' to the term 'Ukraine' marked a clear break with Ukrainian historiographic tradition. Since it occurred in a work that generations of scholars have considered the pinnacle of early modern Cossack historiography, it deserves further discussion. What made such a break possible, and what motives lay behind it? With regard to the first part of the question, one should take account of the new meaning acquired by the term 'Ukraine' in official discourse and public consciousness of the late eighteenth and early nineteenth centuries. In that period, the term began to be associated first and foremost with lands outside the

Cossack Hetmanate. Thus the 'Ukrainian line' of fortifications was built in the 1730s to the east and south of the Hetmanate. The Sloboda Ukraine gubernia was established in 1765, with its administrative centre in Kharkiv. It kept that name until 1780 and was then restored with different boundaries in 1796; it was renamed the Kharkiv gubernia in 1835. By contrast, the restoration of the Hetmanate's territorial integrity after its liquidation by Catherine II was associated with the brief existence of the Little Russian gubernia, administered from Chernihiv, between 1796 and 1802.[35] The close association of 'Little Russia' with the lands of the former Hetmanate and of 'Ukraine' with the territories of Sloboda Ukraine is well attested in a private letter from a prominent Ukrainian intellectual of the period, Hryhorii Skovoroda. In September 1790, he wrote of 'my mother, Little Russia,' and 'my aunt, Ukraine,'[36] apparently meaning that while he had been born and raised in the Hetmanate, most of his adult life had been spent in neighbouring Sloboda Ukraine. Thus, by the time the 'History of the Rus'' was written, local elites had largely ceased to associate the name 'Ukraine' with the territory of the Hetmanate, and some authors may well have regarded it as a foreign invention.

Let us now turn to the author's motives for breaking with historiographic tradition. The most obvious of them appears to be his anti-Polish attitude, which he does not attempt to conceal. In Polish historiography the term 'Ukraine' preserved its original meaning as first and foremost the land of the Cossacks, giving the author a good opportunity to strike at the Poles. His attack seems to have been well timed. If the author was indeed responding to Berlynsky's textbook, as argued above, then the zeitgeist of his 'History' was that of the first decade of the nineteenth century, which was highly conducive to a renewed confrontation with the Poles. The feverish activity of Adam Czartoryski, who was not only presiding over the increasing cultural Polonization of the Vilnius educational district but also, as de facto foreign minister of Russia, preparing to restore the Kingdom of Poland under the auspices of the Russian tsar, provoked a strong negative response from Russian society. Distrust of Poles grew in the second half of the decade, when Polish exiles in the West sided with Napoleon, and the French emperor, perceived by that time as Russia's worst enemy, carved a Polish polity known as the Duchy of Warsaw out of the Prussian part of the former Commonwealth. In 1806–7 the Poles were submitting proposals to Napoleon to make Podilia, Volhynia, and Right-Bank Ukraine part of a future Polish state.[37] The elites of the former Hetmanate could by no means have endorsed the inclusion of the Right Bank (lands that the author of the 'History of the Rus'' claimed as ancient Rus' territories) into a future Polish polity under Alexander I or Napoleon. Rising anti-Polish sentiment in the Russian Empire gave the Cossack elites of the former Hetmanate a good opportunity not only to settle historical scores with their traditional enemy but also to take credit for their age-old struggle with Poland.[38] At the turn of the nineteenth century, the Cossack elites needed recognition of their former services to the all-Russian cause more than ever before, as the imperial authorities continued to question the nobiliary credentials of most of the lower-ranking Cossack officers.[39] Not surprisingly, in the above-cited extract from the 'History,' its author asked rhetorically whether the Cossack wars with the Poles were 'of insufficient merit that this nation and its chieftains be rendered due justice for their exploits and heroism.'[40]

Maksym Berlynsky, a priest's son and a schoolteacher, is unlikely to have been ready or willing to perform that function for the Cossack officer elites of the former Hetmanate. His general assessment of the Ukrainian past was damning of those who extolled the heroic deeds of the Cossack nation. 'In a word,' he wrote in his article 'On the City of Kyiv,' 'this people groaned beneath the Polish yoke, made war under Lithuanian banners, occupied itself with the Union under Polish rule and contended for privilege under Russian rule, producing nothing for us except descendants.'[41] As Volodymyr Kravchenko has recently noted, Berlynsky was also quite negative in his assessment of the role of Cossackdom, especially the Cossack officer elite – an attitude that caused him difficulty when an excerpt from his 'History of Little Russia' was considered for publication in 1844. On the recommendation of the prominent imperial Russian historian Nikolai Ustrialov, a negative characterization of the Cossacks was removed from the journal publication.[42] It is entirely possible that the anti-Cossack attitudes of Berlynsky, whose writings clearly favoured Ukrainian city dwellers, prevented the publication of his 'History' year after year. Ironically, Berlynsky lived long enough to see the publication of the 'History of the Rus',' which contained an attack on his views and was potentially dangerous to the imperial regime, but not long enough to witness the appearance of his own works, such as the 'History of Little Russia' and the 'History of the City of Kyiv,' which were perfectly loyal to the authorities.

It would appear that Andrei Storozhenko was wrong when he presented (first in 1918 and then in 1924) the unknown opponent of the author of the 'History of the Rus'' in the 'Ukraine vs. Little Russia' debate as a promoter of Polish-led attempts to establish the Ukrainians' distinct origins and separate them from their Rus' roots.[43] In the early nineteenth century, the Ukrainian terminology against which the author of the 'History' protested was indeed associated with the Polish vision of Ukraine as separate from Russia, and from the 1840s on it served to promote the Ukrainian national idea in the Russian Empire. But it would be wrong to assume that the author of the 'History' was combating the Ukrainian or proto-Ukrainian trend represented by Berlynsky's textbook. While the Ukrainian terminology used by Berlynsky implicitly compromised his project of integrating the Cossack elites into the imperial Russian narrative, Berlynsky himself did not threaten the pan-Russian vision of the anonymous author, nor did the historical paradigm employed in his textbook. If anything, Berlynsky's scheme integrated the Cossack past into the imperial Russian narrative more effectively than did the 'History of the Rus'.' Berlynsky, who traced all that was good in Kyiv and Ukraine back to the reign of Catherine II, achieved his integration without claiming any special historical rights for the Cossack elites – an attitude directly opposed to that of the anonymous author of the 'History.'[44]

This explains how the 'History of the Rus'' became a major ideological threat to the empire. Given its long-term impact on the historical imagination of generations of Ukrainian activists, that threat can hardly be denied. Despite the 'anti-Ukrainian' remarks made in the introduction to the book, the author of the 'History of the Rus'' filled his narrative with numerous anti-Muscovite statements, which, like the term 'Ukraine,' he may have taken over from the earlier Cossack chronicles and historical tradition. He also claimed the Kyivan Rus' past, which had been considered part of Russian history alone, and extended the *courte durée* of previous Cossack historiography, whose narrative was mainly limited to the post-1648 history of Ukraine.[45] By celebrating the glorious past of the Cossack Host, the 'History' – either directly or through the works of Taras Shevchenko – inspired Ukrainians to espouse a historical and national identity distinct from that of Russia.

What conclusions may be drawn from the origins of the 'Ukraine vs. Little Russia' debate and its role in the formation of national mythologies in the late eighteenth and early nineteenth centuries? First, it appears that there are grounds to challenge the dominant historiographic trend, which treats the 'History of the Rus'' as a manifestation of growing Ukrainian self-awareness. The delimitation of Russian and

Ukrainian identity was not among the goals of the anonymous author of the 'History of the Rus'.' In all likelihood, as noted above, his immediate goal was to ease the integration of the Cossack elites into the Russian nobility and society at large, as well as to enlist St Petersburg's support in fighting Polish 'intrigues' in Right-Bank Ukraine, by narrating the heroic deeds of his people. His polemic with Berlynsky and his choice of terminology show that the anonymous author wanted to achieve his goal by playing the Rus' card (the title of his work is most eloquent in that regard). He presented his compatriots as more Rus'ian than the Russian themselves, giving former Cossack officeholders a basis to claim equal status with the Great Russian nobility.

If that was indeed the case, how does the 'History of the Rus'' fit into the 'national mythology' and 'national mystification' paradigm? While such mystifications as the *Igor Tale* helped build up pride in the all-Russian nation, tracing the roots of its literary tradition back to the twelfth-century court of the prince of Novhorod-Siverskyi, what was the function of the 'History of Rus',' a work actually produced in the vicinity of that ancient town? It may be argued that originally the 'History's' main function was the creation of a subordinate myth, a historical narrative intended to help Little Russians partake in the larger historical myth of the all-Russian nation. That function, however, changed with the passage of time. As Anthony D. Smith has noted, 'myths, memories, symbols and values,' if viewed as constituent parts of cultures and identities, 'can often be adapted to new circumstances by being accorded new meanings and new functions.'[46] This is what seems to have happened to the collection of heroic stories and images created by the author of the 'History.' Produced for one purpose, they were successfully adapted to serve another: instead of helping to integrate the Cossack past into the all-Russian narrative, they served as a basis for the creation of a new national narrative of Ukrainian history.

The role that the 'History of the Rus'' has played in the formation of Ukrainian historical identity highlights the simple fact that historians have little control over the use of their narratives. As Eric Hobsbawm warned his fellow historians, 'The crops we cultivate in our fields may end up as some version of the opium of the people.'[47] If this metaphor, supplied by one of the last Mohicans of Marxist historiography in the West, can be applied to national ideology, then the reception of the 'History of the Rus'' is indeed a case in point. Like the poetry of Adam Mickiewicz, which inspired proponents of the nineteenth-century Polish, Lithuanian, and Belarusian national movements, the image of the heroic Cossack past produced by the anonymous author of the 'History of the Rus'' clearly captured the imagination of his readers, whatever their national ideologies.[48] It inspired both a proponent of all-Russian identity, Nikolai Gogol, and the father of the modern Ukrainian nation, Taras Shevchenko. In the end it was the latter's interpretation that prevailed, turning the anonymous author of the 'History,' a self-proclaimed enemy of Ukrainian terminology, into the forefather of Ukrainian national historiography.

4 The Missing Mazepa

On 5 November 1708, the terrified inhabitants of the Ukrainian town of Hlukhiv witnessed a shocking ritual. An effigy of their hetman, Ivan Mazepa, who together with his associates had recently defected from Tsar Peter I and joined the advancing army of Charles XII of Sweden, was dragged through the streets of the town. At a freshly built scaffold, Aleksandr Menshikov, the tsar's right-hand man, read out a list of Mazepa's crimes and tore the sash of the Order of St Andrew from the effigy. These events gave the inhabitants of the Hetmanate – the autonomous Cossack polity in the Tsardom of Muscovy (later the Russian Empire) – their last public opportunity to see an image of their elderly hetman. His capital, Baturyn, and his palace were burned, his name was anathematized in all the churches of the empire, and his portraits were banned and destroyed. The same fate befell icons in which Mazepa was depicted as a donor to the numerous churches that he helped build or restore.[1]

Almost thirty years after the Hlukhiv ritual, in 1737, the mere suspicion that Mazepa had been depicted in an icon of the Dormition prompted a major investigation in the Hetmanate. It was alleged that the icon included portraits of Hetman Mazepa, his successor, Ivan Skoropadsky, and Acting Hetman Pavlo Polubotok. Members of the Cossack general staff who had served under the three hetmans testified that none of the images resembled the above-mentioned individuals. They described Mazepa as a carrot-haired man with a longish face and a beard.[2] The seriousness of the investigation and the summoning of high-ranking Cossack officers as witnesses attest to the fact that icons bearing Mazepa's image and portraits of him were systematically hunted down in Ukraine and destroyed long after Mazepa's actual defection, the end of the Northern War with Sweden, and the death of Emperor Peter himself. What helped sustain Mazepa's bad reputation was the anathema proclaimed annually on the first Sunday of Great Lent in the churches of the empire.[3]

Despite the continuing efforts of the imperial secular and church authorities to discredit Mazepa and, more particularly, the idea of the separation of Ukraine from Russia, of which he became a primary symbol, he turned into one of the most emblematic figures of European romanticism. Voltaire, Byron, Ryleev, Pushkin, and Słowacki wrote about him, while Liszt and Tchaikovsky, among others, dedicated musical compositions to him.[4] His upbringing at the court of the Polish king, his capture by the Cossacks and stunning rise to the pinnacle of Cossackdom, his romantic involvement with a younger woman, his flight from the tsar, his death in exile, and, finally, his anathematization by the church – all these subjects proved irresistible to romantic authors. Mazepa's popularity abroad could not but inspire interest in him among the young Ukrainian national awakeners, for whom he was not only the ultimate romantic hero but also a symbol of resistance to the Russian Empire on behalf of their beloved Ukraine.

Among those who showed more than a benign interest in the person of Mazepa was the young Ukrainian painter and poet Taras Shevchenko, a member of the first clandestine Ukrainian political organization who was to become known as the 'father' of modern Ukraine. As a student at the Academy of Fine Arts in St Petersburg, he became interested in Mazepa and searched among the paintings stored in the academy's attic for a portrait of the famous hetman. What he found was a depiction of a Cossack officer with unkempt hair and an unbuttoned coat, often thought in the nineteenth century to be a portrait of Mazepa.[5] While the painting was highly reminiscent of the romantic image of Mazepa as portrayed by Byron and Pushkin, it had nothing to do with his actual appearance. Shevchenko used some elements of it as a model for his portrait of another Cossack enemy of Peter, Acting Hetman Pavlo Polubotok. The latter died in a tsarist prison after appealing to Peter to restore Cossack liberties: unlike the 'accursed' Mazepa, Polubotok was accorded a measure of toleration by the Russian imperial authorities as a symbol of Ukrainian aspirations, apparently because he did not take up arms against the monarch.[6]

In the conflict between Peter and Mazepa, Shevchenko's sympathies were unquestionably on the side of the latter. In the poem 'Irzhavets'' (1847), written after his arrest and exile on political charges, Shevchenko called the emperor a 'hangman' (*kat*) and regretted that the Cossacks of the Hetmanate had not emulated the Zaporozhians in giving unanimous support to their hetman, Mazepa, in his struggle with Peter at Poltava.[7] During the years preceding his arrest, Shevchenko lived for a while in Pereiaslav, one of the centres of the former Hetmanate. There he painted pictures of local architectural monuments, including the local Church of the Holy Protection (*Pokrova*) of the Theotokos.[8] He also had the opportunity to study the large painting of the *Pokrova* in the church, whose iconographic composition was drawn from the *Life of St Andrew the Holy Fool.* Figuring prominently in that *vita* was the story of the appearance of the Mother of God in the Byzantine church of Blachernai to protect the people of Constantinople from a barbarian siege. Judging by the names of newly consecrated churches, the Feast of the *Pokrova* became popular in Ukraine during the late seventeenth and early eighteenth centuries. The iconography of the *Pokrova* developed in Ukraine under strong Western influence, allowing painters to depict the Mother of God and the saints along with images of tsars and tsarinas, which replaced depictions of Byzantine emperors and empresses, as well as images of the Cossack officers who sponsored the icons.[9] One such Cossack icon was the Pereiaslav *Pokrova*, which was transferred from wood to canvas. It showed Tsar Peter I, Catherine I, representatives of the Orthodox clergy, and a number of Cossack officers, their wives, and relatives under the protection of the veil (*pokrov*) of the Theotokos.

Shevchenko was clearly impressed by the icon: years later, he included a description of it in his Russian-language novel *The Twins* (1855). One of the main characters, Nikifor Sokira, a descendant of an old Cossack family who embodies Ukrainian patriotic traditions, is presented there as a great admirer of that particular icon. Shevchenko described the church and the painting itself as follows: 'The Church of the Pokrova, clumsy and nondescript in construction, was built in honour of Peter I's conquest of Azov by Colonel Myrovych of Pereiaslav, a friend and contemporary of the anathematized Mazepa. Preserved in that church is a remarkable historical painting, perhaps a work of Matveev, if not of some foreigner. The painting is divided into two parts: above, the Protection of the Most Holy Mother of God; below, Peter I with Empress Catherine I; and around them, all his eminent associates. They included Hetman Mazepa and the founder of the shrine in all his regalia.'[10]

Shevchenko was correct in his identification of the portraits of Peter and Catherine, but his belief that the icon included a portrait of

Pokrova icon from Pereiaslav. Igor' Grabar', *Istoriia russkogo iskusstva,* vol. 6 (Moscow, 1914), 473.

Mazepa was a mere figment of his imagination. The very fact that the icon included a portrait of Peter together with Catherine suggests that it could not have been painted before the announcement of their wedding in 1712. By that time, Mazepa had already been anathematized, and a depiction of the victorious tsar and his 'betrayer' in the same icon would have been simply impossible. As the investigation of 1737 indicates, even if such an icon had been painted, it would not have survived until Shevchenko's times.

Still, if Mazepa is not depicted in the icon, who is? There is good reason to believe that the Pereiaslav icon was commissioned by members of the Sulyma family, which gave Ukraine a number of prominent Cossack officers during the seventeenth and eighteenth centuries. The Pereiaslav icon closely resembles the *Pokrova* icon from the village of Sulymivka commissioned by Semen Sulyma, who was colonel of Pereiaslav from 1739 to 1766. It was either he or his father, Ivan, the acting colonel of Pereiaslav during the reign of Peter I, who most probably commissioned the Pereiaslav icon, so reminiscent of the *Pokrova* icon displayed at their estate in Sulymivka. What we now know about the Sulymas and the general atmosphere in the Hetmanate after 1712 indicates that the Pereiaslav icon manifested the loyalty of the Cossack officer stratum to the tsar, not the notion of rebellion against him symbolized by the image of Mazepa.[11]

Clearly, that is not how Shevchenko saw the icon and understood its historical and political message. After all, his Nikifor Sokira willed that the icon be placed at the head of his coffin at his funeral – not, of course, for its portrait of the imperial couple but because of the images of the Cossack officers. For Shevchenko and his contemporaries in the ranks of Ukrainian national awakeners, those images, especially that of Mazepa, symbolized the glorious Cossack past, which was emerging as a cornerstone of modern Ukrainian historical memory and identity.[12] Shevchenko's identification of one of the personages in the Pereiaslav *Pokrova* icon as Hetman Mazepa had a lasting effect on the study of the Cossack *Pokrova* in general and the Pereiaslav icon in particular.

As the Cossack mythology gained a stronger hold on the imagination of adherents of the Ukrainian national movement in the late nineteenth and early twentieth centuries, so did the images of its hetmans. One of the main developments in the field was the de facto rehabilitation of Mazepa by the leaders of the national movement. Under new circumstances, he replaced Polubotok as a symbol of Ukraine's struggle for autonomy and independence. Numerous real and alleged portraits of

Mazepa were included in the surveys of Ukrainian history that began to appear in the Russian Empire in the first decade of the twentieth century. The most popular of them was Mykhailo Hrushevsky's *Illustrated History of Ukraine*,[13] which included seven different portraits of Mazepa.

An important role in the conceptualization of early modern Ukrainian icon painting was played by Evgenii Kuzmin's essay 'Ukrainian Painting of the Seventeenth Century,' which appeared on the eve of the First World War as part of the sixth volume of Igor Grabar's *History of Russian Art*.[14] Kuzmin suggested that Ukrainian art of the second half of the seventeenth century had been shaped by the rise of national identity, owing to the influence of Metropolitan Peter Mohyla and, as Kuzmin put it, 'the definitive unification of Ukraine with Moscow under Bohdan Khmelnytsky.' In his opinion, the latter development 'promoted the vindication of all that was characteristically Orthodox, i.e., Byzantine-Russian, as a counterweight to Polish Latinization.'[15] Kuzmin maintained that the defining feature of Ukrainian art in the first decades of the eighteenth century was the growing impact of West European art forms – a process associated with Hetman Mazepa. Although the hetman figured as a 'scoundrel' (*getman-zlodei*) in Kuzmin's text, the author used quotation marks to dissociate himself from that characterization. Kuzmin stressed the impact of Mazepa's activities on Ukrainian art, comparing it with that of Metropolitan Mohyla. He associated another important development in art, the advance of secularism at the expense of religion, with the transforming activity of Peter. Those were the elements that Kuzmin discerned in the *Pokrova* icon from Pereiaslav, which was reproduced in the volume. He claimed that the secularism of the new era was reflected in the centrality of the figure of Peter in the icon, while the advance of Western influence was apparent in its style.[16]

The study of Cossack icon painting in the former Russian Empire was halted by the events of the First World War and the Revolution. The rise of militant atheism in the USSR and the intensification of government attacks on the cultural intelligentsia further hindered research on the subject. In Ukraine, the situation was exacerbated by the incessant official search for manifestations of Ukrainian nationalism in art and scholarship, with Mazepa serving as the embodiment of 'Ukrainian separatism.' Thus a revival of the study of Cossack icon painting in Ukraine became possible only in the 1950s, and then only within the context of research on the liberation struggle of the popular masses and the paradigm of the 'reunification' of Ukraine with Russia. It was in these terms that the Ukrainian art historian Pavlo Zholtovsky, freshly released from the GULAG, attempted to rehabilitate Cossack painting of the period in his study of early modern Ukrainian art (1958). In it Zholtovsky defined the ideological significance of the Cossack *Pokrova* icons (including the one from Pereiaslav) as follows: 'The Cossack *Pokrovas*, uniting religious and historical subjects, were a specific affirmation in church painting of the idea of the reunification of Ukraine with Russia.'[17] Thus Kuzmin's and, later, Holubets's interpretation of the conditions that influenced the development of Ukrainian art in the second half of the seventeenth century were transferred by Zholtovsky to the era of Ivan Mazepa and treated not as a cultural but a political phenomenon. Ironically, if one ignores the official 'reunification' terminology imposed on Zholtovsky, he was not too far off the mark, as the icons indeed reflected the nature of Russo-Ukrainian relations of the period.

Fedir Umantsev, the author of the section on early modern Ukrainian painting in the collective volume *Essays on the History of Ukrainian Art* (1966), also regarded the Cossack *Pokrovas* as manifestations of the reunification of Ukraine with Russia and the unity of 'two fraternal peoples.' The editors of the volume published a black-and-white reproduction of the Pereiaslav icon, a colour image of a *Pokrova* icon that included a portrait of Bohdan Khmelnytsky, and a detail of the Sulymivka icon – the most representative collection of reproductions of the Cossack *Pokrovas* at the time. In discussing the Pereiaslav icon, Umantsev claimed that, along with the image of Peter I, it included portraits of Catherine II (an obvious confusion with Catherine I) and the architect of Peter's church reform, Teofan Prokopovych. He also claimed that the icon had been commissioned by the builder of the church, a certain Nemyrych, confusing the name of the famous seventeenth-century Cossack general chancellor with that of the eighteenth-century colonel of Pereiaslav, Ivan Myrovych.[18]

The late 1960s witnessed a revival of interest in early modern Ukrainian icon painting, which prompted numerous publications and republications of the *Pokrova* icons. Most prominently featured was the icon with the portrait of Bohdan Khmelnytsky, while the Pereiaslav icon was reproduced only once, in the above-mentioned one-volume history of Ukrainian art. There are several reasons why the Khmelnytsky icon not only overshadowed but completely eliminated the Pereiaslav *Pokrova* from histories of Ukrainian art. First of all, the Pereiaslav icon itself was destroyed in the Second World War, leaving scholars and publishers with a mere copy. Second, although Peter I, whose portrait appeared in the icon, was regarded as a progressive figure in the 1960s, he was no match for the leader of a popular uprising, Hetman Bohdan Khmelnytsky, especially when it came to representing the idea of Russo-Ukrainian friendship – a key concept in post–Second World War Soviet historiography. And last but not least, the Pereiaslav icon was blemished by its association with the name of Ivan Mazepa, the antihero of the historiographic myth of the 'friendship of peoples.' Shevchenko's identification of one of the Cossacks in the icon as Hetman Mazepa, whom Soviet ideological watchdogs proclaimed a traitor to the Ukrainian people, was not forgotten. Shevchenko's works were reissued in large print runs throughout the Soviet period, and some Soviet scholars, such as Hryhorii Lohvyn, continued to list Mazepa among the historical figures depicted in the Pereiaslav icon.[19]

At the end of the 1960s, Platon Biletsky published his groundbreaking study of the early modern Ukrainian portrait, in which he did not associate the flourishing of Ukrainian art in Left-Bank Ukraine (a Soviet euphemism for the Hetmanate) with the consequences of the Pereiaslav Council of 1654, which, according to the Soviet historical imagination, proclaimed the 'reunification of Ukraine with Russia,' or with the friendship of the two fraternal peoples. Rather, Biletsky saw it as a consequence of Khmelnytsky's 'wars of liberation' and of the economic independence of the Cossack polity.[20] From that statement, it was only one step to the assertion that the Ukrainian state had been independent under Khmelnytsky – a notion regarded by the Soviet watchdogs as the ultimate manifestation of 'Ukrainian bourgeois nationalism.' Biletsky, for his part, made use of the Soviet paradigm of class struggle to assert his national agenda. In the tradition of Ukrainian populist historiography of the pre-revolutionary era, he attacked the representatives of the Cossack officer stratum, such as the Sulymas, claiming that they had 'rejected' their glorious Cossack ancestors and invented a foreign ancestry to prove their noble status. Although Biletsky did not write specifically about the Cossack *Pokrovas*, his attitude to the likely commissioners of the Pereiaslav and Sulymivka icons leaves no doubt that he did not approve of their servility towards the Russian tsars.[21]

In his book of 1981 on early modern Ukrainian art, Biletsky elaborated his critique of the social egoism of the Cossack officer stratum, which betrayed the interests of the people (and, one should understand, the nation as well) in its pursuit of the privileges and estates granted by the Russian government. In a decade of government-sponsored hunting for manifestations of Ukrainian nationalism and 'idealization' of Cossackdom, which cost the first secretary of the Communist Party of Ukraine, Petro Shelest, his career, Biletsky could not write as he had in the late 1960s about the economic independence of Bohdan Khmelnytsky's state as the basis for the flourishing of Ukrainian art. At most, he could limit the number of obligatory references to the impact of the 'historical act of the reunification of the Russian and Ukrainian peoples' on art and continue his class-based critique of the pro-Russian elites of the Hetmanate.[22] In his new book, Biletsky briefly discussed the Pereiaslav and Sulymivka icons, noting the Russian roots of their composition. He also quoted from Shevchenko's description of the Pereiaslav *Pokrova* but failed to mention Mazepa among the figures possibly depicted in it.[23]

While Ukrainian art historians under Soviet rule struggled with state-imposed limitations on what they could say in their works, their few counterparts in the ranks of the Ukrainian diaspora in the West sought to ignore the Russian aspect of the Cossack *Pokrovas* altogether, focusing on the genre of Cossack *Pokrovas* as an expression of Ukrainian art. What resonated very strongly among historians of Ukrainian art in the West (all of them recent émigrés from Ukraine) was the interpretation of Ukrainian art of the first half of the eighteenth century as a phenomenon closely associated with the activities of Hetman Mazepa. If in Soviet Ukraine association with Mazepa could relegate a particular work of art to decades of obscurity and neglect, in the diaspora this association had the opposite effect, since Mazepa emerged there as a forerunner of Ukrainian independence. It was through this prism that the architecture, painting, and engraving of the era were interpreted in Volodymyr Sichynsky's book on Mazepa as a patron of the arts.[24] The same approach was taken by the historian of the Ukrainian icon (and an active icon painter himself), Sviatoslav Hordynsky. In his popular book on the history of the Ukrainian icon, published in 1973, Hordynsky noted the wealth of *Pokrova* iconography in Cossack Ukraine and associated it with the development of portrait painting during the Cossack era. Like other diaspora scholars, he preferred not to focus on the political and ideological message conveyed by the Cossack *Pokrovas*.[25]

The dissolution of the USSR in 1991 and the rise of independent Ukraine resulted in the lifting of ideological controls on publications dealing with the history of Ukrainian art. The collapse of state-sponsored atheism and the religious revival, on the one hand, and growing interest in the history of Ukrainian culture, with icon painting as one of its components, on the other, resulted in the publication of an impressive number of books and illustrated collections on the history of the Ukrainian icon. The 1990s saw an avalanche of publications that included reproductions or discussions of the Cossack *Pokrovas*. When it comes to quantity of reproductions, the *Pokrova* with the portrait of Bohdan Khmelnytsky remained in the lead, with the Pereiaslav *Pokrova* as sorely neglected as before 1991 – this time, apparently, not because of the alleged association with Mazepa but because of the portrait of Peter I, whose empire-building efforts find little admiration among Ukrainian scholars. Given that the original icon did not survive, it has been easy for contemporary Ukrainian scholars to avoid including it in their illustrated collections.[26]

Contemporary Ukrainian writing dealing with Cossack iconography presents a curious mix of old and new approaches to the subject. Some scholars remain attached in one way or another to their Soviet-era stereotypes, while others are prepared to pull out all the stops in attempting to complete the nationalization of the Cossack *Pokrovas* as symbols of Ukrainian identity. The first tendency is represented by the most recent work of Fedir Umantsev, the author of the 1966 essay on early modern Ukrainian art that includes a reproduction of the Pereiaslav *Pokrova*. In 2002 Umantsev published a general survey of medieval and early modern Ukrainian art in which he essentially repeated his previous assessments of *Pokrova* iconography and his earlier factual errors. He characterized the *Pokrova* icon with the portrait of Khmelnytsky as consonant with ideas expressed in Ukrainian *dumy* (epic songs) 'that extol the events of the Pereiaslav Council.' Sadly for the elderly scholar, there are no such *dumy*. In discussing the Pereiaslav *Pokrova*, Umantsev repeated his old errors whereby the church builder Colonel Myrovych was confused with Nemyrych, and Catherine I with Catherine II.[27]

The scholarly standards of proponents of the complete nationalization of the Cossak *Pokrovas* would appear to be no higher. In an illustrated history released by the same Kyiv publisher that issued Umantsev's book, the art historian and Orthodox activist Dmytro Stepovyk presents the *Pokrova* icons as the embodiment of Ukraine's incessant struggle with its three oppressors: the Ottoman Empire, the Polish-Lithuanian Commonwealth, and Muscovy (later the Russian Empire). He also denies the possibility that Peter I is depicted in the *Pokrova* icon from Sulymivka (obviously confusing it with the one from Pereiaslav). Stepovyk writes that the *Pokrova* icons were meant to depict the Byzantine emperor and empress, not the Russian tsars. He goes on to reject the possibility of Peter I's depiction on patriotic grounds, stating: 'And what artist of sound mind would depict a bitter enemy of Ukraine, a despot and an insane maniac in a Ukrainian icon after what he did to Ukraine following the Battle of Poltava?'[28]

If one compares the attention paid to the Cossack *Pokrovas* in the course of the twentieth century in terms of number of reproductions with the amount of actual research done on them in the same period, the result is quite disappointing. That research was minuscule indeed, especially as compared to the body of work done in neighbouring Poland and represented by Mieczysław Gębarowicz's book on *Pokrova* iconography. The Pereiaslav *Pokrova*, associated in one way or another with the figures of Emperor Peter I and Hetman Ivan Mazepa, who are highly symbolic in modern national and social mythologies, exemplifies the difficult plight of art-historical research in modern Russia and Ukraine. It also focuses attention on the ideological and political currents that have influenced the interpretation of East European art over the last two centuries, including the rise of competing national projects that sought to 'nationalize' the artistic heritage of multinational empires and the advance of radical socialist doctrines that emphasized class struggle, striving to eradicate all manifestations of religious belief and its reflection in the fine arts. It appears that meticulous research into the rich legacy of the Cossack iconographers and the discovery of the multilayered significance of their work remains largely a task for the future.

PART TWO

Between Class and Nation

5 The Historian as Nation Builder

'Пишу Вам по-русски, не умея писать по-малороссийски,
и думая, что неприятно Вам будет, если напишу по-польски.'
Nevill Forbes to Mykhailo Hrushevsky,
Oxford, 27 June 1911[1]

Most of Ukraine's history since the early modern period has been determined by its location between the two major political, economic, and cultural powers of Eastern Europe, Poland and Russia. Their competition for the 'lands between' naturally involved military, political, and economic dimensions, but our concern here is with culture, particularly questions of religion, language, literature, and history, which became especially pronounced in the nineteenth century, after the destruction of the Polish-Lithuanian Commonwealth. The nascent Ukrainian national movement was profoundly influenced by the clash between Ukraine's two powerful neighbours. Inspired by the ideas of Poland's 'Great Emigration' of the nineteenth century, it also took advantage of the Russian imperial struggle against Polish cultural influence in the wake of the Polish uprisings of 1830 and 1863. Ukrainian activists, who were persecuted in the Russian Empire, found better conditions for their publishing activities in the Habsburg province of Galicia, which was largely controlled by the Poles in the last decades of the nineteenth century. To survive and extend its influence over the Ukrainian masses, the Ukrainian national movement had to make its way between the two East European cultural giants, who regarded the Ukrainians as raw material for their respective nation-building projects. The task facing the Ukrainian national 'awakeners' was never easy and always full of internal contradictions. But without finding the right course between Ukraine's West, represented by Poland, and its

East, represented by Russia, the Ukrainian national project would never have come to fruition.

Among Ukrainian activists of the late nineteenth and early twentieth centuries, no one was more involved in negotiating Ukraine's political course and formulating its historical and national identity vis-à-vis Poland and Russia than Mykhailo Hrushevsky (1866–1934), the greatest Ukrainian historian of the twentieth century and the first head of an independent Ukrainian state (1918). Hrushevsky was born in the Kholm region of the Russian Empire. His father, a prominent Ukrainian pedagogue, was sent to the Ukrainian-Polish borderlands to de-Polonize and Russify the local Ukrainian population in the aftermath of the Polish uprising of 1863. The young Hrushevsky obtained his historical education at Kyiv University, where his professor was the well-known Ukrainian historian Volodymyr Antonovych (1834–1908). Antonovych forsook Roman Catholicism for Orthodoxy and abandoned the 'high' Polish culture of his home to embrace the 'low' Ukrainian culture of the local peasantry and become one of the leaders of the Ukrainian national movement in the second half of the nineteenth century. Upon graduation from Kyiv University, Hrushevsky accepted a position in East European history at Lviv University, where he taught Ukrainian history from 1894 until the outbreak of the First World War. During that time, he served as president of the Shevchenko Scientific Society in Lviv, founded the Ukrainian Scientific Society in Kyiv, and edited Ukraine's most influential monthly of the period, *Literaturno-naukovyi vistnyk* (Literary and Scholarly Herald).[2]

Hrushevsky had been regarded as the leader of the Ukrainian cause by its proponents and opponents in the Habsburg Monarchy and the Russian Empire alike. What helped him cross the boundaries between the two empires and the two branches of the national movement as easily as he did was that for all the differences in tactics, the movement had a common ideology and long-term goal: national-territorial autonomy within the respective empires. It was Hrushevsky, the recognized exponent of the Ukrainian movement on both sides of the border, who led it to the achievement of its immediate and prospective goals. Hrushevsky was a villain for Polish and Russian nationalists and a national prophet in the eyes of his followers. His friends were impressed with his ability to withstand continuous attacks from the Russian and Polish nationalist camps. Hrushevsky moved into the public spotlight once he decided to abandon the realm of 'cultural' work and began to take part in politics. His insistence on the use of Ukrainian at the Russian archaeological congress in Kyiv (1899) and his participation in the founding of the

Ukrainian National Democratic Party in the same year turned him into a symbol of the Ukrainian national revival. When in 1906 he joined the Ukrainian deputies of the First Russian Duma, they accepted him as their unquestioned leader and symbol of the unity of eastern and western Ukraine.[3]

Hrushevsky's main achievement, the separation of Ukrainian history from Russian as a field of study, turned the Ukrainian historical narrative from a subnational into a national one and immediately plunged the historian into a maelstrom of controversy. The first to attack Hrushevsky were representatives of Polish national historiography, who severely criticized his attempt to construct a Ukrainian national narrative at the expense of the Polish one. The latter continued to include significant parts of the Ukrainian past in both territorial and ethnocultural terms. While the confrontation between Polish and Ukrainian political elites in the Habsburg Monarchy before the First World War encouraged the critical assessment of Hrushevsky's works by Polish historians,[4] co-operation between Ukrainian national parties and Russian liberals in the Russian Empire often shielded him from attack by his Russian opponents.[5] That situation changed in 1917, when Hrushevsky became a principal target of proponents of the all-Russian idea and was deemed the main culprit behind the efforts of the empire's foes to divide 'Russia, one and indivisible.'[6]

This chapter, which grew out of my work in the Hrushevsky Translation Project – the collective effort of an international group of scholars led by Frank E. Sysyn to make available to the English-speaking reader Hrushevsky's ten-volume *History of Ukraine-Rus'* – takes a close look at the historian's political writings during the first revolution in the Russian Empire (1905–7). At that time, Hrushevsky tried to chart a middle course for the nascent Ukrainian national movement between Russian liberalism and Polish nationalism, applying different tactics in dealing with these two political currents. In discussing this stage of Ukrainian nation building, the essay seeks to attain a better understanding not only of the role played by Hrushevsky in this process but also of the challenges faced by the Ukrainian national revival of the late nineteenth and early twentieth centuries.

Mykhailo Hrushevsky was elected to the chair of European history at Lviv University in 1894 owing to a deal between the Polish political elites of Galicia and the Ukrainian populists. Apart from the Austrian government, the Polish political circles of Galicia, and the Ukrainian populists, major actors in the 'new era' were the Ukrainophile leaders of Russian-ruled Ukraine, represented by Hrushevsky's mentors in Kyiv, Volodymyr Antonovych and Oleksander Konysky. They established good relations not only with the Ukrainian populists but also with the Polish political circles of Galicia. In the mid-1880s, when Austro-Russian relations were deteriorating, the Kyiv Ukrainophile leaders even attracted the attention of the Austrian government and Polish politicians in Galicia, who were looking for possible allies in Russian-ruled Ukraine in case of war between the two states. Disillusioned with the prospects of a federative order in Russia, Antonovych and Konysky placed their hopes in the creation of a Central European federation of Slavic states. They also sought ways to circumvent the restrictions on Ukrainian publications and cultural activity in the Russian Empire, which became especially severe after the assassination of Emperor Alexander II in 1881.[7]

The plans worked out by Antonovych and Konysky, on the one hand, and the leaders of the Ukrainophile movement in Galicia, on the other, envisioned the transfer of Ukrainophile activities from Kyiv to Lviv and the creation of a 'Ukrainian Piedmont' in Galicia. Consequently, it is not surprising that as soon as the Revolution of 1905 in the Russian Empire permitted, Hrushevsky sought to go beyond his Galician base and began to take an active part in promoting the Ukrainian cause in the Romanov realm. He even applied for a position in Russian history at Kyiv University, but the Russian nationalists who dominated Kyiv political life did all they could to prevent the appointment of a 'Ukrainophile' as a professor at Kyiv University. They claimed that his scholarly achievements were difficult to evaluate, as his works were written in the obscure dialect developed by the Galician Ukrainophiles, and that his desire to lecture in Ukrainian would provoke conflicts at Kyiv University. Some authors of anti-Hrushevsky articles even stated that there was no place for him at Kyiv University and that Kyiv, the 'cradle of Russia,' had never been and would never become the centre of an autonomous Ukraine.[8] Nor did Hrushevsky's application benefit from his active participation in the 1907 campaign to establish chairs of Ukrainian studies at Ukrainian universities in the Russian Empire. During the first months of 1907, Hrushevsky raised his voice in support of the student movement for the introduction of such chairs and for the use of Ukrainian as a language of instruction. In a long article published in *Literaturno-naukovyi vistnyk*, Hrushevsky discussed the teaching of Ukrainian subjects in the Habsburg Monarchy and advocated the establishment of chairs of Ukrainian studies (history, geography, language, literature, folklore, art, etc.) at the universities of Kyiv, Kharkiv, and Odesa.[9] A tsarist censor posited a direct link between Hrushevsky's article and student unrest at Kyiv University.[10]

Hrushevsky began his political activity in the Russian Empire by issuing a number of articles that advocated the lifting of the ban on Ukrainian publications. He addressed his writings to the broadest possible audience, but his primary target in the spring of 1905 was the Russian government, which was then giving consideration to lifting the ban.[11] This was a continuation of the campaign that he had begun with demands to legalize the import into the Russian Empire of Ukrainian-language books published in Galicia, including his own works, especially the first volumes of the *History of Ukraine-Rus'*. With the first signs of the liberalization of Russian censorship in 1904, Hrushevsky addressed the new minister of internal affairs, Prince Petr Sviatopolk-Mirsky, with a letter in which he tried to turn the anti-Polish sentiments dominant in Russian ruling circles at the time to the benefit of the Ukrainian cause. Concerning the ban on importing the latest volume of his *History* into Russia, he wrote as follows: 'I find it not only painful but, as a Russian subject, simply shameful to see that, for example, my university colleague's book on the history of Poland and Lithuania in the fifteenth century, which appeared at the same time as the fourth volume of my *History,* has been allowed to circulate in Russia without restriction because it is written in Polish, while my fourth volume, devoted to the same Polish-Lithuanian period of South Russian history, has been banned unconditionally, without even an inspection by the censors, merely because it is written in the Little Russian language.'[12] The revolution hastened the liberation of the Ukrainian word in the Russian Empire. The prohibition was silently dropped from the new regulations on publishing activities issued by the government in the spring of 1906. Hrushevsky, like other activists of the Ukrainian movement, had every reason to celebrate.[13]

The language question, however, was only one of the issues on the activists' agenda. Dubbed 'the resolution of the Ukrainian question,' that agenda envisaged the achievement of territorial autonomy for the Ukrainian provinces of the Russian Empire. However, with the opening of the First Duma in the spring of 1906, the government was no longer prepared to entertain any demands from the Ukrainian movement. The only hope of resolving the reformulated 'Ukrainian question' was to convince the opposition parties in the Duma – the representatives of liberal Russia – to put the national question on their political agenda. The Russian liberals, not the government, became the primary audience of Hrushevsky's articles, though the proponents of Russian nationalism continued to be the object of his attacks. Particularly worrisome to Hrushevsky were the arguments of the Russian rightists, who were attempting to convince the public that the liberalization of political life would result in the disintegration of the Russian Empire, as the non-Russian nationalities would take advantage of the newly granted freedoms to secede. In the spring of 1906, Hrushevsky travelled to St Petersburg to advise Ukrainian deputies of the Duma and stayed there into the summer. Through his numerous contributions to the *Ukrainskii vestnik* (Ukrainian Herald), the mouthpiece of the Ukrainian Club at the Duma, he influenced political debate on the Ukrainian issue in Russian society.[14] In his article 'Unity or Disintegration,' published in June 1906, Hrushevsky sought to calm the Russian liberal public. He acknowledged that political independence was indeed the ultimate goal of any national movement but stated at the same time that 'a nationality does not necessarily require political independence for its development.' The only way to save the Russian state, according to Hrushevsky, was to adjust it to the demands of the national movements and turn it into a 'free union of peoples.' Hrushevsky wrote: 'Aspirations to establish one's own state can only be held in check by the awareness that membership in a given political union offers too many advantages and conveniences. The absence of restrictions on the full and universal development of national forces; the absence of their exploitation by the state for the interests of others or for unproductive ends is a necessary condition for such consciousness.'[15]

For Hrushevsky, such conditions could be achieved only through the restructuring of the Russian Empire on the basis of autonomy for its constituent nations – an idea that he put forward in the summer of 1905 in the debate then taking place on the future Russian constitution. At that time, Hrushevsky proposed to apply the principle of national-territorial self-government, which had previously been discussed only in relation to the Polish provinces of the Russian Empire, to the empire as a whole. He envisioned the Russian state divided into national regions governed by local diets.[16] Hrushevsky also continued to promote the idea of Ukrainian territorial autonomy in a number of articles published in *Ukrainskii vestnik* in the spring and summer of 1906. There he legitimized his demand for the federalization of the Russian Empire by noting that in the spring of 1905 the congress of Russian journalists had adopted a resolution calling for the decentralization of the Russian state and the organization of its future political life on the basis of self-governing national territories.[17] Hrushevsky also referred to the history of Ukrainian-Polish relations in Galicia, claiming that what the Ukrainians needed was not just regional autonomy, which might leave them subject to another nationality, but national-territorial autonomy, which could ensure their dominance in a given autonomous unit and guarantee their future national development.[18]

In August 1906, Hrushevsky specifically addressed the issue of the Ukrainian intelligentsia's duty to serve its own people, discussing it in relation to the authorities' dissolution of the First Duma and the prospects of the liberation movement in the Russian Empire. One of his articles dealing with that theme, 'On the Following Day,' appeared in the eleventh issue of *Ukrainskii vestnik* on 2 August 1906.[19] Another, 'Against the Current,' was written for the fifteenth issue of the same newspaper, which was never published.[20] Hrushevsky's main purpose was to convince the liberal Ukrainian intelligentsia, which had supported Ukrainian aspirations during the first stage of the revolution, not to abandon that cause in a period of official reaction and repression. He argued that in continuing to work for the liberation of Russia and opposing reactionary government policies, there was no need to forsake the Ukrainian cause. Service to broader goals did not contradict the idea of serving one's own people. Hrushevsky called on the Ukrainian intelligentsia to join the ranks of the Ukrainian movement in its effort to liberate Russia.[21] He argued that the alleged sacrifice of the Ukrainian intelligentsia for the benefit of the 'all-Russian' cause in fact amounted to a betrayal of the interests of the Ukrainian people and that the long tradition of such Little Russian 'self-sacrifice' earned the Ukrainian intelligentsia no respect in Russian liberal circles, while the Poles earned such respect by serving the interests of their nation. Hrushevsky maintained that the Russian government and Russian progressive circles did not differ greatly in their attitude to the Ukrainian movement, which they saw as naturally subordinate to all-Russian/Great Russian culture and society, intended to serve as building material for the development of both.

The significance of the ideas that Hrushevsky expressed in these two articles went far beyond the specific circumstances created by the dissolution of the First Russian Duma. In 1907, Hrushevsky reprinted both articles in *The Liberation of Russia and the Ukrainian Question*. They touched not only upon the enormously important question of the loyalty of the Ukrainian intelligentsia to its own people, without which the Ukrainian movement was doomed to extinction, but also on the interrelation between Ukrainian, Russian, and so-called all-Russian culture and society. In his political and historical writings of 1905–7, Hrushevsky postulated the 'Ukrainian question' as part of the national question in the Russian Empire in general, while divorcing it from the 'all-Russian' context. That postulate had highly important consequences for the future of the Ukrainian movement, but for the time being the consciousness of the Ukrainian intelligentsia remained predominantly 'Little Russian,' regarding the Ukrainian people and culture as part of the all-Russian nation and culture. Hrushevsky's strategy under the circumstances was not to counterpose the goals of the Ukrainian and all-Russian (all-imperial) movements for the 'liberation of Russia' but to present them as complementary. The Ukrainian movement was too weak to set goals antithetical to those pursued by the Russian liberal intelligentsia, or even significantly different from them.

Hrushevsky adopted a different strategy in dealing with the Polish movement in the Russian Empire. As early as May 1905, Hrushevsky had raised the alarm about the unequal treatment of Russia's nationalities in connection with an imperial edict permitting the use of the Polish and Lithuanian languages in the secondary schools of the western gubernias.[22] While welcoming the edict in general, he noted that it was rather limited in scope, excluding elementary schools, as well as languages other than Polish and Lithuanian. Hrushevsky argued that the Ukrainians of the western gubernias were just as entitled as the Poles and Lithuanians to be taught in their own language. He made reference to the opinion of the Imperial Academy of Sciences that the 'all-Russian language' was in fact Great Russian, which was foreign to the Ukrainian population of the empire.[23] Hrushevsky considered an imperial policy that helped Polonize the Ukrainian masses not only harmful to the Ukrainians but also absurd from the government's own viewpoint, asking the rhetorical question: 'Is a Polonized Ukraine less dangerous to Russia than a Ukraine loyal to her own nationality?'[24]

Hrushevsky's trip to the Russian Empire in the spring of 1906 and his sharing of the experience of the Ukrainian cultural and political struggle in Galicia with the Ukrainian deputies of the First Duma caused alarm among the Polish political elite in Austria, resulting in the publication of a number of articles commenting on Hrushevsky's visit to St Petersburg. It was implied there that Hrushevsky's efforts to strengthen links between Russian and Austrian Ukraine were dangerous to the Austro-Hungarian state. Readers were also reminded that the Shevchenko Society was receiving subsidies from the Galician diet and that Hrushevsky would do well to remember that the Poles were still masters in Galicia. The real concern of the authors of those articles was that by disseminating information about the abuses suffered by the Ukrainian movement at the hands of the Polish masters of Galicia, Hrushevsky could compromise Polish prospects in the Russian Empire. Hrushevsky, who did not attempt to conceal his dissatisfaction with Polish attacks on him and the Ukrainian movement in general, made the whole story public in St Petersburg.[25]

In 1907, when plans for granting autonomy to the former Congress Kingdom of Poland were being widely discussed in the Russian Empire, Hrushevsky published a number of articles in which he once again discussed the history and current status of Polish-Ukrainian relations in Galicia, protesting plans to include the Kholm region in the prospective autonomous realm. Hrushevsky's essay on the issue, 'For the Ukrainian Bone (The Question of the Kholm Region),' was printed in Ukrainian in the Kyiv newspaper *Rada* (Council), then appeared as a separate brochure, and finally was included in Russian translation in *The Liberation of Russia and the Ukrainian Question*.[26] The essay was a response to an article published by one of the leaders of the Polish National Democratic Party, Count Antoni Tyszkiewicz, in the newspaper *Rech* (Speech), the mouthpiece of the Russian Constitutional Democrats. Tyszkiewicz argued against the Russian government's attempts to make the Kholm region a separate province, claiming that the whole enterprise had been thought up by Russian nationalist circles and local elites that would benefit from the elevation of Kholm to the status of a provincial capital. Tyszkiewicz was certainly right in his evaluation of official intentions: facing the prospect of having to grant autonomy to the lands of the former Kingdom of Poland, the government wanted to save the Ukrainian population of the Kholm region for the 'all-Russian' cause. It is hardly surprising that Tyszkiewicz's argument found support in the oppositional Constitutional Democratic circles, whose representatives argued that the whole issue should be taken out of the hands of the government and submitted to the State Duma for decision.[27]

Hrushevsky, for his part, was clearly alarmed that the Polish National Democrats and the Russian Constitutional Democrats might reach an agreement at the expense of the Ukrainians. In his article he rebuffed Tyszkiewicz's argument, pointing out that by playing the pan-Slavic and liberal cards, it failed to take into account the interests of the local population, which was neither Russian nor Polish and had the right to separate national and cultural development. Hrushevsky argued that granting autonomy to Poland within its ethnic boundaries was a just cause, but not within the boundaries of the former Congress Kingdom of Poland, which included non-Polish ethnic territories. Hrushevsky believed that Russian and Polish policies towards the Ukrainians were intended to promote the assimilation of the Ukrainian population to their own cultures and societies. Nevertheless, along with a significant number of Ukrainian activists, he continued to believe that there were better prospects for the development of Ukrainian culture under Russian than under Polish rule. Once again, the interests of the Ukrainian movement and those of the central government in St Petersburg coincided on the issue of Polish dominance in the ethnic Ukrainian territories, but this time, unlike after the Polish Uprising of 1863, the Ukrainian activists did not have to hide their true intentions. They no longer presented themselves as proponents of the all-Russian cause; instead, they joined the battle under their own flag.

A close reading of Hrushevsky's political writings leaves no doubt that during the Revolution of 1905 in the Russian Empire his main goal, like that of the whole Ukrainian movement, was the achievement of Ukrainian autonomy. The strategies that he adopted to achieve it depended on whether he was dealing with Russian liberals or Polish nationalists. In the first case, he subscribed to the broadly defined goals of the democratic movement throughout the empire, arguing that the 'liberation of Russia' required a solution to the empire's national question and the granting of territorial autonomy to the ethnic minorities. By posing the 'Ukrainian question' as part of the 'national question' facing the empire as a whole, Hrushevsky gave new legitimacy to the Ukrainian demands for autonomy, even as he sought to persuade the Ukrainian intelligentsia within the ranks of the 'liberation of Russia' movement that it had not only 'all-Russian' but also specifically Ukrainian goals at stake in the success of that movement.

The self-awareness and political maturity of the Polish national movement served as an example to the nascent Ukrainian movement in the Russian Empire, and Polish activists were important allies in the struggle for federalization. But they were also dangerous competitors in the contest to 'nationalize' the empire's western borderlands and outright enemies of the Ukrainian movement in Austrian Galicia. As Hrushevsky considered developments in the Russian Empire from the perspective of Polish-Ukrainian relations in Galicia, he became more alarmed than his Kyivan colleagues at the prospect of Russia's solving its 'Polish question' at the expense of the Ukrainians. The introduction of Polish as a language of school instruction in lands where ethnic Ukrainians constituted the majority or plurality of the population would mean further cultural Polonization of the Ukrainian peasantry unless the schools were Ukrainized. If the Kholm region were included in autonomous Polish territory, Polish culture would again become dominant in that traditionally Ukrainian land. Official 'accommodation' of Polish political and cultural demands rather than those of the other nationalities would diminish the prospects of national 'autonomists' in Russian politics.

Hrushevsky's proposed solution to the complex political dilemmas that faced the Ukrainian movement in its dealings with its much stronger Russian and Polish counterparts was quite simple. During the Revolution of 1905 he emerged as a formidable supporter and tireless propagandist of the unity of all democratic forces in their struggle for the 'liberation of Russia.' For Hrushevsky, that slogan implied the achievement of territorial autonomy by the non-Russian nationalities. There was no place in this struggle for any separate deals between individual members of the anti-autocratic camp or between them and the government. Hrushevsky believed that the 'liberation of Russia' would bring freedom not only to Russia and Poland but to Ukraine as well.

6 Renegotiating the Pereiaslav Agreement

On 8 January 1654, a Cossack council assembled by Hetman Bohdan Khmelnytsky in the town of Pereiaslav approved his proposal to submit the Cossack polity to the authority of the Muscovite tsar. There have been very few topics as important to and contested in Ukrainian and Russian historiography as the Russo-Ukrainian agreement of 1654. The 'Articles of Bohdan Khmelnytsky,' as the Cossack conditions and the tsar's response of March 1654 became known in historical tradition, served as the basis for the creation of one of the most powerful myths of Ukrainian historiography. Writing in 1920, Viacheslav Lypynsky, a prominent Ukrainian historian and conservative rival of Mykhailo Hrushevsky, distinguished the Pereiaslav Agreement of 1654 from the Pereiaslav legend. According to Lypynsky, the latter was constructed by the Cossack officers after the Khmelnytsky Uprising and further modified after the defeat of Hetman Ivan Mazepa at Poltava (1709). The legend held that what happened at Pereiaslav was a voluntary union of Cossack Ukraine with Muscovy. Those who promoted the legend first treated the Muscovite tsardom as a country that shared the same religion as Ukraine and, later, as one that shared the same nationality. According to Lypynsky, the Pereiaslav legend helped the Ukrainian elites survive the demise of the Cossack state while preserving their rights and privileges, but it also helped lay the foundations for the imperial concept of one Russian nation and the theory of the 'reunification of Rus'.' Moreover, it had little to do with the true history of the Pereiaslav Agreement.[1]

There can be little doubt that the Pereiaslav legend influenced the development of Ukrainian political thought and historiography; it also promoted the integration of the Cossack elites into imperial Russian society with no loss of rights and privileges. But the legend had another important function as well. After the death of Bohdan Khmelnytsky, every Ukrainian Cossack leader regarded his 'Articles' as the Magna Carta of Ukraine. As successive Muscovite and Russian imperial governments infringed on the rights guaranteed to the Cossacks in 1654, the Pereiaslav legend was invoked to defend not only the rights and privileges of the Cossack estate but also the autonomous status of Ukraine. Ironically, the Pereiaslav legend continued to perform that function long after the full absorption of the Hetmanate into the Russian Empire in the final decades of the eighteenth century.[2]

In fact, the first appeal for Ukrainian independence in the modern era used the 'Pereiaslav Constitution' as a point of reference in its attempt to establish grounds for Ukraine's separation from Russia. The essay in question, 'Independent Ukraine' (1900), was written by the Ukrainian lawyer and political activist Mykola Mikhnovsky, who argued that the 'Pereiaslav Articles' had established the union of Russia and Ukraine as two equal states. Mikhnovsky admitted that Ukraine (the Ukrainian republic, as he termed it) had not been fully independent at the time, as it paid tribute to the tsar, but insisted that it was nevertheless a state under international law. He went on to claim that at Pereiaslav Ukraine had been looking for protection, not submission, and had joined the Muscovite monarchy without relinquishing any of its prerogatives either as a state or as a republic. The 'Pereiaslav Constitution,' which, according to Mikhnovsky, could not be changed without the agreement of both parties, had been violated by Muscovite infringements on the rights of Ukraine. Consequently, Ukraine was free of its obligations under the 'Pereiaslav Constitution.' Moreover, its agreement had been made with the Muscovite tsar, not the Russian emperor, allowing Mikhnovsky to claim that Ukraine could now become free and independent.[3]

Mikhnovsky's essay is a good example of the political use of the Pereiaslav legend by the rising Ukrainian national movement at the turn of the twentieth century. It was rooted in the tradition of Cossack chronicle writing and provided inspiration to Ukrainian activists, whether they were pursuing independence or autonomy within a reformed Russian Empire – the latter being the main demand of the Ukrainian movement at the time. Despite its political appeal, Mikhnovsky's interpretation of the 'Pereiaslav Constitution' was questionable, to say the least, from the historical viewpoint and potentially boded more harm than good for the Ukrainian cause, especially in academic circles. There the task of presenting and defending the Ukrainian perspective on the Russo-Ukrainian agreements of 1654 fell to Mykhailo Hrushevsky, then a young professor of Ukrainian history at Lviv University in Austrian-ruled western Ukraine.

This chapter deals with the development of Hrushevsky's views on the history of the Pereiaslav Agreement of 1654 – views that shaped the Ukrainian outlook on Russo-Ukrainian relations of the early modern era and that Soviet historians considered a major threat to their concept of the 'friendship of peoples' in the USSR. The article 'Reunification of Ukraine and Russia' in the Soviet-era encyclopedia of Ukrainian history noted that 'Ukrainian bourgeois nationalist historians, especially M.S. Hrushevsky, sought in all possible ways to depreciate the great historical act of reunification of Ukraine with Russia; to deny its significance in the history of the two fraternal peoples.'[4] What were Hrushevsky's views on the Pereiaslav Agreement, and why were they so dangerous to generations of Soviet historians?

Hrushevsky's Critique of the Pereiaslav Decisions

Hrushevsky's first essay on the Khmelnytsky Uprising and the Pereiaslav Agreement appeared in 1898, two years before the publication of Mikhnovsky's brochure, on which it apparently had no impact.[5] The young Hrushevsky treated the Russo-Ukrainian agreement of 1654 as an outcome of the confluence of Muscovite and Ukrainian interests at a particular moment. The tsarist government wanted to weaken Poland and attach Ukraine to Muscovy, while Khmelnytsky wanted to involve Muscovy in his military struggle with Poland. To achieve that goal, Khmelnytsky was prepared to make all sorts of promises to the Muscovite ruler while maintaining good relations with the Ottomans, who considered the Cossack hetman their vassal. While pursuing that course, Khmelnytsky created intractable long-term problems for his newborn polity. According to the young Hrushevsky, the Pereiaslav Council witnessed the clash of two very different political world views, the Muscovite autocratic tradition and Cossack constitutionalism. The latter, he argued, was accompanied by a rough-and-ready attitude towards the rule of law – the product of Cossack experience under Polish rule. Discussing the Muscovite boyars' refusal at Pereiaslav to swear an oath in the name of the tsar, Hrushevsky pointed out that the Cossack officers generally paid little attention to matters of form. Khmelnytsky had the same failing, making him a good diplomat but a bad politician in Hrushevsky's eyes. 'Having grown up in a state without executive power,' wrote the historian, 'where law and the courts were powerless, especially "as things are done in Ukraine," the Cossack officers became used to disregarding the legal aspect of things, paying attention only to the actual state of affairs and relying on that alone. They carried over this disregard into their new relations with an entirely different kind of state, one with a strong executive and the pettifogging pedantry and formalism of a bureaucratic machine. The results, of course, were most unfortunate.'[6]

Hrushevsky emerges in his essay of 1898 as a principled critic of Khmelnytsky's policies at Pereiaslav, accusing the hetman of advocating the interests of the Cossack stratum alone and neglecting the needs of the popular masses. Thus, reasoned Hrushevsky, in 1654 Moscow recognized the autonomy of the Cossack estate but not that of the whole nation. Khmelnytsky and his advisers failed in their duty to represent all of Ukraine in its ethnic boundaries.[7] In his interpretation of the Russo-Ukrainian agreement of 1654, Hrushevsky clearly departed from the paradigm used by the creators and interpreters of the Pereiaslav legend in both its pro-Russian and pro-Ukrainian versions. His view shows the influence of ideas developed by the two leading Ukrainian intellectuals of the nineteenth century, Mykhailo Drahomanov and Volodymyr Antonovych. Drahomanov discussed the history of Russo-Ukrainian relations in his essay of 1878, 'The Lost Epoch: Ukrainians under the Muscovite Tsardom, 1654–1876,' treating Pereiaslav as the starting point of a long series of troubles besetting Ukraine. Many of the ideas set forth in his work were restated and further developed by Hrushevsky twenty years later. These included the treatment of the Pereiaslav negotiations as a contest between Cossack constitutionalism and Muscovite despotism. Drahomanov's discussion of the 'Pereiaslav Articles' has much in common with Hrushevsky's critique of Khmelnytsky as a representative of the Cossack stratum alone who refused to champion the peasantry and other social groups.[8]

Volodymyr Antonovych was Hrushevsky's professor at Kyiv University and the historian who had the greatest influence on him. In 1896, two years before the publication of Hrushevsky's essay on the Khmelnytsky Uprising, Antonovych's students issued a collection of his lectures on the history of Cossack Ukraine. Some of Antonovych's ideas directly influenced Hrushevsky's interpretation of the Pereiaslav Agreement. Not unlike Drahomanov before him and Hrushevsky after him, Antonovych believed that the Pereiaslav Articles demonstrated the limitations of the social agenda pursued by Khmelnytsky and his entourage. He maintained that Pereiaslav was the result of one of many foreign policy combinations undertaken by Khmelnytsky. He also believed that the Cossacks failed to obtain autonomy for Ukraine, as they paid little attention to the formal side of the agreement – something not overlooked by the experienced Muscovite diplomats.[9] These views of Antonovych's found their way into Hrushevsky's essay on the Khmelnytsky Uprising. Generally speaking, the young Hrushevsky proved a much harsher critic of Khmelnytsky than his former professor. If Antonovych consided Khmelnytsky a representative of the whole Ukrainian people and explained the shortcomings of his policies by the prevailing state of political culture, Hrushevsky treated the famous hetman as a representative of the Cossack stratum who pursued a policy of social egoism often directed against the interests of the popular masses.

Hrushevsky adopted a more balanced approach to Khmelnytsky and his Pereiaslav legacy in works written during the first two decades of the twentieth century. In the *Illustrated History of Ukraine*, a popular survey published on the eve of the First World War, Hrushevsky explained Khmelnytsky's decision to enter into the agreement with Muscovy by the difficult military situation in which Ukraine found itself at the time. He offered no criticism of the hetman or his entourage for the mistakes that they allegedly committed at Pereiaslav: instead, he wrote that they expected assistance from Moscow in their struggle against Poland. They counted on the preservation of their freedoms under Muscovite rule and were disappointed by the tsar's aspirations to establish control over Ukraine.[10] Hrushevsky was also supportive of Khmelnytsky's actions at Pereiaslav in his best-selling brochure, *The Pereiaslav Agreement*, which was reprinted several times during the Ukrainian Revolution of 1917. Hrushevsky's earlier critique of social egoism on the part of Khmelnytsky and the Cossack elites gave way to a portrayal of the hetman as an advocate of the all-Ukrainian cause. Both the *Illustrated History of Ukraine*, which was first published in 1912, and the brochure of 1917 on the Pereiaslav Agreement were written with an eye to educating the Ukrainian public and mobilizing it in support of the major Ukrainian political causes – first autonomy and then independence. But the popular character of those publications was not the only reason for Hrushevsky's gentler treatment of Khmelnytsky and the Cossack officers. By the time of the 1917 revolution, Hrushevsky the political activist had completed his evolution from devoted populist to proponent of the unity of the Ukrainian nation. That metamorphosis could not help but influence his historical writings.[11]

Nevertheless, Hrushevsky's old criticism of Khmelnytsky, first manifested in his essay of 1898, reemerged in his postrevolutionary writings, especially in the new volumes of his *History*. The revolution radicalized Hrushevsky, who became not only a staunch supporter of Ukrainian statehood but also a committed socialist. Moreover, the attempts of some conservative historians like Viacheslav Lypynsky to represent Khmelnytsky as a forerunner of Ukrainian monarchism inspired Hrushevsky to renew his critique of the hetman and his policies at Pereiaslav. Thus, in volume 9 of his *History of Ukraine-Rus'*, which was issued in two books in the years 1929–31, Hrushevsky revived and further developed some of the negative observations on Cossack policy at Pereiaslav that he had first made thirty years earlier. 'The Cossack officers,' he wrote, 'had made irreparable errors, having failed to counter Muscovite aspirations with an explicit constitutional formula of mutual relations. Having failed to realize the complete dissimilarity of the new relations to their old pre-revolutionary status within the Polish Commonwealth, occasionally they regressed from the new state pinnacles to the old precedents of their agreements with the king and the senators. While relations between the vassals of the Ottoman Porte and the sultan served as their lodestar, and the Cossack officers wished to establish relations between the "Zaporozhian Host" as a state and the new protector, the Muscovite tsar, on that model, in practice they occasionally strayed into the old administrative scheme of the Commonwealth, in which the Zaporozhian Host was only one of the social strata, and not the primary or the ruling one. They lost their way in establishing relations not only with Muscovite tsardom but also with other social strata of their own Cossack Ukraine. From this standpoint, the procedure of establishing direct relations between the tsarist government and the estate (class) institutions of Ukraine had great significance for the future.'[12]

Was There an Agreement?

'The Pereiaslav Agreement' is the title that Hrushevsky gave his brochure on the establishment of the Muscovite protectorate over Cossack Ukraine in the first months of 1654. The title amounted to a statement of Hrushevsky's position on one of the most hotly debated questions about Russo-Ukrainian relations of the period: was a treaty negotiated in Pereiaslav or not? This is related to the larger question of whether the Hetmanate joined the Muscovite state on particular conditions that the tsars promised to honour or whether the union amounted to an act of the tsar's generosity towards part of the Rus' population oppressed by foreign (Polish) occupation, and thus had no conditions attached to it. Sergei Soloviev, Russia's best-known nineteenth-century historian, believed that the unification of Great and Little Russia was a 'national/popular act' and that the tsar took on no obligations towards his new subjects.[13] Mykola Kostomarov, his counterpart in Ukraine, took a different approach. Continuing the eighteenth-century Ukrainian historiographic tradition, he claimed that in January 1654 negotiations took place in Pereiaslav, resulting in the conclusion of an agreement confirmed by a reciprocal oath.[14] Kostomarov's position on the existence of a Muscovite-Cossack agreement was inherited by Hrushevsky. In volume 9, book 2 of the *History*, he stated that Kostomarov had been right to speak of an 'agreement of Pereiaslav.'[15]

Although Hrushevsky accepted Kostomarov's position on the issue, he was critical of the way in which his predecessor had gone about proving his case. Summarizing the historiographic discussion between Kostomarov and his Russian opponent, Gennadii Karpov, Hrushevsky agreed with the latter that Kostomarov had uncritically followed the tradition established by the Cossack chroniclers, including Samiilo Velychko, and the anonymous author of the *History of the Rus'*.[16] Not only had Kostomarov accepted without criticism their claims that the Muscovite envoys at Pereiaslav confirmed the conditions of the agreement with the Cossacks by swearing an oath in the name of the tsar, but he had gone so far as to provide a list of those conditions and assert that they had been read at the council. 'However,' wrote Hrushevsky, 'as for those "pacts read at the council," Kostomarov, without offering any explanation to the reader, took the liberty of concocting a fabrication of his own invention, all the while creating the impression that he was using a documentary source, and in very detailed fashion set forth the contents of those conditions on which Ukraine was supposed to unite with Muscovy.'[17] What Kostomarov actually did was to take the conditions presented by the Cossacks to the tsar in March 1654 and project them back to the Pereiaslav Council. While Hrushevsky could hardly accept such a 'creative' approach to the sources, he never doubted that negotiations of some sort had taken place at Pereiaslav.

As early as 1898, in his first essay on the Khmelnytsky Uprising, Hrushevsky used Muscovite documents published by Karpov but disregarded by Kostomarov to reconstruct the scope of the Cossack conditions at Pereiaslav. These included a request for the tsar's protection against the Commonwealth, the preservation of Cossack rights and freedoms, the acceptance of a Cossack register of sixty thousand, and the confirmation of the rights and privileges of the clergy, nobility, and burghers.[18] However, expressing no doubt that there had been negotiations between the Cossacks and the Muscovite boyars, Hrushevsky did not speak of a Pereiaslav treaty or agreement. Only in his best-selling brochure of 1917 on the 'Pereiaslav Agreement' did Hrushevsky fully embrace Kostomarov's interpretation of the Pereiaslav negotiations as having resulted in a treaty.[19] He stressed there that Cossack Ukraine had only accepted the Muscovite protectorate under certain conditions. In his interpretation of the Muscovite-Cossack agreements of 1654, Hrushevsky relied on research conducted by the leading Russian legal historian Boris Nolde and his student I.B. Rozenfeld. Nolde stated in his *Essays on Russian State Law* (1911) that the Muscovite boyars gave some assurances to their counterparts at Pereiaslav and had to fulfil them in the later negotiations. In a special study of the legal aspects of Ukraine's absorption by Russia (1915), Rozenfeld claimed that the oath sworn by the Ukrainians in Pereiaslav marked the opening stage of negotiations, not their conclusion. Hrushevsky reviewed both works positively upon their publication and adopted some of their arguments in his brochure of 1917.[20] It was these arguments that allowed him to adopt Kostomarov's view on the existence of a 'Pereiaslav Agreement.'

In volume 9 of the *History*, Hrushevsky, who often quoted from his brochure of 1917, restated the main conclusions of that work. He wrote that 'Kostomarov was entirely correct when he spoke of the "agreement of Pereiaslav," and more recent historians and legal experts admit that independently of the formal aspect, i.e., the lack of a written treaty sanction of what had been agreed upon, the process that was initiated in Pereiaslav and concluded in Moscow had the character of an agreement and was recognized as such by the Muscovites themselves, even though they endeavoured to imbue it with the character of a tsarist "grant" in response to the Ukrainian "petition."'[21] There was a certain tension in this argument of Hrushevsky's, as Kostomarov (and Hrushevsky after him) spoke of a Pereiaslav Agreement, while the legal specialists referred to the agreements of 1654, which included the Pereiaslav negotiations but were mainly based on Cossack petitions to the tsar and his replies to them in March of the same year. Hrushevsky dealt with this anomaly by treating the 'agreement' as a set of formal and informal understandings. The latter were negotiated at Pereiaslav and were the most important ones, at least from the Cossack viewpoint. This was the main line of Hrushevsky's argumentation concerning the Pereiaslav Agreement.

The idea of distinguishing formal and informal aspects of the Cossack-Muscovite agreement was one that Hrushevsky most probably borrowed from Veniamin Miakotin's book on Ukrainian social history (1894). Hrushevsky quotes Miakotin's opinion about the Kostomarov-Karpov debate in volume 9 of the *History*. According to Miakotin, Karpov was formally right, as the conditions of the agreement could not have been read at Pereiaslav, the Muscovite boyars had refused to take an oath on behalf of the tsar, and the agreement was expressed in the form of a grant from the tsar. Nevertheless, this did not mean that Little Russia had unconditionally accepted the tsar's rule.[22] In his brochure of 1917, 'The Pereiaslav Agreement,' Hrushevsky argued that both the Cossack hetmans and the Muscovite rulers, as well as their seventeenth- and eighteenth-century successors, considered the conditions of 1654 a de facto agreement. Khmelnytsky, for his part, had placed special emphasis on the Pereiaslav negotiations – 'treaties' (*traktaty*), as he called them – and insisted that the freedoms and liberties guaranteed to the Cossacks at Pereiaslav be confirmed by decrees from the tsar.[23] Hrushevsky revived these arguments in volume 9 of the *History*, writing that 'in his subsequent relations with Muscovy the hetman considered himself and the Host bound only by those points on which he and Buturlin had come to an understanding ('agreed upon') in Pereiaslav.'[24] Hrushevsky believed that there had been an agreement at Pereiaslav between the Cossacks and the Muscovite boyars that led to Ukraine's acceptance of the tsar's protectorate; further specifications were made to that agreement in the course of the later deliberations in Moscow. Consequently, the appropriate name for the accords of 1654 was 'the Pereiaslav Agreement,' which Hrushevsky used as the title both of his brochure of 1917 and of the corresponding chapter of volume 9 of the *History*.

Long before Hrushevsky, the question of whether the Pereiaslav talks amounted to an agreement had been closely associated with the set of issues surrounding the Muscovite oath in Pereiaslav and the legal status of Ukraine under the accords of 1654. The oath had been a bone of contention in the debate between Kostomarov and Karpov.

Kostomarov used evidence derived from the Cossack chronicles, written more than half a century after the event, to argue that an oath had indeed been sworn, while Karpov cited the ambassadorial report and other Muscovite documents to prove that the envoys had refused to take an oath in the name of the tsar. Karpov's point of view won the support of most historians, including Hrushevsky, but there was still no explanation for the legend maintaining that there had been an oath. Hrushevsky was the first historian to pose the question of the origins of the legend and suggest an answer. He accepted the version presented in the ambassadorial report and admitted that at Pereiaslav, despite all their efforts, the Cossack officers had failed to obtain from Vasilii Buturlin and other envoys either an oath or a written declaration confirming their rights and privileges. Had there been such an oath, argued Hrushevsky, it would have been mentioned in the letters that Khmelnytsky and Ivan Vyhovsky wrote to the tsar after Pereiaslav. He traced the origins of Samiilo Velychko's story about the oath to rumours that circulated in Ukraine after the Pereiaslav Council. In 1659, on the occasion of new Cossack-Muscovite negotiations in Pereiaslav, those rumours led the Cossack officers, now headed by Bohdan Khmelnytsky's son Yurii, to demand a reciprocal oath from their counterparts. The Muscovites refused, and the Cossack side renounced its demand. In Hrushevsky's opinion, the rumours about the oath had been spread in 1654 by Bohdan Khmelnytsky and his entourage as part of an effort to present the agreement to Ukrainian society in the best possible light. Those rumours later became part of the Ukrainian historiographic tradition and the Pereiaslav legend.[25]

In volume 9 of the *History,* Hrushevsky referred to the events of 1654 as the transfer of Ukraine to the tsar's protectorate. He also claimed that at the time of the Pereiaslav Council Ukraine had enjoyed de facto independence – a fact recognized by Muscovy and one that figured in its foreign relations.[26] Hrushevsky criticized the position taken on the issue by Nolde and Rozenfeld, who considered the Russo-Ukrainian agreement of 1654 an incorporation of Ukraine into Muscovy either as an autonomous region or as a regular province. He emphasized that Ukraine had maintained all the attributes of a separate polity and supported the view of those historians who treated the relationship between Muscovy and Ukraine after Pereiaslav as a personal union or a protectorate. Hrushevsky regarded Muscovite-Cossack relations as those between a suzerain and a vassal. He also believed that Khmelnytsky was trying to model his relations with Moscow on those between the Ottoman Turks and their Danubian dependencies. Moscow, on the contrary, was advancing its claim to Ukraine as a patrimonial possession of the tsar and thus preparing the ground for full incorporation of the Cossack polity.[27]

It took Hrushevsky some time to arrive at this position: his earlier writings on the subject proposed a number of alternative views. In his essay of 1898, he maintained that the Muscovite government had accepted the full autonomy of Ukrainian Cossackdom but not of the whole Ukrainian nation, a goal that had not even been pursued by Khmelnytsky and his circle. On the other hand, referring to the work of the Russian legal historian V.I. Sergeevich, Hrushevsky claimed that after Pereiaslav Ukraine had treated its relationship with Muscovy as a personal union.[28] A few years later, in his essay on the 250th anniversary of the Pereiaslav Agreement (1904), Hrushevsky repeated his reference to Sergeevich and personal union but also argued that Moscow had not been prepared to grant Ukraine even the status of provincial autonomy, while the Cossacks had allegedly desired full autonomy for their country.[29] Ukrainian autonomy also emerged as Khmelnytsky's main goal in Hrushevsky's essay of 1907 on the 250th anniversary of Khmelnytsky's death. There the historian directly associated Khmelnytsky's struggles of the mid-seventeenth century with the desire of his own contemporaries to obtain autonomous status for Ukraine in a free union with other nations.[30] Autonomy was one of the demands of the Ukrainian national movement during the Revolution of 1905 in the Russian Empire, and Hrushevsky was prepared to see Khmelnytsky as a forerunner in that tradition. Not surprisingly, in 1915 he wrote a highly positive review of Boris Nolde's work, which made reference to the autonomous status of Ukraine after Pereiaslav.[31]

By the time of the 1917 revolution, Ukrainian autonomy had become a background theme in Hrushevsky's discussion of the legal nature of the agreement of 1654. In his brochure of 1917, he emphasized Ukraine's de facto independence before the Pereiaslav Agreement and claimed that it had preserved the essential features of statehood even afterwards. Ukrainian statehood became the most important theme for Hrushevsky, who now considered discussions on the legal nature of Russo-Ukrainian relations a mere 'debate about words.' In the brochure of 1917, Hrushevsky wrote that his sympathies lay with the legal scholars and historians who argued that relations between Cossack Ukraine and Muscovy were those of vassalage.[32] This was a position that he restated and developed a decade later in volume 9 of the *History*. Hrushevsky noted that he was not alone in adopting this interpretation, which was shared by such scholars as Mykhailo Slabchenko, Viacheslav Lypynsky, and Andrii Yakovliv in Ukraine and Venedikt Miakotin and Mikhail Pokrovsky in Russia.

The Price of Pereiaslav

In the *History of Ukraine-Rus'* Hrushevsky provides an account unsurpassed in its attention to detail of diplomatic relations and military action following upon the conclusion of the Russo-Ukrainian agreement. The years 1654–5 were a crucial period in which the strength of the new alliance was tested and the first cracks in its structure began to show. In dealing with the military side of the story, Hrushevsky brings in new sources and reinterprets the known ones to reconstruct the course of the joint Muscovite-Cossack campaign against the Commonwealth in the summer and autumn of 1654, the disastrous battle at Dryzhypil in early 1655, and the devastating Polish and Tatar raids on Right-Bank Ukraine. Hrushevsky also relates the complex history of diplomatic relations in the region on the basis of painstaking research. This involves an account of the further development of Russo-Ukrainian relations, as well as Cossack contacts with the Crimea, the Danubian principalities, and Sweden.

Hrushevsky dates the emergence of the first tensions between the Muscovites and the Cossacks to the autumn of 1654, when Khmelnytsky disregarded the tsar's order to bring his army to Lutsk in support of the Muscovite troops that were supposed to operate in that region. The hetman, who did not consider such a move advantageous to the Cossack Host, offered excuses for not doing what the tsar expected of him. More importantly, the Muscovite troops that he was supposed to support were never actually dispatched to the Lutsk region: had Khmelnytsky followed the tsar's initial orders, a major military disaster would have ensued. The whole episode might be considered a simple misunderstanding, but it also demonstrated Moscow's disregard for its ally, as well as Khmelnytsky's reluctance to follow orders that did not correspond to his own understanding of the situation. In Hrushevsky's opinion, this was a sign of troubles to come. 'Thus,' wrote the historian, 'disagreement, mistrust, and, from the Muscovites' point of view, "inconstancy," if not outright "treason," had emerged at the very outset on this most important point of establishing a joint foreign policy, which was the actual reason behind this alliance or union.'[33] Further problems in Muscovite-Cossack relations were caused by the actions of the Cossack colonel and acting hetman of the Siverian region, Vasyl Zolotarenko, who was sent to assist the tsar's forces in Belarus. Zolotarenko's undeclared goal in the region was to extend the Cossack social and military order to the upper Dnipro and Sozh territories. Hrushevsky followed the development of Russo-Ukrainian competition in Belarus with close attention, bearing in mind Bohdan Khmelnytsky's later efforts to extend his authority over southern Belarus.

Hrushevsky was clearly upset when he described the devastation of the Bratslav and Kyiv regions by Polish and Tatar troops in the first months of 1655. He laid most of the blame for the atrocities on the Poles, commenting sarcastically that they betokened Poland's civilizing mission in Ukraine – an echo of Hrushevsky's polemics with Polish historians in the previous volumes of the *History*. This time, however, Hrushevsky attacked not his traditional opponents but their forerunners, the authors of seventeenth-century Polish chronicles, Samuel Twardowski and Wespazjan Kochowski.[34] Hrushevsky correctly regarded the Polish-Tatar expeditions against the Hetmanate as the price that the Cossacks had to pay for their alliance with Muscovy, and he was aggrieved by Muscovy's failure to provide effective assistance to Cossack Ukraine. In Hrushevsky's words, 'The first weeks of the new year were one bloody orgy carried out by the Polish army. The Bratslav region was perishing in full view of everyone. The anniversary of Ukraine's transfer to "the high hand of the great sovereign" was marked by a great demise "of the holy churches of God and Orthodox Christians," such as Ukraine had not experienced in a long time. On balance, the first year of the military alliance between Ukraine and Muscovy appeared extremely dismal.'[35]

The only historical account of this period that appears to have brought Hrushevsky excitement and delight was the description of Ukraine in the diary of Paul of Aleppo, a son of Patriarch Makarios of Antioch who visited the Hetmanate in 1654 and 1656 on his way to and from Moscow. In Paul of Aleppo's diary Hrushevsky found what he missed in other sources – the story of everyday life in Ukraine, especially the lives of ordinary people, or 'the masses' in the class-conscious vocabulary of Hrushevsky's day. The historian also found there an optimistic attitude that he ascribed, also in accordance with the conventions of his day, to the revolutionary enthusiasm of the masses liberated by the Khmelnytsky Uprising. '[A]s a representative of a people who had been oppressed throughout the ages,' wrote Hrushevsky, 'Paul had, to a remarkably intense degree, grasped the beauty of this heroic age in the life of the Ukrainian people: the pathos of revolution, popular revolt, and the struggle for liberation, full of sacrifice, self-denial, and idealism. To the Poles and anyone else looking through their prism, as well as to the Muslims and Muscovites, who supported the Cossacks for political reasons, both the Cossacks and the Ukrainian masses in general were nevertheless nothing more than rebellious slaves, despite all their acts of heroism, military prowess, and so on. However, in the eyes of this uncultured Arab they were bearers of the noblest human qualities, fighters for the dreams of liberation that are most precious to every individual.' Hrushevsky clearly preferred Paul's account not only to those of the Poles and Muscovites but also to those of the Ukrainians themselves, including the author of the famed Eyewitness Chronicle, who, according to the historian, 'querulously tallied the number of windowpanes that were smashed during this great conflagration.'[36]

Hrushevsky's often uncritical reliance on Paul of Aleppo, as well his readiness to quote page after page from his diary, later made his account an easy target for critics. Indeed, in volume 9 Hrushevsky too often resorted to endless quotations from documents, leaving little space for synthesis. This is especially true of chapters 8 and 9, which teem with narrative detail, while Hrushevsky's interpretation of the main themes discussed in that part of the volume is deliberately reserved for the concluding chapter.

Class and Nation

When the last issue of the journal *Ukraïna* appeared in print in 1932, it included none of the articles written or edited by Hrushevsky prior to his arrest and exile. Instead, it contained vicious attacks on the founder of the journal and his legacy. The whole interpretation of Ukrainian history developed by Hrushevsky was now thrown into question. One of the critics of Hrushevsky's work was Lev Okinshevych, a former graduate student in the Ukrainian Academy's department of history, chaired by Hrushevsky. In an article entitled 'The National-Democratic History of the Law in Ukraine in the Works of Academician M. Hrushevsky,' Okinshevych accused his former superior of subscribing to principles enunciated by Ukrainian statist historiography, led by Viacheslav Lypynsky. Okinshevych did not take account of the latest installment of Hrushevsky's *History* but attacked his brochure of 1917 on the Pereiaslav Agreement.[37] According to Okinshevych, that work served the interests of the Ukrainian bourgeoisie. He labelled the academician a 'national democrat,' which in that period was tantamount to a political denunciation. Okinshevych claimed that while Hrushevsky had presented his brochure as a response to requests addressed to him by representatives of all strata of Ukrainian society, he was in fact using the 'faded old scrap of paper' of the Pereiaslav Agreement as proof of the existence of a bourgeois Ukrainian state. 'The whole work, aside from its narrative and descriptive character,' wrote Okinshevych about the brochure of 1917, 'is meant to establish that Ukraine was a state after 1654; to prove that the Russian nobiliary government violated the constitutional status of the Ukrainian land. Behind these features it is not difficult to discern the political line of the Ukrainian bourgeoisie in 1917: its striving for constitutional autonomy within the framework of bourgeois Russia and sovereign independence of the land of the proletarian revolution.'[38]

Okinshevych's political accusations had much in common with the attack on Hrushevsky by another representative of the Ukrainian Marxist milieu, Fedir Yastrebov. In 1934, when the anti-Hrushevsky campaign was stepped up, Yastrebov published a long article under the title 'The National-Fascist Conception of the Peasant War of 1648 in Ukraine.' This was a critique of volume 9, book 2 of Hrushevsky's magnum opus.[39] Its tone was even harsher than that adopted by Soviet propaganda in 1932: Hrushevsky's views were now treated not as those of a 'national democrat' but of a 'fascist.' By 1934, Hrushevsky's Marxist critics had abandoned even the pretence of objectivity and were prepared to attack their victims not only for actual deviations from the party line but also for imagined ideological 'crimes.' Yastrebov's article was largely based on the prevailing Soviet interpretation of the Khmelnytsky Uprising. The founder of Marxist historiography in Russia, Mikhail Pokrovsky, considered Pereiaslav a union between two proximate social strata, the Cossack officers and the Muscovite gentry (*deti boiarskie*), with whom the Cossacks had more in common than with the Polish nobility. The union could not take place as long as the Khmelnytsky Uprising developed along the lines of a peasant war but became almost inevitable once the Cossacks managed to establish their control over the masses. This view of the Pereiaslav Agreement was adopted by the leading Marxist historian in Ukraine, Matvii Yavorsky, who developed Pokrovsky's interpretation by asserting that the Cossacks were seeking foreign assistance to maintain their dominance over the masses. At Pereiaslav they allegedly received that help.[40]

For what failings did Yastrebov condemn Hrushevsky's treatment of the Pereiaslav Agreement? First of all, Hrushevsky allegedly ignored manifestations of class struggle and emphasized strivings for national liberation. He ignored documents that contained information about social conflicts and supposedly praised Paul of Aleppo for presenting the exploiters' viewpoint in his diary.[41] According to Yastrebov, Hrushevsky's account of diplomatic and military relations was in fact a paean to the creation of a Ukrainian nation-state, with the Cossack officer stratum as the protagonist of the story. In order to mislead his readers, Hrushevsky occasionally criticized the Cossack officers, but he actually considered them a positive force, bearers of the idea of Ukrainian independence and builders of an independent state. Yastrebov agreed with Hrushevsky that at Pereiaslav the Cossack officers had yielded too much to Moscow and shared his criticism of the Cossack elites for forcing the masses to swear an oath of loyalty to the tsar. Nevertheless, he dismissed Hrushevsky's criticism of the Cossack officers' actions as mild and misdirected. Yastrebov claimed that the elites should be criticized not because they had conducted a weak foreign policy but because they acted in their class interests. For him, opposition to the Pereiaslav Agreement in Ukrainian society was a manifestation either of the social struggle of masses against elites or of tensions among the exploiters themselves. Since official Marxist dogma of the period maintained that a nation-state could only be the product of a bourgeois revolution, and the Khmelnytsky Uprising was no longer so defined by Marxist historians, Yastrebov insisted that the Cossack officers at Pereiaslav could not have been striving to establish a Ukrainian nation-state. Instead, he asserted, the officers had sought 'to obtain firm guarantees of a warm place for their class.'[42]

Interestingly enough, Yastrebov never questioned Hrushevsky's term 'Pereiaslav Agreement' (*Pereiaslavs'ka umova*), which he used throughout his review. At the same time, he dismissed Hrushevsky's discussion of the legal nature of that agreement as 'idealism' and 'Talmudism,' asserting that its content had been determined by the balance of social forces. He accepted Hrushevsky's claim that Muscovy recognized the 'all-national' authority of Bohdan Khmelnytsky but maintained that it could not have been otherwise, as nobody asked the toiling masses whether they wanted the Cossack officers to represent their interests or not. In Yastrebov's opinion, the Pereiaslav Agreement itself demonstrated the absence of a national program, for the Cossack officers were pursuing their own 'feudal program.' This proved the absence of an 'all-national' front in Ukraine, contrary to Hrushevsky's claims but in full conformity with the laws of history. The same laws determined the timing of the Pereiaslav Agreement itself: it came into being when the class struggle of the popular masses, coupled with international factors, made such an agreement possible. Yastrebov claimed that Hrushevsky, as a nationalist and a bourgeois historian, did not recognize the laws of history and drew his conclusions on the basis of 'an idealist dissolution of historical causality and conformity to laws in the accidental wherever this is inconvenient for his conception – and that is, in effect, everywhere.'[43]

Yastrebov's review fully demonstrated the shift in Bolshevik propaganda and historiography away from the policy of coexistence with national historiographies towards their suppression. Given the party's complete control over media and scholarly publications, by the early 1930s opponents of that course had no forum in which to challenge the new approach. Thus the attacks on Hrushevsky went unanswered in the USSR, and favourable responses to book 2 of the *History* were published only abroad. The reviewer in the *Prager Presse* called Hrushevsky's *History* 'a Cyclops' edifice to which his latest work has added a new rough-hewn stone slab.'[44] The Lviv-based *Literary and Scholarly Herald*, a journal once edited by Hrushevsky, welcomed the publication of the latter book of volume 9 as the 'most eminent phenomenon in the field of Ukrainian historiography, both in significance and in the labour invested in it.' Semen Narizhny, the historian of the Ukrainian emigration and the author of the review in the *Herald*, noted that the volume was devoted to the study of a great transformation – Ukraine's transition from the rule of the Commonwealth to that of Muscovy, and the corresponding shift of the centre of political gravity in Central Europe. He praised Hrushevsky for his improved literary style but also noted that the text was overloaded with source quotations and discussion of details that might be the focus of a separate monograph. Narizhny observed that the last chapter of the volume was the most interesting but also the most controversial. He stopped short of endorsing or challenging Hrushevsky's views on the specific problems discussed there.[45]

The last chapter of the volume was devoted largely to Hrushevsky's polemics with alternative interpretations of the Khmelnytsky Uprising. His opponents were not Polish or Russian historians, as in previous encounters, nor, for that matter, the Marxist and left-leaning historians of the 1920s. Instead, Hrushevsky directed his fire against Viacheslav

Lypynsky, whom he considered his main opponent and challenger. In his *Ukraine at the Turning Point* (1920), Lypynsky presented Bohdan Khmelnytsky as a major protagonist of Ukrainian history who had almost single-handedly built a Ukrainian state.[46] Lypynsky and Hrushevsky were in agreement on some aspects of the Russo-Ukrainian union of 1654. Both referred to it as the 'Pereiaslav Agreement' and considered it one of Khmelnytsky's diplomatic initiatives in the search for allies against the Commonwealth. They disagreed, however, on its significance among Khmelnytsky's policies. If Lypynsky considered it a major achievement that established a basis for the existence of Ukrainian statehood in international law, Hrushevsky claimed that at Pereiaslav Khmelnytsky had shown his inability to defend the interests of the Hetmanate. Hrushevsky claimed that Khmelnytsky lacked the capacity to develop a state-building program and criticized his failure to serve as a representative of the entire Ukrainian nation in his dealings with the tsar, his tendency to make promises to the Muscovite boyars without considering the consequences, his acquiescence in separate deals between Moscow and the Ukrainian estates, and the readiness of his government to allow the extension of the Moscow patriarchate's jurisdiction over the Kyiv metropolitanate.[47]

Hrushevsky's debate with Lypynsky was certainly on the mind of Vasyl Herasymchuk, who wrote the most positive review of the book. A former student of Hrushevsky's and an associate of the archaeographic expedition, Herasymchuk saw the importance of the volume in the data that it offered for a comparison of two of 'our great revolutions,' the Khmelnytsky Uprising and the Ukrainian Revolution of 1917–20. Herasymchuk praised Hrushevsky's work as a 'feat of titanic energy,' noting the complexity of his task and the abundance of literature and sources that he had consulted to produce the most complete narrative of the period. He defended Hrushevsky's decision to incorporate numerous and lengthy quotations from the historical sources into his text and praised his decision to treat the Ukrainian people, rather than Hetman Bohdan Khmelnytsky, as the protagonist of the volume. According to Herasymchuk, Hrushevsky's reevaluation of Khmelnytsky's role was 'one of the most sensational tableaux of the *History* ... [I]t is also an act of courage, in the interest of scholarship and truth, to touch critically on the taboo of an "ideal sanctified by centuries."' 'Many readers here in Galicia,' noted Herasymchuk, having in mind the followers of Viacheslav Lypynsky, 'find it somehow difficult to accustom themselves to this novelty as an "incomprehensible, nonpedagogical act."'[48] Herasymchuk also defended Hrushevsky's work against the attacks of its Soviet critics, which he characterized as 'abusive reviews overemphasizing Marxist dialectics, even appealing for official intervention against the spread of counterrevolutionary attitudes and the glorification of petty-bourgeois ideals.' Herasymchuk claimed that those attacks were unjustified, as it was impossible to study the seventeenth century without touching upon the question of nationality, which in his opinion was the leitmotif of the period. Herasymchuk questioned the Marxist credentials of Hrushevsky's critics, claiming that true Marxism did not deny the existence of nationality but considered the national question fully resolved. He concluded his review by asking whether 'feigned concern for the proletarian cause is not allowing the poorly concealed old black militant nationalism of imperialist vintage to emerge.'[49]

Herasymchuk's review, written soon after the publication of volume 9 of the *History*, was not published during his lifetime. There were probably too many people in Lviv who did not appreciate his praise of a work that challenged taboos and removed the halo from heroes such as Khmelnytsky. After all, it was a direct attack on views held by most leading Ukrainian Galician historians of the day. Many of them, including former students of Hrushevsky's such as Ivan Krypiakevych and Ivan Krevetsky, rejected the left-leaning concepts of their professor and embraced the anti-egalitarian doctrines of his opponent. This explains in part why Hrushevsky concentrated his attack on Lypynsky's view of Bohdan Khmelnytsky in general and of his role in the Pereiaslav Agreement in particular. As the last volume of the *History* demonstrates, at the end of his career Hrushevsky was no longer primarily concerned with Polish attacks on Khmelnytsky, nor did he polemicize with Russian historians, new or old. He also completely ignored Franciszek Rawita-Gawroński's new writings on the subject and even cited Kliuchevsky in support of his own interpretation of the Pereiaslav Agreement of 1654 and its consequences. Was this because Hrushevsky no longer considered Polish or Russian interpretations of the Khmelnytsky era a threat to the Ukrainian national paradigm? Or did he think Rawita-Gawroński and Russian émigré historians unworthy of attention, given the poor professional quality of their writings on the subject?[50] Hrushevsky's lack of interest in Marxist interpretations of the Khmelnytsky era seems less surprising, given the lack of professional historians in their ranks.

Thanks to his prominent position in the academy and his editorship of a number of scholarly publications, Hrushevsky effectively controlled a significant portion of academic activity in the historical field, including the training of specialists in early modern Ukrainian history and the conduct of much of the research on that period. A number of 'progressive' left-leaning historians who worked in close contact with Dmytro Bahalii and included Mykhailo Slabchenko in Odesa, as well as Oleksander Ohloblyn and Nataliia Polonska-Vasylenko in Kyiv, avoided Hrushevsky's domain of pre-eighteenth-century history and occupied themselves predominantly with socio-economic topics. As a result, Hrushevsky had no rivals in the field of seventeenth-century Ukrainian history. The only real challenge came from western Ukraine, where some of Hrushevsky's own students, who had grown into first-class historians of early modern Ukraine under his guidance, went on the offensive against their former professor. Their attack was led by Viacheslav Lypynsky, and it was his views on the Khmelnytsky era with which Hrushevsky polemicized in the last volumes of the *History*. The vigour of his response shows that while he considered his former students' rebellion a continuation of the prerevolutionary conflict in the Shevchenko Scientific Society, he also treated the advent of elitism and social conservatism in historiography as a political and intellectual challenge powerful and influential enough to deserve a response in the pages of his academic *History*.

The Legacy

When it comes to the long-term impact of Hrushevsky's views on the historiography of the Pereiaslav Agreement, Fedir Yastrebov was naive at best when he wrote in 1934 that the issue of the character of the Khmelnytsky Uprising had been definitively resolved by Marxist historiography. By the late 1930s the nation was again an element of the Soviet Ukrainian historical narrative, with Bohdan Khmelnytsky emerging as the main representative of the Ukrainian people. The theory of the 'lesser evil' was now recast in national terms.[51] By the early 1950s, the concept of the 'reunification' of the Ukrainian and Russian peoples had emerged as the only 'true' approach in Soviet historiography. The Pereiaslav Council of 1654 was now regarded not as the embodiment of a 'lesser evil' but as a symbol of the triumph of friendship between the two fraternal peoples. That view was promoted by the 'Theses on the Three-Hundredth Anniversary of the Reunion of Ukraine with Russia,' which were approved by the Central Committee of the Communist Party of the Soviet Union (1954).[52] In the USSR the time had come to criticize Hrushevsky's interpretation of the Pereiaslav Agreement not only as devoid of class analysis but also as undermining the age-old friendship of the Russian and Ukrainian peoples.

The section of the 'Theses' devoted to the events of 1654 may be considered an 'antithesis' to Hrushevsky's interpretation of the Pereiaslav Agreement. The term itself was replaced with the references to the 'Pereiaslav Council' and the 'reunification of Ukraine with Russia.' Contrary to Hrushevsky's research, it was claimed that the Pereiaslav Council 'was attended by representatives of various social strata of all the Ukrainian territories liberated from the Polish nobility.' The 'Theses' also stated that 'the decision taken at Pereiaslav was enthusiastically received by the Ukrainians.' Hrushevsky's assertion of Ukrainian statehood was countered with a statement on the historical importance of the Pereiaslav Council, which 'lay primarily in the fact that union with Russia within a single state, the Russian state, saved Ukraine from subjugation to the Polish nobility and from annexation by the Turkish sultans.' Countering the earlier Marxist interpretation of the Pereiaslav Agreement, the 'Theses' proclaimed that 'though Russia in those days was governed by the tsar and the landlords, the reunion was of immense progressive importance for the political, economic and cultural development of the Ukrainian and Russian peoples.' Finally, the interpretation of Pereiaslav as a product of elite politics – one of the few issues on which Hrushevsky and his early Soviet critics agreed – was replaced with an almost mystical treatment of the Pereiaslav Council as an event that 'crowned the people's struggle for the reunion of Ukraine with Russia' and constituted the realization of the 'age-long hope and aspiration of the Ukrainian people.'[53]

Not surprisingly, Hrushevsky was portrayed in Soviet historiography of the 1950s–1980s as the main opponent of the theory of the 'reunification of Ukraine and Russia.' The article on the 'Reunification of Ukraine and Russia' in the Soviet-era encyclopedia of Ukrainian history noted that 'Ukrainian bourgeois nationalist historians, especially M.S. Hrushevsky, sought in all possible ways to depreciate the great historical act of reunification of Ukraine with Russia; to deny its significance in the history of the two fraternal peoples.'[54] When in the 1960s, in the wake of the Khrushchev cultural thaw, the Ukrainian historian Mykhailo Braichevsky attacked the Russocentric concept of 'reunification,' using arguments drawn from Ukrainian Marxist historiography of the 1920s, he was fired from his position at the Institute of History of the Ukrainian SSR Academy of Sciences and condemned by his colleagues in a 'scholarly dispute' not unlike those staged by the authorities to 'unmask' the views of Hrushevsky himself in the 1930s. In fact, Braichevsky, whose view of Pereiaslav was far removed from that of Hrushevsky, was accused of following Hrushevsky's line in the interpretation of developments in the second half of the seventeenth century – the so-called Ruin.[55]

With the advent of Ukrainian independence in 1991, Ukrainian historians rejected the concept of the reunification of Ukraine with Russia. Also discarded was the notion of the age-old drive of the Ukrainian people to reunite with the Russians, as well as the concept of 'the people' as the main agent of Ukrainian history. Instead, most Ukrainian historians advanced new interpretations of the Khmelnytsky Uprising that adopted numerous features of Hrushevsky's outlook. Today Ukrainian historians generally treat the Khmelnytsky Uprising as a national revolution or as a war of national liberation. Under the influence of statist historiography, special attention is paid to the role of the revolt in creating a national state that obtained legitimacy through the Pereiaslav Agreement. New research has been done on the international situation that contributed to the conclusion of the agreement. Not unlike Hrushevsky, contemporary Ukrainian historians regard the Pereiaslav act as one of Khmelnytsky's diplomatic measures intended to promote the interests of the Cossack polity created by him or by his nascent dynasty.[56]

Not all of Hrushevsky's interpretations are equally accepted in the present-day historiography of Pereiaslav. A case in point is the use of the term 'Pereiaslav Agreement,' which is crucial to Hrushevsky's argument. It was promoted by Hrushevsky in his brochure of 1917 and in volume 9 of the *History* and subsequently adopted by most twentieth-century Ukrainian historians writing outside Soviet Ukraine. With some qualifications, the term was used by Viacheslav Lypynsky, Rostyslav Lashchenko, Andrii Yakovliv, and Oleksander Ohloblyn.[57] On the other hand, while not questioning the existence of the agreement, modern Ukrainian historians try to avoid the notion itself, opting instead for terms like 'Pereiaslav Council,' 'Russo-Ukrainian treaty,' or 'Pereiaslav-Moscow Agreement.'[58] The same holds true for modern Russian historiography. One of its leading representatives in the 1990s, Lev Zaborovsky, argued in favour of abandoning the term 'Pereiaslav Agreement.' In his opinion, verbal promises made by the Muscovite envoys at Pereiaslav could not be considered a treaty. Instead, he suggested the term 'Moscow Agreement,' referring to the negotiations and complex of documents adopted in Moscow in March 1654.[59] A different situation emerged in the West. In the 1950s, through the works of Yakovliv and Ohloblyn, the term entered English-language historiography, where it was rendered for some time as 'Pereiaslav treaty.'[60] This was replaced in the 1980s and 1990s with the term 'Pereiaslav Agreement,' which is widely used in the introduction to this book.[61] The same term has also been used occasionally in Polish historiography.[62] Whatever the term used by historians to describe the Russo-Ukrainian union of 1654, none of them seems to question the existence of the agreement itself or its negotiated character – a clear indication that Hrushevsky's understanding of the agreement, if not the term itself, is widely accepted by present-day Ukrainian historians.

Hrushevsky's copious use of primary sources allowed him to give the most complete available account of political, military, and diplomatic developments in Cossack Ukraine during a crucial period of its development.[63] Moreover, his discussion of diverse ways in which the Pereiaslav Agreement was understood by its authors and contemporaries introduced a new theme into the study of an 'old' subject. Hrushevsky's research on the development of national consciousness, based on the analysis of official documents and rumours circulating among the populace at large, helped open a new stage in the development of Ukrainian historiography. His work on the Pereiaslav Agreement continues to be the most important influence on present-day Ukrainian historiography of the problem both in Ukraine and abroad. This influence is likely to continue. Even the shift of Ukraine's foreign policy towards Russia during the last years of the rule of President Leonid Kuchma and his half-hearted attempts to mark the 350th anniversary of the Pereiaslav Council in January 2004[64] did not change the dominant trend in Ukrainian historiography of the Pereiaslav Agreement.

7 Bourgeois Revolution or Peasant War?

In the autumn of 1920 Mikhail Pokrovsky, the leading Marxist historian of Russia, published the first Marxist textbook of Russian history to appear in the postrevolutionary Russian Empire, entitled *Russkaia istoriia v samom szhatom ocherke* (Russian History in Briefest Outline).[1] The book was based on Pokrovsky's lectures delivered a year earlier at the Yakov Sverdlov Communist University in Moscow and reworked during a brief leave from his duties as deputy people's commissar of education of the Russian Federation. Lenin himself welcomed its publication, suggesting that it be adopted as a textbook and translated into various European languages.[2] The book was indeed translated into numerous foreign languages, as well as the languages of the USSR, and reprinted more than ninety times, making it the most popular textbook of Russian history in the 1920s. It employed some of the basic ideas developed in Pokrovsky's five-volume *Russkaia istoriia s drevneishikh vremen* (Russian History from the Earliest Times). Special emphasis was placed on the history of the class struggle, the rise of the working class, and the role of commercial capitalism in early modern Russian history.[3]

Pokrovsky's *Russkaia istoriia v samom szhatom ocherke* turned out to be a history of Russia proper to a degree not matched by any of the prerevolutionary histories of Russia. In a sense Pokrovsky's neglect of non-Russian history in his popular survey was the logical culmination of an earlier tendency, associated with the names of Vasilii Kliuchevsky and his students at Moscow University, to 'Russify' the Russian imperial grand narrative. The outbreak of the 1917 revolution, the disintegration of the empire, and the establishment on its ruins of new independent states, including the Russian Federation, removed the old constraints that hindered the 'purification' of the Russian imperial paradigm by the removal of non-Russian elements. After all, the lecture course that served as a basis for Pokrovsky's new textbook of Russian history was delivered in Moscow, the new capital of the Russian Federation, by a deputy people's commissar of the Russian government at a time when the Moscow authorities had in effect lost control of a significant part of the Russian Empire. Ukraine in particular was lost first to the forces of the Ukrainian People's Republic, whose government was led by Mykhailo Hrushevsky, then to German troops, the Ukrainian Directory, and the White armies of General Anton Denikin. There existed (at least formally) a separate communist party of Ukraine and a separate Soviet Ukrainian government, while the formation of the USSR was at least two years away. Whatever Pokrovsky's intentions at the time he wrote his lectures, by focusing on Russia proper he left a vacuum to be filled with narratives produced locally by party historians in the non-Russian borderlands of the former empire.

In Ukraine there was a particularly strong demand for such a narrative, as evidenced by the hundreds of thousands of copies of brief textbooks and popular historical studies produced during the revolution that presented Ukrainian history from the Ukrainian national point of view. Mykhailo Hrushevsky's *Iliustrovana istoriia Ukrainy* (Illustrated History of Ukraine) alone was reissued six times between 1917 and 1919.[4] The task of constructing a Soviet Marxist narrative of Ukrainian history fell to one of the leading ideologues of the Soviet regime in Ukraine, Matvii Yavorsky. He was occasionally called the 'Ukrainian Pokrovsky,' but unlike his older colleague in Moscow, he was neither a professional historian nor an old Bolshevik. A lawyer by training, he formally joined the Communist Party only in 1920. Yavorsky was an ethnic Ukrainian who came to Eastern Ukraine from Galicia, where he had graduated from Lviv University (having attended Hrushevsky's lectures on Ukrainian history) and, in addition to his law degree, had completed a doctorate in political science (1912).[5]

Among the major battlegrounds in the struggle between the young Marxist historians and representatives of Ukrainian national historiography was the history of the Ukrainian Cossacks, especially of the Khmelnytsky Uprising. The meaning of that uprising, particularly the Muscovite tsar's taking of the Cossack polity under his 'high hand,' was also contested by historians of the Russian imperial school, who viewed the Khmelnytsky era through the prism of the reunification of Rus'. Ukrainian historians, for their part, regarded the uprising as a turning point in the development of the Ukrainian nation. During the 1920s, the topic attracted special attention from Marxist historians, since it constituted the main focus of the scholarly activity of their principal opponent in Ukraine, the dean of Ukrainian national historiography, Mykhailo Hrushevsky. The Khmelnytsky Uprising was discussed in the two books (more than 1,500 pages in toto) of volume 9 of his *Istoriia Ukraïny-Rusy*. The volume, which was researched, written, and published between 1924 and 1931, was among the great scholar's works attacked by the Marxist establishment.

It is the historical debates on the history of Ukrainian Cossackdom and the Khmelnytsky Uprising that illuminate better than any other historiographic discussion of the period the main tendencies in the 'construction' of the Ukrainian historical narrative by Marxist historians in Ukraine. Consequently, the present chapter analyses the 'construction' of that narrative, as well as the formulation and reformulation of the Marxist paradigm of Ukrainian history.

Let us begin our discussion of that historiographic process by assessing the resources that Ukrainian Marxist historians could bring to bear against Hrushevsky's interpretation of the Khmelnytsky Uprising as a milestone in the formation of the Ukrainian nation. When it came to actual historical research, they could offer very little. None of them was a specialist in pre-nineteenth-century history, and those like Yavorsky, Volodymyr Sukhyno-Khomenko, and Mykhailo Svidzinsky, who dealt with the history of the uprising in their general surveys of Ukrainian history, lacked a basic grounding in the premodern period. The forte of the young Marxist cadres was the construction and reconstruction of various schemes of Ukrainian historical development, all of which were based on class as the main agent of historical progress and class struggle as its 'motive force.' Marxist historians of the 1920s acted first and foremost as critics of the old bourgeois historiography. They were trained to expose the 'true' ideological faces of their class enemies, deconstruct the latter's historical narratives by means of the class-based approach, and build their own historical schemes on the basis of factual material 'expropriated' from the bourgeois historians. In the course of the 1920s, a whole generation of Ukrainian Marxist historians was trained according to that model. As Hrushevsky wrote to Viacheslav Molotov in September 1934, defending his own work and the traditional values of the profession, 'one should have a critically assessed pool of facts in order to make it possible for party propagandists to produce books for mass consumption.'[6]

It is hardly surprising that in their analysis of the Khmelnytsky Uprising Ukrainian Marxist historians took the works of Mikhail Pokrovsky as their point of departure. Before the outbreak of the First World War, living as an émigré in France, Pokrovsky wrote a multivolume history of Russia, *Russkaia istoriia s drevneishikh vremen*, which followed the tradition of Russian imperial historiography by including a number of chapters on Ukraine (southwestern Rus').[7] In his book, Pokrovsky developed a Marxist scheme of Russian history, applying a monistic, class-based approach to 'unlock' the meaning of Russian and Ukrainian history.

Pokrovsky strongly believed that until the sixteenth century Russia developed along the same path as the West but deviated from it once capitalism began to make headway in the West.[8] He based his periodization of 'Russian' history on the Marxist idea of successive socio-economic formations: 'Russian' history, as part of world history, began with the dominance of the clan system of social relations, which was followed by feudalism, merchant/commercial capitalism, and eventually industrial capitalism. Seeking to present Russian history as a process subject to the same socio-economic laws as the history of Western Europe, Pokrovsky argued that feudalism in Russia was replaced by a capitalist economy in the sixteenth and seventeenth centuries. To prove the point, he developed a theory of 'commercial capitalism,' a socio-economic stage in Russian history in which commercial capital was used to acquire land. The advance of commercial capitalism resulted in the displacement of the old landowning class, the boyars, by a new one, the gentry (*dvorianstvo*). The new economy, based on corvée labour (*barshchina*) as opposed to the 'feudal' quit-rent (*obrok*), led to the enserfment of the Russian peasantry. According to Pokrovsky, the possessors of commercial capital and the gentry were also mainly responsible for creating the new Muscovite autocracy. The theory of commercial capitalism, whose principal agent was the burgher, was devised in order to guide Marxist historiography through the labyrinths of early modern Russian history.

Although Pokrovsky did not use the term 'commercial capitalism' in his overview of early modern Ukrainian history, reserving it mostly for his discussion of the history of Russia, clear traces of the commercial capitalism approach can also be found in his discussion of the Ukrainian past. Commenting on the history of religious and social struggle in early modern Ukraine, Pokrovsky claimed that the main social conflict of the age resulted from competition between two forms of landownership and colonization: the Polish (magnate) model and the Ukrainian/'Russian' (Cossack) one. That competition acquired an ethnic and religious colouration: accordingly, Pokrovsky interpreted the church union of 1596 as little more than an instrument in the hands of the large landowners.[9] If prior to the 1917 revolution Pokrovsky's view of Ukrainian history was only one of many, after the revolution, especially with the tightening of party control over historical scholarship in the course of the 1920s, his class-based approach to the history of Russia and Ukraine came to be considered the only legitimate one.

What was Pokrovsky's 'vision' of the Khmelnytsky Uprising?[10] To begin with, he called it a revolution. He defined Cossack landownership and the economy based on it as bourgeois and considered the Khmelnytsky Uprising a revolt of the Ukrainian bourgeoisie against Polish feudalism. The bourgeoisie, according to Pokrovsky, was composed of Cossacks and Ukrainian burghers, who not only served as one of the sources for the formation of Ukrainian Cossackdom but also had their own economic and political agenda. As a social group whose rights in the Polish-controlled towns were threatened by the church union, the burghers, he claimed, transferred their national religious ideology to Cossackdom. That development occurred in late 1648 and early 1649, when Khmelnytsky entered Kyiv after his spectacular victories of the first year of the uprising. It was allegedly at that time that the 'bourgeois intelligentsia' took ideological control of the uprising, shifting its goals and slogans from exclusively Cossack ones to national and religious motifs. Setting a precedent for future Marxist historians, Pokrovsky downgraded the heroic image of Khmelnytsky, whom he characterized as a representative of the Ukrainian bourgeoisie and a leader despised by the popular masses.[11]

In his account of the Khmelnytsky Uprising, Pokrovsky often drew on Hrushevsky's publications related to the Cossack era. While he took a generally positive attitude to Hrushevsky's findings, he disagreed on several points. He questioned Hrushevsky's view that the alliance with the Crimean khan had contributed substantially to Khmelnytsky's early achievements, claiming instead that its significance had been purely military: it was Khmelnytsky's alliance with the peasantry that prepared the political ground for the Cossack victories over the Poles. Pokrovsky thought it superficial of Hrushevsky to have asserted that Khmelnytsky failed to understand the importance of popular support for the success of the uprising. In Pokrovsky's opinion, Khmelnytsky's lack of interest in the popular masses was more a reflection of the incompatibility of Cossack and peasant class interests. Unlike Hrushevsky before him, Pokrovsky went on to claim that only a continuing alliance with the popular masses could have ensured the success of the Khmelnytsky Uprising: once Cossackdom decided to reject that important ally after the victories of 1648–9, Khmelnytsky had no choice but to seek foreign support from Muscovy, Turkey, or Sweden.

Muscovy became a logical focus for Cossack diplomacy, in Pokrovsky's opinion, not for religious or national reasons but for social ones. The tsar's realm, which Pokrovsky defined as a gentry state, was allegedly closer to the hearts of the Cossack officers than nobiliary Poland. To prove his point, Pokrovsky indicated that the Cossack officers and the Muscovite gentry (*deti boiarskie*) lived under similar economic conditions. Nevertheless, Pokrovsky argued, negotiations between the Cossacks and Muscovy were fruitless during the first years of the uprising, as the Cossack revolution was also a peasant one at that time – a circumstance that frightened the Muscovite court. After 1649, when the Cossacks demonstrated that they could control the masses, the conclusion of a Russian-Ukrainian alliance became, in Pokrovsky's opinion, simply a matter of time. Owing to the social bond between the Cossack officers and the Muscovite gentry, in the course of the next century Ukraine became as much a gentry-run territory in social and economic terms as Muscovy itself.[12]

Pokrovsky's views on the bourgeois character of the Cossack uprisings were so unorthodox and so grossly contradicted historical fact and historiographic tradition that initially even leading Ukrainian Marxists refused to accept them in their entirety. For example, writing in 1923, a leading Ukrainian 'national communist,' Oleksander Shumsky, accepted Pokrovsky's interpretation of the Khmelnytsky Uprising as an antifeudal revolt but refused to consider Cossackdom a bourgeois phenomenon. 'As for the bourgeois character of the old Cossack movements, this statement is probably too strong,' Shumsky remarked in an article that claimed the Ukrainian Cossack past for the new authorities.[13] Those doubts, however, were soon dismissed as the leading Marxist historian Matvii Yavorsky, who began working on a survey of Ukrainian history in the early 1920s, decided to follow in Pokrovsky's footsteps. Like Pokrovsky, Yavorsky relied on the class-based method to uncover the 'true' meaning of historical events in Ukraine. He also fully introduced Pokrovsky's concept of 'commercial capitalism' into his interpretation of Ukraine's early modern history. When it came to the history of the Khmelnytsky Uprising, Yavorsky not only repeated some of the main points of Pokrovsky's analysis of the 'Cossack revolution' but also reinterpreted and further developed some of them.

In Yavorsky's opinion, the main reason for the Khmelnytsky Uprising was the inefficiency of Polish nobiliary agriculture, which hindered the development of a money economy. Nobiliary dominance led to the growing exploitation of the burghers and enserfment of the peasants: the latter escaped this ever more severe exploitation by fleeing to the unpopulated areas of eastern Ukraine and joining the Cossacks. Yavorsky regarded Cossackdom as a defender of the interests of the burghers and peasants. He divided it into three major groups: the registered Cossacks, who wanted to acquire equal rights with the Polish nobility; the Zaporozhians, who wanted to do away with all restrictions on their foraging rights (in their social aspirations they were close to the burghers and runaway peasants); and, finally, the unregistered poor Cossacks of the settled area. According to Yavorsky, it was only the registered Cossacks who represented the interests of merchant capital, and as such it was they, with the assistance of the burghers, who became the driving force of the Khmelnytsky Uprising.[14]

Like Pokrovsky, Yavorsky called the Khmelnytsky revolt a Cossack revolution. In the opinion of both historians, it was a revolution because it brought about the end of one stage of human development, feudalism, and initiated a new capitalist era. Following Pokrovsky, Yavorsky claimed that the Cossack revolution had defeated feudalism, opening the door to the development of a money economy, the enserfment of the peasantry, and the advance of commercial capitalism with the autocratic monarchy as its political superstructure. Nevertheless, Yavorsky was not satisfied with the definition of the revolution as a Cossack one: following Pokrovsky's lead in his post-1917 writings, he attempted to find a more politically correct term for it. He eventually defined it as a gentry revolution, implying that the Cossack officers actually represented the emerging new class of the Ukrainian gentry. Yavorsky claimed that in the course of the Khmelnytsky Uprising the Cossack officers were fighting not only for land but also for the eventual enserfment of their comrades-in-arms.

There were some important differences between Pokrovsky and Yavorsky in their treatment of the role played by the leader of the uprising, Bohdan Khmelnytsky. If in Pokrovsky's opinion Khmelnytsky was not a hero, but still an important actor in the unfolding events of the uprising, for Yavorsky he was just one of the Cossack officers who happened to be in the right place at the right time. There were also minor differences in Pokrovsky's and Yavorsky's views on the Cossacks' relations with the rank-and-file rebels. Following Pokrovsky's main argument, Yavorsky claimed that because the Cossacks (in his interpretation, only the registered ones) did not want to free the peasants from their obligations to the landlords, the Cossack leaders had to look for outside support. Unlike Pokrovsky, however, Yavorsky maintained that the Cossack officers sought foreign support not to win their struggle with Poland but to establish and maintain their control over the rebel masses. In his discussion of the Pereiaslav Agreement with Muscovy (1654), Yavorsky basically repeated Pokrovsky's interpretation, claiming that the Cossack officers and the Muscovite gentry were socially related groups.

Yavorsky's views on the nature of the Khmelnytsky era evolved as he produced one account of Ukrainian history after another with remarkable speed in the course of the 1920s. In the final revisions of his historical scheme he even tried to incorporate Pokrovsky's interpretation of the role played by the Ukrainian burghers in the Khmelnytsky Uprising. It did not entirely work, as he was never able to reconcile his own interpretation of the registered Cossacks as the driving force of the revolution with the role attributed by Pokrovsky to the burghers and the 'bourgeois intelligentsia.' Generally speaking, Yavorsky proved a rather loyal student of Pokrovsky in his interpretation of the Khmelnytsky revolt. The differences between their interpretations were not significant and can be explained at least partly by the fact that Pokrovsky never returned to the study of Ukrainian history after the 1917 revolution, leaving it to Yavorsky and other Marxist historians to extrapolate his new approaches to Russian history to the realm of Ukrainian historiography.

Although Yavorsky generally adhered to the historical method developed by Pokrovsky, in the late 1920s the two historians clashed over control of Marxist scholarship in Ukraine. In the atmosphere created by the major shift in Communist Party policy on the non-Russian nationalities, Pokrovsky accused his Ukrainian counterpart and his followers of sharing Mykhailo Hrushevsky's views on Ukrainian history. Yavorsky's 'deviations' from Pokrovsky's scheme were then exploited by Pokrovsky's supporters to derail Yavorsky's academic and political career. During the discussions of Yavorsky's scheme of Ukrainian history organized in Kharkiv in May 1929, Yavorsky's interpretation of the history of the Khmelnytsky Uprising was challenged by two Marxist scholars, Volodymyr Sukhyno-Khomenko and Heorhii Karpenko. The former criticized Yavorsky for underestimating the role of towns and burghers, while the latter stressed the importance of the peasantry.

Sukhyno-Khomenko presented his views on the Khmelnytsky era in detail in a collection of lectures delivered during the 1927–8 academic year at a school for party functionaries organized by the Central Committee of the Communist Party of Ukraine. The lectures were published as a book in early 1929.[15] Sukhyno-Khomenko also took an active part in the discussion of Yavorsky's historical scheme in May 1929, generally defending his former professor while presenting his own views on the Khmelnytsky Uprising. Later, he published a number of articles in which he presented a mild critique of Yavorsky and called upon Yavorsky's opponents to fight Yavorskyism (*Iavorshchyna*) together with Yavorsky, while seeking to shield him from further hostile criticism. This was of no avail: not only was Yavorsky soon constrained to leave Ukraine, but Sukhyno-Khomenko himself and Mykhailo Svidzinsky, another of Yavorsky's students who tried to protect him from critical attacks during the May 1929 discussion, were accused of sharing their professor's views and succumbing to Yavorskyism.[16]

Sukhyno-Khomenko was much better prepared to deal with the Khmelnytsky Uprising than Yavorsky or any other of his students, as he was specifically assigned by his supervisor to research the seventeenth-century history of Ukraine (especially the period of the so-called Ruin). In his interpretation of the uprising, Sukhyno-Khomenko adopted and further developed Pokrovsky's view of the role of the burghers. He considered the growth of the towns in sixteenth-century Ukraine to be the most important factor in its early modern history. According to Sukhyno-Khomenko, the towns had become an arena of fierce struggle of representatives of local commercial capital against the aggression of Polish and Jewish commercial capital. The competition between these two groups acquired strong religious overtones. By accepting the church union with Rome, he asserted, the Orthodox hierarchy had sought to undermine the control established over ecclesiastical affairs by Ukrainian commercial capital. The brotherhoods, which, by that logic, represented Ukrainian capital, did not want to give up religion as a means of rallying support in their struggle against foreign capital and managed to regain control over the church with the restoration of the Orthodox hierarchy in 1620.

According to Sukhyno-Khomenko, Cossackdom came into existence as a result of the development of commercial capital, which accelerated the pauperization of the poorest strata of the population in towns and villages alike. Those paupers eventually fled to the steppe regions, where they formed the first Cossack bands. Sukhyno-Khomenko stated in his lectures that he did not share the views of those historians (apparently meaning Yavorsky) who claimed that the Cossacks represented the avant-garde of Ukrainian capital because of their involvement in the Black Sea trade. He referred to the Cossacks as the brigands of the Ukrainian steppes and claimed that there was little commercial motive for their attacks on the Ottoman ports of the Black Sea littoral. According to Sukhyno-Khomenko, because the Cossacks accepted many burghers into their ranks, some of whom eventually settled in the steppes and formed a group of well-to-do Cossacks, Cossackdom in general also incorporated some elements of burgher ideology, specifically the idea of religious struggle against church union and Polish-Jewish capital. This development allegedly occurred during the times of Hetman Petro Konashevych-Sahaidachny. Sukhyno-Khomenko maintained that the struggle between the two commercial capitalisms, domestic and foreign, was reflected in the rulings of the Orthodox council of 1640, which forbade the Orthodox to buy merchandise from Polish and Jewish merchants.

The Khmelnytsky Uprising was defined by Sukhyno-Khomenko as a great Ukrainian bourgeois revolution, a term that associated it with other 'bourgeois' revolutions of that period, including the English one. The historian rejected Pokrovsky's and Yavorsky's definition of the uprising as a Cossack revolution (and identified Nikolai Rozhkov as the first scholar to introduce the term).[17] One could not define a 'great antifeudal, broad social revolution in Ukraine' as a gentry revolution, he claimed, because 'gentry' (*dvorianstvo*) was a legal concept. Nor could it be called a Cossack revolution, for Cossackdom was the name of a social order, not a class. In Sukhyno-Khomenko's opinion, there could be a Cossack or peasant revolt or a gentry coup d'état, but not a revolution, for the latter could be defined only in class terms.

Sukhyno-Khomenko shared Yavorsky's scepticism about the significance of heroes in history and considered Bohdan Khmelnytsky's role in the uprising to have been rather marginal. Unlike Yavorsky, though, who limited the Khmelnytsky Uprising to the years 1648–54, effectively terminating it with the Pereiaslav Agreement of 1654 between the tsar and the Cossacks, Sukhyno-Khomenko preferred to write and speak of the revolution of 1648, which in his opinion extended also to subsequent years and was not chronologically limited by the Pereiaslav

Agreement. In his view, the first stage of the uprising was dominated by the registered Cossacks. From 1649, however, the leading role was assumed by the burghers. The peasantry was the driving force of the revolution but was unable to take control of it.

The historian's overall assessment of the outcome of the Khmelnytsky Uprising, based on changes in the status of the burghers, was quite pessimistic. He believed that Ukrainian commercial capital had managed to mount a great revolution, even more radical in its consequences than the English one, but proved incapable of leading it to victory and perished in the struggle, as the revolution eventually led to the decline of the Ukrainian towns. The reasons for the defeat of the burghers, in Sukhyno-Khomenko's opinion, were the unreliability of their allies, the passivity of the village, the inconstancy of the lumpen elements, and the treachery of the Cossack officer stratum. The latter sought support from either Moscow or Warsaw. The class struggle, claimed this national communist, was exploited by foreign elements to establish the rule of foreign (Muscovite) commercial capital in Ukraine.[18]

Sukhyno-Khomenko was in fact the main proponent of Pokrovsky's theory of 'commercial capitalism' in Ukraine. He applied it to the analysis of the Khmelnytsky Uprising much more systematically than Yavorsky. Later, when political circumstances required, he employed his interpretation of 'commercial capitalism' as a means of criticizing Yavorsky for alleged inconsistencies and deviations from the Marxist approach to Ukrainian history.[19] Sukhyno-Khomenko claimed that Yavorsky was mistaken in arguing that the main cause of the uprising was the inability of the Polish nobility to establish an effective agricultural economy – the factor that allegedly forced the Cossacks, a new landowning elite, to rebel. In Sukhyno-Khomenko's opinion, the Polish nobility was, on the contrary, too effective in its pursuit of new land and new serfs, which led eventually to peasant revolts. But it was the burghers who, according to Sukhyno-Khomenko, managed to turn the isolated peasant revolts into a successful revolution.

He maintained that Yavorsky's gravest mistake was his neglect of the role of the burghers, who fought the advance of Polish and Jewish capital during the Khmelnytsky Uprising. He also rejected Yavorsky's attempt to introduce the 'commercial capital' factor into his analysis of the uprising not through the burghers but through the Zaporozhian Cossacks, whose headquarters in the lower Dnieper region (the Zaporozhian Sich) Yavorsky regarded as a commercial outpost. Sukhyno-Khomenko claimed that, while the Sich indeed performed that role in the eighteenth century, in the mid-seventeenth century it attracted more fugitive peasants and Cossack rabble than merchants. Indeed, Sukhyno-Khomenko ridiculed Yavorsky's claim that the Khmelnytsky Uprising had cleared the way for nobiliary landholding represented by the Cossack officer stratum, asserting that in fact it had helped destroy feudalism and undermine the nobility to clear the way for the capitalist mode of production.

In a number of his writings and public disputes (especially during the May 1929 discussion of Yavorsky's scheme of Ukrainian history), Sukhyno-Khomenko not only made use of Pokrovsky's earlier views on Russian and Ukrainian history but also developed them in a manner hardly intended by the founder of Russian Marxist historiography. Sukhyno-Khomenko's main departure from Pokrovsky's scheme was his definition of the Khmelnytsky Uprising as a national revolution or a revolution of national liberation. To be sure, Pokrovsky had written about the national and religious character of Cossack conflicts with the Polish authorities, but for him the Cossacks were 'Russians,' representatives of the all-Russian nationality, not Ukrainians. Sukhyno-Khomenko, by contrast, argued for the Ukrainian national character of the Khmelnytsky Uprising, heavily loading his argument with Marxist terminology. He maintained that, because the Khmelnytsky revolution took place during the era of commercial capitalism, there was sufficient reason to define it as a national revolution. It was general knowledge, argued the young Marxist historian, that nations were formed in the era of commercial, not industrial, capitalism. 'The Ukrainian nationality takes part in this revolution as a nation and stands up against the Polish lordship with the demands of national liberation,' stated Sukhyno-Khomenko during the Yavorsky discussion. He countered the accusations of his opponents, who claimed that his definition of the revolution as a national one reflected the views of Hrushevsky, with the words: 'So what? Certainly we cannot reject everything that the bourgeois historians say when it is the truth.'[20]

It can scarcely be doubted that Sukhyno-Khomenko was influenced by many elements of Hrushevsky's interpretation of early modern Ukrainian history in general and the Khmelnytsky Uprising in particular. Not only did he avoid criticizing Hrushevsky, but he also tacitly favoured some of Hrushevsky's interpretations of the Ukrainian past over those of his Marxist teachers and colleagues. For example, he ignored Yavorsky's attempt to divide Ukrainian Cossackdom into three groups on the basis of their social status and instead followed

Hrushevsky's less confrontational approach, which divided the Cossacks into two groups: well-to-do and rank-and-file Cossacks. Following Hrushevsky, Sukhyno-Khomenko wrote about the denationalization and Polonization of the Ukrainian elite and used the term 'Ukrainian national revival' to define Ukrainian cultural activity of the 1620s. Like Hrushevsky, he referred to that period as the 'first revival,' viewing the rise of the national movement in nineteenth-century Ukraine as the 'second revival' of the Ukrainian nation.[21] Sukhyno-Khomenko depicted Ukrainian burghers and commercial capital in general as champions of the idea of Ukrainian nationhood and statehood, and even implicitly blamed the class struggle for the loss of Ukrainian independence.

In presenting his views on the Khmelnytsky Uprising, Sukhyno-Khomenko made heavy use of Marxist argot, often applying anachronistic terminology borrowed from the Soviet analysis of the 1917 revolution. That clearly undermined his argument in the eyes of non-Marxist historians of Ukraine, who must have considered him just another communist propagandist, but legitimized the national version of Ukrainian history in the eyes of the regime and the Ukrainian political elite of the day. Needless to say, that legitimization of the national paradigm of Ukrainian history was eventually challenged and condemned by the official establishment. Even Yavorsky ridiculed his former student's insistence on the leading role of the burghers in the Khmelnytsky Uprising. Much more important, however, during the Yavorsky discussion of May 1929, Sukhyno-Khomenko was severely criticized for overestimating the role played by national movements in the age of commercial capital. It was also claimed that he had emphasized the national factor at the expense of class – one of the most serious accusations that could be made against a Marxist historian at the time.[22]

A very different paradigm of the Khmelnytsky Uprising was put forward during the Yavorsky discussion of 1929 by Heorhii Karpenko, Sukhynko-Khomenko's colleague at the Kharkiv Institute of Marxism-Leninism. In presenting his interpretation of the uprising, Karpenko criticized Yavorsky for failing to understand and appreciate Pokrovsky's views.[23] Karpenko defined the Khmelnytsky Uprising as a Cossack war, claiming that it was the peasants who had actually won it. In the long term, he argued, Ukraine was indeed heading in the direction of capitalist development, but at the time of the Khmelnytsky Uprising there were two ways to reach that goal. One was associated with the destruction of feudalism and the development of a peasant-based economy. The other way consisted in adjusting the feudal economy to the demands of capitalist development. According to Karpenko, it was the peasantry that fought for the first option, while the Cossack officers preferred the second, which would have turned them into a new class of land- and serf-owners. In Karpenko's opinion, the peasants originally won the competition and the war, but in the subsequent decades serfdom was reintroduced into Ukraine with Russian connivance.[24]

Karpenko claimed that Yavorsky had misinterpreted the Khmelnytsky Uprising as a gentry revolution, which implied that during the war the peasants were fighting for their own enserfment. Yavorsky's error, argued Karpenko, lay in a misguided approach to analysing the class nature of the uprising. Allegedly, Yavorsky assessed it from the perspective of economic development instead of class struggle, thereby following Rozhkov and not Pokrovsky. In his attack on Yavorsky, Karpenko referred not to Pokrovsky's interpretation of the Khmelnytsky revolt, which Yavorsky basically followed, but to his interpretation of the Time of Troubles in Russia, which he had further developed during the 1920s. Karpenko claimed that Pokrovsky viewed the Time of Troubles as a peasant war like the one that took place in Germany in the sixteenth century and that Marxist historians should regard the Khmelnytsky Uprising in the same way. Karpenko's emphasis on Pokrovsky's new approach and his critique of Pokrovsky's 'old' theory of commercial capitalism showed that he was well acquainted with the latest developments on the 'historical front' in Moscow.

Back in 1925, in an article published in *Pravda*, Pokrovsky had changed his definition of Emelian Pugachev's uprising from 'early bourgeois revolution' to 'great peasant uprising.'[25] He had also revised his earlier interpretation of the Time of Troubles from a peasant revolution to a peasant war. In 1928–9 Pokrovsky was attacked for maintaining that commercial capitalism was a distinct socio-economic formation. His critics claimed that it had not in fact constituted a mode of production and was incapable of developing a superstructure of its own. Pokrovsky tried to defend himself and his theory but eventually was forced to recognize his 'errors' and admit that his definition of the Muscovite autocracy as 'commercial capital in a Monomakh hat' was wrong, as it failed to take account of the feudal mode of production dominant at that time.[26] In his critique of the theory of commercial capitalism during the May 1929 discussion in Kharkiv, Karpenko repeated the main points raised against it in Moscow but avoided criticizing

Pokrovsky directly and turned his wrath against Yavorsky, whose interpretation of the Khmelnytsky Uprising he forcefully rejected.

Even though Karpenko's views on the Khmelnytsky Uprising as a peasant war were gaining influence and eventually even became the 'only correct' interpretation of the Khmelnytsky era, in the late 1920s the most popular interpretation of the Khmelnytsky revolt was still that of a revolution – the key term used by both Pokrovsky and Yavorsky. 'Revolution' became the battle cry of Marxist and leftist historiography in general, for revolutionary transformations of society were endlessly fascinating to historians who had survived one of the bloodiest revolutions in history. Not surprisingly, that was what almost all of them found in the Khmelnytsky Uprising. The only question was what kind of revolution it had been – bourgeois, gentry, Cossack, peasant, or national. At the time Karpenko and Sukhyno-Khomenko were presenting their views on the Khmelnytsky Uprising, the outcome of the Moscow-based discussions on the role of commercial capitalism in Russian history was far from clear, and Sukhyno-Khmenko was in no hurry to change his assessment of the social character of the Khmelnytsky Uprising. Nevertheless, echoes of the Moscow discussions on the mode of production and its relation to socio-economic formations may be heard in his statements in the discussion. These included his views on the inadmissibility in the discussion of the Khmelnytsky Uprising of such terms as 'Cossack revolution' or 'gentry revolution,' which were widely used first by Pokrovsky and then by Yavorsky. One can also discern traces of the Moscow discussions in Sukhyno-Khomenko's rejection of both Pokrovsky's and Yavorsky's views on the 'Cossack revolution' as a precondition for the victory of the gentry-based economy and the enserfment of the peasants.

While Sukhyno-Khomenko used Marxist theory and the class-based approach to history in order to present the Khmelnytsky period as one of the most important periods in the early modern history of Europe, legitimizing the interpretation of that uprising as a national revolution in Marxist terms, one of his younger colleagues, Fedir Yastrebov, also a beginning Marxist historian, took the class-based approach as a point of departure in deconstructing and discrediting the national paradigm of the revolt in the eyes of Marxist historians and the political establishment alike.

Fedir Yastrebov's review of volume 9, book 1 of Hrushevsky's *Istoriia Ukraïny-Rusy,* which covered the Khmelnytsky Uprising from 1650 to 1653, appeared in the journal *Prapor marksyzmu* (Banner of Marxism) in early 1930. That review should be considered a direct echo of the discussion of 1929 concerning Yavorsky's scheme of Ukrainian history. Yastrebov, an apprentice Marxist, was in fact the first historian to offer a Marxist critique of Hrushevsky's *Istoriia Ukraïny-Rusy.* The charges he made differed considerably from those presented in previous indictments of Hrushevsky. If earlier Marxist authors had criticized Hrushevsky for neglecting Marxist methods of historical analysis and ignoring the role of class divisions and class struggle in Ukrainian history, Yastrebov now accused him of being a nationalist historian and an ideologue of the Ukrainian bourgeoisie. 'This work is to the advantage of nationalism. And that is why we draw the conclusion that the first book of volume 9 is a book hostile to us,' concluded Yastrebov.[27]

Yastrebov argued that Hrushevsky regarded nationalism as the principal motive force of history and denounced him with all the naivety and aggressive fervour of a convert: 'It was proved almost a century ago that the main driving force of human history is class struggle, by means of which mankind proceeds first to the dictatorship of the proletariat and then to socialism.'[28] Developing his argument, Yastrebov linked Hrushevsky's nationalism with his alleged sympathies for social oppression and those responsible for it. He argued that Hrushevsky refused to admit the counterrevolutionary nature of some of the actions taken by Cossack officers in the course of the Khmelnytsky Uprising, thereby expressing solidarity with the oppressors. 'We say that it is the predicament of every nationalist to become an ideologue of the oppressors, not of the oppressed,' asserted Yastrebov.[29]

Yastrebov's review was written after the Kharkiv discussion on Yavorsky's historical scheme but before the publication of its proceedings. It is interesting in its own right as an attempt to develop, in the midst of the ongoing discussion, a coherent Marxist account capable of competing with Hrushevsky's interpretation of the Khmelnytsky era. What Yastrebov attempted was to bring together all the existing Marxist interpretations of the uprising, as long as they did not directly contradict one another. The starting point for the writings of all Ukrainian Marxist historians on the history of Ukraine was the corpus of Pokrovsky's writings. Not surprisingly, in his extensive review of Hrushevsky's *Istoriia*, Yastrebov wrote that Pokrovsky's brief chapter on the Khmelnytsky Uprising had done more to reveal its true significance than Hrushevsky's voluminous treatment. Thus Yastrebov based his interpretation of the Khmelnytsky era on Pokrovsky's theory of commercial capitalism and defined the Khmelnytsky revolt as a commercial capitalist revolution. In examining its causes, he also drew on the views of Yavorsky and Sukhyno-Khomenko, claiming that the revolution had been brought about by two factors: competition between large Polish and small Ukrainian landowners and the struggle of Ukrainian commercial capitalists against Polish, Jewish, and other foreign competitors.

His definition of the revolution's driving force was also far from original: according to Yastrebov, it was the commercial bourgeoisie, assisted by the Cossack landowning elite and the popular masses – poor peasants, tradesmen, and rank-and-file Cossacks. The bourgeoisie and the popular masses allegedly strove for the complete victory of the revolution, while the Cossack elite was prepared to betray the revolutionary cause. According to Yastrebov, the Cossack officers were enemies of the popular masses and double-dealers who could not decide whether they wanted an independent Ukrainian state or would settle for a foreign protectorate. As Yastrebov described the revolution, it began with a revolt of the registered Cossacks (the Cossack elite), who used the Zaporozhians as their 'military specialists.' By early 1649, following Khmelnytsky's triumphant entrance into Kyiv, the commercial bourgeoisie had taken control of the revolution, but the Cossack officers remained its official leaders. In this case, as in other instances, Yastrebov sought to reconcile Sukhyno-Khomenko's and Yavorsky's views on the social leadership of the Khmelnytsky Uprising.

If Yastrebov made use of Sukhyno-Khomenko's and Yavorsky's works to present a Marxist view of the Khmelnytsky Uprising, he drew on Pokrovsky's comments about Hrushevsky's alleged misunderstanding of the uprising to launch a critical attack on Hrushevsky. Yastrebov summarized the differences between Ukrainian Marxist historiography and Hrushevsky in the following statement: 'Thus, for Academician Hrushevsky the revolution of 1648–54 was a national revolution that led to the national liberation of Ukraine from Poland. He does not see the class-based, bourgeois nature of that revolution. For us this is one of the many revolutions brought about by commercial capital in many countries of the world. The revolution of 1648–54 destroyed the remnants of feudalism in Ukraine and cleared the way for the development of commercial capitalism, which was [previously] severely obstructed by magnate landownership, Polish commercial capital, and the semi-feudal Polish state with its *szlachta* particularism.'[30] As I have noted, Yastrebov's views on the Khmelnytsky Uprising lacked the originality shown by some of his Marxist predecessors. His only contributions to the Marxist interpretation of the era were the suggestion that the Orthodox struggle against church union was a struggle for a 'Ukrainian bourgeois state independent of Poland' and the assertion that, while the Cossack officers chose to ally themselves with the Muscovite gentry, the Ukrainian bourgeoisie preferred an alliance with Sweden. Yastrebov's interpretation of the Khmelnytsky Uprising was far more anachronistic than those of his Marxist predecessors, and his text was loaded with expressions borrowed from the vocabulary of the Bolshevik revolution, including terms such as 'military specialists,' 'unprosperous peasants' (*nezamozhnyky*), and 'the rightward wavering (*khytannia*) of the revolutionary forces.'

In 1934 Yastrebov produced a long review of the second book of Hrushevsky's ninth volume. Its title, 'Natsional-fashysts'ka kontseptsiia selians'koï viiny 1648 roku na Ukraïni' (The National-Fascist Conception of the Peasant War of 1648 in Ukraine), was a clear indication not only of a new stage in the officially sponsored demonization of Hrushevsky but also of the unequivocal triumph of the 'peasant war' conception in Marxist historiography of the Khmelnytsky era. That conception had been advocated by Karpenko in 1929 but virtually ignored by Yastrebov at the time. In his new review, Yastrebov did not limit himself to criticizing Hrushevsky's ideas, as in 1930, but admitted and repented his own 'errors' in the interpretation of the Khmelnytsky Uprising. He wrote that he had shared some of the assessments of the uprising made by Mykola Skrypnyk and had viewed it as a 'great bourgeois revolution' along the lines suggested by Sukhyno-Khomenko. By that time, both Skrypnyk and Sukhyno-Khomenko had been condemned by the authorities.

With regard to the nature of the Khmelnytsky Uprising, Yastrebov wrote that since his first review of Hrushevsky's *Istoriia*, the issue had been 'finally settled.' 'It has been shown,' he stated, 'that this revolutionary movement was a peasant war and that along with the peasant masses, the oppressed artisan element in Ukrainian towns participated in it.'[31] Yastrebov referred specifically to the resolutions of the Ukrainian Society of Marxist Historians, in which Yavorsky's interpretation of the uprising, first as a gentry revolution and then as a revolution of commercial capital, was condemned and rejected, and Sukhyno-Khomenko's interpretation of it as a bourgeois and national revolution was dismissed as erroneous. The 'final settlement' of the issue completely removed the Cossacks from the leadership of the uprising, in which they were now overshadowed by the peasantry. References to Cossackdom remained only in the official name given to the Cossack revolts of the late sixteenth and early seventeenth centuries, now designated as the 'era of peasant-Cossack wars of 1591–1638.'

In his 1934 review of Hrushevsky's *Istoriia*, Yastrebov found it necessary to repudiate the 'erroneous' position he had taken in his review of book 1, published four years earlier. This time he tried to be more careful in his assessments, but again he was in no position to predict future turns in the party line and their ramifications for historiography. Ironically, many of the historical issues that Yastrebov considered 'finally settled' in 1934 were soon reinterpreted by Soviet historiography, and Yastrebov was again obliged to adjust his views to the new orthodoxy. For example, in *Narys istorii Ukraïny* (Survey of Ukrainian History), written in 1942, the Khmelnytsky Uprising was presented not as a 'peasant war' but as a 'national-liberation war of the Ukrainian people,' and Khmelnytsky was treated as a major hero. Ukraine's incorporation into the Muscovite state after the Pereiaslav Council was viewed as a 'lesser evil,' not in comparison with a popular uprising, as Yastrebov had maintained in 1934, but in relation to the conquest of Ukraine by Poland or the Ottoman Empire.[32]

Yastrebov's review of 1934 was one of the last examples of an exclusively class-based critique of Hrushevsky. The historian was not yet accused of being an enemy of the Russian people and of Russo-Ukrainian brotherhood and friendship – accusations that soon became obligatory in Soviet propaganda attacks on Hrushevsky. In his review, Yastrebov consistently presented Muscovite policy as a 'gradual takeover of Ukraine.'[33] 'For us,' he wrote with reference to the Pereiaslav Agreement of 1654, 'this is a pact between two exploitative forces – Muscovite landowners and Ukrainian (to some extent also Polish) landowners.'[34] Yastrebov's treatment of the Pereiaslav Agreement as a 'lesser evil' casts light on the prevailing balance between class-based and nation-based elements in the Marxist interpretation of Ukrainian history. For him, Pereiaslav was a lesser evil from the viewpoint of the Ukrainian Cossack officers, who had to choose between Muscovite suzerainty and the prospect of a popular uprising.[35]

What does the Marxist critique of Hrushevsky's views on the Khmelnytsky Uprising indicate about changes in the Marxist interpretation of Ukrainian history as a whole? One point that emerges quite clearly from a reading of the officially sponsored reviews of Hrushevsky's works and Marxist debates on the history of the Khmelnytsky Uprising is that after a relatively short period of unsupervised and chaotic efforts on the part of various groups of Marxist historians to apply the Marxist paradigm to Ukrainian history, the centre succeeded in imposing a uniform and obligatory interpretation of the Ukrainian past. That interpretation would change dramatically in the course of the 1930s, but open competition among various interpretations of history was effectively banned and became a thing of the past. The main victim of the new uniformity was the concept of nationhood and all historical symbols considered too closely related to the national paradigm of Ukrainian history. Cossackdom, for example, became a symbol of all that was wrong with the national paradigm in the eyes of Marxist historians: nationalism, statism, elitism, and lack of interest in problems of social differentiation and class struggle in Ukrainian society.

The rejection of Pokrovsky's theory of commercial capitalism and the refusal to see the burghers as leaders of the Khmelnytsky Uprising ('bourgeois revolution') reflected a major shift in party discourse on the bourgeoisie, which was no longer considered a progressive force. The bourgeoisie was now regarded not only as the main enemy of the Soviet state but also as a major antagonist of the proletariat and the toiling masses in the past. The peasantry emerged as a major beneficiary of all these changes. On the one hand, the shift towards treating the peasantry as the protagonist of premodern history was influenced by a rereading of Marx and Engels, especially the latter's classic study of the peasant war in Germany. On the other hand, the further politicization of scholarship meant that the peasant issue, so crucial to the communist politics of the 1920s, was read back into the history of Ukraine. As a result, the new Marxist interpretation of the Khmelnytsky Uprising, as it emerged in late 1920s and early 1930s, had much more in common with the interpretation of that event in populist historiography of the late nineteenth and early twentieth centuries than it did with Marxism.

8 The People's History

Alternative History

In the early 2000s, when members of the Archaeographic Expedition of Zaporizhia State University, led by Professor Anatolii Boiko, went to the villages of southern Ukraine to collect oral testimonies about the Ukrainian famine of 1932–3, they were in for a surprise. Nothing that they had known or read previously prepared them for what they found in the attics and back rooms of peasant homes. Waiting to be discovered were memoirs, histories, and personal notes written by generations of Ukrainian peasants between 1917 and the mid-1970s. It started with one manuscript; then came another and another. In 2005 Boiko and his colleagues published their unexpected bounty in a two-volume collection of more than a thousand folio pages.[1]

The Zaporizhia collection includes diaries, family histories, and reminiscences that passed into journal entries and memoirs of people born in the southern Ukrainian steppes in the late nineteenth and early twentieth centuries. Some of them stayed in the village all their lives, while others moved to the towns, and some even found themselves abroad after the Second World War. In an era when the official confiscation of diaries or memoirs could cost the author his liberty or even his life, it was fairly uncommon to keep such records. Quite a few autobiographies were written, but usually not for the purpose of telling the truth about one's life – rather to conceal it, explain it in an appropriate light, or deny an utterly 'incorrect' social origin, presence on occupied territory, or the existence of relatives abroad. Diaries were usually kept by schoolchildren, scholars, and writers; memoirs were written by generals and certain political figures. That was known to all even in Soviet times, but few (including the authorities) suspected that such efforts had also been made by 'people from the street.'

Historians of the Soviet period have lately begun to publish studies of diaries and memoirs written 'from below.' Featured here are the records of workers who wanted to become writers; participants in the revolutionary events of 1917; autobiographies of party members and Communist Youth League activists or Baptists (many of whom came from Ukraine).[2] The emphasis in present-day humanities scholarship and historiography on the study of cultural development and identity formation (social, national, cultural, gender, and so on) makes these sources particularly interesting to the researcher. To be sure, sources of this kind cannot be considered wholly reliable in elucidating many events of the past. Nevertheless, such sources are indispensable when it comes to studying the imaginings, views, and cultural identities of broad social strata. It has been argued that when the authors of so-called autobiographical narratives took up their pens, they did so in an attempt to make sense of the cultural disintegration and social disorder of the early decades of the twentieth century. Given the total ideological control that prevailed in Soviet times, autobiographical narratives gave their authors a chance to maintain and cultivate a certain degree of spiritual autonomy. At a time when all members of society were supposed to become faithful believers in a radiant communist future, even declarations of 'unbelief' in ideals officially proclaimed and inculcated by the repressive machine, to say nothing of clearly articulated protests against officialdom, should be considered a form of intellectual resistance. The narratives published in the Zaporizhia collection provide examples of just such resistance and demonstrate the illusory nature of the totalitarian control exercised by the communist utopia over the thoughts of Soviet citizens.

Most of the autobiographical narratives published to date come from every milieu but that of the peasantry. There have been publications of memoirs of former peasants who later made brilliant careers, mainly in the Soviet army, as well as of many anti-Soviet emigrants, including General Petro Hryhorenko (who also came from southern Ukraine),[3] but documents written by peasants themselves were either unknown or generally remained beyond the ken of scholars. The authors of all seven autobiographical narratives included in the Zaporizhia collection came from the village. To some degree, all the authors retained features of the peasant mentality, and in this sense, in one way or another, they reflect the attitude of the southern Ukrainian peasantry to the social upheavals and perturbations of the twentieth century. This is characteristic of the diary of Ivan Yaroshenko (1885–1956), who moved to the city rather late and, even as an urban dweller, remained above all a peasant in his interests and preferences. The same applies even more strongly to the family history of Vasyl Rubel (1897–1966), continued by his brother Tykhin (1916–2002), and to the memoirs of Mikhail Alekseev (1893–1986) and Oleksandr Zamrii (1890–1972), who spent their whole lives in villages or, as in Alekseev's case, in a small town. They all received only a primary education, and in this respect they represent the views of a rather numerous stratum of the first twentieth-century generation of literate peasants. The memoirs of Mykola Molodyk (1906–92) and Serhii Cipko (1917–2001), who left their villages as young men and received much better educations, offer interesting comparative material for studying the transformation of the world of the 'urbanized' peasant. Molodyk's memoirs exemplify the reminiscences of a first-generation intellectual, while Cipko's are those of an emigrant cast out of Ukraine by the events of the Second World War. All the authors come from the same region of Ukraine, and the juxtaposition of their narratives is thus of particular interest: the material published in the Zaporizhia collection offers grounds for preliminary but rather well-founded generalizations on a whole host of questions associated with images, views, and evaluations of twentieth-century developments in southern Ukrainian society.

Before examining some of these views and images, it would be useful to determine why our authors took up the pen in the first place. The question can be answered rather easily in the cases of Zamrii, Molodyk, and Cipko: their records belong to a fairly large category of memoir literature dating from the second half of the twentieth century, generally produced by authors nearing the end of their lives for the purpose of drawing conclusions from their experiences and leaving a spiritual legacy to their descendants. Alekseev's memoirs can also be included in this category, but only in part. It is apparent from his records that he began to make entries as early as 1915: they later fell into the hands the GPU (General Political Directorate, a predecessor of the KGB), and Alekseev had to start writing all over again. Yaroshenko began to keep his diary in 1917. In the 1920s, far from the end of his life and any idea of drawing conclusions on the basis of it, Vasyl Rubel wrote his family history. What was it that drove these people? Most probably, the very idea of creating autobiographical family narratives came to them from the upper strata of society, where memoir and diary literature had been especially popular at least since the 1860s.

Hundreds of diaries and memoirs dating from the late nineteenth and early twentieth centuries, written by members of the gentry and representatives of the intelligentsia who sprang from various social origins, are known today. The recently published diaries of Mykhailo Hrushevsky may serve as one of many examples of such popularity.[4] Apparently, the urge to write spread to the peasant milieu before and during the First World War and the Revolution of 1917. Several factors may be considered responsible for this. First, the developing network of zemstvo and parochial schools brought education to the village in the latter half of the nineteenth century, opening up the very possibility of writing autobiographical works. Second, the war brought members of the intelligentsia in officers' greatcoats and peasants in soldiers' cloaks into close direct contact. This was the people's 'going to the intelligentsia,' as it were. Third, the war and the revolution constituted dramatic life experiences that, in the eyes of our authors, were worth recording and lent themselves to being set down in writing (this becomes particularly apparent when one reads Yaroshenko's diary). Finally, the cultural revolution of the 1920s not only brought a previously unheard of level of education to the village but also encouraged the peasant to take part in cultural life, participate in programs of folklore collection, contribute to newspapers, and so on.

What came from the pens of our authors impresses one with the freshness, range, and unconventionality of their historical palette, captivating the reader with the candor and openness with which they recount their own experience and that of the epoch. In many respects, of course, the authors are less than exact in conveying the developments and atmosphere of the time. Later impressions and experiences left their stamp (especially in the case of memoirs); perspectives changed; there was interference from Western radio broadcasts that advanced their own interpretations of events (as in the case of Alekseev, who lived 'in the back of beyond' and was therefore able to listen to the Western 'voices' without jamming, to the envy of all city dwellers). For all that, the significance of our authors' testimony for recreating the history of the 'little people' can hardly be exaggerated. The structure and dynamics of the history presented in these narratives are completely different from those familiar to us from the history textbooks. The First World War, forgotten, ignored, and overshadowed by the revolution in the minds of younger generations, appears in our narratives as an event of the greatest importance, formative for many authors. Compared with it, the Second World War, which occupies such an important place in all current historical narratives, seems no more than a reprise of what was already part of our authors' experience. In their records, the revolution appears not in the trappings of heroic uprisings, as presented in Soviet-era textbooks, but of human tragedies, while the Bolsheviks are just as criminal as other participants in the conflict – to be sure, with the proviso that they managed to establish order of a kind and even gave the peasants land. What our authors could not forgive them was collectivization and famine. Here the peasants were completely at odds with the new order and its official narrative. Their opposition became implacable, and uncovering the gap between official discourse and the actual deeds of the authorities was the principal means of intellectual resistance.

The historical vision that emerged from the authors' life experience is sometimes strikingly original. To judge by some of Alekseev's generalizations, Lenin could figure perfectly well in the 'people's history' along with Stolypin as a ruler who gave land to the peasants, while Khrushchev, for example, might be lumped together with Stalin, since peasant land and private plots were subject to restrictions under his rule. For our authors, collectivization, famine, and war were not merely the crimes of one regime or another. Those crimes had faces, and the criminals had names. The struggle with abstract evil and lies, personified by concrete individuals – fellow villagers and neighbours – was a lifelong occupation, and the behaviour of representatives of one family or another was a memory to be handed down to descendants. That was also part of the motivation for writing peasant narratives.

The materials published in the Zaporizhia collection are a unique source for the study of many aspects of twentieth-century Ukrainian and Soviet history. Of these, it is worth specifying such major themes as the family history of the Ukrainian village and the industrialized city; the history of soldiers' perceptions and everyday life during the First World War; the peasantry's attitude to the revolution and the political forces that fought one another at the time; the Sovietization and atheization of the village in the 1920s and 1930s; and the man-made famines of 1932–3 and 1947. Among other subjects deserving special attention are the campaigns of repression in the 1930s, strategies of individual survival and social resistance under Stalinism, popular loyalty towards various political and military forces during the Second World War, the cult of the Great Fatherland War in the Soviet Union, public opinion and internal opposition in the times of Khrushchev and Brezhnev, and everyday life in the USSR. This list of possible subjects whose study would certainly be aided by the material published in the Zaporizhia collection is of course far from exhaustive. It remains incomplete even today, but the future will bring new questions and approaches to which answers may be found in these sources. In the space of this chapter, it is clearly impossible to elucidate or even touch upon all the themes and subjects noted above. The task here is far more modest: to explore only one of the many themes that the sources published in this collection help illuminate.

What I have in mind is the history of the transformation of cultural and national identities in southern Ukraine. Autobiographical narratives offer a unique opportunity to reconstruct the formation of these identities, since they reflect the way of thinking of a relatively broad stratum of the region's population over a considerable period. They make it possible to raise the curtain to some extent on the making of modern Ukrainian and Russian identity and to establish, in general terms at least, the role of history and historical memory in the formation of these identities. Our authors did not set themselves the specific task of discussing problems of national identity: for some of them, the national question was of less than secondary importance, and they cared more whether their friends or opponents were peasants or workers, rich or poor, rank and file or bosses, politically nonaligned or party members, than they did about the language they spoke or the nationality to which they belonged. And therein lies the value of the narratives analysed below, for they reflect the generally unconscious or only partly articulated manifestations of a complex hierarchy of cultural identities that was only gradually being transformed into modern national consciousness.

National Projects

In the second half of the nineteenth century, the peasantry of the western and southwestern gubernias of the Russian Empire became a bone of contention between two national projects. Alexei Miller has defined the first of these as the project of the 'great Russian nation.'[5] Supported and carried out by the government, it was meant to create one modern Russian nation out of the Great Russians, Little Russians, and Belarusians. This program, which we shall call 'pan-Russian,' was opposed by projects for the creation of individual East Slavic nations – Russian, Ukrainian, and Belarusian. The clearest and best articulated of them was the Ukrainian project, which duly became the main competitor of the pan-Russian idea on Ukrainian ethnic territory. In the course of the nineteenth century, the peasantry had a fairly definite social and religious identity but lacked any feeling of modern national identification, for which ethnic and local loyalties served as partial substitutes. Alternative national identities could be – and were – established on that basis.

The educational system became the principal agent of 'nationalization' of the peasant masses that had recently been emancipated from serfdom, while the question of the language in which the peasants were to read and study became the central issue in a confrontation between supporters of the pan-Russian project, the imperial government, and the Ukrainophiles. The Valuev Circular of 1863 and the Ems Ukase of 1876 prohibited Ukrainian-language teaching and the publication of educational, religious, and popular literature in Ukrainian, considerably impeding the realization of the Ukrainian project and creating favourable conditions for its pan-Russian competitor.[6] The latter posited the replacement of Church Slavonic as the literary language of educated strata of the Ukrainian peasantry with Russian. Even if the existing idiom could not be eliminated entirely, Russian language and literature were definitely to constitute the basis of high culture in the new pan-Russian nation, leaving the lower cultural sphere – everyday life, folklore, and so on – to the local (in this case, Ukrainian) language, whose official status was that of a 'dialect' (*narechie*), and to the literature written in that 'dialect.'[7]

The peasant histories published in the Zaporizhia collection give a good idea of the progress of linguistic Russification in southern Ukraine in the latter half of the nineteenth century and the early decades of the twentieth. Four of the seven authors obtained their education in Russian in their native villages before the revolution, and three of them wrote their histories and diaries in Russian, laced (even in the case of the ethnic Russian Alekseev) with a considerable admixture of Ukrainisms. Even the greatest 'Ukrainophile' of the whole group, Vasyl Rubel, who wrote in Ukrainian, still had the intention of 'translating' (*perevodyty* – a Russianism) his text – into Russian, of course.[8] The 'History' of Rubel, who came from a family of village 'literates,' offers a good example of the gradual transition from Church Slavonic to Russian as the language of rural education. Vasyl's great-great-grandfather Danylo and his great-grandfather Ivan 'understood letters well according to the Psalter.' His grandfather Kuzma not only 'knew the Psalter straight through but could sign his name in Russian.' According to Vasyl Rubel, in Mala Bilozerka, where there had previously been one school offering instruction only in Church Slavonic, two parochial schools that also used Russian as a teaching language opened in the 1880s. Thus Kuzma's sons could not only read the Psalter but 'also knew Russian.' The peasants evidently welcomed the transition from Church Slavonic to Russian; even if it was not their native language, it was still closer than Church Slavonic. Judging by the memoirs of one of Vasyl Rubel's relatives, the study of Church Slavonic according to the Psalter left particularly unpleasant impressions, with a large number of incomprehensible words.[9] Moreover, the peasants, with no thought of pursuing ecclesiastical careers, had much more reason to study Russian than Church Slavonic. It was Russian that opened doors for them to the wider world, which in the peasants' case was represented by the Russian-speaking state administration and the army. The educational system promoted Russian as the language whereby the peasants were introduced to high culture. This was symbolized by the gift – the Gospels and 'a book by [Nikolai] Gogol'[10] – presented to Mikhail Alekseev in May 1907 together with a certificate of completion of a four-year school. Pupils from Ukraine were attracted to Russian culture by reading the works of one of their most famous countrymen, who had contributed greatly to the formation of pan-Russian identity through the medium of the Russian language and literature.

But what did the peasants themselves – the objects of attention of the two competing national projects – think of Russo-Ukrainian unity or difference? The coexistence of Ukrainian and Russian settlements in the northern Black Sea region made linguistic and cultural differences between the two ethnic groups particularly apparent in that region of Ukraine. At times, as Rubel recounts in his 'History,' Ukrainian wagoners and Russian traders came to blows.[11] Citing his father, Alekseev recounts how Russians resettled from the Kursk gubernia and Ukrainians resettled from the Poltava and Chernihiv gubernias quarrelled and finally proved unable to live together in the same village. As a result, the village of Petropavlivka was divided into the Russian Petrovka and the Ukrainian Pavlivka.[12]

Ethnic identity became the basis for differentiating 'one's own' from 'foreigners.' Alekseev's use of the terms 'Russians' and 'Ukrainians' – terms of modern national identity – was rooted in concepts characteristic of the revolutionary and postrevolutionary era. His own records, as well as those of other contemporary authors, attest that the names most often used by peasants of the prerevolutionary era with reference to ethnic Ukrainians and Russians were *khokhly* (referring to Cossack topknots) and *katsapy* (a derogatory term). These terms, which hardly excluded negative connotations, were used to denote the two ethnic groups *faute de mieux*: as Rubel's own 'History' attests, Ukrainians used *khokhol*, inter alia, as a self-definition.[13] The official term *maloros* (Little Russian) did not, however, gain currency among the peasants. When Alekseev served in the army during the First World War, Moldavians called him a *katsap*, but then, he himself applied the term to a Russian from Penza.[14] That *khokhly* and *katsapy* were terms for ethnic groups, not for well-defined modern nations in the present-day sense of the word, is attested by the dominance of local or regional identities in the early decades of the twentieth century, which is established in the peasant histories.

Local Identities

Given the military operations of the First World War and the soldiers' absence from home, regional identity – feelings of closeness to compatriots and loyalty to the *rodina*, which in our sources more often meant a small fatherland than a great state – took on particular significance. In such a context, group loyalty took shape according to the formula: family (first immediate, then extended, including godparents, and so on), village, county, gubernia. In the case of our authors who participated in the First World War (here we should also include Andrii Rubel, from whose letters his brother Vasyl quotes generously in his 'History'), their compatriots were above all fellow villagers (from Bilozirka, Petrovka, and other settlements), then those from the same county (Melitopol), followed by those from the same gubernia (Tavriia). Andrii Rubel found it difficult to part with the boys from his village.[15] Oleksandr Zamrii and Ivan Yaroshenko also write about informal contacts and mutual assistance among compatriots.[16] Throughout his military career, Mikhail Alekseev stayed in close touch with his compatriots and even impressed his superiors by agreeing to command a platoon feared by other young commanders and made up mostly of 'Tavriians.' Compatriots whom the authors of the Zaporizhia collection concordantly identify as having come from the Tavriia gubernia are contrasted with those from other gubernias and regions of the empire: residents of Penza, Siberians, Muscovites, and so on. At times they are also contrasted with representatives of other ethnic groups, especially Moldavians and Poles, but as a rule national differentiation among compatriots themselves remains little articulated. The compatriots include people with both Ukrainian and Russian surnames, and the authors' attitudes to them are not determined by ethnic or national solidarity. Andrii Rubel, for example, was extraordinarily glad to encounter a Jewish compatriot.[17]

Not only did the category of compatriots not accent ethnonational and religious differences among those who came from the same area, but it was also potentially capable of giving rise to a system of loyalties in which people from Katerynoslav would be as 'foreign' to Tavriians as those from the Kursk gubernia. The next storey, or even roof, in such a structure is not a modern national but a transnational one, or an imperial identity. Our authors associated that level of identity with the term 'Russia' or *rodina* when the matter at hand did not concern the small fatherland (the village) but the defence of the state. In the context of the war, Russia stood opposed to Germany and Austria, and the cases noted by our authors in which 'Austrians' spoke Ukrainian, 'Russian Germans' fought on the side of the tsar, 'Russian Poles' readily went over to the 'Germans,' and 'German Poles' spoke Russian with a Polish accent remain in our sources with no particular explanation.[18] In the soldiers' mentality, wartime conditions and official propaganda tended to level national differences within the same political and military camp while highlighting differences of state and policy with regard to the opponent, who was constantly 'othered' and demonized under conditions of military conflict.

In the Romanov army, the idea of defending the larger *rodina* was popularized, and the formation of imperial identity proceeded at an accelerated pace. Conditions for the development of the pan-Russian project were thus particularly favourable. For example, an officer imputed to Andrii Rubel that his surname sounded German. Ultimately, in one of the letters notifying Rubel's family of his demise, he was given an authentically Russian name, Porublev. Andrii, who initially complained in his letters from the army that the soldiers were being 'driven' into battle, later began to write that the *rodina*, Holy Rus', had to be defended and generally noted that he was leading a hero's life. Having found it so difficult to part with his fellow villagers at the beginning of the war, he later enjoined his younger brother not to long for his village comrades – after all, everyone was a comrade in the army. And indeed, when Andrii was killed, there was not a single Tavriian among the comrades who notified his family of his death.[19]

From Local to National

It was only the February Revolution of 1917 and the swift politicization of the army that brought about the activization of hitherto suppressed ethnic loyalties and the actualization of Ukrainian national identity and its alternatives in the army.[20] This change came too late to affect the letters of Andrii Rubel, who fell near Kovel on 25 September 1916. Nevertheless, it was reflected at various levels and in a number of ways by authors who survived the First World War. Yaroshenko, who attended a demonstration on Cathedral Square in Katerynoslav on 12 March 1917, saw Ukrainian flags among the other banners displayed there.[21] Alekseev later recalled the transfer of Ukrainians from the northern to the southern front and the dispatch of 'northerners' from the 'Ukrainian' to the northern front but left that report without comment.[22] An author who did comment on the formation of Ukrainian units at the front was Oleksandr Zamrii, who, judging by his memoirs, was transferred from Pskov to Brovary near Kyiv and dispatched to the front from there. Like other Ukrainians, Zamrii first went to Petrograd, where a soldiers' meeting decided to dispatch natives of the southern gubernias to Ukraine. Zamrii later regretted having obeyed that decision, for he left Pskov without even stopping to examine its historical monuments. One reason for his dissatisfaction was that he had to abandon the peaceful post of quartermaster, far from the front, and set out on the 'untrodden way' that led to the front. But that was not his only reason to be dissatisfied.[23]

Looking back on those events from the perspective of the 1960s, Zamrii considered that the soldiers in Petrograd were poorly versed in politics and had been duped by agitators sent by Symon Petliura, the organizer of the Ukrainian army and later head of the Ukrainian state. 'As we understood later and today, that was the voice of Petliura and his stooges; it was they who wanted to tear Russia apart and did so,' wrote Zamrii in his memoirs. For our purposes, it is extraordinarily important to determine what the author understood 'then' and what he accepted post factum under the influence of later events, his own experiences, and Soviet propaganda. Recalling the events of 1917, Zamrii wrote that one of the officers had advised him not to 'follow the abovementioned clique,' as 'they will simply involve you in a fight and you will beat one another, that is, Ukrainians will beat Russians and vice versa.' Post factum, Zamrii considered that the officer had been right, noting that 'the same thing is now going on in African countries, in the Congo and Laos, where blood is being shed as it was shed among us during the Civil War – not only nation against nation but also brother against brother.' That was later, but in the summer of 1917 Zamrii clearly yielded to the call of the national idea and allowed the national awakeners in the army to mobilize and prioritize his ethnic identity, even contrary to considerations of his own peace and security. He also accepted the new national identity and the new national designation with regard to his compatriots from Tavriia. 'The soldiers among us are more Siberians and Permians. Of the Tavriians – or, rather, Ukrainians – there is no more than one around each gun. And even so, they were gunners and gun commanders,' wrote Zamrii in the 1960s about the events of 1916.[24]

Regional loyalty, based on the origin of soldiers from certain gubernias, now became a building block in the structure of the new national identity. This was fairly simple in practice, considering that both the Central Rada in Kyiv and those who formed Ukrainian units at the front defined Ukraine and Ukrainian identity in terms of gubernias. Nevertheless, the Tavriia gubernia, with the Crimea as one of its constituent parts, posed a special problem, for as of August 1917 (by which time Zamrii had already decided to return to Ukraine) the Provisional Government in Petrograd would not hear of recognizing the authority of the Central Rada over 'New Russia,' which was considered to include the Tavriia gubernia.[25] That gubernia (not including the Crimea) was only proclaimed a constituent part of the Ukrainian People's Republic in November 1917, when the Central Rada issued its Third Universal.[26] The status of the Crimea, separate from the rest of the Tavriia gubernia, which became part of Ukraine, was registered in Alekseev's memoirs: recalling the events of December 1917, he not only wrote of transfers from one front to another and the demobilization of the Ukrainians but also made separate mention of the demobilization of 'the Crimeans.' He celebrated Christmas 1917 with a friend from Simferopol, Fedor Lysykh, who stopped in Alekseev's native village on his way home.[27] It would appear that all the authors of the Zaporizhia collection who wrote about the events of 1917, including the ethnic Russian Alekseev, found their newly acquired Ukrainian identity and the definition of their villages as part of Ukrainian territory completely natural.

A Choice Delayed

For many residents of Ukraine, the establishment of a Ukrainian state and its conflict with the Russian Reds and Whites squarely posed the question of choice of political loyalty and national allegiance. As our sources attest, however, this challenge of the time was generally ignored in southern Ukraine. Alekseev and Zamrii (who later developed a pan-Russian orientation) considered that the Civil War, which all the authors regarded as an internal political conflict within the Russian Empire, had begun with the conflict between the Ukrainian government and the Bolsheviks. Post factum, both authors identified the Central Rada, formed in Kyiv in the spring of 1917 and dissolved by the German military in the spring of 1918, with Symon Petliura, the head of the Ukrainian state in 1919–20, but their evaluation of events was somewhat different. If Zamrii, as noted earlier, accused Petliura and his supporters of attempting to divide Russia, Alekseev was inclined to represent the conflict more in political and regional colours than in national ones. He wrote that in January 1918 rumours reached his village to the effect 'that in Kyiv there was organized – in a word, in Ukraine – Petliura, and in the north the Red Guard after October, still in the year [19]17, and the Civil War was beginning.'[28]

A different assessment of events was given post factum by Mykola Molodyk, who was an elementary-school pupil in 1917. He associated the beginning of the conflict with the illegal Bolshevik seizure of power and the rising of all other parties (among which the author enumerates the Mensheviks, Socialist Revolutionaries, and monarchists) against them. In the developing conflict, Molodyk clearly sympathizes with the Ukrainian side, and with the Central Rada above all. He is the only author who does not reduce the Ukrainian Revolution to Petliura and Hetman Pavlo Skoropadsky, the head of the Ukrainian state in 1918, but also mentions the names of Mykhailo Hrushevsky and Volodymyr Vynnychenko, the leaders of the Central Rada. Molodyk welcomes the formation of the Ukrainian state and the introduction of Ukrainian as the official language, as well as Ukrainian currency. Writing in the 1960s, he constructs his account of those times as an explicit antithesis to the dominant Soviet historical narrative. While accepting certain tenets of that narrative, such as its negative attitude to the hetman and the German occupation (with the reservation that the Germans initially behaved correctly towards the population), Molodyk represents the Central Rada, not the Bolsheviks, as the major positive force behind revolutionary developments. In his view, it was not the Central Rada but the Soviet government that 'handed Ukraine over to the Germans.' According to Molodyk, the Central Rada and Petliura, who was in charge of its military forces, fought the Germans, who overthrew the Rada and forced Hrushevsky and Vynnychenko to emigrate.[29] This assessment of events from late 1917 to mid-1918 runs counter to historical fact and finds no parallel in the other sources published in the Zaporizhia collection. Nevertheless, it should not be rejected as a purely historiographic construction of a later time. After all, as Molodyk says, his family and the whole village voted for the Socialist Revolutionaries – the leading political force in the Central Rada – in the elections of 1917 to the Constituent Assembly, and Molodyk's later evaluation, in all likelihood, reflected the feelings and attitudes of his fellow villagers in 1917 and early 1918.

For the peasants of southern Ukraine, as the material published in the Zaporizhia collection makes apparent, the outbreak of the Russo-Ukrainian war at the beginning of 1918 remained no more than a distant rumour and was marked only by the introduction of a new military census. Life went on as before until the arrival of German and Ukrainian units in the spring of that year.[30] Judging by Yaroshenko's diary, the Ukrainian-German alliance aroused no particular objection on the part of the peasants. His native village had just undergone the rule of anarchists and Red Guards, which was marked by pogroms and public executions of Jewish petty entrepreneurs and their families. The peasants were clearly awaiting the arrival of a firm authority, and the Germans met that demand in full. The first to arrive in the village at the beginning of 1918 were Ukrainian Cossack-style military detachments, generally known as haidamakas, who were welcomed with bread and salt on the church square. Yaroshenko, who generally avoided any evaluation or show of political sympathies, described the ceremony in detail in his diary. Breaking temporarily with the Russian language, which he used to keep his records, Yaroshenko used Ukrainian to relate the welcoming speech in honour of the arriving soldiers, delivered by the local teacher Karas, and the reply by the haidamaka commander (a former deputy to the Constituent Assembly from the town of Nyzhniodniprovsk), Romanchenko. The haidamakas were thanked for establishing order, and they promised to maintain it, agitated for an independent Ukraine, and called for struggle against the Bolsheviks.[31] The change of language and the detailed account of the arrival of the haidamakas in Yaroshenko's generally laconic diary may indicate that he was receptive to some of the Ukrainian soldiers' appeals, but he was loyal above all not to party or nation but to his village, where he was a member of the self-defence force. On 9 December 1918 Yaroshenko noted in his diary: 'At the moment we are in such a state that we do not know where to go and why. The hetman has mobilized the officers and Petliura the junior officers, and they are going one against the other, brother against brother. The hetman is a Cadet [member of the Constitutional Democratic Party], so they say, and Petliura is a republican, and [Nestor] Makhno is an anarchist, and the

Russians are Bolsheviks, and each is against the other, and they are killing one another. It is terrible to see this sad story. When the end will come, I do not know.'[32]

A characteristic feature of the situation in southern Ukraine reflected in our sources was that neither the Ukrainian nor the Russian national idea was a major factor in the peasants' choice between the warring sides. Just as the Ukrainian idea could not shake Yaroshenko's primary loyalty to his village, so the pan-Russian idea proved of secondary importance to the ethnic Russian Alekseev. If at the end of 1918 Yaroshenko clearly associated the Russians only with the Bolsheviks, 1919 brought a new Russian force to southern Ukraine – General Anton Denikin's Volunteer Army. But Alekseev was clearly opposed to the 'Cadets' – the forces that fought initially under Denikin and then were led by Petr Wrangel, whom he also called 'masters' (*gospoda*) in his records. In spite of his distaste for the 'bosses,' he also was not enthused by the Bolsheviks. At times, but by no means invariably, he associated himself with the Makhnovites, who included a good many of his fellow villagers and friends, but for the most part he kept to his own village. To some extent, the 'hear nothing, see nothing' approach of most of our authors to the conflict reflected the attitudes of the specific demographic group to which they belonged – the peasants who had fought in the First World War and, on their return, had married and established families. They considered that their fighting days were over and that they should now concentrate on their families and homesteads. Loyalty to their native village and participation in local self-defence forces were fully in accord with that hierarchy of values.

The most substantial characterization of peasant attitudes of the revolutionary epoch appears in the memoirs of Molodyk, for whose fellow villagers the true beginning of the conflict came with the pillaging and bloody depredations of the Makhnovites. He writes, 'The first lesson that the peasants learned was not to get involved in that fight. Let them fight one another if they want, but we should keep our families alive, if possible, and save what we can of our property. With a few insignificant exceptions, that was the policy adhered to by the peasants of every village until the end of the Civil War. No one from our village fought in the ranks of Makhno, Petliura, the Red armies, or the Whites. They took shelter ... The following forces fought one another in Ukraine: the Makhnovites, the Petliurites, the Red Army, the Denikinites, various bands and, finally, the Wrangelites. Between 1917 and 1920, all the above-mentioned participants entered the village more than once and took whatever they needed from the peasants – horses, cattle, grain, and even clothing ... Towards the end, people became so sick and tired of the frenzy that they were glad to get it over with – whoever the authorities might be, let them be, as long as they did not make war or engage in robbery.'[33] Other authors attest that significant numbers of their fellow villagers (especially in Alekseev's case) did in fact fight in the ranks of all the above-mentioned factions, but the general assessment of peasant attitudes given by Molodyk is corroborated by the records of the selfsame Alekseev, Yaroshenko, Zamrii, and even Rubel, who makes only occasional mention of revolutionary events in the village.

Ukrainization

Even though the southern Ukrainian village did not come out in definitive support of the forces that propagated the Ukrainian or the pan-Russian idea during the Civil War, the results of those revolutionary developments, especially the existence of independent Ukrainian states and the subsequent formation of the Ukrainian SSR, clearly changed the balance of forces between supporters of the Ukrainian and the pan-Russian national projects.[34] Molodyk was an open supporter of the wave of Ukrainization during the postrevolutionary period. When the revolution broke out, he was eleven years old. He attended a four-year school and was directly affected by the changes in its curriculum. They were introduced by a teacher who exchanged Russian textbooks for Ukrainian ones and announced that instruction would henceforth be given in Ukrainian. The teacher also explained to the pupils that they were Ukrainians and not Little Russians, related the history of Ukraine to them, and 'read some' of Taras Shevchenko's *Kobzar* (Minstrel) in class. According to Molodyk's memoirs, the transition to Ukrainian was problem-free, as the students spoke the language and easily acquired the alphabet. Molodyk even specifies the date on which Russian textbooks were exchanged for Ukrainian ones: 22 February 1917.[35] In all likelihood, the textbooks appeared somewhat later, and the author's memory played him false in this instance, conflating the events of several months (for example, at the meeting of 12 February [Old Style] there could as yet have been no mention of the Central Rada under the leadership of Vynnychenko and Hrushevsky, as Molodyk writes), but his reminiscences about the dramatic yet fluid reorientation of the pupils' identity deserve to be trusted: the teacher's personality, his Ukrainian history lesson, and his reading from the *Kobzar* obviously imprinted themselves on the author's memory.

In the course of the 1920s, the balance of forces in the contest between the pan-Russian and Ukrainian national projects in Ukraine was clearly changing in favour of the latter. The prohibitions of 1863 and 1876 were receding into the past, and the Ukrainian project was steadily taking control of a new and potent instrument – the educational system. If Vasyl Rubel's grandparents had been schooled in Church Slavonic and he himself, as well as Zamrii, Yaroshenko, and Alekseev, in Russian, Molodyk was already acquiring the rudiments of knowledge in Ukrainian. Part of his memoir is written in literary Ukrainian, while Rubel wrote in dialect, and the older writers (graduates of Russian elementary schools), whose language contained a heavy admixture of Ukrainisms, nevertheless wrote in Russian. The *Kobzar* and the Ukrainian history lesson were instruments of national mobilization and cultural reorientation of the Ukrainian peasantry, but they still had to compete with the Russian-language Gospels and the 'book by Gogol' mentioned in Alekseev's memoirs. It was no easy competition. Molodyk, for instance, having completed the four-year school in 1919, continued his education privately at first, and then, from 1922, at the Oleksandrivsk (later Zaporizhia) vocational school in Russian: there were no Ukrainian-language textbooks, and the Ukrainian language was taught only as a subject. Recalling his education at that school, he automatically went over to Russian, in which he wrote most of his memoirs. Before enrolling in the vocational school, Molodyk read the Russian classics – not only Gogol but also Chekhov, Tolstoy, and Goncharov, whose works he found in his uncle's library.[36] Oleksandr Zamrii also found the works of Leo Tolstoy in a relative's private library. He read twelve volumes of the classic writer's works and even decided to name his son, born in 1923, Lev. The name was clearly unknown to his fellow villagers, and some registry official wrote it down as 'Leonid.' The offended Zamrii noted in his memoirs: 'Such was the level of our literacy.'[37] In this context, literacy was associated with the Russian language and Russian literature.

The field in which Ukrainian culture made definite progress was that of the theatre, where the previous tsarist prohibitions on the Ukrainian language had been less effective than in relation to the printed word, while the genre itself did not require such costly measures as the printing of Ukrainian textbooks and literature. Under the date of 21 January 1918, Yaroshenko noted that he had attended a theatrical performance of *V chadu kokhannia* (In the Vapours of Love). His comment was reserved: 'a cheerful little experience, but not overly so.'[38] Molodyk dates the beginnings of Ukrainian theatre in his village to 1924, when economic and cultural life revived under the influence of the New Economic Policy: 'Songs again resounded in the village; weddings, revelry, and evening parties began again. Reading rooms and clubs opened, and amateur choirs, music groups, and drama groups appeared in them. People staged Ukrainian plays on their own initiative: *Natalka-Poltavka* [Natalka, the Girl from Poltava], *Svatannia na Honcharivtsi* [Matchmaking in Honcharivka], *Nazar Stodolia*.' According to Molodyk, peasants were glad to go to clubs, and churches and clubs even became involved in a kind of competition for attendance.[39] Clearly, both institutions competed for the same blocks of time – Sundays and holidays. In this connection, it is interesting that on the day after attending the theatre Yaroshenko went to church and to the bazaar and then took part in a village meeting.[40]

The linguistic and cultural Ukrainization proclaimed in 1923 and intensified in 1926 clearly influenced the southern Ukrainian village and found its reflection on both the conscious and unconscious levels in the peasant 'histories.' Most interesting in this regard is Yaroshenko's diary, where, beginning with the entries for 1924, the number of Ukrainian words increases sharply, and the language gradually turns from Russian with numerous Ukrainisms into Ukrainian with numerous Russianisms. This becomes particularly apparent in the brief meteorological records towards the end of the diary. Here, the transition to Ukrainian may be dated as having occurred in June 1924. If the entry for 1 June notes, in Russian, *redkie dozhdi* (infrequent rain) and *khoroshuiu pogodu* (good weather), the following entry (for 15 June), in Ukrainian, reads *zharko i vitry, doshchiv malo* (hot and windy; little rain).[41] In the diary itself, the author goes over mainly to Ukrainian in his entries for 1926.[42] The Russian language makes an ever more confident return to the diary in the late 1930s, which can be explained by the cumulative effect of the author's functioning in the generally Russian-language milieu of industrial Zaporizhia: he moved to a suburb of that city, the settlement of Khortytsia, in 1930. The change reflected the defeat of linguistic Ukrainization in the cities. In education and culture, the Soviet Ukrainian leaders of the 1930s sought to do no more than maintain the achievements of the late 1920s.

Another witness of the advance of Russian in Ukrainian towns of the 1930s was the youngest of our authors, Serhii Cipko. The only book in his parents' village home was Shevchenko's *Kobzar*, but once in town, where the author found himself after his father had been dekulakized and arrested, it was necessary to learn Russian. The Russian language was dominant on the streets of southern Ukrainian cities, as well as in all official institutions, and the peasants gradually began to use a creole called *surzhyk*. As Cipko says about his forced move to Dnipropetrovsk (formerly Katerynoslav) in the early 1930s, 'the city was highly Russified, and people in the city spoke Russian; at first their language seemed strange to me, but in time I, too, began to speak *surzhyk*.'[43] When Cipko enrolled in the Mariupol technical college, the language of instruction was Russian. Ukrainian was taught as a subject, the hours devoted to it were progressively reduced, and after the academic year 1935–6, when the teacher of Ukrainian was arrested, the language ceased to be taught. But even earlier, as Cipko attests, the technical college treated Ukrainian as a second-class language: there was no requirement to pass an exam in it, as there was, for example, in the case of Russian. The whole atmosphere in the city was hostile to the Ukrainian language and culture. Cipko was long galled by the mockery that he endured from Russian girls for his occasional use of Ukrainian words, and, as he himself notes, it helped strengthen his Ukrainian consciousness. Recalling this episode towards the end of his life, Cipko wrote, 'It angered me greatly, and I thought to myself: you intruders have come to our Ukraine; you eat our bread; and yet you have the effrontery to make fun of our language.'[44]

Although insults to the native language aroused indignation, yesterday's peasants did not venture to express it aloud: after all, as Cipko writes, 'Later they began to try people for their nationality.'[45] Thus waves of peasant migrants like Yaroshenko and Cipko, forced out of the village by the policy of collectivization and attracted to the towns by the advance of industrialization, were introduced to higher culture through the medium of the Russian language and literature. The lower rungs of peasant migrant culture were served by Ukrainian-Russian *surzhyk*, which in most cases did not develop into any literary language. The creole in which Yaroshenko wrote the concluding sections of his diary may serve as a good illustration of these realities of the post-Ukrainization era.

Peasant Historiography

Rubel's 'History' – most of which, judging by the text, was written in the late 1920s, just as linguistic Ukrainization reached its peak, may be considered a product of that policy. As noted above, the text of this work was written in demotic Ukrainian. Many elements of Ukrainizing discourse can readily be discerned in it, most notably the author's particular attention to Ukrainian folk tradition and lore, to which more than a few pages of the 'History' are devoted. In parts of Rubel's work, one feels the influence of programs of folklore collection carried on in many Ukrainian villages in the late 1920s by the All-Ukrainian Academy of Sciences. But the zeitgeist is most apparent in Rubel's attempt to incorporate the story of his family and village into a broader historical canvas – in this case, Ukrainian national history. To that end, Rubel makes use of a book lent to him by a neighbour, the Reverend Dmytro Popov.[46] Textual analysis reveals that this was a copy of Mykhailo Hrushevsky's *Illustrated History of Ukraine*, first published in 1912 and reprinted several times in huge press runs in 1917–18.[47] Excerpts from Hrushevsky's *History* endow Rubel's work with a clearly Ukrainian countenance as regards its conceptualization and even terminology. The people, who figure as *khokhly* in fragments written independently by Rubel, are transformed into Ukrainians in unmarked quotations from Hrushevsky, giving Vasyl Rubel's 'History' an entirely different tendency.

If Rubel accepts Hrushevsky's idea of Ukrainian history completely and without contradiction, he makes only selective use of the historical narrative created by Hrushevsky. Rubel copies only the account of developments in Dnipro Ukraine, beginning with the second half of the seventeenth century, into his work, and he devotes most attention to the *Koliivshchyna* (haidamaka) rebellion (1768) and the history of the Zaporozhian Sich (the Cossack headquarters on the lower Dnipro) and its abolition in 1775 by the tsarist government. These are the components of Hrushevsky's all-Ukrainian narrative that find an echo in the family history of the Rubels or pertain to the history of southern Ukraine and are thus easily accepted and adapted by the peasant historian from Mala Bilozirka. For Rubel, Ukrainian history really begins only with the haidamaka revolts. In the family legend that he recounts, the founding father, a Cossack captain named Andrii Rubel, is presented as a participant in the most important events associated with the historical memory of Cossackdom and the haidamaka period. He supposedly joined the haidamaka forces of Ivan Gonta before the slaughter of the Jewish and Polish population at Uman, made his way to the Sich after the defeat of the rebellion, and established himself in the Poltava region after the liquidation of the Sich and the imprisonment of its otaman, Petro Kalnyshevsky. From there his elder son,

Havrylo, moved to Mala Bilozirka. Andrii Rubel allegedly maintained a good opinion of Maksym Zalizniak (another leader of the 1768 uprising), Gonta, and Kalnyshevsky to the end of his life and inveighed against the Russians.[48]

It is hard to say what is true and what is invented in the Rubel family chronicle, but in Vasyl's account it is given a twist that makes it compatible not only with Hrushevsky's historical narrative but also with the official Ukrainian communist narrative of the day, propagated by Matvii Yavorsky and his students, which placed particular emphasis on the role of the toiling peasants and class warfare in the history of Ukraine.[49] Judging by Rubel's 'History,' the founder of the Rubel line, Andrii, lamented Gonta, Zalizniak, and Kalnyshevsky not as abstract heroes of some kind but as 'fine defenders of the oppressed common people.' As for the Russians, Andrii Rubel was allegedly dissatisfied not with Russians in general but with plundering 'Muscovite generals.' Rubel explained his moderate antagonism towards 'Moscow' by its role in suppressing the struggle of Ukrainians against their overlords, inasmuch as it 'interfered and put an end to the whole cause of liberation from serfdom.' Such a class-oriented critique of Moscow was an entirely legitimate component of Ukrainizing discourse and of the Soviet Ukrainian historiography associated with it. Such an approach also eased the acceptance of Hrushevsky's historical conception and its adaptation to new conditions. Hrushevsky himself had devoted considerable attention to the struggle of the popular masses for 'social and national liberation.'[50]

Rubel, however, went much further than Hrushevsky in stressing the social aspects of Ukrainian history. With all due respect to the Cossack mythology and its role in the history of Ukraine and of his own family (the author emphasized that his family had never been 'cattle,' as the serfs were called, but was descended from a free Cossack haidamaka), he devoted his attention primarily to the peasantry, with which he identified himself and whose social identity he fully shared and articulated in his records. Rubel copied precisely those fragments of Hrushevsky's work that concerned the fate of the peasantry. He begins his excerpts from the *Illustrated History* with the subsection that Hrushevsky titled 'Cossack Officers and Commoners.' Rubel calls it 'The Beginning of Serfdom' and precedes the text borrowed from Hrushevsky with the phrase, 'We shall begin with the political measures applied to the peasantry.' His most interesting borrowing is from a subsection of Hrushevsky's work titled 'National Life in Eastern Ukraine,' which he reduces to two words, 'National Life,' while condensing the whole subsection to one single paragraph that bears no relation to national life but relates Hrushevsky's view of the gentrification of Cossack families. Khmelnytsky's name is deleted from the text at this point. Perhaps this was done because Rubel had written nothing about the Khmelnytsky Uprising earlier and did not wish to complicate the reader's reception of his narrative, but more probably the author was echoing the prevailing tendency in the representation of Khmelnytsky in the 1920s: as an exploiting lord and an enemy of the toiling masses he was not, of course, entitled to a place in peasant history.[51]

Rubel's presentation of Russo-Ukrainian conflicts in class terms was also in keeping with the spirit of the times. Having recorded a family story about a fight between *khokhol* wagoners and *katsap* traders that had allegedly begun when one of the Russians called Danylo Rubel a '*khokhol* mug,' Vasyl Rubel noted: 'Not infrequently, the police had to intervene in these clashes between nat[ional] minor[ities] that were irreconcilable on class grounds; in this hatred and struggle.' The fight was thus presented as one that had arisen on the basis of class, not nationality: after all, in this instance the Ukrainians were peasants and wagoners, while the Russians were peddlers and traders.[52] Judging by the preface to Rubel's 'History,' his work would have had a very definite class orientation if it had been completed. Rubel was setting out to relate 'how people, having divided into classes, fought over that well-known "serfdom"'; how Andrii Rubel and the haidamakas had 'slaughtered the lords' (that part of the plan was carried out); the beginnings of the revolutionary movement in 1904–5; the Revolution of 1917–19; the 'partisan warfare' and the violence inflicted on the peasants by a [probably White] 'punishment detail.' Although the author wrote of the revolutionary events: 'It is not life but torment; the devil only knows what it is,' he greeted the reader with the 'new life' and planned to bring his history up to the 1930s so as to relate 'what fine things they had given people.'[53]

Rubel's very purpose and programmatic idea, as well as its realization in his 'History,' give a good general impression of the penetration of the Ukrainian national idea into the southern Ukrainian peasant milieu during the years of Ukrainization. That penetration was due in part to the influence of works written by the leaders of the Revolution of 1917 (in this case, Mykhailo Hrushevsky's *Illustrated History*). Another channel whereby the Ukrainian national idea penetrated the village was the Soviet press of the day. The official discourse of Ukrainization was based on the primacy of the social factor and the idea of class struggle, and the Ukrainian idea was sometimes perceived by the peasantry in that particular coloration. In Rubel's work, the social aspect clearly prevailed over the national one, in complete accordance with official Soviet dogma of the time. However, it is obvious from the concluding lines of Rubel's 'History' that the famine of 1933 forced him to reconsider his former optimistic prognoses about the 'new life' and to condemn the new order – if not entirely, then at least its key symbol, the five-year plan, which should be interpreted as meaning the policy of collectivization and exacting grain from the village by force.[54] It appears that Rubel and his wife remained independent farmers until 1936, thinking it better to pay exorbitant taxes than to join a collective farm.[55] One may conclude that in the case of Vasyl Rubel and those of like mind, the wave of enthusiasm for class-based ideology passed relatively quickly.

Competing Identities

The autobiographical narratives published in the Zaporizhia collection demonstrate that Ukrainian identity, if not the Ukrainian language, managed to overcome its largely peasant character and orientation in the USSR. This is particularly apparent in the memoirs of Mykola Molodyk, who, like Vasyl Rubel, reacted positively to the Ukrainization of the 1920s. Molodyk's personal story, like the life histories of Yaroshenko and Cipko, is that of Ukrainian urbanization of the 1920s and 1930s: the decay of the village, which was ruined by collectivization, and the migration of the Ukrainian peasantry to the towns, which were industrializing. In Yaroshenko's case, as initially in Molodyk's, it was Zaporizhia, with its dam on the Dnipro and its accelerated pace of industriaization, that became the urban magnet. Yaroshenko managed to buy a house in a suburban village and effectively combine features of urban and rural life, working now in an agricultural cooperative, now in an urban brick factory when village occupations did not suffice for survival. Most peasants, however, found themselves in town with no prospect of returning to the village and were obliged to live either in overcrowded collective apartments or in earthen dugouts. Alekseev, who visited Zaporizhia in 1934, described his brief call on a former fellow-villager in the course of the 'phenomenal' first five-year plan:

'And I went to Nove Zaporizhia to search for people from Petrovka. And whom should I come upon but Egor Rodionovich Tutov? He had a dugout in a gully, one side of it in the earth. He invited me in. I entered. I had a look: there was snow on the inside walls, and I could not stay the night because it was damp and cold. And I went off to the Zaporizhia railway station and rode to Petrovka.'[56] Living conditions in the village, destroyed by collectivization and ruined by hunger, struck Alekseev as preferable to conditions in the socialist town.[57]

Molodyk enjoyed a measure of luck, as his personal 'urbanization' began before the mass collectivization of the village, the industrialization of the towns, and the influx of tens of thousands of unfortunate peasant migrants into Zaporizhia. Even so, the peasant boy's encounter with the city was by no means easy or free of drama. As noted above, Molodyk, who came to Zaporizhia to study at a vocational school in 1922, had to switch from the Ukrainian language to Russian – a shift that would lead to an unconscious change of language in his memoirs decades later. He also had to cope with the condescending attitude of city boys – former gymnasium students – towards peasants. Molodyk would long remember their 'mean questions': 'You're so interesting: what sort of backwoods did you come from? How many cows are there on your farm, and what do you do with them? Have you started chasing girls yet?' Only the extensive knowledge that Molodyk possessed made it possible to change the city schoolboys' attitude towards him and make the gap between rural and urban culture less apparent. Ironically, the authorities' new social policy, oriented towards restricting the rights of the former 'lords,' including representatives of the upper and middle classes from which most of the gymnasium students came, not only did not promote but, on the contrary, actually impeded the capable peasant boy's climb up the social ladder. For example, Molodyk was denied enrollment in the 'prestigious' industrial vocational school, for it accepted only children of workers and farm labourers, while Molodyk's family belonged to the 'prosperous peasants.' Molodyk was obliged to return to the village and put off his further education for three years.[58]

Not until 1926 did he move to Zaporizhia again, this time to enroll in the less prestigious pedagogical training school, which accepted peasant children, clearly without regard to their financial circumstances. By that time Ukrainization was under way, and the language of instruction in the training school was Ukrainian. A capable student, Molodyk was also in charge of courses intended to Ukrainize the government apparatus. It fell to him to teach courses in the Ukrainian language to staff members of the newspaper *Selians'ke zhyttia* (Peasant Life), whose readership was the Ukrainian-speaking village. It may be assumed that the staff members either did not know Ukrainian at all or spoke it poorly; had it not been for the Ukrainization of the 1920s, they would have continued to Russify the Ukrainian village, intentionally or not. It is clear that even though Ukrainization was defeated in the towns, partly as a result of the change in official policy, it managed to protect the Ukrainian village from Russification and propagate the Ukrainian national project there to a considerable degree. Molodyk associated the end of Ukrainization (according to the official party line, it was never terminated and continued successfully throughout the 1930s) with actions of the authorities. Referring to his career as a Ukrainizer, he noted (in Russian): 'Later all those Ukrainization courses were broken up and their organizers arrested.'[59]

Molodyk, who taught Ukrainian and Russian in the 1930s, as well as mathematics in primary and secondary schools, was fortunate enough to escape the fate of many members of the Ukrainian intelligentsia of that day and avoid imprisonment. But he was not spared that fate in the mid-1940s, when Soviet forces returned to eastern Ukraine. In November 1944 Molodyk was arrested by agents of the MGB (Ministry of State Security, the successor of the GPU and predecessor of the KGB) in Dnipropetrovsk on a charge of belonging to the Organization of Ukrainian Nationalists (OUN). The charge was completely false, and the arrestee did not even know what the OUN was. To all appearances, the investigating officer did not remind him of his activities during the period of Ukrainization. But Molodyk was sentenced to long years of imprisonment, as was his wife, who was also completely innocent. Naturally, the bitter experience of the camps could not fail to infuse Molodyk's later recollections with an oppositional attitude. Nor could he avoid contact with actual OUN members from western Ukraine in the camps, although there is no mention of this in the memoirs. What one does find here, however, is a positive assessment of the western Ukrainian resistance movement – quite rare for an eastern Ukrainian – that is sharply at odds with the view promoted by Soviet propaganda and the official historiographic discourse of the age. Although Molodyk confuses certain historical facts, he gives a generally accurate depiction of the followers of Stepan Bandera as proponents of an independent Ukraine who hoped at first for German support but then, having become disillusioned with the Germans, who had no use for an independent Ukraine, turned their weapons against them. Molodyk explained their struggle with the Soviet authorities by citing their desire to establish an independent Ukraine. 'Although the Banderites are considered a band of some kind and every effort is made to shame and slander them,' he wrote, 'this was a struggle of Ukrainians for national liberation, and I consider that there was nothing shameful about it. It is another question whether it was appropriate at the time or not, but history will decide that in the future.'[60]

The notion that the very idea of Ukrainian national liberation was legitimate and that there was, consequently, nothing 'shameful' about fighting for it is present directly or indirectly in Molodyk's view of Ukrainian history in general. At times he interprets even the Soviet historical narrative of the 1950s and 1960s in a manner that allows him to leave space for the idea of Ukrainian independence. In Molodyk's memoirs, Ukrainian history begins in 1654, but the 'reunion' of Ukraine with Russia, glorified in Soviet historiography of that day, was not intended, in his opinion, 'to abolish the independence of Ukraine.' According to Molodyk, after 1654 there remained a Ukrainian state whose attributes were a government, the Ukrainian language, and an army. In defining the territory of that state, Molodyk included not only the Hetmanate per se but also the latter-day Sumy, Kharkiv, and Donetsk oblasts, thereby legitimizing Ukraine's historical claim to those lands. Speaking of the 'free and prosperous' life of the Ukrainians of that time, Molodyk refers to the works of Nikolai Gogol, who is thus transformed from a symbol of pan-Russian identity into a pillar of the Ukrainian historical narrative. The question of Mazepa's 'treason,' a complicated matter for traditional Ukrainian historiography, was one that Molodyk resolved by means of a compromise. In his version, Mazepa was indeed a traitor – not to the Ukrainian people, as official propaganda had it, but only to Tsar Peter I. It is Peter who becomes the truly negative figure of Molodyk's historical excursus, since he inflicted cruel punishments on the Cossacks and curtailed the rights of the Ukrainian government. Another negative figure is Catherine II, under whose rule the Zaporozhian Sich was destroyed. After that, according to Molodyk, 'Ukraine was given the name "Little Russia," the Ukrainian language was prohibited, the hetmancy abolished, and Cossackdom abolished as well. They began to take young men into the Russian army, only now they were called soldiers. In a word, Ukraine lost its independence completely, and the word "Ukraine" was forbidden.'[61]

Molodyk's assessment of the course of Ukrainian history is only partly reminiscent of Vasyl Rubel's no less patriotic synthesis dating from the 1920s. What they have in common is the representation of Ukraine as a victim of the policies of Russian ruling circles, as well as attention to the history of Left-Bank Ukraine and of the Zaporozhian Sich – the native grounds of both authors. What sets them apart is the absence in Molodyk's brief synthesis of Ukrainian history of the primacy of the social factor, so important to Rubel. Molodyk presents a narrative of Ukrainian history somewhat adapted to official historiography but clearly national in character. The poetry of Taras Shevchenko, with one of whose verses Molodyk concluded his memoirs, could have been only a partial source for that narrative. Shevchenko did indeed cast the Russian tsars in a negative light – Catherine and Peter above all – but he was far removed from the spirit of Ukrainian statism with which Molodyk's historical excursus is thoroughly imbued. (Hrushevsky, whose work Rubel used, was no less distant from the statist spirit, at least in his *Illustrated History*.) It is quite apparent that Molodyk's 'synopsis' was influenced by the ideas of the Ukrainian statist school, which was dominant in western Ukrainian historiography until the Second World War and in Western émigré communities thereafter. Molodyk does not say how he became acquainted with these ideas. One may assume, however, that he encountered them either in Stalin's camps or by listening to programs broadcast by the Ukrainian bureaus of Western radio stations. What is important in this case, however, is the irrefutable fact that the ideas of Ukrainian statist historiography, which constituted a well-developed alternative to the official historical narrative, were known in southern Ukraine in the 1960s and considered perfectly legitimate by certain people.[62]

As far as one can judge from the memoirs of Serhii Cipko, he was more influenced by a populist than a statist conception of history. For him, the leitmotif of Ukrainian history was the martyrdom of a peasant nation oppressed by a national and social yoke that ultimately turned into collective-farm slavery. The prophet of that kind of history was Cipko's beloved Taras Shevchenko, whom he cites at the beginning of his memoirs. Generally speaking, that idea was inherent in the Ukrainian national narrative of the early decades of the twentieth century and was employed and adapted according to circumstances, both by promoters of Ukrainization in the 1920s and by leaders of the Ukrainian national movement outside the USSR. Undoubtedly, the transformation of the ethnocultural identity of Cipko's parents, whose national consciousness, by his account, 'was on a very low level,'[63] into the author's own modern national identity began in Ukraine. It most probably culminated in the Displaced Persons' camps, where members of the Ukrainian intelligentsia worked actively to create a common all-Ukrainian identity for Galicians and Dnipro Ukrainians.[64] That consciousness was tempered in the émigré community in Great Britain, where Cipko headed a local Ukrainian school in his spare time. A distinguishing feature of the postwar Ukrainian emigration in Britain was a considerable preponderance of men over women and a much higher incidence of inter-ethnic marriage than in other countries. Serhii Cipko was one of the Ukrainian boys who married non-Ukrainian women, but the national feeling awakened in him by the events of the 1930s and reinforced by years of emigration proved so strong that he managed to maintain a Ukrainian spirit in his family and bring up his children accordingly. Since it is usually women and not men who act as guardians of family tradition, Serhii Cipko was extraordinarily grateful to his wife for her understanding and support.[65] In his memoirs, Cipko interpreted his past in Ukraine through the prism of the Ukrainian idea; hence Ukraine's achievement of independence and the author's visit to Ukraine after 1991 figure as the climax of his narrative.[66]

How unique or, conversely, typical of southern Ukraine were the views of Molodyk and Cipko? A general knowledge of the situation in that region during the final decades of Soviet rule suggests uniqueness as the likelier characteristic. Molodyk was schooled not only by the Ukrainization of the 1920s but also by the camps. Cipko wrote his memoirs in the emigration after Ukraine's achievement of independence. The existence of very different attitudes in the southern Ukrainian society of Soviet times is indicated by the memoirs of the ethnic Russian Alekseev, which are extraordinarily rich in detail. Reading them, one becomes aware of a 'contextualization' of personal, family, and local history very different from that of Molodyk, Cipko, and Rubel. For Alekseev, history begins not with the heroics of Cossackdom, as it does for Rubel and Molodyk, but with the conquest of the southern Ukrainian steppe by the Russian Empire during the rule of Catherine II.[67] It emerges from Alekseev's memoirs, however, that in southern Ukraine Ukrainian identity competed not so much with a well-developed Russian identity as with the muted but nevertheless influential all-Russian project. As regards nationality, the Russian self-identification of Alekseev, who grew up and lived his life in close contact with Ukrainians, remained less than fully formed. He is perfectly aware of the differences between Russians and Ukrainians but does not regard his Ukrainian neighbours as 'other' and, as noted earlier, refers to Russians from Russia as *katsapy*, thereby setting himself apart from them. Towards the end of his life, listening to Western radio broadcasts, Alekseev is pained by the prohibitions on the Ukrainian language and associates himself with the Ukrainians when it comes to Stalin's crimes.[68] Alekseev uses the term *russkie* to denote both nationalities, employing it when Eastern Slavs are contrasted with other ethnic groups, such as Germans.

Zamrii's memoirs exemplify similar thinking, considering that he constructs his identity as that of an ethnic Ukrainian. Alekseev and Zamrii share a greater preponderance of social concerns over national ones than one finds in the other authors: both are seekers after truth, formerly poor peasants who hate the rich but are also dissatisfied with the Soviet-era bosses and outraged by the cynicism of the communists. Like Alekseev, Zamrii is a bearer of all-Russian consciousness. For him, the Soviet troops are 'liberators, glorious warriors of Mother Russia.' Just like Alekseev, Zamrii uses the collective term *russkie* when both ethnic groups are contrasted with a third – in Zamrii's case, with Jews. Zamrii is the only author in the Zaporizhia collection who comes across as an anti-Semite. For example, he explains his dismissal from the post of prison-camp guard by the appointment to the prison administration of Jews who began 'to throw out us Russians, including me, for no reason at all.'[69] Alekseev describes his own participation in the mass robbery of Jewish shopkeepers in Berdychiv in 1914 but expresses no anti-Jewish sentiments, blaming the whole incident on the encouragement of an unidentified warrant officer in charge of a detachment of recruits being shipped to the front.[70] Although the available sources are not comprehensive enough to warrant any conclusions about the spread of anti-Semitic sentiments in southern Ukraine, it is noteworthy that anti-Semitic statements and/or descriptions of pogroms are encountered in the works of authors who shared prerevolutionary types of national identity.

The roots of the all-Russian identity assimilated by Alekseev and Zamrii should naturally be sought in the achievements of the all-Russian project in the years preceding the Revolution of 1917, but its vitality can be explained above all by the authorities' termination of the Ukrainization policy of the 1920s, residual elements of Russian nationalism in official propaganda during and after the war, and the advance of the Russocentric Soviet project during the final decades of

Soviet rule. In southern Ukraine, the idea of one Soviet people, propagated in the 1970s and 1980s, amounted to little more than the camouflaged idea of one Russian people that predated the revolution.

Most of the material presented in the Zaporizhia collection attests to the inarticulateness of the national identities of Ukrainians and Russians in their mutual relations over the greater part of the twentieth century. The authors of diaries and memoirs who internalized Ukrainian identity rarely considered it exclusive. In formulating that identity, they did not 'other' Russians in general but only greedy Russian tsars, or Stalin. Southern Ukrainian Russians, for their part, lacked the possibility of counterposing themselves to Ukrainians even in this fashion. The inadequate articulation and non-exclusive character of national identities in southern Ukraine led in the 1960s and 1970s to the formation of a common field of identity in which the Russian language and culture were dominant but still allowed for the existence of a distinct Ukrainian historical, ethnic, and territorial identity. The existence of Ukraine as a separate republic of the USSR created conditions favouring the retention of a distinct regional identity attached to that territory and of certain republican institutions. The distinct republic also provided an umbrella for remnants of Ukrainian identity in the sphere of high culture and education: in eastern Ukraine these remnants were a legacy of the Ukrainization of the 1920s that no longer threatened the regime, while in the west they were a concession to the 'nationalist' sympathies of the population. In southern Ukraine, the new identity encompassing both Ukrainians and Russians included certain elements of both cultures. As the cases of Yaroshenko and Zamrii indicate, not only did Ukrainians read Tolstoy, but Russians, as one may deduce from Alekseev's memoirs, knew Ostap Vyshnia. It was this combination of contradictory but not mutually exclusive loyalties and cultural orientations that created the basis for the identity with which southern Ukraine entered the age of Ukrainian independence.

PART THREE

Post-Soviet Debates

9 History and Territory

The dissolution of the USSR brought to the fore the whole range of problems that usually accompany the dissolution of empires. The disintegration of the Ottoman, Habsburg, and, to some extent, French empires took place in the midst of war. Despite the fact that Britain and, later, Portugal withdrew from their colonial territories almost peacefully, the national, tribal, and religious conflicts that commenced after the departure of colonial administrations eventually resulted in bloody conflicts and wars.

Among the many problems that followed from the dissolution of the USSR was the border question. Although the border disputes in the former USSR were not as acute as in the former Yugoslavia, they constituted a serious threat to peaceful relations between the former Soviet republics. It was hardly accidental that the first major manifestation of national unrest in the USSR came with the events in Nagorno-Karabakh, a region claimed by two former Soviet republics, Armenia and Azerbaijan. The long war that they waged for control over Nagorno-Karabakh demonstrated how dangerous border conflicts in the former USSR can be. The frozen conflicts in Transdnistria and Abkhazia serve as another indication that the transformation of administrative borders into state borders turned out to be a very complicated and uneasy process.[1]

With the disintegration of the USSR, the border question raised relations between two other republics of the former Soviet Union, Russia and Ukraine, to a level of special importance. The problem came to light in late August 1991, after the proclamation of Ukrainian independence. On 29 August a spokesman for the Russian president, Pavel Voshchanov, announced that if Ukraine seceded from the USSR, Russia would reserve the right to revise its borders with Ukraine.[2] In fact, the new Russian authorities claimed Russia's right to the eastern and southern oblasts of Ukraine, areas that underwent a high degree of Russification during the communist regime, and to the Crimean peninsula, a region transferred from Russia to Ukraine in 1954.

Since the results of the Ukrainian referendum (held in December 1991) demonstrated overwhelming support for the idea of Ukrainian independence (more than 90 per cent of those who took part in the referendum voted for independence), the 'empire-saviours' (to use Roman Szporluk's expression) in the Russian leadership were forced to abandon previous Russian claims to the eastern Ukrainian oblasts and concentrate specifically on the issue of the Crimea. This is the only region of Ukraine where ethnic Russians constitute the majority of the population, and the vote for independence there was the lowest in Ukraine (54 per cent in favour). As the 'all-Union resort' and home of the Black Sea Fleet, the Crimea was viewed by many Russian politicians as 'ancient Russian territory.' Leaders of nationalist factions in parliament have used every single opportunity to publicize their opinion that the transfer of the Crimea to Ukraine in 1954 was carried out in violation of the Russian constitution and that there were more than enough legal arguments in place to demand its return to Russia.[3]

In April 1992, when the confrontation over the Crimea had reached its peak, Vice-President Aleksandr Rutskoi of Russia made a direct claim to the peninsula while on a visit there, using historical arguments. Rutskoi rejected one aspect of Crimean history – the transfer of the peninsula to Ukraine in 1954 – and emphasized another, the annexation of the Crimea by the Russian Empire and its military presence there: 'If one turns to history, then again history is not on the side of those who are trying to appropriate this land. If in 1954, perhaps under the influence of a hangover or maybe of sunstroke, the appropriate documents were signed according to which the Crimea was transferred to the jurisdiction of Ukraine, I am sorry, such a document does not cancel the history of the Crimea.'[4]

In another remark made by Rutskoi during his visit of April 1992 to the Crimea, he asserted that the Black Sea Fleet was and would remain Russian.[5] The myth of Sevastopol as a 'city of Russian glory' has often been used as the cornerstone of the historical justification of Russian territorial claims to the Crimea. That myth is based on the events of the Crimean War (1853–6) and presents the heroism of the multinational Imperial Army during the siege exclusively as the heroism of Russian soldiers. It was used to justify and protect the imperial aggrandizements of the Russian Empire in the eighteenth and nineteenth centuries and was revived under the Stalin regime, especially during the Second World War, and then during the Cold War. With the disintegration of the USSR and the rebirth of Russian imperial ideology, the myth of Sevastopol, like other imperial myths that survive from the Soviet period, was invoked to defend Russian interests beyond the territory of the Russian Federation.[6] It was in the tradition of Sevastopol mythology that Admiral Igor Kasatonov proudly asserted in his interview with *Literaturnaia Rossiia* that the tomb of Admirals Lazarev, Nakhimov, Kornilov, and Istomin, who were killed during the siege of Sevastopol (1854–5), was restored at the St Volodymyr (St Vladimir) Cathedral during his tenure as fleet commander.[7]

The exploitation of the Sevastopol myth by leading Russian politicians and military commanders in their territorial claims to Ukraine obliged the Ukrainian side to fight back with the same weapon – historical arguments and justifications. In his interview with Sevastopol television in January 1993, President Leonid Kravchuk of Ukraine proposed to solve the Sevastopol question peacefully by avoiding the issue of whose glory is symbolized by the city. 'Otherwise,' he said, 'one might return to the times of Alexander of Macedon and Julius Caesar.' And he continued: 'Why do we limit ourselves to a hundred-year period? Could we not take a thousand years into consideration? Really, there are no limits. One person might like to start with the 1920s, and another with the 1940s.'[8] Thus Kravchuk tried to avoid questioning the history of the Russian presence in the region, while emphasizing the legitimacy of claims made on the basis of a relatively short period in the history of the peninsula, although its history is in fact very long and includes the period of Greek colonization. In order to counter the Russian position, Ukrainian historians and politicians chose to base their policy of preserving their country's territorial integrity on a highly elaborate Cossack mythology.

From the historiographic point of view, Ukrainian nation builders of the nineteenth and early twentieth centuries based the idea of an independent Ukrainian state on two main myths: that of Ukraine as the only direct successor to medieval Kyivan Rus' and that of the Ukrainian Cossacks. Mykhailo Hrushevsky, the head of the Ukrainian People's Republic in 1918 and, like many other leaders of the national awakening in Eastern Europe, a prominent historian, contributed much to the development of both myths. It was his initiative to adopt the trident – the political symbol of the medieval Kyivan princes – as the national coat of arms. Hrushevsky can also be considered the most prominent twentieth-century student of the Cossack era.[9]

This chapter takes as its point of departure John A. Armstrong's definition of myth as 'the integrating phenomenon through which symbols of national identity acquire a coherent meaning.'[10] The present author also shares Armstrong's approach to the study of the myths, based on the method of Claude Lévi-Strauss. 'I am utterly incompetent to judge whether the version of Kiev and its successors that Hrushevsky presented is "truer" than other versions,' argued Armstrong in his discussion of Ukrainian historical mythology. 'The basic insight provided by the anthropological approach is that such questions are irrelevant for identity except insofar as they affect a constitutive myth.'[11]

Thus the main goal of this chapter is not to decide whether the Cossack myth is 'true' or 'false' but to determine how it was created and subsequently transformed to meet the challenges of the Russo-Ukrainian border dispute of the early 1990s.

Cossacks and Borders

Cossack mythology, which was based on accounts of the most glorious pages of Cossack history and the Cossack struggle against the Crimean Tatars and the Russian Empire, became an important part of the ideology of the Ukrainian national awakening in the nineteenth century. The leaders of the movement were searching for examples of their illustrious national past and for periods of history in which their nation had been independent or semi-independent. It is hardly surprising that they chose the history of Cossack uprisings and the Hetmanate in the mid-seventeenth century as a basis for a new national mythology.[12]

In the Ukrainian grand narrative, the Cossack era covers the period from the sixteenth to the eighteenth century. In fact, the first accounts of Ukrainian Cossack activity come from the last decade of the fifteenth century, but only a century later did the Cossacks emerge as a significant military and, to some extent, political force. As a social group, the Cossacks came into existence following an eastward movement of the local Ukrainian population to colonize the steppe territories of southern Ukraine. Many of them were fugitive peasants looking for new lands to cultivate and trying to avoid the serfdom imposed on them by the Polish and local Ukrainian nobility. Relatively soon the Cossacks became strong enough to oppose Commonwealth policies in the frontier region. A series of Cossack uprisings against Polish rule began in the late sixteenth century and culminated in 1648 with the Cossack revolt led by Hetman Bohdan Khmelnytsky. He managed to create a separate Cossack polity – the Hetmanate. For a short period the Hetmanate enjoyed independent status, but in 1654, unable to resist a Polish offensive on his own, Khmelnytsky recognized the suzerainty of the Muscovite tsar.[13] The Hetmanate became an autonomous part of the Muscovite state, and its eastern borders, based on those of the Kyiv and Chernihiv palatinates of the Polish-Lithuanian Commonwealth, became the basis of the first Russo-Ukrainian boundary. The origins of that boundary go back to the turn of the sixteenth century. In 1503, during a war between Muscovy and the Grand Duchy of Lithuania, the Chernihiv princes transferred their loyalty from Lithuania to Muscovy, and the Chernihiv territory was incorporated into the Muscovite state. It was lost by Muscovy to the Polish-Lithuanian Commonwealth in the first two decades of the seventeenth century. Owing to the Deulino truce of 1618, the Chernihiv region was transferred to Poland.[14]

Muscovy's drive to the west and its incorporation of the Ukrainian territories began after the conclusion of the Pereiaslav Agreement in 1654. The prolonged war that followed the treaty established a new international order in Eastern Europe. As a result of the Truce of Andrusovo (1667), Ukrainian territories were divided between Muscovy and the Commonwealth. The Dnipro River was chosen as the major line of demarcation. Left-Bank Ukraine came under the tsar's rule, and the existence of an autonomous Cossack polity, the Hetmanate, was allowed there. Right-Bank and western Ukraine remained under Polish control. In the Polish zone the autonomy of the Cossack formations was at first significantly restricted and then completely abolished. The same process was under way in Russian Ukraine. A Cossack uprising led by Hetman Ivan Mazepa in 1708 tried to reverse the decay of the Hetmanate with the help of Sweden. Mazepa and his ally, Charles XII of Sweden, were defeated by Tsar Peter I at the Battle of Poltava (1709), which resulted in the further limitation of the Hetmanate's autonomy. The Russo-Polish border along the Dnipro continued to exist for more than a century, and in some areas on the left bank of the river, such as the Chernihiv region, it laid the foundations for the present-day Ukrainian-Belarusian border.[15]

The second half of the eighteenth century witnessed the further extension of Russian imperial territory to the west and south. The empire's victorious wars with Turkey resulted in the annexation of vast areas along the coast of the Azov and Black Seas and, finally, in the annexation of the Crimea in 1783.[16] The subsequent partitions of Poland (1772–95) brought most of Ukrainian ethnic territory, including Right-Bank Ukraine, Volhynia, and Podilia, under the tsar's rule.[17] The Ukrainian Cossacks played an important role in the acquisition of these new territories, especially the areas annexed as a result of the Russo-Turkish wars. The Ukrainian elite, which collaborated with the imperial government, showed special support for Russian actions against its traditional enemies – the Tatars, Turks, and Poles. A principal architect of Russian foreign policy in the last quarter of the eighteenth century was Prince Oleksander Bezborodko, a descendant of a well-known Ukrainian family and initially a Cossack officer himself, who was especially anxious to annex to the Russian Empire territories in western and southern Ukraine that had once belonged to Poland and Turkey.[18]

The Russo-Turkish wars of the second half of the eighteenth century resulted not only in the opening of new territories for Ukrainian colonization but also in the abolition of autonomous Cossack bodies in Ukraine. By the 1780s, both the Hetmanate and the Zaporozhian Sich – the Cossack Host of the lower Dnipro region – ceased to exist as a result of actions taken by Empress Catherine II. The Zaporozhian Cossacks were resettled (or migrated) partly on territories along the coast of the Azov and Black Seas that they had helped gain for the empire and partly in the Kuban (now in the Russian Federation) and the trans-Danube region (now part of Romania). The empire's new territorial acquisitions opened the way for Ukrainian peasants to emigrate from densely populated parts of Left- and Right-Bank Ukraine to southern and eastern Ukraine, as well as to the Voronezh, Don, Kuban, and Stavropol regions, which are now in Russia. This resettlement, which began in the seventeenth century, continued until the early twentieth and defined the boundaries of Ukrainian colonization in the east.[19]

The Formation of the Cossack Myth

Despite the initial spread of Cossack formations over the vast territories of Left- and Right-Bank Ukraine, Volhynia, and Podilia, the origins of Cossack mythology are associated with the relatively small part of Left-Bank Ukraine once controlled by the Cossacks – the Hetmanate. This was the only Cossack region that enjoyed a degree of autonomy for a relatively long period and in which the maintenance of the historical memory of the Cossacks was essential for the survival of the ruling elite.

There is enough evidence to assert that the creation of certain elements of Cossack mythology began as early as the first decades of the seventeenth century. Nevertheless, until the turn of the eighteenth century there was a lack of 'bearers of high culture' closely associated with the Cossacks to create any semblance of elaborated mythology. The process began on a large scale only in the first decades of the eighteenth century. This period saw the emergence in the Hetmanate of a new social stratum comprised of a mixture of Cossack officers and the older nobility, defined by Zenon Kohut as the Ukrainian gentry.[20] The gentry strived to maintain the autonomy of the Hetmanate and to legitimize it on the basis of past Cossack treaties with the tsars, thereby laying a foundation for the development of Cossack mythology. In fact, the myth was shaped in such a way as to support the power of the emerging gentry, which needed the Cossack past to secure not only the political rights of the Hetmanate but also its own economic rights, based on the Cossack-Muscovite treaties of the second half of the seventeenth century.[21]

The defeat of Hetman Ivan Mazepa at the Battle of Poltava in 1709 was in many ways a turning point in the development of Cossack mythology. Threatened by Peter I, the gentry mobilized in defence of the rights of Cossack officers first obtained from the tsar by Hetman Bohdan Khmelnytsky. It was in the atmosphere of the Poltava defeat that the Cossack chronicles of Hryhorii Hrabianka and Samiilo Velychko were written and the cult of Bohdan Khmelnytsky reemerged, acquiring new characteristics. It would later develop into one of the pillars of Ukrainian national ideology.[22] The next wave of commemoration and celebration of the heroic Cossack past came in the second half of the eighteenth century. This was the period in which the gentry made its last attempt to preserve and extend the Hetmanate's autonomy and found itself involved more deeply than ever before in a struggle for official recognition of its nobiliary rights by the imperial authorities. Historical arguments were considered extremely important in both cases, and a number of works recalling the glorious Cossack past were written at this time, beginning with Semen Divovych's 'Conversation between Great Russia and Little Russia' and ending with the anonymous 'History of the Rus'.'[23]

It was the gentry of the Hetmanate – the ruling elite of a comparatively small part of what is now Ukrainian territory – that created the Cossack myth as a reflection of its own political needs and historical beliefs. A new generation of Ukrainian patriots would have to enter the political arena to turn that myth from a local cult into a national ideology extending to the remotest parts of Ukrainian ethnic territory. That task was accomplished by the nation builders of the nineteenth century.

The most prominent role in the development and popularization of Cossack mythology belongs to the apostle of the nineteenth-century Ukrainian national revival – the poet and artist Taras Shevchenko (1814–61).[24] His views on the Cossack past were based on two main sources – popular memory and the Cossack mythology elaborated by the Hetmanate elite and popularized by the 'History of the Rus'.' The outstanding event in Cossack history remembered by the simple peasants of Right-Bank Ukraine (Shevchenko's homeland) was the Koliivshchyna of 1768–9, a popular uprising against Polish rule led by the Cossack officers Ivan Gonta and Maksym Zalizniak. Shevchenko described it in his poem *Haidamaky*. This revolt was launched under the slogan of protecting Orthodoxy against a Uniate offensive and was accompanied by massacres of Jews and Catholics. Shevchenko also brought into his poems the popular memory of the Zaporozhian Cossack Host on the lower Dnipro, generally viewed without heroization by the authors of the Hetmanate. Although Shevchenko challenged the Khmelnytsky myth because of the hetman's pro-Russian policy, he managed to combine the historical experience and views on the Cossack past of two social strata, the descendants of the Left-Bank Cossack officers and the Right-Bank peasants, and presented this unified vision in his historical verses and poems, first published in the 1841 edition of the *Kobzar* (Minstrel), the bible of the Ukrainian national revival.

Without a doubt, the new type of Cossack mythology created and popularized by Shevchenko's poetry won the hearts of readers in eastern and central Ukraine, where the Cossack past still lived in popular memory, much more easily than in western Ukraine, where the Cossack experience was but a short-lived phenomenon of the seventeenth century. Shevchenko's poetry was also a much better vehicle for propagating the new Cossack mythology than the writings of the Hetmanate elite. Unlike the 'History of the Rus',' which was written in the highly Russified, bookish language of the late eighteenth and early nineteenth centuries, read and understood only in Russian Ukraine, Shevchenko's poems were written in the Ukrainian vernacular. This opened the way for the dissemination of his writings and the Cossack mythology that they promoted in Ukrainian ethnic territories under Austro-Hungarian rule.

Especially important for the fate of the Ukrainian national movement was the case of Galicia in the Austro-Hungarian Empire.[25] For a host of political, confessional, and historical reasons, it was difficult for

Cossack mythology to make its way into Galicia, where there had never been any Cossack organization, even though many of its natives, such as the seventeenth-century Hetman Petro Konashevych-Sahaidachny, had taken part in the Cossack movement in Dnipro Ukraine. Presenting Galicians as active participants in Cossackdom was the only logical approach to linking the Galician national revival with the Cossack past. Special subsidiary myths and family legends were created in Galicia to bring the Cossack past closer to its population: for example, a theory of migration from Galicia to Dnipro Ukraine and then back to Galicia was developed and popularized among the Galician intelligentsia.

This situation was complicated not only by the fact that the Cossack system had never existed in Galicia but also by the pro-Orthodox and very often anti-Uniate character of Cossack mythology. Accepting that mythology full-blown, with all its anti-Uniate trappings, was no easy task for the Ukrainian movement in Uniate Galicia. The myth was accordingly modified and reshaped for adaptation to local circumstances. In a very short time, owing to the spread of the Shevchenko cult and the activity of the *narodovtsi* (populists), Galician Ukrainians became even more zealous adherents of the Cossack mythology than their eastern Ukrainian counterparts.

The triumph of Cossack mythology as the unifying factor of the Ukrainian national revival came with the Ukrainian Revolution of 1917–20. Detachments of Sich Riflemen, named after the traditional headquarters (*Sich*) of the Zaporozhian Cossack Host on the lower Dnipro, were formed in Galicia during the First World War and later played an important role in the struggle for independence in both western and eastern Ukraine. In 1918 eastern Ukraine, occupied by German forces after the Treaty of Brest-Litovsk, witnessed the rule of Hetman Pavlo Skoropadsky, who sought to restore Hetmanate traditions. The armed forces of the Directory, the Ukrainian government that took over from Skoropadsky after the withdrawal of German troops, were also dedicated to the preservation of Cossack tradition. Even the Bolshevik army that fought Ukrainian forces for control of Ukrainian territory claimed to be an heir to the Cossack tradition: special units of 'Red Cossacks' were formed as an integral part of the Red Army.[26]

When the Bolsheviks took over eastern and central Ukraine, they initially tolerated and then attempted to take over the Ukrainian national and cultural revival, but finally crushed it in the early 1930s. Cossack mythology was restructured by Soviet historians to meet the demands of vulgar Marxism and growing Russian nationalism. Only those Ukrainian hetmans who had served Russia were tolerated in the new textbooks of Ukrainian history. Peasants replaced Cossacks as the principal heroes of the seventeenth and eighteenth centuries: since they had little connection with the tradition of Ukrainian nation building, they presented no threat to the communist rulers.[27] 'Independentist' Cossack mythology survived only in western Ukraine (Galicia and Volhynia), which was under Polish occupation from 1920 to 1939. In 1943–4, when Soviet troops fighting the Germans entered western Ukraine, official Soviet propaganda was forced to take account of the national aspirations of the local Ukrainian population. The Ukrainian government began to present itself as independent; Soviet army groups (fronts) that fought in Ukraine were renamed 'Ukrainian fronts'; and, finally, a special military award named after the Cossack hetman Bohdan Khmelnytsky was introduced by the Soviet authorities in the autumn of 1943.[28] This was only a temporary liberalization of official Soviet ideology. After the war, most expressions of Ukrainian national ideology tolerated in the course of the war were officially banned.

Cossack mythology, revived in Ukraine after Stalin's death, became quite popular in the 1960s but was banned again in 1972. At that time, Petro Shelest, the first secretary of the Communist Party of Ukraine, was accused of 'idealization of the past' and replaced by his rival Volodymyr Shcherbytsky. A purge of 'Cossackophiles' began in the institutes of the Ukrainian Academy of Sciences and in the universities, and many of the academics who specialized in Ukrainian history and the literature of the Cossack era were removed from their positions or forced to shift to the study of other topics unconnected with the officially condemned Cossack past.[29] Despite the persecution of Cossack studies, Cossack mythology appeared to be deeply rooted in the historical consciousness of Ukraine and reemerged with the beginning of perestroika and glasnost.

Territorial Integrity and Historical Claims

In the spring of 1990 in the southeastern Ukrainian city of Nikopol, in an area where most of the Zaporozhian strongholds (*Sich*) were established, the local branch of the Ukrainian Republican Party – one of the most anti-communist organizations of that day – endorsed the idea of a local student of Cossack history, Pavlo Bohush, to celebrate the five-hundredth anniversary of the Ukrainian Cossacks. The initiative for what developed into an extensive political campaign called the 'March to the East' came from the Dnipro region, but it was actively supported and realized by the national-democratic organizations of Galicia that came to power there after the first relatively free elections in the USSR. They employed the Cossack myth as their main weapon in the political struggle for eastern Ukraine. Thousands of people from all parts of Ukraine, especially Galicia, travelled to the lower Dnipro region in the summer of 1990 to take part in these festivities.[30]

One of the ironies of history was that Galicians, who had no direct links to the Cossack past, were bringing the Cossack myth back to eastern Ukraine, the homeland of the Ukrainian Cossacks. The communist functionaries in eastern Ukraine tried to fight back, challenging the Galicians' right to the Cossack heritage and exploiting the anti-Uniate motifs of nineteenth-century Cossack mythology. For example, in Dnipropetrovsk oblast they did not want to allow Greek Catholic (Uniate) priests to serve a liturgy on the grave of the Cossack otaman Ivan Sirko.[31] But all these attempts to split the movement and isolate the Galician participants of the march from the local population had little if any effect. Government officials found themselves under pressure to join the Cossack celebrations; a year later, in 1991, seeking to take control of the Cossackophile movement, they organized conferences and festivities of their own to mark the Cossack anniversary. The official celebrations took place in the lower Dnipro region – Dnipropetrovsk, Zaporizhia, and Nikopol – and near Berestechko in Volhynia, at the site of the Cossack battle of 1651 with the Poles.[32]

The rise of Ukrainian national aspirations in 1990–1 and the massive eastward offensive of national-democratic forces from Galicia provoked some Russian separatist initiatives on the part of the communist elite of the eastern and southern oblasts of Ukraine. These separatist moves were also based on historical arguments. They attempted to prove that the eastern and southern Ukrainian territories had never been part of Ukraine but were colonized and settled by Russians. Similar ideas were expressed around the same time by Aleksandr Solzhenitsyn, who claimed in an article entitled 'How Shall We Reconstitute Russia,' which was widely distributed in the USSR, that New Russia, the Crimea, and the Donbas 'were never part of old Ukraine.'[33] The term 'New Russia,' first introduced in the second half of the eighteenth century, referred to the territory of the southern Ukrainian oblasts. Although that territory included the lands of the Zaporozhian Cossacks, which they had colonized long before the imperial authorities made their first appearance in the region, the idea of establishing New Russia as a Russian polity in southern Ukraine was put forward by some scholars and historians, including the Odesa professor A. Surilov. Around the same time, the idea of restoring the Donetsk-Kryvyi Rih and Crimean republics, proclaimed by the Bolsheviks in 1918 to stop German seizures of territory after the Treaty of Brest-Litovsk, was advanced in some eastern and southern Ukrainian newspapers.[34] These initiatives were a direct challenge to the historical arguments used by the national democrats to accelerate the Ukrainian national awakening in the region.

The adherents of Cossack mythology accepted the challenge and published a dozen articles in the national and local press in an effort to adjust Cossack mythology to the new political demands. Since the territory of the Zaporozhian Sich even at its apogee did not cover all the eastern and southern oblasts of Ukraine, the Cossack myth had to be modified. In order to provide historical justification for Ukraine's right to those territories, Cossack mythology was obliged to challenge Russian imperial mythology, on the one hand, and its own anti-Tatar orientation, on the other.

Ukrainian historians placed new emphasis on the role of Cossack detachments in the Russo-Turkish wars of the second half of the eighteenth century. Numerous publications issued in 1990–1 emphasized that it was not so much the imperial forces as the Ukrainian Cossacks who had conquered and colonized Ukrainian territories during the Russo-Turkish wars. This was true in part, especially in the case of colonization, for otherwise Ukrainians would never have come to constitute a majority of the region's population, but as regards military history it was an exaggeration of the Cossack role in those actions and a diminution of the role played by the well-trained Russian imperial army. Ukrainian authors wrote about the participation of Cossack detachments in Russian attacks on the Turkish fortresses of Ochakiv, Izmail, and Akkerman and their capture of other forts, Berezan and Khadzhibei. On the site of the latter, Cossacks and their families were the first inhabitants of the newly founded city of Odesa.[35] Some articles even attempted to challenge the 'cornerstone' of Russian imperial ideology – the myth of Sevastopol. A historian of the Ukrainian navy, Volodymyr Kravtsevych, citing an eighteenth-century description of Sevastopol, claimed that the 'city of Russian glory' was built by Cossacks and local Ukrainian peasants and that in the first decades of its existence Sevastopol looked like a typical Ukrainian settlement.[36]

Another modification of Cossack mythology was connected with the reexamination of the history of Cossack-Tatar relations. The Cossack was usually regarded by the creators of Ukrainian national mythology as a defender of his homeland, Ukraine, from Ottoman and Tatar attacks. Accordingly, Tatars were treated in this context as the worst enemies of Ukraine. That part of the myth was fully accepted by Soviet historiography. During the 1950s and 1960s, Tatars were usually portrayed in official Soviet historiography as the main adversaries of the Ukrainian Cossacks. It was almost prohibited at that time to study Cossack conflicts with Russia or to pay too much attention to Cossack-Polish conflicts. Socialist Poland was a close ally of the USSR, and one could hardly find any remarks about Cossack-Polish conflicts or Ukrainian-Polish wars. Instead of making such references, official Soviet historiography used the formula 'peasant-Cossack uprisings against the gentry (*shliakhta*) and magnates.' By contrast, official historians spoke of 'Tatar attacks' on Ukrainian lands.[37]

In the 1960s, representatives of the Ukrainian democratic movement introduced a new approach to the Tatar problem. The role of General Petro Hryhorenko in defence of the rights of the Crimean Tatars is well known in the West, but he was not alone in his attempts to 'rehabilitate' the Tatars. In 1968 the well-known Ukrainian writer Roman Ivanychuk published a novel, *Mal'vy* (Mallows), in which he attempted to reexamine the history of empires and the role of janissaries, who were regarded as traitors to the nation. He also took a new approach to the dramatic history of Ukrainian-Tatar relations in the sixteenth and seventeenth centuries. The novel was severely criticized, banned, and confiscated from bookstores and libraries.[38]

With the beginning of glasnost, Ukrainian historians renewed their attempts to reexamine the history of Cossack-Tatar relations. This initiative was launched by publications of scholars from Dnipropetrovsk University, the only centre of Cossack studies that survived the persecution of Ukrainian historiography in the 1970s and 1980s. In his articles on the history of the Cossack army, the Dnipropetrovsk historian Ivan Storozhenko pictured the Tatar troops of Tughay Bey, the ally of Bohdan Khmelnytsky, in predominantly positive terms. Storozhenko's colleague Yurii Mytsyk, whose main works have also been devoted to Cossack history, published a series of articles on Tatar history in a Crimean Tatar newspaper.[39] In other Ukrainian publications of this period the history of Cossack-Tatar collaboration in the struggle against Russia and Turkey received special attention.[40] It was also claimed that in the seventeenth century most of the Crimean population was not made up of Tatars but of Ukrainians captured by the Tatars during their attacks on Ukrainian territories. According to some sources, there were 920,000 Cossacks (Ukrainians) and 180,000 Tatars in the Crimea in the mid-seventeenth century.[41]

These and other attempts to reexamine the history of Cossack-Tatar relations represented something of an effort to modify Cossack mythology so as to meet new demands for the creation of a Ukrainian-Tatar political union to oppose Russian claims to the peninsula. For this reason, those promoting the Cossack myth have been giving up some features of ethnic exclusivity in order to help build a multinational civil society and preserve Ukraine's territorial integrity. In Ukraine, the Cossack legacy was also regarded as an important means of legitimizing Ukrainian claims to the USSR Black Sea Fleet. Proponents of Ukrainian national ideology began the history of the Ukrainian Navy with the period of the Kyivan princes Askold, Dir, Oleh, and Ihor, who attacked Constantinople by sea on a number of occasions in the ninth and tenth centuries, but most attention was devoted to the history of Cossack activity in the Black Sea region. After independence, organizations of Ukrainian Cossacks established close relations with the newborn Ukrainian Navy and its commander, Admiral Borys Kozhyn. He then promised that the first anniversary of the Ukrainian Black Sea Fleet would be celebrated on the island of Khortytsia on the Dnipro River – the legendary homeland of the Zaporozhian Cossacks.[42]

Ironically, Cossack mythology has found it much less difficult to claim some Ukrainian territories beyond the country's borders than to secure the territorial integrity of the Ukrainian state. Among the territories settled by the Cossacks in the seventeenth and eighteenth centuries are the Kuban peninsula and parts of the Stavropol region of the Russian Federation, as well as trans-Danube territory now in Romania. The Kuban, which is separated from the Crimea by the Strait of Kerch, was initially settled by former Zaporozhian Cossacks in the 1790s. Later, more Cossacks and Ukrainian peasants moved into the region, together with Don Cossacks and Russian settlers. During the Revolution of 1917 there was a strong pro-Ukrainian movement in the Kuban, and the local government negotiated with Hetman Pavlo Skoropadsky on conditions of a Ukrainian-Kuban federative treaty. After the revolution, the Kuban was included in the Russian Federation. In 1926,

47.1 per cent of the region's inhabitants considered themselves Ukrainian and 41 per cent Russian. Ukrainian schools, newspapers, and even a Ukrainian department of the local university existed for a brief period, but a policy of Russification of the Ukrainian population was launched by the communist authorities in the 1930s, and, with the introduction of a passport system, all residents of the Kuban were declared to be Russian.[43]

Kuban Cossack organizations like those of the Don and Stavropol regions were reestablished in 1990, with some support from local authorities who wanted to use Cossacks to counter the growing political activity of non-Slavic peoples in the North Caucasus and to fight crime. With the proclamation of Ukrainian independence, pro-Ukrainian sentiment emerged among some leaders of the Cossack movement in the Kuban region – a development that was not welcomed by the local authorities. Unlike their Don colleagues, the Kuban Cossacks developed close ties with Cossack organizations in Ukraine. It is quite symptomatic that in March 1993, when a leader of the Kuban Cossacks, Yevhen Nahai, was arrested by local authorities in the Kuban on charges of plotting a Cossack coup, another high-ranking officer of the Kuban Cossacks, the kish otaman Pylypenko, stated that in the event of further violations of his colleague's civil rights the Cossacks would call for support from their historical homeland, Ukraine, and the Ukrainian diaspora in the United States and Canada, and would even use arms to defend themselves. A special Committee for the Return of the Kuban to Ukraine, led by General Siverov, was established in the Kuban region in 1993.[44]

From the outset, Ukrainian Cossack organizations declared the Kuban a sphere of special interest. There in 1992 they employed tactics similar to those used by Galician Ukrainian organizations in eastern and southern Ukraine in 1990: a Cossack march to the region was organized to mark the bicentennial of Cossack resettlement to the Kuban. The idea was supported by the hetman of the Ukrainian Cossacks, General Volodymyr Muliava, who also headed the socio-psychological directorate of the Ukrainian Army and served as its chief ideologist. In August 1992, forty-four men, representing not western but eastern and southern Ukrainian oblasts, including the Donbas and Zaporizhia regions, took part in a cavalry march to the Kuban. The march was reportedly met with enthusiasm on the part of the local population.[45]

In the early 1990s, Ukrainian Cossack mythology began to spread to former Cossack territories outside Ukraine. The Cossack past of those regions, which include parts of the Voronezh oblast in Russia and Transdnistria in Moldova, was regarded by proponents of Ukrainian nationalism as an important means of rekindling Ukrainian national identity among the Ukrainian diaspora of more than six million in the former Soviet Union. On a number of occasions Ukrainian officials have rejected claims by proponents of Ukrainian nationalism to territories outside Ukraine, but the development of Cossack movements in the Russian regions of the Don and the North Caucasus presented a challenge to the leaders of the Russian Federation. Although the Russian Cossacks are generally considered partisans of the restoration of the Russian Empire, in the 1990s their demands for self-government of the Cossack regions, including the Don area, promoted tendencies towards the decentralization and, potentially, the disintegration of the Russian Federation.

One can hardly exaggerate the significance of national territory for the belief system of modern nations. Of no less importance to that system is the complex of historical myths that provides a nation with its own view of its past and tries to explain and justify its territorial possessions or claims against its neighbours. With the collapse and disintegration of world empires, the problem of the division of territories between 'old' imperial and 'young' stateless nations has arisen. Historical arguments and myths are of special importance in justifying the conflicting territorial claims of different nations.

Russian politicians have often challenged the demarcation of Ukrainian borders on grounds of historical legitimacy. Most of these challenges are rooted in the highly developed Russian historical mythology. In the case of Ukraine, as in other cases of territorial claims against former Soviet republics, Russian politicians of the 1990s proceeded from the borders of the Russian Empire of the late eighteenth to early twentieth centuries, when the empire had attained its greatest territorial extent, and ignored periods that did not fit their agenda. A student of foreign policy, N. Narochnitskaia, indignantly posed the rhetorical question: 'Why in the case of the Crimea do we follow the borders of 1954, in the case of the Baltic region those of 1939, and in the case of the Kurile Islands those of 1855?'[46] There is nothing new in this approach. For instance, Romanian nationalists usually claim the territory once united under the leadership of Michael the Brave at the beginning of the seventeenth century, while Poles used to claim the territory that belonged to their state in the sixteenth and seventeenth centuries.[47]

From the Ukrainian perspective, Cossack mythology was used to protect the territorial integrity of Ukraine. The myth emerged locally in Dnipro Ukraine in the early eighteenth century and was then disseminated all over Ukrainian ethnic territory by nineteenth-century nation builders, including the celebrated poet Taras Shevchenko. It was preserved best of all in a historically non-Cossack territory, Galicia, and with the beginning of glasnost it made a successful return to the historical Cossack lands – the eastern territories of Ukraine along its current border with Russia. Cossack colonization of most of these territories in the course of the seventeenth and eighteenth centuries helped Ukrainian historians make the case that they belonged to Ukraine. Another argument was Cossack participation in the Russian military campaigns that helped annex the vast territories of southern Ukraine to the empire in the second half of the eighteenth century and open them to Ukrainian colonization. In view of the eruption of the Russo-Ukrainian dispute over the Crimea in the early 1990s, the traditionally anti-Tatar character of Cossack mythology has changed dramatically. In order to foster cooperation between the Ukrainian and Tatar national movements, episodes of such cooperation in the past have been recalled, bringing traditional Cossack mythology into conflict with its newest variant.

Not unlike other border disputes, Russo-Ukrainian territorial disputes of the 1990s were based on conflicting historical arguments and mythologies. The periods of greatest territorial expansion of the Russian Empire and the autonomous Cossack polities have been taken as points of departure in making territorial claims. Russo-Ukrainian conflict over the future of the Crimea, Sevastopol, and the Black Sea Fleet developed in an atmosphere of economic decline and the deterioration of the standard of living in Russia and Ukraine, as well as the activization of nationalist and pro-communist forces. Both these potentially dangerous processes were under way in the early 1990s and threatened to bring territorial disputes between Russia and Ukraine to the brink of military conflict. Conflicting territorial claims based on Russian imperial mythology and the Ukrainian national myth could have dangerous consequences if one side were to try to assert its 'historic right' by force. Fortunately, this has not happened, although political debates over the presence of the Russian Black Sea Fleet on Ukrainian territory are still going on.

10 The City of Glory

The demise of world empires and the loss of colonies by West European states is often regarded by students of nationalism 'as a central feature of the post-war Western European experience.'[1] In Eastern Europe, the end of the Cold War resulted in the disintegration of the multinational Russian/Soviet empire and two 'pan-Slavic' states, Yugoslavia and Czechoslovakia. In the case of Russia, the loss of empire was accompanied not only by loss of access to raw materials and markets and great damage to its prestige, as had been the case with the West European colonial powers, but also by military conflicts both beyond and within the Russian Federation.

At the core of the differences between Russia and the West in dealing with the loss of empire lies the specific character of Russian imperialism, whose peculiarities have been strongly manifested over the last two centuries and noted by students of the region. John Dunlop, who has written extensively on the 'loss' and 'fall' of the Soviet empire,[2] has even questioned the usage of the term 'empire' in regard to the tsarist state and the USSR. He writes that 'imprecise use of terminology serves to skew and to distort the position of Russians under both the Tsars and the Soviets.'[3] Richard Pipes, for his part, believes that the Russian Empire acquired special characteristics owing to the fact that in Russia 'the rise of the national state and the empire occurred concurrently, and not, as in the case of the Western powers, in sequence.'[4]

A number of specific characteristics distinguish Russian imperialism from the classical imperialisms of countries like Britain and France. These characteristics include the absence of Russian colonies overseas, active incorporation of the elites of the conquered borderlands into the Russian imperial elite, prevalence of empire-building tendencies over nation-building ones, employment of a federal façade for the highly centralized state of the Soviet period, etc.[5] It can also be argued that the very concept of 'Russianness' that replaced the old Muscovite identity in eighteenth-century Russia was constructed not only by the Great Russians but also by the Little Russians/Ukrainians, who were recruited into the imperial ruling elite and were looking for ways to formulate their new empire-oriented identity.[6] As a result, 'Russian,' as opposed to 'Muscovite,' often meant not Great Russian but all-Russian or East Slavic. During the following centuries all-Russian (imperial) and particular Russian (ethnic) identity became almost indistinguishable in the consciousness of the average Russian. Soviet experience certainly strengthened this tendency, making the term 'Soviet' synonymous with 'Russian,' both in the eyes of the outside world and to Russians themselves. That led inevitably to a situation in which, in the words of John Breuilly, 'the fusion of Russian with Soviet institutions has meant that any sense of Russian superiority has been associated with the maintenance of the USSR, not the creation of an independent Russia.'[7]

The 'conflict of borders,' in which political boundaries cut across ethnic and cultural ones, is one of the inevitable consequences of the demise of any empire. Although in most cases it is the colonial and not the imperial peoples who suffer most, in the case of the disintegration of the USSR it has been the Russians who have claimed to be the most victimized, with millions of their brethren effectively cut off from the Russian state by the new state borders. The old imperial tradition of Russian national identity and the feeling of being victimized by the demise of the USSR account for many characteristics of contemporary Russian nationalism.

If indeed, in the words of Geoffrey Hosking, Western powers like Britain *had* empires but Russia *was* an empire, for Russia the dissolution of the USSR has meant not only the loss of imperial possessions but also the loss of its very being. In no other area has this been as obvious as in the realm of national identity. The 'sacred space' of the empire, the cultural and historical map created by Russian imperial nationalists of the nineteenth century and Russian proletarian internationalists of the Soviet era, has been torn apart by the events of 1991. Numerous cultural and political symbols of old imperial Russia (such as Kyiv and Narva) and twentieth-century Soviet Russia (such as the Baikonur Cosmodrome and the Brest fortress) were displaced beyond the borders of the Russian Federation almost overnight. Conversely, the new Russian state includes a number of Muslim-populated republics, foreign to Russia both ethnically and culturally, which have had hardly any place on the historical and cultural map of the nation.

When independent Ukraine left the USSR, it effectively took with it a number of prominent imperial 'sacred places' on the Russian cultural map. They included traditional 'all-Russian' places of religious worship and pilgrimage, such as the Cave Monastery and St Sophia Cathedral in Kyiv, and places associated with the history of the Russian Empire during its 'golden age' of the eighteenth and nineteenth centuries, like Poltava and Sevastopol. Kyiv, Odesa, and Sevastopol also served as places of new government-sponsored pilgrimages in the Soviet era as Soviet municipalities awarded them the status of 'hero-cities' to commemorate the heroism of their defenders during the Second World War.

The results of the December 1991 independence referendum in Ukraine came as a major surprise not only to Mikhail Gorbachev but also to his adversaries among the Russian political elite, who were grouped around Boris Yeltsin. The overwhelming success of the referendum in eastern Ukraine was totally unexpected. Even in the Crimea the referendum vote was 54 per cent in favour of independence, signalling a serious threat to Russian interests in the Black Sea region. This was especially the case in Sevastopol, the home of the Soviet Black Sea Fleet. Support for independence in Sevastopol was slightly higher than in other areas of the Crimea: 57 per cent in favour. There was also another indication that voters in Sevastopol were more pro-independence than those in other parts of peninsula. Viacheslav Chornovil, a pro-Western candidate for the presidency and a former dissident, received more votes in Sevastopol (10.93 per cent) than the ethnic Russian Vladimir Griniov, a representative of the highly Russified city of Kharkiv (8.38 per cent).[8]

The possibility of Sevastopol and the Crimea allying themselves with Kyiv and leaving the USSR to become part of Ukraine alarmed the Russian leadership and caused it to intensify its efforts to maintain the Black Sea Fleet under Moscow's unilateral control. Since 1992 the issue of the Crimea, Sevastopol, and the Black Sea Fleet has remained on the agenda of Russian-Ukrainian relations in one form or another. The issue was raised anew every time the political struggle in Kremlin intensified. From Aleksandr Rutskoi to Yurii Luzhkov, every 'strong man' in Moscow would exploit the issue of Sevastopol, thereby appealing to the nationalistically oriented electorate.[9] Only the growing contacts of the Ukrainian military with NATO and the latter's expansion into Eastern Europe forced the Russian leadership to abandon its claims to the Crimea and sign a comprehensive treaty with Ukraine in May 1997 confirming its current borders.

The cornerstone of all Russian claims to the Crimea and Sevastopol is the myth of Sevastopol as an exclusively Russian city, the 'city of Russian glory,' the symbol of the Russian fleet and Russia's glorious past. For many Russian politicians the history of the Russian presence in the Crimea is closely connected to the history of the fleet and hence to the history of its main base in the Crimea, Sevastopol. The former commander of the fleet, Admiral Igor Kasatonov (recalled from Sevastopol to Moscow in December 1992), stressed in an interview to the Russian newspaper *Literaturnaia Rossiia* that Russia cannot be imagined in any form without its glorious Black Sea Fleet. To deprive Russia of the Black Sea Fleet and its naval bases in the Crimea and Black Sea region would mean setting it back three centuries to the times before Peter I.[10] In the autumn of 1996, when the status of Sevastopol was once again under discussion in the Russian parliament, Russian newspapers published an appeal from A.P. Nakhimov, G.V. Kornilova, and A.P. Istomin – allegedly descendants of Sevastopol heroes – to the president, government, and parliament of Russia. The appeal called on the authorities to bring Sevastopol under Russian control.[11] The names of Admirals Nakhimov, Kornilov, and Istomin – the commanders of the fleet and defenders of Sevastopol during the Crimean war of 1853–6 – symbolize, perhaps better than anything else, the core of the Sevastopol myth as it exists in contemporary Russia.

This chapter seeks to explain the Sevastopol phenomenon in the history of the Russian Empire and the USSR. The two principal concepts employed for that purpose are the 'territorialization of memory' and historical myth as an important element of national memory. The study takes as its point of the departure Anthony Smith's definition of the territorialization of memory as 'a process by which certain kinds of shared memories are attached to particular territories so that the former ethnic landscapes (or ethnoscapes) and the latter become historic homelands,'[12] and John A. Armstrong's definition of myth as 'the integrating phenomenon through which symbols of national identity acquire a coherent meaning.'[13]

At the centre of this chapter is the development of the Sevastopol myth (the complex of historical interpretations related to the defence of the city during the Crimean War of 1853–6), which is examined in its relation to the history of Russian national identity.

Modern Russian national mythology began to take shape in the first decades of the nineteenth century with the growth of national awareness and the formulation by Count Uvarov of the 'theory of official nationality,' the triad of autocracy, Orthodoxy, and nationality.[14]

In the nineteenth-century Russian Empire, the major battlefields of the imperial army were effectively turned into places of national veneration and served as important components of the new national mythology. From that perspective Russia was not an exception to the general rule, as it simply followed the universal pattern of the territorialization of memory and national myth making. According to Anthony Smith, battlefields historically have played an important role in the process of territorialization of national memory, as they 'marked critical turning-points in the fortunes of the community, be they victories like Marathon, Lake Peipus, Bannockburn or Blood River or defeats like Kosovo, Avaryar, Karbala, or the fall of Jerusalem or Constantinople.'[15] The Borodino myth in Russia serves as a good example of the 'battlefield' type of mythology. The myth arose from the account of the decisive battle of Napoleon's campaign of 1812 in Russia. The trick with the Borodino myth is that the battle could hardly be considered a Russian victory, even though it cost the French a great many casualties. After Borodino, the Russian imperial army continued its retreat and surrendered Moscow to Napoleon.[16] Nevertheless, the Borodino battle site was established as one of the most venerated 'sacred places' on the cultural map of Russia.

The Sevastopol myth that was formed in the second half of the nineteenth century in many ways resembles the myth of Borodino. This myth, as it exists in contemporary Russia, is based predominantly on the events of the Crimean War (1853–6). The war resulted from international conflict over the partition of the Ottoman Empire. In 1853, St Petersburg began a successful campaign against the Turkish protectorates of Moldavia and Wallachia, but very soon the Ottomans received crucial support from two powerful West European states, Britain and France. Neither of these powers wanted Russia to strengthen its position in the Balkans or take control of the Black Sea straits. With the entry of Britain and France into the war, the centre of the conflict moved to the territory of the Russian Empire. In 1854 the allies invaded the Crimea and besieged Sevastopol, the main base of the Imperial Black Sea Fleet. This turn of events came as a major surprise to the Russian government, which, forty years after its victories over Napoleon, still believed that the Russian army and fleet were the most powerful in

Europe. As the war showed, that was by no means the case, and the only enemy forces against which the imperial army and fleet could launch successful campaigns were those of the declining Ottoman Empire.

The Russian fleet could not withstand that of the allies and was forced to retreat to the Sevastopol harbour. The only factor that helped the Russian Empire in the war and rescued it from immediate defeat was the heroism of the defenders of Sevastopol. The siege cost the allies thousands of soldiers and officers killed and wounded, humiliating the elite forces of the two colonial powers. Nevertheless, in 1855, after a long and exhausting siege, the imperial army had no choice but to withdraw from Sevastopol. The war was over. Russia was forced to sign a humiliating Paris peace treaty with the allies that did not allow it to maintain a Black Sea fleet or fortresses on the shores of the Black Sea. This military defeat, the first on such a scale since the Muscovite-Polish wars of the seventeenth century, created the atmosphere in which the Sevastopol myth came into existence.[17]

The veneration of the heroes of Sevastopol began at the initiative of participants in the Sevastopol defence themselves, apparently with no support from the government. It was thanks to donations from the sailors of the Black Sea Fleet that the first monument to Admiral Lazarev (who died before the outbreak of the war) and Admirals Kornilov, Istomin, and Nakhimov (all three killed during the siege) was erected in August 1856. In 1869, it was again on private initiative that a committee for the organization of a Sevastopol military museum was established in St Petersburg. The tradition of venerating the victims of the Crimean War was influenced by one of the main trends of Russian political thought, Pan-Slavism. Such Pan-Slavs as Mikhail Pogodin supported government policy towards the Ottoman Empire insofar as it reflected their own agenda of taking control of Constantinople and liberating the Orthodox Slavs under the Ottoman yoke.[18] The Russian public at large viewed the siege of Sevastopol as a symbol of the heroism of the Russian people, which had saved Russia from foreign invasion despite the inefficiency and corruption of the tsarist administration.[19]

Although as early as 1869 Tsarevich Aleksandr Aleksandrovich visited Sevastopol on his trip to southern Russia and was given a tour of the former battlefield by General Totleben,[20] the court apparently was not involved in the creation of the new sacred place until the Russo-Turkish War of 1877–8, which was launched by the government under Pan-Slavic slogans.[21] Benedict Anderson regards 'official nationalisms' of the European states in the nineteenth century as a 'willed merger of nation and dynastic empire' and stresses that 'it developed *after* and *in reaction to* the popular national movements proliferating in Europe since the 1820s.'[22] The history of the formation of the Sevastopol myth in imperial Russia helps to explain problems that the court encountered when taking, in Benedict Anderson's words, 'to the streets.' While reluctantly participating in the creation of the Sevastopol myth, the court wanted to stress the role played in the defence of Sevastopol by such government-appointed officials as the commander of the Russian army in the Crimea, Prince Mikhail Gorchakov. The Russian public, on the contrary, came up with a hero of its own, Admiral Pavel Nakhimov.

Nakhimov, a hero of Sinope (a successful navy battle against the Turks in the autumn of 1853), in fact played a secondary role in the defence of Sevastopol. He was clearly demoralized by the allied control of the Black Sea and, according to numerous accounts, sought death on the fortifications of Sevastopol. Apart from that, he was never in charge of the defence, and only in 1855 was he appointed to serve as commandant of the port.[23] The rules of myth making nevertheless required that Nakhimov be transformed from the hero of the successful attack on Sinope into a hero of the defence of the motherland. During and after the siege of Sevastopol, Nakhimov became known to the general public through newspaper and journal publications as 'the soul of the defence of Sevastopol' and a friend of the common people. Nakhimov, reprimanded by superiors early in his career for brutality towards sailors, became extremely popular among his subordinates by the end of his life because of his genuine attention to their needs. More important to this study is that, given the general atmosphere in Russian society after the emancipation of the serfs in 1861 and the growing influence of the populists, the new hero of the Russian public was almost fated to be a 'friend of the people,' and the young Nakhimov's harsh treatment of sailors, recruited by the authorities predominantly from peasant serfs, was rarely mentioned.[24]

A strong 'populist' element was also introduced into the Sevastopol myth by its best-known propagandist, Count Leo Tolstoy. In his 'Sevastopol Sketches,' Tolstoy presented the defence of Sevastopol as a story of the suffering, sacrifice, and heroism of the common people – rank-and-file sailors, soldiers, and civilians.[25] The 'Sevastopol Sketches' became very popular with the Russian public, surviving even the collapse of the empire. Thanks to Bolshevik populist rhetoric, Tolstoy's sketches made their way into the Russian literature curriculum in

Soviet schools. By the turn of the twentieth century, Sevastopol had become one of the most venerated places of the empire. In the 1890s, monuments to Admirals Kornilov and Nakhimov were erected, and the new building of the Sevastopol military museum was opened. This was, in fact, the first step towards the creation of a new imperial sacred place, the first on recently conquered territory to rank with St Petersburg, Moscow, and Kyiv. The ritual complex that was developed in Sevastopol through joint efforts of the public, the court, and the Black Sea Fleet played an important role in the creation of a new historical tradition shared by the throne and emerging Russian civil society alike.

Probably it was not accidental that the veneration of the heroes of Sevastopol reached its peak when Russia became involved in a new imperialist conflict, the Russo-Japanese War of 1904–5. To commemorate its fiftieth anniversary, numerous monuments to the defenders of Sevastopol were erected in the city, and a museum featuring a panoramic depiction of the 'Defence of Sevastopol, 1854–5' was opened. The Russian government was still at pains to present its own version of the defence, as opposed to the populist one, in the panoramic painting. Court officials demanded that the artists remove the figure of Admiral Nakhimov and replace it with the figure of Prince Gorchakov. As a result, Nakhimov never made it to the largest and most elaborate painting depicting the Sevastopol defence.[26]

Despite the many similarities between the Sevastopol myth and the equally populist myth of Borodino (which also made its way through the collapse of the empire into the civil religion of the new Bolshevik regime), there is an important difference between them. Even though both can be called 'defence of the motherland' myths, the Sevastopol myth was the first to be based on the events of a war conducted on previously non-Russian territory that had been annexed to the empire only seventy years before the outbreak of the Crimean War. From that perspective, the Sevastopol myth presents a new type of Russian mythology, one that justified and glorified the defence of new imperial possessions acquired by the tsars during the eighteenth and nineteenth centuries. The Russian defeat in the Russo-Japanese War gave rise to a new imperial myth – that of the heroic defence of Port Arthur, which in many ways resembled the old Sevastopol myth. Port Arthur served as the base of the imperial fleet in the Far East and was besieged by the Japanese army. Eventually, after a long siege, it was surrendered by the Russian imperial army and fell to the Japanese. The popular Port Arthur myth, like that of Sevastopol, condemned the inefficiency and corruption of the tsar's generals and praised the heroism of the Russian soldiers. Like the Sevastopol myth, that of the heroic defence of Port Arthur came into existence in an atmosphere of defeat and national humiliation.[27]

The prerevolutionary Sevastopol myth praised the heroism of the Russian people, which, according to the official view, consisted of three branches: the Great Russians, the Little Russians, and the Belarusians. This concept of a tripartite Russian people did not survive the events of the 1917 revolution. The new Bolshevik authorities were forced to recognize the existence of three separate peoples – the Russians, Ukrainians, and Belarusians. What remained almost intact after the revolution was the myth of Sevastopol. As before, it was based on the heroism of the Russian people, now understood not as the heroism of a tripartite nation but as that of the Great Russians alone. The first years after the Bolshevik takeover brought predominantly negative attitudes towards imperial Russian history. Lenin's view of tsarist Russia as a prison-house of nations was developed in the writings of the leading Soviet historian of that time, Mikhail Pokrovsky, and his school. The consolidation of power by Stalin in the early 1930s resulted in a dramatic change of official attitudes towards the Russian past. Not only were the old negative approaches to imperial Russian history abandoned, but the followers of Pokrovsky were persecuted and often sent to the Gulag. The beginnings of the national revival in the non-Russian Union republics were crushed by the authorities, and Stalin employed Russian nationalism to extend the power base of his oppressive regime.[28]

Russian nationalism was employed as a means of mobilizing Soviet society on the eve of the Second World War. The atmosphere of preparations for war set the stage for recalling images of the imperial past and the comeback of the Sevastopol myth. Soviet aggression against Finland, whose allies were Britain and France (Russian adversaries in the Crimean War), also helped create an appropriate atmosphere for the myth's reemergence. The first major Soviet historical work on the siege of Sevastopol was issued in 1939. Its publication coincided with the outbreak of the Second World War and the Soviet invasion of Poland.[29]

German aggression against the USSR and the outbreak of the Soviet-German war accelerated the reorientation of the Soviet propaganda machine towards heroic images of the imperial Russian past. The war was officially called the Great Patriotic War, a designation based on the official name of the Russian war against Napoleon in 1812. New myths based on the events of the war came into existence, and old ones made their comeback in a big way. One of them was the myth of Sevastopol, whose reemergence was of special significance for the war effort, as Sevastopol was again besieged in 1941–2, this time by the Germans, and the defenders of the city again displayed true heroism.[30] Admiral Nakhimov, a participant in the first defence of Sevastopol, was elevated to the status of national hero by Soviet propagandists. In 1944 an order and a medal named after Nakhimov were introduced to decorate Soviet Navy officers and rank-and-file sailors. In the same year, special cadet schools for the training of naval officers, also named after Nakhimov, were established.[31] He was thus transformed into an icon in the Soviet Russian iconostasis, taking his place next to Aleksandr Nevsky, Aleksandr Suvorov, and Mikhail Kutuzov.

The new wave of Sevastopol veneration came in 1955 with the commemoration of the hundredth anniversary of the Crimean War and the defence of Sevastopol. The commemorations were held in the atmosphere of the Cold War, in which the old Sevastopol enemies, Great Britain, France, and Turkey, were NATO members and adversaries of the USSR. Dozens of books and hundreds of articles dealing with the history of the Sevastopol siege of 1854–5 were published during the first postwar decade. It was then that the standard Soviet work on the Sevastopol siege was written by a well-known Soviet historian of the Stalin era, Evgenii Tarle. Entitled *The City of Russian Glory: Sevastopol in 1854–55,* it was issued in 1954 by the publishing house of the USSR Defence Ministry.[32] The book was based on Tarle's earlier two-volume study, *The Crimean War,* and was addressed to the general public.

Tarle began working on the history of the Crimean War in the late 1930s, as Soviet relations with Britain and France were deteriorating. The authorities gave him exclusive use of otherwise inaccessible Russian foreign-policy archival files. The first volume, published in 1941, was awarded the Stalin Prize. The second volume appeared in 1943, and the work was frequently reprinted. In his introduction to the fourth edition of the book in 1959, Nikolai Druzhinin praised Tarle for successfully refuting the concepts of Mikhail Pokrovsky and his school. According to Druzhinin, Pokrovsky had failed in his writings on the Crimean War to reveal the aggressive character of French and British imperialism, exaggerated the superiority of West European technology and military training over their Russian counterparts, and neglected to distinguish between popular and official Russian patriotism. In Druzhinin's opinion, Tarle had managed to correct all these mistakes of his predecessor.[33]

In the title of his new book, *The City of Russian Glory,* Tarle coined the currently popular designation of Sevastopol, based on its Greek name, which means 'city of glory.' Tarle's general approach to the history of the Crimean War is a mixture of criticism of the imperialist character of the war (a tribute to the works of Marx and Engels) and glorification of the Russian nation. The book begins with the statement that the Crimean War introduced a glorious page into the history of the Russian people. This is followed by an attack on 'British imperialism.'[34] In another passage, Tarle compares the siege of 1854–5 to the defence of Sevastopol in 1941–2 and attacks the 'heirs' of Hitler and Hitlerism in Washington and West Germany.[35] Following the writings of Marx and Engels, Tarle often blames imperial Russia, not for its own imperialist ambitions but for its weakness and backwardness, which prevented the empire from winning the war. The Crimean War was presented by Tarle to the Soviet reader as a war launched by the Western states 'against our Motherland.'[36] According to the historian, in 1854–5 the defenders of Sevastopol not only fought for the city but also defended 'the annexations made by the Russian state and the Russian people in the times of Peter I and during the eighteenth and nineteenth centuries.'[37]

The title of Tarle's book, *The City of Russian Glory,* reflected one of the work's main characteristics: it praised Russian glory and Russian heroism in a context in which 'Russian' was viewed exclusively as Great Russian. There was no attempt to interpret 'Russian' in any broader manner. The campaign against Jews and 'cosmopolitans' in the late 1940s and early 1950s brought to the fore the practice of glorification of ethnic Russians and denial of any attention to historical figures of non-Russian origin. One of the most venerated historical figures in Stalin's USSR was a participant in the Crimean War, the brilliant Russian surgeon Nikolai Pirogov. A special feature film was produced at that time to glorify Pirogov, whose achievements were supposed to prove the superiority of Russian science and scholarship to those of the West. It is not surprising that Pirogov was among the most venerated heroes of the Crimean War, and Tarle's book was no exception in its treatment of the famous surgeon. At the same time, the names of generals and officers who played an important role in the defence of Sevastopol but were of non-Russian background were barely mentioned in the book.[38]

An example of Tarle's nationalistic approach is the case of the military engineer Eduard Totleben, who was in charge of the fortifications at the time of the siege and whose talent and activity contributed immensely to the success of the imperial army. Totleben, who had received a great deal of attention in Tarle's earlier books on the Crimean War, was randomly mentioned in *The City of Russian Glory.* The historian now accused Totleben of depriving officers with Russian surnames of the glory they had earned during the war.[39] Instead, Tarle devoted many pages of his book to the glorification of Admiral Nakhimov. The official version of the history of the Sevastopol siege, employed by Tarle, was written along Russian populist lines and claimed that after the death of Admiral Kornilov, who was killed during the very first attack on the city, Admiral Nakhimov became the 'soul' of that defence.[40]

Tarle's book, which became perhaps the most popular Soviet publication about the Sevastopol siege and contributed immensely to the creation of the image of Sevastopol as a city of Russian glory, displayed the symbiosis of Marxist phraseology and ideas of Russian nationalism that formed the ideological base of Stalin's policies from the 1930s to the 1950s. In the 1960s, owing to the change in the Soviet ideological approach under Nikita Khrushchev and the transfer of the Crimea to Ukraine, the celebration of Russian heroism in the Sevastopol siege of 1854–5 was overshadowed by glorification of the heroism of the Soviet people in the Sevastopol siege of 1941–2. Sevastopol's heroic defence against the invading Germans served as one of the sources of a new mythology, that of the 'Great Patriotic War.' In the 1960s Sevastopol, along with Moscow, Leningrad, Odesa, and a number of other cities, was awarded the Gold Star of Hero of the Soviet Union. Subsequently, the principal focus of historical literature devoted to the Crimea and Sevastopol shifted to the history of the Soviet period.[41]

Around the same time, the exclusively Russian character of the Sevastopol myth was effectively challenged by the glorification of Sevastopol heroes of non-Russian origin. The heroism of the ethnic Ukrainian Petro Kishka (in Russian transcription, Petr Koshka) was highly praised in all books about the Sevastopol siege published in Ukraine.[42] In the 1980s, a book by A. Blizniuk devoted to the heroism of Belarusians in the Sevastopol siege was published in two editions in Belarus. (The most prominent of the ethnic Belarusians who fought at Sevastopol during the Crimean War was Aleksandr Kozarsky.)[43] The reclamation of parts of the Sevastopol myth by Ukrainians and Belarusians continued until the dissolution of the USSR but never managed to shake the exclusively Great Russian character that the myth had acquired in the Soviet Union from the 1930s to the 1950s.

The fate of the Sevastopol myth in post-Soviet Russia offers a striking example of a sharp conflict between cultural and state boundaries on the territory of the former USSR. The territorialization of Russian national memory that took place within the boundaries of the Russian Empire and then of the Russian-led USSR had to face the challenge of the newly shrunken Russian territory after 1991. The confusion of the Russian public at large with regard to the new state boundaries was profoundly expressed in the words of a poem by A. Nikolaev:

> On the ruins of our superpower
> There is a major paradox of history:
> Sevastopol, the city of Russian glory,
> Is outside Russian territory.[44]

The Sevastopol myth, though restructured and reshaped after the fall of the USSR, is alive and well in contemporary Russia and constitutes an important part of current political discourse. One of the best examples of the modification of the Sevastopol myth in post-Soviet Russia was presented by Aleksandr Solzhenitsyn, the patriarch of Russian nationalism, in his pamphlet *'The Russian Question' at the End of the Twentieth Century.* For Solzhenitsyn, Russia's appropriation of the Crimea marked the attainment of her 'natural southern boundary.'[45] He refuses to attribute responsibility for defeat in the Crimean War to Russia's backwardness, siding instead with the nineteenth-century Russian historian Sergei Soloviev, who advocated the continuation of the war in 1856.[46] Solzhenitsyn also attacks the West for interfering in the Russo-Ukrainian debate over Sevastopol. He wrote in that regard: 'The American ambassador in Kyiv, Popadiuk, had the gall to declare that Sevastopol rightly belongs to Ukraine. Based on what historical erudition or relying on what legal foundations did he pronounce this learned judgment?'[47] Aleksandr Solzhenitsyn's view of the history of Russian presence in the Crimea is not an isolated phenomenon. In many respects it follows the current trend in Russian historiography towards rewriting Soviet-era Russian history along neo-imperialist lines.

Since the dissolution of the USSR, the Russian myth of Sevastopol has made use of the prerevolutionary mythology of the Crimean War and largely dismissed the Soviet-era mythology of the Second World War. The most likely explanation of such a modification of the Sevastopol myth lies in the different relation of the two Sevastopol myths to the Russian national idea in general. The Soviet-era component of the

Sevastopol myth, based predominantly on the events of the Second World War, appears quite limited in its ability to provide a basis for the mobilization of Russian nationalism in its dispute with another Slavic nation, Ukraine, over the Crimea and Sevastopol. The Crimean War mythology that represents the heroism of the Russian imperial army exclusively as the heroism of the Russian people, on the other hand, does offer such a basis.

There can be little doubt that the modification of the Sevastopol myth in the 1990s exemplifies important trends in the development of Russian national identity in the post-communist era. Such trends include nostalgia for the lost empire, confusion over the issue of Russianness (whether it includes Ukrainian and Belarusian components), and growing anti-Western sentiments among contemporary Russian elites.

11 The Ghosts of Pereiaslav

In March 2000 the Ukrainian section of the BBC aired a special program devoted to Hetman Bohdan Khmelnytsky and his historical legacy. A number of historians in Ukraine, Russia, and Canada, as well as people on the streets of Kyiv, Moscow, and Warsaw, were asked the same question: what did the name of Khmelnytsky mean to them? While in Warsaw the hetman's name was associated first and foremost with the Cossack rebellion of 1648, in Kyiv and Moscow his legacy was viewed almost exclusively through the prism of the 1654 Pereiaslav Agreement, which placed the Ukrainian Cossack state under the protection of the Muscovite tsar and initiated a long era of Russian domination in Ukraine.[1]

In Moscow Khmelnytsky was seen both by professional historians and by the 'man in the street' as the one who had brought Russia and Ukraine together by means of the Pereiaslav Agreement. A distinguished Russian historian, Gennadii Sanin, stated that he considered Khmelnytsky a great man, as he had not only united Russia and Ukraine but also conceived of a larger East European federation that would have included Moldavia, Wallachia, and the Balkans as well.[2] Khmelnytsky's Pereiaslav legacy was viewed from a different perspective in Kyiv. A woman interviewed by a BBC correspondent in the Ukrainian capital was not even sure whether Khmelnytsky could be considered a Ukrainian, as she believed that he was also claimed by the Russians. Other Kyivans interviewed for the program strove to present the Pereiaslav episode of Khmelnytsky's career as an act forced upon him by unfavourable circumstances. One of them claimed that Khmelnytsky had been confronted with three choices – to accept the Turkish, Polish, or Russian yoke – and had chosen the Russian one.

The same opinion was expressed by another interviewee, who stated that Khmelnytsky's choice was the right one for his time. Similar ideas are to be encountered in the Ukrainian press, as well as in the writings of Ukrainian historians.[3] Overall, despite a fair amount of sympathy for Khmelnytsky among these interviewees, his status as a national hero has been seriously shaken in independent Ukraine, first and foremost because of his role in bringing about the Russo-Ukrainian agreement at Pereiaslav.

Before the beginning of glasnost and the dissolution of the USSR, the Pereiaslav Agreement was unanimously viewed by Soviet historians in both Russia and Ukraine as an important and positive event in their nations' histories. Why do scholars and ordinary people in Russia and Ukraine now regard its legacy so differently? The answer to this question is closely related to the fate of Soviet historiography in general and to the changes that affected historians and historiographic concepts in the post-Soviet space after the dissolution of the USSR and Moscow's loss of control over non-Russian cultures and historiographies. It also touches upon the more theoretically informed question of the interrelation between historical and national identities in the newly independent states of Eurasia in general, and in the Slavic republics of Russia, Belarus, and Ukraine in particular. To what degree did changes in historical paradigms in these countries influence nation-building projects (and vice versa), and to what degree did they promote or, on the contrary, retard the development of a common identity in the countries of the *Slavia Orthodoxa*? In this chapter I do not intend to provide answers to all these questions but instead will try to enrich my analysis of a particular historiographic debate by adopting this broader theoretical approach.[4]

It would be difficult to find a better point of departure for discussing the importance of the Pereiaslav legacy in post-Soviet Ukraine than the events that took place in the town of Pereiaslav in the summer of 1992. On 21 June, 338 years after the conclusion of the Pereiaslav Agreement between Bohdan Khmelnytsky and the Muscovite boyars, activists of the Ukrainian Cossack brotherhood from all over Ukraine descended on that sleepy provincial centre to convene a new Cossack council. There were only two points on their agenda: a denunciation of the oath given by the Ukrainian Cossacks to the Russian tsar and the swearing of an oath of loyalty to the Ukrainian people. In the text of the declaration adopted by the Pereiaslav Council of 1992, Muscovy in general and the Muscovite tsars in particular were accused of betraying the naive and God-fearing Cossacks, conspiring with their enemies, taking over their lands, destroying their language and customs, and, most recently, attempting to rend Ukrainian territory with the talons of a two-headed eagle, the central element in the old tsarist coat of arms that was readopted by the Russian Federation under Boris Yeltsin. The council's proclamation stated that the Ukrainian Cossacks were denouncing their oath to the tsar so that those seeking to place Ukraine under a new yoke would not be able to exploit their old oath in Pereiaslav.[5]

In historical and legal terms, the whole undertaking was completely anachronistic, as the Russo-Ukrainian treaty of 1654 was officially denounced by Hetman Ivan Vyhovsky in his 'Manifesto to Foreign Rulers' less than five years after the original Pereiaslav Council. Nevertheless, the symbolic importance of the event becomes clearer when placed in the context of Ukrainian nation-building efforts, Ukraine's relations with Russia, and internal debates on both issues in the Ukrainian parliament. In that context, it comes as no surprise that the person who read the Pereiaslav declaration denouncing Cossack allegiance to the tsar was none other than Viacheslav Chornovil, a Soviet-era dissident and a contender in the 1991 presidential elections. In 1992 he was also the hetman of the Ukrainian Cossacks and the leader of the Rukh party, the main opposition force in the Ukrainian parliament. The presence at the ceremony of a deputy speaker of the Ukrainian parliament also added to the symbolic significance of the event. The stain of Pereiaslav was something that the activists and supporters of the Ukrainian national movement obviously wanted to remove from what they saw as the otherwise spotless image of Ukrainian Cossackdom.

The Ukrainian Cossacks' active intervention in the process of nation-building and Russo-Ukrainian relations did not end with the 1992 denunciation of the Pereiaslav Agreement. In 1995 the Cossacks, now led by the former head of the Political and Educational Administration of the Ukrainian Armed Forces, General Volodymyr Muliava, took an active part in the commemoration of the Battle of Konotop (1659), where Cossack detachments led by Hetman Ivan Vyhovsky and assisted by the Crimean Tatars defeated a numerically superior Muscovite army. The celebrations in Konotop featured, among other things, a scholarly conference on the history of the battle that was attended by some of Ukraine's leading experts on the Cossack past. The message that the participants were sending to their compatriots and the outside world was quite clear. They were turning to history in order to reveal the most glorious episode of their anti-Muscovite struggle, deliberately suppressed by Russian imperial and Soviet authorities. On the political level, Cossackdom, a non-governmental organization that had forged close links with the national-democratic political parties and organizations, was also taking a strong stand against threats to Ukrainian territorial integrity then emanating from the Russian political establishment.[6]

The 'return' of the Cossack myth during the last years of Soviet rule in Ukraine proved significant for the revival of the suppressed Ukrainian national identity on the eve of the disintegration of the USSR. Since then, the myth has faced a number of challenges in newly independent Ukraine. One of them is related to the fact that the Cossack period left a somewhat confusing legacy when it comes to Ukrainian relations with Russia, traditionally an important 'other' in Ukraine's self-identification. On the one hand, the Cossacks are known for numerous uprisings and wars waged against Russian rule: the revolt led by Hetman Ivan Mazepa in the early eighteenth century is seen as the most vivid example of Cossack antagonism towards Russia. On the other hand, it was also a Cossack hetman, this time Bohdan Khmelnytsky, who accepted the protectorate of the Muscovite tsars. For centuries, the attitude of Ukraine's political groupings and leaders to the Pereiaslav Agreement was considered a significant indicator of their political orientation. The same holds true for post-Soviet Ukraine.[7]

In Ukraine, the legacy of Pereiaslav and the Khmelnytsky revolt in general has been viewed as an important factor in the formation of a new paradigm of Ukrainian national history, closely linked with Ukraine's nation-building project.[8] Since the early 1990s, the history of the Pereiaslav Agreement has become a politically sensitive topic in the sporadic but continuing discussions between Russian and Ukrainian historians. Generally speaking, since the disintegration of the USSR, representatives of the two national historiographies have taken profoundly different attitudes towards the historical role and importance of the agreement.

One of the most controversial topics in Russo-Ukrainian discussions on the legacy of Pereiaslav has been the usage of the term 'reunification.' Ukrainian historiography has effectively rejected the old Soviet cliché of the Pereiaslav Agreement as a reunification of Russia and Ukraine, which was imposed on scholars by the *Theses* approved by the Central Committee of the Communist Party of the Soviet Union on the three-hundredth anniversary of the event in 1954. In Soviet historiography, the Khmelnytsky Uprising was known as the 'Ukrainian people's war of liberation.' This official term implied that the uprising was a war of the toiling masses against their overlords, as well as the climax of the struggle of Ukrainian society as a whole against Polish oppression and for 'reunification' with fraternal Russia. That message was also strengthened by the officially adopted chronology of the war, which allegedly came to an end with the decision of the Pereiaslav Council in January 1654. At that time, Ukraine's war aims were allegedly achieved: the Polish yoke was thrown off, reunification took place, and the toiling masses of Russia and Ukraine joined forces in a common struggle against social oppression and foreign subjugation.[9]

In independent Ukraine, the term 'reunification' has been completely abandoned by scholars and politicians alike, resulting in its disappearance from scholarly and popular literature and the media. 'Reunification' has also been dropped from the official name of Dnipropetrovsk University, which was named in 1954 for 'the three-hundredth anniversary of the reunification of Ukraine with Russia,' as well as from the official titles of other Ukrainian institutions.[10] Despite the clear unpopularity of the term in Ukraine, it continues to be used in Russia on both the popular and scholarly levels. The Moscow historian Gennadii Sanin stated in his previously mentioned BBC interview that he liked the term and was in favour of using it, since, in his opinion, it indicated the voluntary nature of the Russo-Ukrainian alliance.[11]

Qualified support for the term was also expressed by another Russian historian, an expert on the history of Russian foreign policy of the mid-seventeenth century, Lev Zaborovsky. In his presentation at a conference of Russian and Ukrainian historians held in Moscow in May 1996, he stated that Russian historians had fewer reasons than their Ukrainian colleagues to revise their earlier approaches to the history of the Pereiaslav Agreement. He claimed that Soviet political control had been much stronger in Ukraine than in Moscow, and that he personally had never even read the notorious 1954 *Theses*.[12] Zaborovsky also said that he had always considered the term 'reunification' artificial and preferred not to use it in his writings. Nevertheless, in the last few years he had begun to rethink the matter, as new historical sources recently discovered by him and his colleagues revealed that if not the term itself, then its ideological significance was quite popular at the time of the Pereiaslav Council. According to Zaborovsky, this was reflected in statements by residents of the Cossack state recorded by Muscovite diplomats who visited Ukraine at the time. Zaborovsky suggested maintaining the term 'reunification' but freeing it from the ideological baggage of the past.[13]

What accounts for the continuing attractiveness of the term 'reunification,' which represents a set of views clearly misused by Soviet historiography, in the eyes of Russian historians? One possible explanation of ongoing Russian attempts to retain this part of the Soviet heritage is to be found in the fact that 'reunification' was not a Soviet invention. The term was borrowed from the works of nineteenth-century historians, including the Ukrainian author Panteleimon Kulish, who wrote about the 'reunification of Rus'.' In the 1950s, the 'reunification of Rus'' was replaced with the concept of the 'reunification of Ukraine with Russia,' which combined some elements of the old pre-Soviet Russian nationalism with Soviet-era recognition of the existence of a separate Ukrainian nation.

It is hardly surprising that the politically motivated approaches to the Khmelnytsky revolt and the history of the Pereiaslav Agreement influencing the writings of Russian specialists on the seventeenth century were most articulately expressed in the works of those who wrote on policy issues. Some striking views on the history of Russo-Ukrainian relations, apparently shared by the Russian foreign-policy establishment, were presented by Sergei Samuilov, the head of a department of the Russian Academy's Institute of the USA and Canada. Writing in the Russian foreign-policy journal *SShA: ėkonomika, politika, ideologiia,* he attacked the position taken by John Mroz and Oleksandr Pavliuk in their article on Ukrainian foreign policy that appeared in *Foreign Affairs* in the summer of 1996. Samuilov set himself the primary task of proving that the Ukrainians were not a fully developed people and that Ukraine was never an independent state; hence it was never 'forcefully incorporated by imperial Moscow.' The more practical goal of his article was to challenge mistaken stereotypes of Ukraine and its history that allegedly enjoyed broad currency in the United States, as well as to warn 'interested circles' in the United States against possible errors in American foreign policy.[14]

In dealing with the history of Ukrainian statehood, Samuilov could not avoid a discussion of the Khmelnytsky Uprising and the meaning and consequences of the Pereiaslav Agreement. Seeking to revisit and revise the history of Russo-Ukrainian relations, Samuilov did not conceal his main source of ideological inspiration. He found it in the works of a well-known nineteenth-century Ukrainian historian and writer, Mykola (Nikolai) Kostomarov,[15] who, despite his important contribution to modern Ukrainian historiography, generally treated Ukrainians and Russians as parts of one Rus' nation. Not surprisingly, Samuilov praises Kostomarov highly as a 'true scholar,' counterposing him to the founder of Ukrainian national historiography, Mykhailo Hrushevsky, whom Samuilov accuses of every conceivable deadly sin, including alleged racism.[16] Inspired by Kostomarov's concept of the age-old struggle between Poland and Rus', as well as by his Orthodox religious sympathies, Samuilov writes that the Khmelnytsky revolt was motivated by Ukraine's desire to 'save and protect itself as a Russian Slavic Orthodox ethnos from forcible Polish Catholic assimilation.'[17]

Samuilov, in fact, rejects the Soviet-era image of Khmelnytsky as a leader who allegedly dreamt of 'reunification' with Russia. Instead, he claims that Khmelnytsky conducted a pro-Polish foreign and domestic policy but was forced to conclude an agreement with the tsar owing to pressure from the 'popular masses.' In his attempt to undermine the thesis of Ukraine's forcible incorporation into the Russian state, Samuilov questions the independent status of Khmelnytsky's polity on the eve of Pereiaslav and claims that Ukraine joined the Russian state voluntarily. Seeking to counter the Ukrainian foreign-policy establishment's European option and Ukrainian intellectuals' belief in the European character of their culture, Samuilov claims that Ukrainians have much more in common with Russians than with Poles, which allegedly explains why they emigrated in significant numbers not to the Catholic West but to Orthodox Russia during the Khmelnytsky Uprising. In bizarre fashion, Samuilov even finds an argument against Ukraine's claim to be a European nation in the well-known fact that Khmelnytsky often fought the Poles in alliance with the Crimean Tatars.[18] In Samuilov's opinion, 'the Little Russians (Ukrainians) were saved by Orthodox Russia, as a Russian, Slavic, and Orthodox ethnos, from the threat of complete assimilation according to the Polish Catholic model.'[19]

Samuilov's views on the causes and outcome of the Khmelnytsky revolt not only reflect the influence of Kostomarov's ideas about the importance of nationality and religion in the forging of the Russo-Ukrainian alliance but also evince clear parallels with the *Theses* of 1954. According to the *Theses*, 'for the Ukrainian people, the historic importance of the Pereiaslav Council's decision lay primarily in the fact that union with Russia within a single state, the Russian state, saved Ukraine from subjugation to the Polish nobility and from annexation by the Turkish sultans.'[20] One of the major differences between the *Theses* and Samuilov's approach to the Pereiaslav Agreement lies in the fact that, unlike his communist forerunners, Samuilov rejects the existence of a separate Ukrainian nation and revives the nineteenth-century imperial paradigm, which treated Ukrainians as a subdivision of the Russian nation. The conclusion that Samuilov draws from his historical excursus is quite simple: Ukraine belongs to 'all-Russian culture and Slavic Orthodox civilization' and is destined to exist in 'close union with Russia.'[21]

The apparent return of many Russian authors and politicians to the pre-Soviet concept of the existence of one Russian nation, which, in their opinion, has been unjustifiably divided by post-Soviet borders but will be reunited in the future, should be seen as one of the conditions contributing to the survival of 'reunification' terminology in post-Soviet Russia. By reviving ideas of pre-revolutionary authors on the unity of the 'all-Russian' nation and Orthodox Slavic solidarity, and by keeping the term 'reunification' alive, the Russian academic and foreign-policy elite has been leaving the door open to new 'reunifications' in the future.

What are the main features of post-Soviet Ukrainian writing on the history of the Khmelnytsky Uprising? In independent Ukraine, the approach of the 1954 *Theses* to the history of the Khmelnytsky revolt was promptly rejected. The development of a new terminology and a new interpretation of the uprising has not, however, proved an easy task.[22] One might assume that the easiest way for post-Soviet Ukrainian historiography to deal with these problems would be to go back to the pre-Soviet Ukrainian historiographic tradition or to borrow from diaspora writings on the topic, as Ukrainian historians have often done since 1991.

Indeed, in the case of the Khmelnytsky Uprising, post-Soviet Ukrainian historians have actively borrowed from the diaspora writings of adherents of the 'statist school' in Ukrainian historiography, often adopting the statist approach to the history of the uprising and the activities of its leader. According to that paradigm, the main outcome of the uprising was the formation of the Cossack Ukrainian state, and Khmelnytsky's principal accomplishment was the successful realization of the state-building project. The elements of the statist approach to the history of the uprising made their way to Ukraine in the late 1980s and became the dominant factor in historical and political discourse after Ukraine acquired its independence in 1991. In the autumn of 1995, the Ukrainian government sponsored official celebrations of the four-hundredth anniversary of Khmelnytsky's birth. Both the president of Ukraine and the head of its parliament took part in these celebrations, which were held in Khmelnytsky's capital, the town of Chyhyryn. In official pronouncements and articles published on the occasion, Khmelnytsky was praised first and foremost as a state builder, the founder of early modern Ukrainian statehood.

Ukrainian views on the history of the Khmelnytsky Uprising at the turn of the twenty-first century present a curious combination of pre-Soviet, Soviet-era, and diaspora approaches to the history of that important era in Ukrainian history in general, and Cossack history in particular. While actively borrowing from diaspora writings, post-Soviet Ukrainian historians have also shown their dissatisfaction with some of the terms and concepts employed by the statists. This applies particularly to the official name given to the Khmelnytsky Uprising. The traditional term used in Ukrainian populist and statist historiography alike was 'Khmel'nychchyna,' which diaspora authors translated into English as 'Khmelnytsky Uprising' or 'Khmelnytsky Revolt.'

For a number of reasons, the term 'Khmel'nychchyna' was not revived in Ukrainian historiography after 1991. According to Yurii Mytsyk, one of the leading Ukrainian specialists on the period, 'Khmel'nychchyna' was politically unacceptable to the new Ukrainian historiography because of the negative connotation attached in Soviet-era discourse to the name of any movement or event derived from the surname of its leader. The communist authorities often used labels derived from the names of Ukrainian political leaders to discredit movements led by them. This was the case, for example, with 'Petliurivshchyna,' the term used to define the Ukrainian state of 1919–20 led by Symon Petliura, and 'Banderivshchyna,' the term applied to the Ukrainian Second World War-era insurgency associated with the name of the leader of the Organization of Ukrainian Nationalists, Stepan Bandera. Another possible reason for the rejection of the term 'Khmelnychchyna' is the obvious reluctance of post-Soviet historians to use a conceptually neutral term to designate a revolt that played such a crucial role in Ukrainian history. Post-Soviet historians have clearly been looking for a term and chronological frame of reference that would reflect their new, independence-minded view of the Ukrainian past.[23]

There is little doubt that the search of Ukrainian historians for a conceptually loaded and politically acceptable term for the Khmelnytsky Uprising should be viewed as a legacy of the old Soviet historiography. In the Soviet tradition, the discussion of terminological issues pertaining to the politically correct labelling of the Khmelnytsky Uprising can be traced back to the late 1920s, when the school of Ukrainian Marxist historians led by Matvii Yavorsky was defeated by the leader of Russian Marxist historiography, Mikhail Pokrovsky, and his followers. At that time, at least three competing views on the name to be given to the Khmelnytsky Uprising were under discussion: Yavorsky defended the term 'Cossack revolution,' his student Volodymyr Sukhyno-Khomenko defined the uprising as a bourgeois and national revolution, and Karpenko, another participant in the discussion, defended Pokrovsky's definition of the uprising as a peasant war. In the long run, it was Yavorsky and Sukhyno-Khomenko who lost the argument and Karpenko who won it,[24] for in the 1930s Soviet historians were forced to adopt the view according to which the peasants, supported by the urban toiling masses, were the 'hegemon' of the Khmelnytsky Uprising. This approach to the history of the uprising remained dominant in Soviet writing on the subject until the late 1980s. As the *Theses* had it, 'The chief and decisive force in this war was the peasantry, which was fighting both social oppression by the Polish and Ukrainian feudal landlords and alien subjugation.'[25]

There are other parallels as well between the writings of post-Soviet Ukrainian historians and the ideas developed by their predecessors during the Soviet period. Consciously or not, some post-Soviet Ukrainian historians echo the official dogma of 1930s Soviet historiography, which considered the acceptance of the Russian protectorate a 'lesser evil' for Ukraine than the incorporation of the Cossack state into Poland or the Ottoman Empire. It was in this vein that Academician Petro Tolochko, one of the politically most active Ukrainian historians, stated in 1991 that there was no need to make a new hero of Ivan Mazepa so as to put him in the place traditionally occupied in Ukrainian historical consciousness by Bohdan Khmelnytsky. According to Tolochko, Khmelnytsky's contribution to the Ukrainian national renaissance was much more significant than Mazepa's. He also stated that, given the aggressive policy adopted against Ukraine in the mid-seventeenth century by Poland, Turkey, and the Crimean Khanate, and taking into account the allegedly unfavourable conditions of a possible Swedish protectorate, Khmelnytsky's choice at Pereiaslav was 'the only correct decision, that of union with Russia, with which we shared not only a common history but also one Orthodox faith.'[26]

To a degree, variants of the same idea can be found in the writings of Tolochko's younger colleague, the director of the Institute of Ukrainian History of the National Academy of Sciences and a former vice-premier responsible for humanitarian issues, Valerii Smolii. In his scholarly writings Smolii declines to evaluate Pereiaslav as a mistake on Khmelnytsky's part. He maintains that Khmelnytsky, faced with a choice between the Ottomans and Russia, decided on the Muscovite alternative, taking the religious factor into account. His acceptance of the Muscovite protectorate was, in Smolii's opinion, a step conceived 'in the process of painful reflection on the fate of Ukraine and its future.'[27] Smolii does not treat the Pereiaslav Agreement as one that subordinated Ukraine to Russia, thereby downplaying the controversy over the wisdom of the choice made by the hetman in Pereiaslav.[28]

Probably the single most influential factor in post-Soviet Ukrainian historical writing on the Khmelnytsky Uprising is the impact of the ideas formulated back in the mid-1960s by the then dissident Ukrainian historian and later patriarch of Ukrainian national historiography, Mykhailo Braichevsky. He was the first in Soviet Ukraine to challenge the official paradigm of 1954. In the mid-1960s Braichevsky wrote an essay arguing in favour of replacing the politically loaded term 'reunification' with a more neutral one, 'incorporation.' Braichevsky also advocated the restoration of the class-based approach to Ukrainian history and attacked the legacy of Stalinism and Great Russian chauvinism in historical scholarship. The essay was never published in Ukraine but first found its way into *samizdat* and then was smuggled to the West, where in the early 1970s it appeared in print in Ukrainian and English. The author, meanwhile, was forced by the authorities to issue a statement protesting the publication of his work abroad and subsequently dismissed from his position at the Institute of History of the Academy of Sciences.[29]

In his pamphlet Braichevsky undertook a generally successful attempt to deconstruct the pan-Russian 'reunification' myth by means of a class-based methodology. He claimed that the term 'reunification' had helped establish the idea of the superiority of the Russians to other peoples of the USSR, idealized the Russian autocracy, and neglected the positive aspects of the Ukrainian people's liberation struggle. While deconstructing the pan-Russian myth, Braichevsky attempted to develop a Ukrainian national paradigm of the Khmelnytsky Uprising, making use of the class-friendly national-liberation mythology. Braichevsky suggested replacing the officially approved definition of the Khmelnytsky Uprising as the 'Ukrainian people's war of liberation' with a new one, 'war of national liberation.' He was not alone among Soviet Ukrainian historians in suggesting this change. About the same time as Braichevsky wrote his pamphlet, some of his colleagues, including the subsequently persecuted historian of Ukrainian Cossackdom Olena Apanovych, attempted to apply this politically attractive term to early modern Ukrainian history, thereby stressing the priority of the national factor in the war over the officially favoured social ones.[30] The use of the term 'war of national liberation' had clear positive connotations in the USSR of the mid-1960s, when national-liberation movements in the Third World were viewed as a positive phenomenon by Soviet ideologists.

The ideas expressed by Braichevsky in the 1960s managed to influence a relatively large number of Ukrainian historians in the 1970s and 1980s and naturally found their way into the writings of historians in independent Ukraine. This was the case not only with Braichevsky's use of 'national-liberation' terminology but also with his employment of a class-based method to deconstruct the pan-Russian paradigm of the Khmelnytsky Uprising. It was with the aid of this method that in the late 1980s a historian from Kamianets-Podilskyi, Valerii Stepankov, challenged the Soviet-era chronology of the Khmelnytsky revolt, declining to accept the Pereiaslav Agreement as the end of the uprising. In the course of his study of peasant revolts of the mid-seventeenth century, Stepankov became convinced that the peasant war that began in 1648 did not end after the Pereiaslav Agreement but continued into the 1670s. He initially suggested the later terminus of the war on the basis of a class-oriented approach but later modified his position and made an argument grounded in the Ukrainian statist paradigm to support his original view. He claimed that the resignation of Hetman Petro Doroshenko in 1676 signalled the failure of Cossack attempts to reunite the Ukrainian lands into a single state and should be seen as marking the end of the period that began with the Khmelnytsky Uprising in 1648.

The new term suggested by Stepankov to define the period of Ukrainian history between 1648 and 1676 was 'Ukrainian national revolution.' This term, as well as Stepankov's periodization of the Khmelnytsky Uprising, gained considerable notice in Ukraine, partly because he often published his works in co-authorship with Academician Valerii Smolii. Stepankov's idea of a Ukrainian national revolution also found its way into the seventh volume of the multi-volume series 'Ukraine through the Centuries,' written by Stepankov and Smolii and entitled *The Ukrainian National Revolution of the Seventeenth Century (1646–1676).*[31] In adopting the term 'revolution,' Stepankov actually outdid Braichevsky in his application of the class-based approach and returned to the Ukrainian historiographic tradition of the post-revolutionary decade, when that term was accepted and used both by representatives of the old populist school, led by Mykhailo Hrushevsky, and by some practitioners of Ukrainian Marxist historiography, including Volodymyr Sukhyno-Khomenko.[32]

Not surprisingly, in the new post-Soviet Ukraine, Stepankov's reliance on the 'revolutionary' terminology closely associated with the old regime met with reservations. Stepankov's colleague Yurii Mytsyk rebelled against the use of the term 'revolution,' declining to use terminology implying the primacy of the social factor in the uprising. Challenging Stepankov's choice of 1676 as the terminal date of the revolution, Mytsyk took a statist approach to the problem. He argued that the Cossack state did not disappear with Doroshenko's resignation but continued to exist in Right-Bank Ukraine until the 1720s, while in Russian-ruled Left-Bank Ukraine it survived even longer, until the second half of the eighteenth century. Instead, Mytsyk suggested that the Hadiach Agreement of 1658 between Poland and the Cossacks be taken to mark the end of the Khmelnytsky Uprising. In Mytsyk's opinion, that agreement officially ended the Polish-Ukrainian conflict that began in 1648 and terminated the short-lived period of Ukrainian independence.[33] Following in the footsteps of Braichevsky and Soviet Ukrainian historiography of the 1960s, Mytsyk defined the period between 1648 and 1658 as a 'war of national liberation.'

Mytsyk's revival of this term reflects the trend that became dominant in post-Soviet Ukrainian historiography.[34] Nevertheless, Ukrainian historians are far from unanimous on this point, with Stepankov and occasionally his co-author Smolii continuing to use the term 'revolution.' Both terms and chronological divisions are used concurrently. For example, Stepankov has published a paper on the Ukrainian national revolution in a collection of articles that not only bears the title 'The National-Liberation War of the Ukrainian People of the Mid-Seventeenth Century' but also includes an article by his colleague Valerii Smolii entitled 'The National-Liberation War in the Context of Ukrainian Nation-Building.' In that article, contrary to all of Stepankov's arguments and even to some of his own writings, Smolii defined a short period at the beginning of the uprising, between January and May 1648, as a national revolution.[35]

Despite obvious sloppiness in the use of historical terminology, the disagreements among Ukrainian historians on the character and chronology of the Khmelnytsky revolt point to a number of major changes occurring in post-Soviet Ukrainian historiography. First of all, they indicate the growing maturity of the historical profession, which is gradually overcoming the Soviet heritage of ideological uniformity. They also reveal not only differences among historians in treating the course of the revolt and the Pereiaslav Agreement but also signs of growing consensus on a number of important issues pertaining to the problem. Quite obviously, most Ukrainian historians reject the view that the Pereiaslav Agreement was the paramount event of the war and accept the use of the term 'national' in their definition of it. The latter point may serve as an indication of an important development that was under way in Ukrainian historical discourse in the 1990s. In the second half of that decade, Ukrainian scholars began to pay special attention to the role of the national factor in the history of the Khmelnytsky revolt and other Cossack uprisings of the period. If in the late 1980s and early 1990s Ukrainian historians mainly emphasized the state-building element of Khmelnytsky's policies,[36] in the late 1990s significantly more effort went into portraying Khmelnytsky as a nation builder.

In Valerii Smolii's article 'The National-Liberation War in the Context of Ukrainian Nation-Building,' which appeared in 1998, when Smolii was serving as vice-premier, he made the following statement in that regard: 'Today, hardly anyone needs to be convinced that the liberation epic of the mid-seventeenth century began a new epoch in the people's struggle for independence. Its main goal was the creation of an independent national state that would include all Ukrainian ethnic territories.'[37] Smolii, in fact, was not only summarizing previous debates in Ukrainian historiography on the history of the Khmelnytsky revolt but also giving his official blessing to the 'nationalizing' approach to the history of the uprising. As the Russian historian Lev Zaborovsky noted with respect to the nationally oriented Ukrainian interpretation of the Khmelnytsky Uprising, it has acquired clear characteristics of an official dogma and become a standard definition of the goals of the Khmelnytsky Uprising in textbooks and popular writings alike.[38] Interestingly enough, some Russian scholars, including Zaborovsky himself, have accepted the term 'war of national liberation,' popularized by Ukrainian historians. Applied to the Khmelnytsky Uprising in order to denote a war for the liberation of the East Slavic population from the Polish yoke, this term apparently does not contradict the paradigm of the reunification of Rus'.

Ukrainian and Russian historians dealing with the Pereiaslav Agreement have focused mainly on issues of terminology and chronology.

Paradoxically, the legal nature of the Pereiaslav Agreement and the subsequent Muscovite-Cossack agreement concluded in Moscow in March 1654 has received little if any recent attention in either Russia or Ukraine. While Russian and Ukrainian historians of the early decades of the twentieth century could hardly agree whether the Pereiaslav Agreement constituted a protectorate, suzerainty, military alliance, personal union, real union, or complete subordination, post-Soviet historians have preferred to leave this topic alone. In Russia, Zaborovsky declared the whole discussion of the issue a 'scholarly pathology,' while other historians, such as Sanin, agreed with the Ukrainian definition of the Ukrainian-Russian agreement of 1654 as a kind of confederation.[39] Even though this definition is clearly a historical anachronism that does not correspond to the realities of the 1654 treaty, it is considered politically expedient by Ukrainian historians, as it satisfies their desire to underline the de facto independence or semi-independent status of the Hetmanate within the Muscovite state in Khmelnytsky's day.[40]

The debates over the legacy of the Pereiaslav Agreement in Russian and Ukrainian historiography show that both Russian and Ukrainian historians are heavily dependent on approaches to the history of Russo-Ukrainian relations developed by their predecessors. No participant in this debate has yet managed to reject the heritage of Soviet historiography in its entirety. On the contrary, by making selective use of the Soviet heritage and 'recycling' ideas associated with different stages of development of Soviet historiography, both sides have attempted to legitimize and strengthen their respective arguments in the course of the discussion. If Ukrainian authors build upon the internationalist and class-based approach of Soviet historiography in order to deconstruct the Russian nationalist and imperial paradigm of Ukrainian history, Russian authors develop those aspects of Soviet historiography that gained prominence in the last years of Stalin's rule and were influenced by prerevolutionary Russian historiography.

No less selective has been the use by both Russian and Ukrainian historians of the heritage of non-Soviet historiography. While post-Soviet Ukrainian authors readily adopt many concepts produced by the 'statist' school of Ukrainian historiography, which perforce developed for most of the twentieth century beyond the borders of Soviet Ukraine, Russian authors go back to the writings of the prerevolutionary imperial historians. In particular, they rely on the intellectual heritage of some nineteenth-century Ukrainian writers and scholars who regarded

Ukraine and its history as parts of a larger all-Russian national and historical tradition. The changing assessments of the historical legacy of Pereiaslav advanced by post-Soviet Russian and Ukrainian historians reflect and coincide with major changes in the development of national identities and nation-building projects in both countries.

It may be said that in Ukraine official historiographic discourse has followed the major trends of state-sponsored ideology, gradually strengthening state-building and nation-building elements of the national historical narrative. It became quite clear in 2002, when President Leonid Kuchma of Ukraine, unpopular both at home and abroad, decided to make a gesture of good will towards one of his major supporters in the international arena, President Vladimir Putin of Russia. Kuchma signed a decree on plans for the official commemoration of the 350th anniversary of the Pereiaslav Council. The Kremlin liked the idea, and in January 2004 a delegation headed by Putin descended on Kyiv to take part in celebrations marking the anniversary of the agreement and the beginning of the Year of Russia in Ukraine. The celebrations, however, had to be scaled down because of the controversy that the decree provoked in Ukrainian society. Kuchma's critics accused him of reviving the tradition of celebrating anniversaries of the 'reunification of Ukraine and Russia' and selling out Ukraine's national interests to its northern neighbour. A significant portion of the Ukrainian intellectual and political elite rebelled against the spirit, if not the letter, of the decree, and the authorities were obliged to listen. A Russian television crew sent to Kyiv to cover Putin's participation in the Pereiaslav celebrations had to report back that 'nothing in the streets of Kiev reminds one either of the 350th anniversary of the Pereiaslav Council, which is described by historians as a moment of union of the two countries, or about the Year of Russia in Ukraine, or about the Russian president's forthcoming visit.' 'Near the monument to Bohdan Khmelnytsky,' stated the RenTV news anchor, 'an old man approached us to ask when picketing in protest against Putin's visit would start.'[41]

The failed celebration of the Pereiaslav Agreement in 2004 demonstrated that even Ukraine's supreme political authorities have not managed to turn back the clock on the major changes that have occurred in Ukrainian historiography and society since independence. In the post-independence years, one of the main characteristics of the Ukrainian nation-building project has been the restoration and reinvention of national tradition, orienting the nation's culture towards the West and stressing its distinctiveness from Russian culture and tradition. In Russia, on the contrary, the nation-building project has recently taken on a clear anti-Western orientation, with a strong emphasis on the idea of the Slavic and Orthodox unity of the Russians, Belarusians, and Ukrainians. So far, it is clear that Ukraine has been the odd man out of this projected civilizational triangle. But it is equally obvious that the ghosts of Pereiaslav, unleashed by the collapse of communist ideology and the advance of Pan-Russianism, have become an ever more corporeal presence in contemporary Russian and Ukrainian political and cultural discourse.

12 Remembering Yalta

On 4 February 2005, military guards welcomed guests arriving at the Livadia Palace near Yalta, as they had done sixty years earlier on the first day of the Yalta Conference, which brought together Franklin D. Roosevelt, Winston Churchill, and Joseph Stalin to discuss the shape of the world after the Second World War. Aside from the guard of honour and the return to the Livadia Palace of some of the former Soviet soldiers and waitresses who had provided security for the conference and helped assure its smooth progress sixty years earlier, there was little resemblance between the events of February 1945 and those of 2005. The organizers of the 2005 Yalta Conference – a symposium entitled 'Yalta 1945–2005: From the Bipolar World to the Geopolitics of the Future' – anxiously awaited but never received greetings from President Viktor Yushchenko of Ukraine, to which Yalta and the Crimea now belong, or from President Vladimir Putin of Russia, the legal successor to the Soviet Union, which hosted the Yalta Conference in 1945. Nor were there greetings from the leaders of Britain or the United States.[1] Every political leader whose greetings never reached Yalta on 4 February 2005 had his own reasons to overlook the anniversary of the conference that shaped the modern world and plunged it into almost half a century of cold war.

In the opinion of the Polish historian Jerzy Jedlicki, the twentieth-century history of Eastern Europe is 'a perfect laboratory to observe how the genuine or apparent remembrances of the past may aggravate current conflicts and how they themselves are modified in the process.' According to Jedlicki, the most intriguing question that the study of Eastern Europe can help answer is 'what factors activate historical reminiscences, and what circumstances would rather allow them to remain dormant and apparently forgotten. In other words, collective "memories" may become "hot" or "cooled," and the course of events may often depend on their emotional temperature.'[2] This chapter examines patterns of collective remembrance and forgetting of historical events of international importance by analysing public debates on the legacy of the Yalta Conference in Russia, Latvia, Poland, Ukraine, and the United States. It looks into interrelations between politics and historical representations in each of these countries. It also discusses the impact of the changing international situation on the ways in which intellectual and political elites interpret the importance of the Yalta agreements. Finally, it looks into the narrative strategies employed by the 'winners' and 'losers' of Yalta in representing their vision of the past.

Since the end of the First World War and the disintegration of the Austro-Hungarian, Russian, and Ottoman Empires, Eastern Europe has been an arena for the competing interests of new nation-states and the ambitions of great powers. After the German vision of *Mitteleuropa* as a Berlin-dominated space between Germany and Russia evaporated in the wake of the German defeat in the First World War, and the Bolshevik revolutionary advance on Europe was thrown back in 1920 by the 'miracle on the Vistula,' the territory between the Baltic and Adriatic Seas became a contested ground between the capitalist West and the communist East. While Britain and France regarded the newly independent countries of the region as a 'cordon sanitaire' against Bolshevik expansion, the Soviets tried to undermine some of the new regimes by turning their republics of Ukraine, Belarus, and Moldavia into a socialist Piedmont for the national minorities of Poland, Czechoslovakia, and Romania. Eventually Stalin used the irredentist argument to divide Eastern Europe with Hitler in 1939. As Britain and France entered the Second World War over the German invasion of Poland, London considered the restoration of Poland's independence and British interests in the region one of its main objectives in the war. The Yalta Conference effectively put an end to those plans, since Soviet armies occupied most of Eastern Europe, and Churchill failed to persuade Roosevelt to back British policy in the region. Yalta initiated the era of Soviet domination of Eastern Europe, which lasted until the end of the Cold War and left bitter memories of Western betrayal and Soviet dominance in the collective memory of the region.[3]

Historians have often treated the events leading to the disintegration of the Soviet bloc in Eastern Europe, the collapse of the USSR, and the emergence of new nation-states on the ruins of the communist empire as a manifestation of 'the revenge of the past.'[4] It would be difficult indeed to exaggerate the role of history in the rearticulation of national identities in post-communist Eastern Europe. The recovery of collective memory suppressed by authoritarian regimes and recollections of the region's traumatic experiences during and after the Second World War not only helped boost the national pride of the newly freed nations but also fuelled ethnic and sectarian conflicts from the Balkans in the west to Nagornyi Karabakh in the east.[5] The European borders established at Yalta generally survived the historical and national resurgence of the late 1980s and early 1990s. Germany was reunited, but there was no adjustment to its eastern border as of 1989. Czechoslovakia split into two states, but their borders remained those established immediately after the Second World War. Nor was there any change in the borders of Poland or the former Soviet republics of Lithuania, Belarus, and Ukraine, all of which 'inherited' part of Poland's interwar territory. Does this mean that the new national elites are satisfied with the map of Eastern Europe as drawn at Yalta, or do they still harbour grudges against the authors of the Yalta agreements? The historical 'amnesia' of the world leaders who forgot to send their greetings to the Yalta symposium in February 2005 indicates that while the Yalta borders generally remained intact, the historical and political consequences of the decisions made at Yalta in 1945 continue to haunt the world's political elites.

The Ghosts of Yalta

Vladimir Putin had more reason than any other world leader to 'forget' the sixtieth anniversary of the Yalta Conference. In early 2005 he faced a growing international crisis whose roots could be traced back to the legacy of Yalta. Russia ended 2004 as a big loser in international relations: its intervention in the Ukrainian presidential elections on the side of a pro-Russian candidate with a well-known criminal record and underground connections backfired. The Orange Revolution brought to power a Western-leaning and pro-democratic Ukrainian opposition leader, Viktor Yushchenko. Russia was losing control over its closest neighbour, whose territory now included the Crimea and the site of the Yalta Conference. In December 2004, the Russian minister of foreign affairs, Sergei Lavrov, suggested to the American secretary of state, Colin Powell, that Ukraine was part of the Russian sphere of influence

– a statement that had all the hallmarks of a Yalta-type approach to international affairs. It was intended to counter Western criticism of Russia's meddling in the Ukrainian elections and persuade the American leadership to give an increasingly authoritarian Russia a free hand in proceeding against democratic governments on the territory of the former Soviet Union. Powell rebuffed Lavrov's suggestion: the United States regarded developments in Ukraine as proof that democracy was on the march all over the world, from the Middle East to the former Soviet Union.[6]

While the American administration rejected the Yalta-inspired principle of the division of the world into spheres of influence, politicians in Germany and Japan – the main 'losers' of the Yalta agreements – rejected not only the principles underlying the Yalta decisions but also the legitimacy of Russian territorial acquisitions approved by the Crimean conference. In October 2004 the opposition parties in the German parliament raised questions about the continuing militarization of the former East Prussia, allocated to Russia by the Big Three in February 1945 and known as the Kaliningrad oblast ever since. They suggested calling an international conference with the participation of organizations representing Germans resettled from East Prussia to discuss the economic development of the region, to which they referred as the Königsberg oblast. They also suggested the creation of a Lithuanian-Polish-Russian cross-border region to be called 'Prussia.' The Russian government was appalled. Stressing that Gerhard Schroeder's government had no territorial claims against Russia, Sergei Lavrov condemned those German politicians who had raised the question of the lost territories.[7] If in Germany the government decided against opening the can of worms represented by the post-Second World War European borders, in Japan there has always been a national consensus favouring the return of territories lost to Russia as a result of the Second World War. The Japanese government never recognized the loss of the southern Kurile Islands, which were 'awarded' to the Soviet Union by the Yalta Conference, and continues to insist on the return of what it calls the 'northern territories.' In the spring of 2005 the Japanese parliament adopted a resolution increasing the number of islands that it wanted back from Russia. The return of those islands is regarded as a precondition for the signing of a peace treaty, the absence of which has clouded Russo-Japanese political, cultural, and economic relations ever since the end of the Second World War.[8]

In early 2005 Russia's neighbours to the west, the Balts and Poles, attacked the Russian government for its failure to apologize for Stalin's occupation of Eastern Europe, which had been sanctioned by the decisions of the Yalta Conference. The attacks came in response to Russia's decision to invite world leaders to Moscow to celebrate the sixtieth anniversary of the victory over fascist Germany in May 2005. Cashing in on the heroism and sacrifice of the Soviet peoples in the Second World War, the Russian government was hoping to carry out a public-relations coup and improve its international image, which was suffering from growing authoritarian tendencies, the persecution of independent-minded business tycoons such as Mikhail Khodorkovsky, and the continuing war in Chechnia. The failure of Russian policy in Ukraine added urgency to the government's resolve to appear in the international arena wearing the mantle of principal victor over fascism and saviour of Europe from Nazi rule. VE Day, however, brought not only liberation from fascism but also the Soviet occupation of Eastern and Central Europe, which lasted in one form or another for more than forty years. The leaders of the 'captive' nations were now determined to remind the world of that episode and, in the process, to encourage Russia to face its Stalinist past and acknowledge the atrocities committed in Eastern Europe by the Soviet Union and its communist allies.

The Baltic Front

The Russian invitation to the leaders of East European nations to attend VE Day celebrations in Moscow aroused heated discussions in the Baltic states. At the core of Russo-Baltic tensions was the question of whether the Soviet takeover of the Baltic states, tacitly approved by the Yalta Conference, was or was not an act of occupation. The answer to that question had serious legal and political repercussions for Russia, as it would affect the status of the Russian minority in Latvia and place on the international agenda not only the issue of Russia's moral responsibility for an act of aggression but also its legal consequences. Potentially, the Russian government faced lawsuits demanding material compensation for the imprisonment, deportation, and death of hundreds of thousands if not millions of citizens of the Baltic states. The Russian political elites took the issue so seriously that they were prepared to soften their demands on the issue of the human rights of Russian speakers in the Baltic states – their main weapon in diplomatic conflicts with the Baltics throughout the 1990s – if Latvia and Estonia would drop their claims for recognition of the Soviet takeover of the Baltic states as an act of occupation. On 3 February 2005 (the eve of the sixtieth anniversary of the Yalta Conference) the Russian side leaked to the press drafts of unsigned joint declarations on Russo-Estonian and Russo-Latvian relations that included a quid pro quo agreement in that regard.[9]

The debate over the participation of the presidents of the Baltic states in the VE Day celebrations in Moscow became especially acute in Latvia, the home of the largest Russian minority in the Baltics. Indeed, it crossed national boundaries and caused an international scandal. The president of Latvia, Dr Vaira Vike-Freiberga – herself a refugee from Soviet rule and a former professor of psychology at the University of Montreal, known in Russian diplomatic circles as a 'Canadian' – has been a strong promoter of the thesis that Soviet rule in her country amounted to an occupation. She has not been reluctant to express that conviction at home and abroad, and in January 2005, at the ceremony marking the sixtieth anniversary of the liberation of the prisoners of the Auschwitz concentration camp, she presented President Putin with a book promoting that interpretation of the history of Russo-Latvian relations. The Russian response was swift and decisive. The publication of the book, entitled *The History of Latvia: The Twentieth Century,* was officially condemned by the Ministry of the Foreign Affairs of the Russian Federation, and when a Russian translation of the volume was subsequently launched in Moscow, one of its authors was denied an entry visa to Russia.[10]

Not surprisingly, Dr Vike-Freiberga was highly reluctant from the outset to participate in the Moscow commemorations. Only later, under pressure from President George W. Bush of the United States, did she change her mind and accept the invitation, becoming the only Baltic head of the state to attend. The Latvian president stated that she would take part in the ceremony in Moscow out of respect for the Russian people and their sacrifice in the fight against Nazism, but she stood firm when it came to the interpretation of Latvian history and Russo-Latvian relations after the Second World War. Speaking on the Latvian radio program *Krustpunkti,* she suggested that Russia's harshly negative reaction to the Latvian viewpoint precluded open discussion on important questions of recent history, while other countries were making attempts to reevaluate their past. According to the Latvian president, Soviet-era stereotypes continued to dominate the Russian interpretation of the Second World War and the postwar era. In an article published in *Der Tagesspiegel* on 6 May 2005, Vike-Freiberga reiterated her earlier statement, arguing that after the expulsion of the Nazis, Latvia and the other Baltic states had become victims of Soviet occupation, which resulted in mass arrests, killings, and deportations of their citizens. She also suggested that both Latvia and Germany had faced their record in the Second World War, while Russia refused to separate its heroes from its tyrants and condemn the atrocities committed in the name of communism.[11]

The Polish Revolt

If in the Baltic states the decisions of the Yalta Conference were seen as a mere confirmation by the Western powers of the Molotov-Ribbentrop Pact, which delivered the Balts into the hands of Stalin, in Poland those decisions were discussed in a different context. There the Yalta debate coincided with discussions about President Aleksander Kwaśniewski's possible visit to Moscow for the VE Day celebrations. The tone and direction of the debate provoked strong criticism on the part of Moscow. As in the case of Russo-Latvian disagreements over the interpretation of the Soviet past, the Russian Ministry of Foreign Affairs took it upon itself to present the Russian point of view on the matter. On 12 February 2005, sixty years to the day after the conclusion of the Yalta Conference, the Information and Press Department of the ministry issued a statement distributed by the government-controlled press agency ITAR-TASS. The authors of the statement took issue with those Polish authors and politicians who regarded Yalta as a symbol of Poland's betrayal by its Western allies and of the subsequent Soviet occupation. The Russian Ministry of Foreign Affairs protested what it called an attempt to rewrite the history of the Second World War and take historical events out of context. It asserted that the participants in the Yalta Conference had wanted to see Poland strong, free, independent, and democratic. The fact that the Soviet Union did everything in its power to turn that country into anything but a strong, free, independent, and democratic state apparently was not considered by the authors of the statement to be part of the historical context. Another Russian argument in favour of the Yalta decisions dealt with the extension of the Polish borders to the north and west and the recognition of those borders by the Big Three at Yalta and Potsdam. The statement conveniently overlooked the fact that Poland lost its eastern lands, and, by incorporating western territories previously settled by ethnic Germans, became an accomplice in Stalin's partition of Europe.[12]

It is not clear what the initiators of the Russian Foreign Ministry's statement expected, but it created a great deal of negative publicity in the Polish media. Critics immediately pointed out that as a result of the Yalta decisions, Poland found itself under the control of a totalitarian regime and not only gained but also lost territory. Still, the Polish media was not prepared to open the Pandora's box of the postwar European border settlements. Some observers even asserted that if Lviv had remained in Poland after the war, it would probably have become a Polish Belfast. Generally, when it came to countering Russian arguments on the significance of the Yalta decisions, the Polish media treated them with a kind of fatalism – what else could one expect of the Russians? Commentators stated that it would be unreasonable to think that Moscow could condemn the decisions made at Yalta with the participation of Roosevelt and Churchill if it still refused to admit its failure to support the Warsaw uprising of 1944 or release all available information on the Soviet execution of thousands of Polish prisoners of war in Katyn Forest in 1940.[13]

The Katyn massacre of more than twenty thousand Polish prisoners of war by Soviet security forces has always been high on the list of Polish grievances against Russia.[14] In the spring of 2005, some commentators even suggested that Kwaśniewski's visit to Russia for the VE Day celebrations would be justified only if he used the occasion to lay flowers at the mass graves of Polish officers in Katyn Forest. Even the last communist ruler of Poland, General Wojciech Jaruzelski, who was invited to attend the celebrations in Moscow and intended to visit his father's grave in Siberia, stated that he did not understand why the Russians were reluctant to tell the whole truth about Katyn and publish the available documents.[15] Opposition leaders in parliament, including the future president of Poland, Lech Kaczyński, declared themselves against Kwaśniewski's visit to Moscow. But the Catholic Church hierarchy and majority public opinion supported the visit, as did the government, which maintained that it would not amount to a ratification of the Molotov-Ribbentrop Pact of 1939 or the Yalta decisions of 1945.

In his interview with the German daily *Die Welt* in late February, Kwaśniewski stated that he intended to go to Moscow to celebrate the end of the bloodiest dictatorship in human history but would not accept the invitation if it were for a ceremony marking either the anniversary of the Molotov-Ribbentrop Pact or of the Yalta Conference. Like the Baltic presidents before him, Kwaśniewski noted President

George W. Bush's earlier statements that Yalta had led to the partition of Europe and failed to bring freedom to significant numbers of Europeans. Kwaśniewski believed that the anniversary of the end of the war in Europe presented Putin with an opportunity to remind the world of the contribution of the Russian and other Soviet peoples to the victory over fascism and to give a just assessment of what had taken place after the war. In early May 2005, before leaving for Moscow, Kwaśniewski addressed his compatriots at the Polish VE Day celebrations in Wrocław. According to the Polish State Information Agency (PAP), Kwaśniewski stated: 'Yalta was painful ... for Poles, above all because the declarations on independent and democratic Poland were not kept.' He added, however, that 'thanks to the Yalta and Potsdam agreements, our country built and continues to build its sovereignty and found new opportunities for development in the west and north.' Kwaśniewski condemned the Soviet killings of Polish patriots after the war, stating that 'We remember with indignation and bitterness that when fireworks exploded in the Moscow sky to celebrate the victorious end of the war, sixteen leaders of the Polish Underground were incarcerated in the Lubianka Prison, and three of them were murdered.' Having calmed public opinion at home and countered his opponents' calls to turn down Putin's invitation, Kwaśniewski was ready to depart for Moscow.[16]

There he was in for a major surprise that strengthened the hand of those who had opposed the visit from the outset and advised him not to go to Russia. In his speech at the festivities President Putin omitted Poland from his list of nations that had contributed to the victory over fascism. This apparently came as a surprise not only to Mr Kwaśniewski but also to his communist predecessor, Wojciech Jaruzelski, who had boasted before his trip to Moscow that he was going to Russia as a representative of the fourth largest army in the anti-Hitlerite coalition. Whether Putin's omission of Poland in his VE Day speech was deliberate or not, it helped bring Polish-Russian relations to a new low. As was later admitted by Artem Malgin, the coordinator of the Polish-Russian Forum on European Politics, official Russia lost a unique opportunity to improve its image abroad. In Poland, according to Malgin, Russian diplomats did not show sufficient flexibility, as they failed to shift discussion from topics harmful to Russo-Polish relations and focus on useful ones instead. One such topic, suggested Malgin, was the current status of veterans of the Ukrainian Insurgent Army, who had fought not only against the

Germans but also against the Poles and Soviets. In Malgin's view, Russia had failed to exploit the generally positive opinion in Polish government and society of the role played by the Soviet Union in the Second World War. In the Baltic states, where the governments adopted an 'anti-VE' stand, the best option for Russia was allegedly to ignore the historical debate altogether. Malgin warned his readers against assuming that there was a coordinated Western information offensive against Russia and called upon them to continue working for the improvement of Russia's image abroad. Given the degree to which that image had been damaged by the debates over the legacy of the Yalta Conference, Malgin's advice was timely indeed.[17]

Meanwhile the Russian authorities preferred to put on a brave face and interpret the criticism of their country's post–Second World War role in Eastern Europe as an indication of the growing strength of the Russian state. Thus the Russian foreign minister, Sergei Lavrov, stated that in 1995, when the world celebrated the fiftieth anniversary of the victory over fascism, no one had bothered to present historical claims against Russia, since it was a weak state at the time. As Russia grew stronger, its neighbours became concerned about its new might and decided to advance their historical claims. According to Lavrov, one of the factors that worried Russia's detractors was its desire to lessen its treasury's dependence on energy exports. This was a peculiar claim to make at a time when much of Russia's economic recovery was fuelled by the country's energy exports and rising oil prices.[18]

The Second Front: The Americans Join In

Lavrov's questionable argument, which linked energy policy with the history of the Second World War, appears less strange if one considers the interplay of two similar factors in the speech given by President George W. Bush in Riga on 6 May 2005. Bush entered the East European historical debate head on, placing the legacy of the Yalta agreements within the broader context of the progress of freedom throughout the world and American support for democracy in countries ranging from former Soviet republics to Iraq, the latter occupied by American troops. As Bush presented it, democracy was the link between America's policy in Eastern Europe after the Second World War and its policy in the oil-rich Middle East. But this is the only parallel that one might draw between the Russian and American positions on the significance of the Yalta decisions.

As he accepted Vladimir Putin's invitation to attend the VE Day celebrations in Moscow and encouraged others, such as President Vike-Freiberga of Latvia, to do likewise, Bush decided to take the opportunity to visit not only Russia but also Latvia and Georgia, two former Soviet republics whose recent relations with Russia were far from smooth. The message was clear. Although the U.S. administration cared about maintaining good relations with Russia, it was not relinquishing its support of democratic processes in former Soviet republics struggling to escape the Russian sphere of influence. In Latvia Bush apparently felt obliged to take a stand on the legacy of the Yalta Conference, given the prolonged debate in that country on the history of Russo-Latvian relations during and after the Second World War. Referring to the conference in his Riga speech, Bush deliberately took the East European side in the ongoing debate. Indeed, he showed his readiness to go further than any of his predecessors in acknowledging American complicity in the Yalta division of Europe.

'As we mark a victory of six days ago – six decades ago, we are mindful of a paradox,' stated Bush. 'For much of Germany, defeat led to freedom. For much of Eastern and Central Europe, victory brought the iron rule of another empire. VE Day marked the end of fascism, but it did not end oppression. The agreement at Yalta followed in the unjust tradition of Munich and the Molotov-Ribbentrop Pact. Once again, when powerful governments negotiated, the freedom of small nations was somehow expendable. Yet this attempt to sacrifice freedom for the sake of stability left a continent divided and unstable. The captivity of millions in Central and Eastern Europe will be remembered as one of the greatest wrongs of history.'[19]

A U.S. administration official later revealed that the Yalta remark was intended as an invitation for Putin to apologize for the Molotov-Ribbentrop Pact. If that was indeed the case, then the White House speechwriters clearly miscalculated, for the remark did nothing to change Russia's position on the issue. Bush certainly scored points with leaders of the 'new Europe,' but he also created unexpected problems for his administration at home. The speech reignited the old debate between Republicans and Democrats over the role of Franklin Delano Roosevelt in what his critics called the 'sellout' of Eastern Europe to Joseph Stalin. Conservative journalists and commentators such as Pat Buchanan and Anne Applebaum praised Bush's remarks as a long overdue recognition of the 'awful truth,' while liberals, represented by a number of historians of American foreign policy and the

Cold War, accused the Republicans of reviving the spirit of Joseph McCarthy. The Democrats maintained that the Yalta Conference had done little more than recognize the reality on the ground, given that by the time of the Crimean summit Stalin had already gained control of Eastern Europe.[20]

The Riga speech was by no means the first public statement in which President Bush criticized the Yalta agreements. He had done so on previous occasions as well, always expressing his criticism in remarks addressed to East European audiences. Those remarks were apparently designed to placate allies of the United States in the new Europe, demonstrating American concern about the consequences of an event crucial to their history. They were also aimed at President Putin, encouraging him to be more honest in his assessment of the role played by the Soviet Union in Eastern Europe in the 1930s and 1940s. In the past, Bush's criticism of the Yalta agreements had failed to convince Putin to alter Russia's official interpretation of the event, but it was clearly appreciated by the East European elites.

When it comes to American discourse on Yalta, Bush's critique did not follow in the footsteps of Joseph McCarthy, as claimed by his Democratic critics, but it echoed statements made by leading figures in President Bill Clinton's administration. In March 1999 Secretary of State Madeleine Albright, the daughter of a former Czechoslovak diplomat who escaped to the West after the communist takeover, stated to representatives of East European governments: 'Never again will your fates be tossed around like poker chips on a bargaining table.' In fact, Albright was developing an argument made earlier by her deputy and Clinton's classmate Strobe Talbott. 'After World War II,' remarked Talbott in May 1997, 'many countries in the east suffered half a century under the shadow of Yalta. That is a place name that has come to be a codeword for the cynical sacrifice of small nations' freedom to great powers' spheres of influence, just as Versailles has come to signify a short-sighted, punitive, and humiliating peace that sows the seeds of future war.'[21]

Why, then, were the liberal opponents of President Bush so critical of his Riga speech? Leaving aside the political dynamics of May 2005, it should be noted that Bush was much more explicit in his critique of the Yalta agreements than his Democratic predecessors, especially as he compared Yalta not to Versailles but to Munich and the Molotov-Ribbentrop Pact. In so doing, he indeed revived some of the ghosts of the McCarthy era. 'The Munich Called Yalta' was the title of a chapter contributed by William H. Chamberlin to a book published in 1950 that criticized American diplomacy for appeasing Stalin and sacrificing the independence of Poland and the national interests of China.[22] By contrast, the comparison with the Molotov-Ribbentrop Pact was a new addition to the decades-old controversy introduced by the author of the Riga speech, the presidential assistant Michael Gerson.[23] It seemed appropriate to mention the division of Europe between Germany and the USSR in 1939 in a speech made in Latvia, where the memory of the Hitler-Stalin deal is alive and well more than sixty-five years after the event, and where every schoolchild knows that at Yalta Roosevelt and Churchill agreed to Soviet territorial acquisitions based on that pact. Not so in the United States. By drawing attention to the connection between the pact and the Yalta agreements, Bush opened the door to possible comparisons of FDR not only with Neville Chamberlain but also with Hitler and Stalin. More than anything else, it was that sacrilegious suggestion that provoked attacks on the administration from the belligerent Democrats – attacks that the White House had not expected and would have preferred to avoid.

What were the arguments on both sides of the Yalta debate in the United States? It would appear that the opposing parties contributed very little new material to the debate that reached its climax in the 1950s and 1960s. On the Democratic side, the old arguments were summarized and reiterated by a participant in the academic debates of the 1960s, Arthur Schlesinger, Jr. In his commentary on Bush's Riga speech, he stated that the president 'is under the delusion that tougher diplomacy might have preserved the freedom of small European nations.' Schlesinger rebuffed that thesis, stating that 'it was the deployment of armies, not negotiated concessions, that caused the division of Europe.' He reminded his readers that at the time of the Yalta Conference Eastern Europe was already occupied by the Red Army, and conflict with the USSR was inconceivable as long as the war with Japan was still going on. Among the achievements of the Yalta Conference, Schlesinger listed Stalin's promise to enter the war with Japan at a time when 'the atom bomb seemed to be a fantasy dreamed up by nuclear physicists,' and FDR's success in making Stalin sign the Declaration on Liberated Europe, which obliged the Soviets to conduct free elections in the countries of Eastern Europe that they occupied.[24] Jacob Heilbrunn, writing in the *Los Angeles Times*, put forward another important argument in favor of Yalta that Schlesinger had overlooked. He claimed that refusing to make a deal with Stalin on Eastern Europe 'would have seriously jeopardized the common battle against Germany.'[25]

The defenders of Bush's Riga speech did not, of course, argue that the West should have gone to war with the Soviet Union, jeopardized the victory over Hitler, or impeded the war effort in the Pacific. Their argument, like the reasoning of their opponents, was deeply rooted in formulas developed in the political and scholarly debates of the 1950s and 1960s. Pat Buchanan, for example, titled his article on the issue 'Was WWII Worth It? For Stalin, Yes,' echoing the title of the chapter 'Stalin's Greatest Victory' in Chester Wilmot's book *The Struggle for Europe* (1952).[26] Buchanan juxtaposed Putin's rhetoric about the Soviet liberation of eleven countries with Bush's admission that many of the European countries liberated from fascism found themselves under another form of oppression as a result of the agreements reached at Yalta. Siding with Bush, Buchanan accused FDR and Churchill of selling out Eastern Europe to one of history's deadliest tyrants, Joseph Stalin. Following in the footsteps of prewar American isolationists, he also questioned the rationale behind American involvement in a war that took fifty million lives. Echoes of the earlier debates were also to be heard in the *National Review* editorial 'Yalta Regrets,' which stated that the United States could have won the war against Japan without Soviet participation.[27]

Anne Applebaum, on the other hand, added some new emphases to the old theme as she attacked 'a small crew of liberal historians and Rooseveltians' who claimed that 'Yalta was a recognition of reality rather than a sellout.' 'Their charges,' according to Applebaum, 'ignore the breadth of the agreement – was it really necessary to agree to deport thousands of expatriate Russians back to certain death in the Soviet Union? – as well as the fact that Yalta and the other wartime agreements went beyond mere recognition of Soviet occupation and conferred legality and international acceptance on new borders and political structures.' The new element in this conservative argument was the conviction with which the author spoke about Stalin's crimes and the complicity of the Western powers in them. Applebaum, who has written an acclaimed book on the Gulag based on archival materials that became available after the collapse of the USSR, knew exactly what she was talking about when she wrote of the 'certain death' awaiting former Soviet citizens shipped back to the USSR by the American and British military. 'The tone was right,' stated Applebaum with regard to Bush's speech, 'and it contrasted sharply with the behavior of Russian president Vladimir Putin, as perhaps it was intended to. Asked again last week why he hadn't made his own apology for the Soviet occupation of Eastern Europe, Putin pointed out that the Soviet parliament did so in 1989. "What," he asked, "we have to do this every day, every year?"'[28]

The Long Shadow of 'Uncle Joe'

Putin was certainly in no mood for apologies during the Moscow celebrations of VE Day, and Bush did not insist on them. He stated in his remarks about his Moscow visit that he was dealing with a friend. The American president remained silent regarding Putin's encroachment on democratic institutions and liberties in Russia – a silence understood by the Russian media as tacit support for Putin.[29]

During the first half of 2005, the decisions adopted by the Yalta Conference were discussed by the Russian media in a number of contexts, including the long-term implications of the disintegration of the international system created at that conference. On the eve of the Yalta commemorations, the Russian state-run news agency Novosti released an interview with Valentin Falin, the former head of the international department of the Central Committee of the Communist Party of the Soviet Union. The veteran of Soviet diplomacy declared the Yalta agreements to be the best chance the world had ever had to end the threat of war. Falin interpreted attacks on the agreement as denunciations of the legacy of President Roosevelt, whom he held in the highest regard. Quoting from Edward R. Stettinius's memoirs of the Yalta Conference, Falin rejected the assumption that Stalin, whom President Roosevelt almost affectionately called 'Uncle Joe,' had outmanoeuvred his American counterpart at Yalta. He noted that both the idea for the creation of the United Nations Organization and the final communiqué on the conference were conceived by the Americans. Falin held President Harry Truman responsible for the failure of the Yalta agreements and the beginning of the Cold War. By reiterating that traditional Soviet-era view, Falin was in effect sending a new message to critics of Soviet expansionism in Eastern Europe: if you do not like Yalta, address your grievances to the United States.

When asked specifically about the partition of Europe into spheres of influence, Falin first tried to dodge the question; when it was repeated, he used Soviet-era arguments to present Soviet actions at the conference in the best possible light. He rejected the interviewer's suggestion that any spheres of interest had been established at Yalta. Following Stalin's argument of 1945, Falin stated that the Curzon Line, which became the basis of the new border between Poland and the USSR, had been drawn not by the Russians but by the leaders of the United States, Britain, and France in 1919 on the basis of ethnographic maps. Answering a question about the Baltic states, Falin reminded his audience that they had been cut off from Soviet Russia during the revolution by pro-German governments and used by the West as a base for intervention against Russia. The United States, according to Falin, did not care about the independence of the Baltic countries as long as they supported the White government of Admiral Kolchak, and Roosevelt had opposed the inclusion of the Baltic states in the USSR only because he did not want to lose the votes of Baltic immigrants in the USA.[30] Falin clearly believed that Russia had nothing for which to apologize in relation to the Yalta decisions. That was also the opinion of Vadim Trukhachev, who commented in *Pravda* on an article by the Polish journalist Marek Ostrowski, noting that the latter had failed to mention that it was thanks to the insistence of the USSR that Poland had acquired its postwar western and northern territories.[31]

The Russian liberal press remained largely silent on the issue of Yalta in February 2005, when it was at the centre of controversy in Eastern Europe. Yalta reemerged in Russian public discourse only in April 2005 within the context of a broader debate on Stalin's role in Russian history. The debate had begun in the late 1980s with the onset of glasnost. It originally focused on the crimes committed by the Stalin regime but acquired new characteristics in the 1990s with the rise of Russian nationalism. More Russians adopted a positive attitude towards Stalin after 2000, as Vladimir Putin took power and authoritarian tendencies came to the fore in Russian politics.[32] In the spring of 2005, the Stalin debate was reignited by Zurab Tsereteli, arguably Russia's most productive and controversial sculptor. In anticipation of the anniversary of the Yalta Conference, Tsereteli created a gigantic bronze sculpture of Stalin, Roosevelt, and Churchill as depicted in numerous photographs taken in front of the Livadia Palace in February 1945. The sculpture, which is four meters tall and weighs ten tons, was originally supposed to be installed at the Second World War memorial near Moscow[33] but was later offered to the Livadia municipal council. The city council first accepted the offer and then turned it down. After that, the sculpture was offered to the war memorial in Volgograd, the site of the Battle of Stalingrad. By April 2004 the issue had attracted the attention of the Russian media and representatives of the Russian liberal elite, who issued an appeal protesting the idea of installing the sculpture on Russian soil.

The authors of the appeal, who included Oleg Basilashvili, Aleksandr Gelman, Daniil Granin, Oleg Tabakov, and the 'grandfather of perestroika,' Aleksandr Yakovlev, regarded Tsereteli's depiction of the Big Three as an attempt to build a monument to Stalin and as a step towards his political rehabilitation in Russia. 'For the first time since the revelation of Stalin's crimes against humanity,' wrote the authors of the appeal, 'an attempt is being made in our country to put up a monument to him, and that on the sacred occasion of the sixtieth anniversary of Victory, which would have cost our nation considerably fewer victims had it not been for Stalin's "purges" of military cadres and his glaring miscalculations in policy and strategy.'[34] The statement was a direct response to those in the Russian nationalist camp and among the public at large who often cite Stalin's contribution to the victory over Nazi Germany as the main argument for his rehabilitation. Ironically, the appeal was addressed not to the Russian public but to President Putin, who brought back the Stalin-era anthem of the USSR as the anthem of the new Russia and whose rule witnessed a rise in the popularity of the once dreaded generalissimo. It would appear that the liberal intellectuals who signed the appeal had no illusions about the presence in Russia of any force other than the authoritarian president capable of stopping the public rehabilitation of Joseph Stalin.

The Stalin controversy and the approaching celebrations of VE Day finally brought the question of the Yalta Conference and the historical responsibility of the USSR (and, by extension, Russia) for its decisions to the attention of Russian liberals, giving them a legitimate voice in a discussion earlier dominated by officialdom. On 3 April 2005 Vladimir Pozner, the host of the popular Russian television program *Vremena* (Times), asked a guest: who was to be credited with victory in the Great Patriotic war, Stalin or the people? The guest refused to distinguish between the two, and Pozner was later criticized by Russian nationalists for trying to separate Stalin and the state from the people.[35] But the liberals were not silenced. Writing in *Izvestiia* in late April 2005, Fedor Lukianov noted the danger of associating the end of the Second World War with the victory of the Russian state. He wrote: 'But if that war is understood not as a heroic feat of the nation but as the political triumph of the Russian state, then we fall into a trap. One would then have to argue, foaming at the mouth, that Stalin acted as he should have done, the pact of 1939 was in accord with international law, and Yalta brought democracy to Eastern Europe.'[36] Writing after the VE Day celebrations in Moscow, Viktor Sheinis, a member of the liberal Yabloko Party, stated that at Yalta the Western leaders had approved the territorial acquisitions obtained by Stalin according to the Molotov-Ribbentrop Pact. Those decisions blocked the progress of democracy in Eastern Europe for more than forty years, and it should come as no surprise that the East Europeans regarded Yalta as another

Munich and refused to participate in the VE Day celebrations in Moscow. In Sheinis's opinion, 'If one is to show respect for Churchill, who understood earlier than others what a mess Stalin's Western allies had made, then I would depict him not in a chair on the Crimean shore but at the rostrum in Fulton. But such a monument should not, of course, be erected at Yalta.'[37]

The Crimean Debate

What happened in and around Yalta in the spring of 2005 that first prompted the municipal council of Livadia, the actual setting of the Crimean conference, first to accept Tsereteli's gift and then to refuse it? The city fathers changed their minds mainly for two reasons. The first was the attitude of the Crimean Tatars, whom Stalin forcibly deported from the peninsula less than a year before the Yalta Conference. They were welcomed back by the government of independent Ukraine and became embroiled in a political struggle with the Russian-dominated Crimean parliament for the restoration of their political, cultural, and economic rights in their historical homeland. The second reason was the position taken by the Ukrainian government, the new master of the Crimea and of the conference site. In 1954 the Crimean peninsula, including Yalta, was transferred from the jurisdiction of the Russian Federation to that of the Ukrainian SSR, and in 1991 it became an autonomous republic within the independent Ukrainian state. Thus, by the spring of 2005, it was not only the citizens of Livadia but also the Mejlis (parliament) of the Crimean Tatars, the authorities in Simferopol, the capital of the Crimea, and the leadership of the Ukrainian state in Kyiv who influenced the Livadia decision.

The decision to commemorate the sixtieth anniversary of the Yalta Conference was made by the Ukrainian parliament on 16 December 2004, less than two months before the event. The reason for this last-minute decision was readily apparent, given that in November and December 2004 the Orange Revolution had thrown the Ukrainian parliament into turmoil. The decision on the Yalta commemoration was made after the resolution of the political crisis but prior to the third round of the presidential elections, which brought the opposition candidate, Viktor Yushchenko, to power. The organizing committee for the celebrations consisted of members of the Crimean government, and in January 2005 its vice-president, Professor Vladimir Kazarin, was busy making a last-minute pitch to raise the public profile of the event. In an interview with Kyiv's most respectable weekly, *Dzerkalo tyzhnia* (Weekly Mirror), Kazarin suggested that by starting late and not committing enough resources to the celebrations, Ukraine, a founding member of the UN, was losing a chance to raise its visibility in world affairs and give a boost to its struggling tourist industry. According to Kazarin, one of the problems encountered by the organizers of the commemoration was opposition to Tsereteli's monument to the Big Three. Kazarin argued that it was a monument commemorating a particular event, not a tribute to Stalin. One could not remove important figures from history or pretend that certain events had never happened. Kazarin also noted that there were monuments to Genghis Khan and Tamerlane, which, in his opinion, was as it should be.[38]

As Kazarin sought to promote the commemoration of the Yalta Conference in the national media and argued in favour of installing Tsereteli's monument in Livadia, he found himself under increasing attack in the Crimea. The leaders of the Crimean Tatar Mejlis accused Kazarin – who, aside from being vice-premier of the Crimean government, was also a member of the communist faction in the Crimean parliament and head of the Russian cultural society of the Crimea – of attempting to rehabilitate Stalin and Stalinism under the pretext of commemorating the Yalta Conference. They reminded the public that two years earlier the communist deputies of the Sevastopol city council had voted in favour of building a monument to Stalin in their city. A leading figure in the Mejlis, Ilmi Umerov, stated that he could not accept the idea of a monument to the Big Three, given the forcible deportation of the Crimean Tatars conducted on Stalin's orders, as well as the controversial nature of the Yalta Conference, which had divided Europe into spheres of influence. The head of the Mejlis, Mustafa Dzhemilev, stated for his part that if such a monument were to be erected in Livadia, the Crimean Tatars would ensure that it would not stay there long. The appeal not to allow the installation of the monument was signed by dozens of former dissidents in Ukraine and Russia. The Crimean branches of Ukrainian political parties that supported the Orange Revolution made a similar appeal to Kyiv. As a result, the office of the Crimean attorney general annulled the decision of the Livadia town council to install the monument, citing a law that gave national authorities the right to make final decisions on the construction of monuments of national significance. Kazarin had to retreat, announcing the postponement of a final decision pending 'public consultation' on the project.[39]

This was not the end of the controversy. On 4 February 2005, the anniversary of the Yalta Conference, communists staged a meeting in Simferopol to protest the refusal of the Crimean authorities to install the monument. They criticized the Crimean premier, Serhii Kunitsyn, for kowtowing to the new 'Orange' government in Kyiv and threatened to initiate a criminal investigation into Kunitsyn's alleged embezzlement of parcels of land on the Crimean shore of the Black Sea. The Crimean Tatars held their own rally in Livadia to protest the installation of the monument. On the eve of the commemoration, Kazarin noted the irony that a bust of President Roosevelt was to be unveiled in Yalta, but that there would be no monument to the Big Three in Livadia. At the Livadia Palace, there was an exhibition featuring the offices occupied by Roosevelt and Churchill during the conference but not Stalin's office. Eventually the organizers of the commemoration compromised, deciding to include Stalin's Livadia office in the exhibition instead of installing the monument to the Big Three. President Mikheil Saakashvili of Georgia even promised to send artefacts from the Stalin museum in his native town of Gori.[40] But the controversy over the monument did not go away entirely. In April, Leonid Hrach, the leader of the Crimean communists, called upon the Livadia town council to install Tsereteli's monument in order to honour the memory of those who had fallen for the 'Great Victory.' The leaders of the Mejlis issued their own statements on the matter, threatening to block the roads along which the monument could be transported to Livadia. By that time the decision not to allow the installation was final, forcing Tsereteli to look for a site in Russia, which led in turn to a major controversy in the Russian media.[41]

'Making Sense of War'

In 2002 Amir Weiner published a book under this title in which he discussed the impact of the Second World War on the elites and general population of Vinnytsia oblast in Ukraine during the postwar era. Judging by recent debates in the Ukrainian media, Ukrainians are still struggling to make sense of their Second World War experience; hence the Yalta debate was not limited to Crimean political and historical discourse. Throughout 2005, articles in the Ukrainian press criticized the artificiality of Stalin's 'constitutional reform' of 1944, which allowed the Soviet dictator to ask for an additional UN seat for the Ukrainian SSR. Such prominent Ukrainian historians as Yurii Shapoval attacked Stalin for the Molotov-Ribbentrop Pact, questioning the dictator's role as 'gatherer' of the Ukrainian lands.[42] The Kyiv authors Serhii Hrabovsky and Ihor Losiev, writing in the American Ukrainian-language newspaper *Svoboda* (Liberty), adopted the Polish-Baltic position on Yalta.[43] That position was shared by the majority in formerly Polish-ruled western Ukraine, which became part of the USSR as a result of the Molotov-Ribbentrop Pact and the Yalta agreements. Eastern Ukraine, however, was not prepared to accept the 'Westerners'' interpretation of the history of the Second World War or of the decisions reached at Yalta. In the spring of 2005, as the Ukrainian government struggled with the question of whether President Yushchenko should accept Vladimir Putin's invitation to the Moscow celebrations, the Ukrainian media kept its readers informed about the controversies provoked by the VE Day anniversary in Poland and the Baltic states. Polish articles debating the issue were published in translation in Ukrainian newspapers, and statements of the Baltic leaders were liberally quoted in articles by Ukrainian authors. Some of them, such as Viacheslav Anisimov, writing at the end of March in *Dzerkalo tyzhnia*, called upon Yushchenko not to fear displeasing the Kremlin, decline Putin's invitation, and celebrate the anniversary in Ukraine with his own people.[44] After long hesitation, President Yushchenko opted for compromise: he flew to Moscow for a few hours, then rushed back to Kyiv on the same day to commemorate VE Day in the Ukrainian capital.

Prior to the VE Day celebrations in Moscow and Kyiv, public debate in Ukraine centred on the issue of whether the country had fought in the Great Patriotic War of the Soviet people or participated in the Second World War. The first interpretation meant sticking to the old Soviet myth of the war, which treated only Red Army soldiers as legitimate combatants and portrayed the cadres of the Ukrainian Insurgent Army (UPA), who fought both the Soviets and the Nazis in western Ukraine, as German stooges. The second option allowed Ukrainian intellectuals to develop a Eurocentric or Ukrainocentric interpretation of the war, as opposed to a Russocentric one. Within that framework, Ukraine emerges as a country that fought against and was one of the major victims of both totalitarian systems of the twentieth century – fascism and communism.[45] The choice of concept was not only important for the interpretation of history but also had serious political implications for the Ukrainian government and society at large.

At President Yushchenko's initiative, the new Ukrainian government sought to do away with the Soviet-era tradition of commemorating

Victory Day with a formal parade and attempted to use the occasion to encourage reconciliation between Red Army and UPA veterans, who had fought one another during the war. Among other things, such a reconciliation was supposed to help bridge the gap between eastern and western Ukraine that had opened up during the divisive presidential elections of 2004. Like many of the plans of Yushchenko's revolutionary government, the high hopes invested in the VE Day commemorations were disappointed. First, the Soviet Army veterans' organization protested against changing the format of the celebrations. Then the idea of reconciliation was opposed by the communists and their allies in parliament, who protested the extension of government benefits enjoyed by combatants in the 'Great Patriotic War' to UPA fighters. The government, trying to avoid a new conflict between the two veterans' groups and their supporters, decided to abandon the idea of changing the traditional VE Day anniversary celebrations. The communists maintained their control over the Soviet veterans' association and preserved their de facto political monopoly on the commemorations.[46] When on 15 October 2005 UPA supporters tried to celebrate the sixty-third anniversary of the founding of the army with a demonstration in Kyiv, they were physically attacked by communists and supporters of radical pro-Russian groups.[47] Once again, worshippers of 'the great Stalin' intervened to oppose Ukraine's attempt to break with the Soviet past. After the VE Day celebrations Ukraine remained as divided as before in its attitudes toward the Second World War and its outcome.

Conclusions

It has become a cliché to state that all politics are local. It is more controversial to state that all historical debates are parochial or are determined by local (national) agendas, traditions, fears, and complexes. The recent Yalta debate, despite its international scope, seems to support the second proposition as much as the first. Remembering, forgetting, and (re)interpreting the Yalta Conference during the winter and spring of 2005 turned out to be a process fuelled as much by national historiographic traditions as by current perceptions of national interests. Nevertheless, the recent Yalta debate allows one to draw some preliminary conclusions of a more general nature, as it sheds light on the interrelation between historical memory and international politics in a dialogue involving great powers and smaller states dependent on their protection. One such conclusion is that if the victims of Yalta stood united in their negative assessment of the Yalta accords, the victors' assessments of the agreements varied by political camp. It has been said that victors are not judged. The debates of 2005 in the United States and Russia show that they are judged not only by others but also by themselves.

For the East Europeans, the anniversary was a chance to express their indignation about an event that had remained at the core of their historical memory and identity for the last sixty years. They could finally begin the process of healing their historical traumas by presenting a list of grievances to the main perpetrator, Russia, and its Yalta accomplices. It seems quite clear that for most of the Polish and Baltic elites, remembering Yalta was necessary not only to recover historical facts suppressed by the communist regimes but also to ensure international recognition of the trauma suffered by the East European nations after the end of the Second World War. The first of these tasks was achieved immediately before and after the collapse of communism, with the consequent delegitimization of the Russocentric communist historical narrative. It was now time to achieve the second goal. By commemorating Yalta in 2005, the East European elites were once again parting ways with their nations' communist past and dependence on Russia – but they were now doing so on the international scene. As the countries of Eastern Europe were admitted to NATO and the European Union, it became safer for them to air their historical grievances against Moscow in the international arena. As the new Russia's activity in the region increased with the start of the new millennium, while a new generation of East European citizens who had never witnessed communist or Soviet domination of their countries came of age, it also became useful for domestic and international reasons alike to remind the world about the trauma of Yalta. As the East Europeans saw it, the new generation should not forget the lessons of the past, while the West should not repeat the errors of Yalta by allowing Russia a special role in Eastern Europe.

No country in the region was more interested in delivering this message to the world than Ukraine, which had just emerged from the drama of the Orange Revolution, in which it rejected Russian interference in its internal affairs. While the new Ukrainian government would have preferred to side with its Polish and Baltic colleagues in unreservedly condemning the Yalta agreements, it had to beware of the lack of consensus on the significance of the Second World War within its own political elite. Remaining pro-Soviet sentiment in the country's eastern regions, as well as the still influential communist opposition in parliament, drastically limited the new government's options with regard to public remembrance of the end of the Second World War. The Ukrainian public debate on the legacy of the Yalta Conference was influenced not only by political dynamics after the Orange Revolution but also by international considerations. None was more important than the issue of Ukraine's borders. While sharing the criticism of Yalta expressed by its western neighbours, the Ukrainian intellectual elites could not fully condemn the conference that had made their country a founder of the United Nations and provided international legitimacy for its western borders. Thus in the Ukrainian media the border question was discussed in the context of the Molotov-Ribbentrop Pact but not in that of the Yalta agreements. The sensitivity of the border issue helps explain Ukraine's reluctance to take advantage of the anniversary to raise its international profile: at Yalta the Big Three had made not only Poland but also Ukraine complicit in Stalin's division of Europe. As a result of the Yalta decisions, Ukraine obtained lands that did not belong to it before the war, although they were largely settled by ethnic Ukrainians. A new nation that could be considered both a beneficiary and a victim of Yalta, Ukraine, as represented by its government, preferred to 'forget' so important an event in its history as the Yalta Conference.

What about the other beneficiaries of Yalta? No country seems more entrapped by the Yalta decisions and the legacy of Stalinism than the Russian Federation. Faced with actual and potential claims against its Yalta booty and post-Yalta policies on the part of Germany, Japan, Poland, and the Baltic states, the Russian leadership is as far today as it has ever been from issuing a public apology for the 'crimes of Yalta.' Russian imperial pride is one reason why President Bush's invitation to President Putin to apologize for the wrongs done to Russia's neighbours has elicited no positive response and will not do so in the immediate future. For the Russian elites, Yalta remains a symbol of their country's glory, reminding them of Moscow's former status as the capital of a superpower rivalled only by the United States. The nostalgic communists continue to see the Yalta decisions as proof of the triumph of communism and the greatness of the communist dictator Joseph Stalin. Only the liberals, now weak and marginalized – an echo of the once powerful popular movement of the Gorbachev and early Yeltsin years – remain critical of both the Stalinist legacy and Russia's continuing imperial ambitions.

All Russian political forces, from nationalists to liberals, approached the Yalta and VE Day anniversaries with their own hopes and political agendas. The ruling elites wanted to raise and embellish Russia's international image by reminding the world of its leading role in defeating fascism. The Russian conservatives complained about the post-Cold War world, rife with unpredictability and danger now that it was no longer held in check by Yalta-type agreements. In the eyes of Russian diplomats, the solution to the world's new insecurities was quite simple: it would suffice to recognize the territories of the former Soviet Union as a zone of Russian responsibility. Russian liberals expected the collapse of the unjust Yalta arrangements to lead to the complete elimination of the Iron Curtain and make Russia a full member of the club of European nations. None of these scenarios materialized, and the negative reaction to the Moscow celebrations in East Central Europe dashed the hopes of Russian conservatives and liberals alike. This failure should not obscure the general trend in the evolution of Russian collective memory since the collapse of the USSR. As the loss of empire becomes more obvious to the Russian elites and society at large, and former clients adopt more independent policies towards Moscow, official Russia becomes less inclined to issue apologies for crimes and injustices perpetrated against the empire's former subjects. On the contrary, it becomes more aggressive both in the interpretation of its historical role in the region and in the pursuit of its current policies there.

Only the United States rose to the occasion when in the words of its president it condemned the Yalta agreements, placing them in the same category as the Munich appeasement and the Molotov-Ribbentrop Pact. Unlike Russia, the United States is prepared to admit its historical error for the sake of building better relations with the countries of the region. President Bush's remarks about Yalta are an interesting case of the use and abuse of history on the international scene. There is little doubt that they were not intended mainly for a domestic audience. Bush appears to have had at least two goals in mind. The first was to support the countries of the new Europe that showed loyalty to the United States and embarrass President Putin, who was in no psychological, political, or economic position to afford a similar admission of guilt. The second was to legitimize his war in Iraq and his policy in the Middle East by pledging never again to abandon support for freedom and democracy – the latter being the major theme of his discourse on Iraq. The president's use of the Yalta anniversary to recognize America's past errors, while promoting his new international agenda, did not sit well with critics of his administration in the United States. Enraged by the comparison of the Yalta agreements to the Molotov-Ribbentrop Pact (a mere recognition that, in the Baltic states at least, the Yalta decisions ratified the borders established by the Stalin-Hitler agreement of 1939), the Democrats rose instinctively to the defence of Franklin Delano Roosevelt, the Democratic president revered even by Ronald Reagan. The Yalta debate in the United States itself demonstrated once again the predominance of the national over the international perspective in the collective memory of the world's only remaining superpower.

Nevertheless, it would appear that the United States is winning not only the geopolitical competition with Russia in its East European backyard but also the historical debate. The ideas of freedom and democracy, which lie at the core of the master narrative of American history, are well suited to the requirements of past and present American policy in the region and find support and understanding on the part of the East European 'losers' of Yalta. As the tone of the Yalta debate in Poland demonstrates, the ideas of liberty and independence remain central elements of the Polish historical narrative and national self-image. They coexist with the tradition of depicting Poland as a quintessential victim of Russia and other world powers from the partitions of the Polish-Lithuanian Commonwealth in the second half of the eighteenth century to the end of the twentieth. In the East European countries discussed in this chapter, only the Ukrainian elite ended up sitting on the fence, in complete accordance with a popular historiographic paradigm of Ukraine as a country positioned on the civilizational divide between East and West, democracy and authoritarianism.

In the case of Russia, its historical narrative lost its universal appeal with the collapse of communism. It is no longer possible to justify the Soviet takeover of Eastern Europe either by the interests of world communism or by those of the toiling masses of the East European countries. The Pan-Slavic idea, employed by Stalin during and immediately after the Second World War, has also lost its appeal. The idea of Russia's great-power status, which works at home, can only frighten the western neighbours of the new Russia. Thus, as was the case during the Yalta Conference, Moscow sought in 2005 to find common ground with the West and its former republics and dependencies by appealing to Russia's role in the struggle against Nazi Germany and the liberation of Eastern Europe from fascist rule. While the anti-Hitler theme clearly worked and apparently has a future, the 'liberation' motif clearly backfired, since it opened Russia to attack by all those who were enslaved by communism after having been liberated from fascism. The only way for Russia to change the dynamic of the historical debate would have been to offer sincere apologies to the victims of the Yalta agreements. Moscow had missed one more chance to improve its image abroad and its relations with its western neighbours.

PART FOUR

The Search for a New History

13 The History of a Non-Historical Nation

Mark von Hagen's essay 'Does Ukraine Have a History?' (1995) initiated a new discussion of Ukrainian history in the pages of the *Slavic Review.* A previous discussion appeared in the *Slavic Review* in 1965 with the participation of Omeljan Pritsak, John S. Reshetar, Jr., and Ivan L. Rudnytsky. All of them, according to von Hagen's definition, were 'professional ethnics,' and the discussion concerned the implications of Ukraine's position between East and West and the problem of continuity in Ukrainian history.[1]

Much has changed in the three decades between 1965 and 1995. Probably the most important change is the emergence of a Ukrainian state and the consequent disappearance of the article 'the' in references to Ukraine (this change becomes obvious when one compares the title of von Hagen's essay with those of Pritsak, Reshetar, and Rudnytsky). Another sign of change is evidenced by the fact that the 1995 discussion of Ukrainian history was initiated not by an 'ethnic' but by a non-Ukrainian historian – a clear indication that Ukrainian studies are emerging from the 'ethnic' ghetto. One more sign of change was the participation of scholars from Ukraine in the discussion.

So much for the good news about Ukrainian history. The title of von Hagen's essay (if not the essay itself) forthrightly challenges the very fact of the existence of a Ukrainian history. This is a clear setback from the previous discussion on the pages of the *Slavic Review,* as well as an ironic turn of events. While the 'professional ethnics,' long disappointed by the unattractiveness of their field to 'non-ethnics,' finally achieved what they wanted, the long-awaited 'Varangians' questioned the very existence of the field almost immediately upon their 'arrival.' Von Hagen begins his essay with the statement that Ukraine certainly has a past, but he questions whether it has a history, which he understands as 'a written record ... that commands some widespread acceptance and authority in the international scholarly and political communities'[2] – an outrageously 'orientalist' approach to the problem.

History as National Myth

Ukraine belongs to the so-called non-historical nations of Eastern Europe, whose nationalism and nation-states (arguably more than those of the West European countries) can be regarded as direct products of a highly elaborated historical myth. Hans Kohn, the founding father of the contemporary study of nationalism, believed that nationalism in the West arose in an effort to build a nation in the political reality and struggles of the present without too much sentimental regard for the past: out of the myths of the past and dreams of the future, nationalists in Central and Eastern Europe often created an ideal fatherland closely linked with the past, devoid of any immediate connection with the present, and expected to become a political reality at some time in the future.[3] Kohn's differentiation between East and West, based on the role of historical mythology in the nation-building process, has since been criticized as unsubstantiated, given that historical mythology was no less important to the rise of national movements in Western and Central Europe than in Eastern Europe. It would be wrong, however, to deny the outstanding role played by history and historians in the legitimization of East European nation-building projects. One may consider it an irony of history that historians, more than representatives of any other profession, were the 'founding fathers' of the 'non-historical' nations of Eastern Europe. Some of them headed national revolutions in the region and even became leaders of the newly established states. As for the role that history and historians played in the formation of East European nations, Ukraine was no exception.

Mykhailo Hrushevsky, a renowned Ukrainian historian and the author of the Ukrainian historical myth, was elected the first head of an independent Ukrainian state in 1918. His ten-volume *History of Ukraine-Rus'* was published between 1898 and 1936, and his main achievement as a historian was that he managed to fill the numerous gaps in the Ukrainian past, transforming Ukraine from a young, emerging nation without a history of its own into a historical nation. Hrushevsky claimed the Kyivan heritage for Ukraine alone and connected the Kyivan period of Ukrainian history to the Cossack period: he presented the Halych-Volhynian Principality, not that of Vladimir-Suzdal (as generally accepted in Russian historiography), as the sole legitimate heir of Kyivan Rus'. Although Hrushevsky's effort was considered revolutionary by his contemporaries, his thesis was not absolutely new. He merely followed the Halych-Volhynian chronicles, as opposed to the Muscovite chronicles that Russian historians followed.[4]

During Hrushevsky's tenure as head of the Ukrainian government, the trident, an emblem of the Kyivan princes, was adopted as the emblem of the newly emerged state. Now it serves as the official symbol of independent Ukraine. The anthem that was adopted by the Ukrainian state under Hrushevsky and now serves as the national anthem of Ukraine also contains direct references to Ukrainian history, particularly of the Cossack era. Its title, 'Ukraine Is Not Yet Dead,' echoes the title of the Polish national anthem, 'Poland Is Not Yet Dead.' Apart from evident Polish influences, the title of the Ukrainian anthem reflects the belief of Ukrainians in their own 'historical' past. That past is reflected in numerous Ukrainian songs, poems, and prayers. 'Bring back the freedom, bring back the glory to our Ukraine,' goes one of the prayers that can be heard today in Ukrainian churches all over the world.

This historical mythology, which could not exist without a highly developed interest in history and at least a partially developed historiography, contributed immensely to the emergence of an independent Ukraine in 1991. The victory of the pro-independence forces in the December 1991 Ukrainian referendum, which put an end to the existence of the Soviet Union, came about as a result of the victory of two principal myths. The first was historical: that of Ukraine as an old nation with a glorious past that was deprived of its statehood by tsars and commissars. The second myth was that of the economic greatness of Ukraine as the 'breadbasket of Europe' and as an industrial colossus.

It is quite interesting (and in many ways characteristic of Ukrainian nationalism of the early 1990s) that none of the components of the historical myth contributing to the outcome of the 1991 independence referendum was anti-Russian (or anti-Jewish, anti-Polish, etc.). The highly developed Cossack mythology that was successfully revived in the pre-independence years had all the characteristics of an inclusive myth that allowed not only Ukrainians but also millions of Russians, many of whom have mixed ancestry, to associate themselves with the mythologized Cossack past. Numerous writings on the man-made famine of 1933 in eastern Ukraine, along with commemorations of the Chornobyl nuclear disaster of 1986, have portrayed Ukraine as the principal victim of the communist system. Sporadic attempts to present that system and its crimes against Ukraine as the product of a Russian or Jewish anti-Ukrainian plot were effectively overshadowed by the inclusiveness of the historical myths of both the famine and Chornobyl, in which all citizens of Ukraine, whatever their national, social, or political affiliation, were viewed as innocent victims of the Soviet system.

Once independence was achieved, the integrity and inclusive character of Ukrainian historical mythology was severely challenged. The pre-independence Cossack and famine mythologies exhausted themselves in the face of the crumbling of the economic-greatness myth and deteriorating standards of living. Nationalistic, exclusive myths like that of the Ukrainian Insurgent Army, which fought both Nazis and Soviets during the Second World War, though vigorously accepted in western Ukraine, were violently rejected in the east. During his last months in power, the first president of Ukraine, Leonid Kravchuk, and later his successor, Leonid Kuchma, tried to reintroduce a modified version of the Second World War myth into the all-Ukrainian historical consciousness and launched a campaign to celebrate the fiftieth anniversary of Ukraine's liberation from Nazi occupation. But these initiatives were openly rejected in western Ukraine, owing to the simple fact that liberation from the Nazis meant reoccupation by the Soviets.

Reintegrating the Past

Mark von Hagen was certainly correct when he wrote that Ukraine needs a new history – and, one might add, a new historical myth. Throughout the nineteenth century, the period of the formation and growth of Ukrainian nationalism, the Ukrainian lands were divided between two major European powers, the Russian and Austro-Hungarian Empires. The ideas of the nationalist movement were formulated mainly in Russian (Eastern) Ukraine and later adopted with only minor modifications by Galicians and Bukovynians in Austria-Hungary. It was another of Mykhailo Hrushevsky's major tasks to write the history of Ukraine in such a way as to offer a sense of common heritage to Ukrainian subjects of two empires who had been separated culturally, politically, and economically for centuries. Hrushevsky, a populist, accomplished that task by choosing as his subject of study the people and their ethnic territory instead of the state and by stressing on every possible occasion the elements of unity between the different parts of Ukraine. This approach to Ukrainian history has been adopted by most historians in post-Soviet Ukraine.

What has been problematic about Hrushevsky's concept is the application of its ethnocentric paradigm to the history of the entire territory claimed by the independent Ukrainian state. By 1991, when Ukraine became independent, the territory that Hrushevsky discussed in his works was settled by millions of non-Ukrainians as well as Ukrainians. Moreover, urbanization, combined with powerful successive waves of Russian colonization, had brought about the linguistic and cultural Russification of millions of Ukrainians in central, southern, and eastern Ukraine. There can be little doubt that independent Ukraine, largely the product of one historical myth, needed a new myth to make its way forward after 1991. The scheme of Ukrainian history that seems to be finding more and more acceptance in Ukraine is one that accepts the basics of the Hrushevsky approach to pre-Soviet Ukrainian history and then shifts to the study of the history of the Ukrainian Soviet Socialist Republic ('the second Soviet republic,' as Yaroslav Bilinsky called it). The Ukrainian SSR is viewed both historically and legally as the predecessor of the independent Ukrainian state. Within its post-Second World War boundaries it united the majority of the Ukrainian lands as defined by Hrushevsky, as well as some non-Ukrainian territories in the south and west.

What has become a problem for historians and society at large is the treatment of the history of the Ukrainian Revolution (1917–20) and, even more so, of the Second World War, when Ukraine was sharply divided, with pro-Russian communists fighting pro-independence members of Ukrainian nationalist organizations. With the reemergence of independent Ukraine, the latter have apparently won, but the majority of the population who voted for independence clearly associate themselves not with the nationalist movement or the independent Ukrainian governments of 1917–20 but with the heritage of Soviet Ukraine. Integrating these two stories told by opposing sides into one 'written record' has proved a difficult task.

History and Historians in Ukraine

The historical profession encountered numerous problems in post-Soviet Ukraine. On the positive side of the change, one could list the end of Soviet-imposed restrictions on the use of the works of Ukrainian prerevolutionary, western Ukrainian, and émigré historians; open access to formerly closed archival materials; and the fact that state support for national historiography, so desperately needed in the past, has finally been granted. The end of communism also meant the end of the

Iron Curtain and the appearance of new opportunities to become acquainted with Western colleagues and Western methodological approaches. These were positive changes, but their effect was diminished by negative factors influencing the state of historical scholarship in post-Soviet Ukraine. One of these factors, pointed out by Von Hagen, was the impact of the recent past, including the dogmatism, provincialism, and methodological backwardness of Soviet Ukrainian historiography. One should also note the severe economic crisis that was driving the younger generation of historians, especially those with a knowledge of foreign languages, out of the field. Since the average salary of a history professor in the early 1990s did not exceed $50 U.S. per month, even a trip to the libraries of Kyiv or Lviv (not to speak of those of Moscow, Warsaw, or St Petersburg) was a major financial problem. To the continuing lack of access to Western books was added lack of access to the scholarly publications of Russia and other former Soviet republics, owing to the complete collapse of the book-trade network. That network collapsed in Ukraine as well. In order to obtain a book published in Lviv, one had to go to Lviv; to obtain one published in Dnipropetrovsk, one had to go to Dnipropetrovsk, etc.

Another piece of bad news for Ukrainian historians was the ongoing decline of the social status of their profession. For generations, historians were viewed in Ukraine as important cultural and political figures, no matter what side they took, communist or nationalist. For the nationally oriented intelligentsia, historians were considered bearers of genuine national values and possessors of the truth about the history of a nation that had been deprived of its political state and natural rights. With the establishment of an independent Ukraine and the emergence of opportunities for any citizen to demonstrate his patriotism if he felt so inclined, the previous political significance and social status of historians were drastically reduced.

Major changes in the status of the profession have been caused by the collapse of the Communist Party and the subsequent movement towards a democratic society and market-oriented economy. The huge complement of historians of the Soviet Communist Party has become in many ways the principal victim of that change. They served as interpreters of 'ever living' Marxist-Leninist teachings and were charged with the task of legitimizing the otherwise illegitimate rule of the Communist Party. Historical education was considered political in the USSR; the historian was expected to be a member of the Communist Party and, if a schoolteacher, he or she was a prime candidate for the post of school principal. Once the ideological society was gone and the bankrupt state found itself without money to support schools and universities, the prestige of the profession drastically decreased.

If in the 1970s and 1980s there were five to seven people competing in the entrance exams for every position, by the 1990s the number had decreased to one or two per position. The low salaries of schoolteachers and university professors have made the profession more and more one for women, while men compete for better-paying jobs. In many ways, these problems of the historical profession resembled the general problems of science and scholarship in Ukraine and the rest of the former Soviet Union. Eventually the historical profession found its place in new societies' 'Tables of Ranks,' but this took time and a great deal of pain. The peculiarities of that process in the post-Soviet republics had a profound impact on historians and the kind of history they write today.

Ukrainian History in North America

Although the general situation of the Ukrainian historical profession in the West, especially in North America, was different from that in Ukraine, the fall of Soviet communism deeply affected it as well. With the collapse of the USSR and the disappearance of the immediate Soviet military threat, the whole field of Soviet studies, of which Ukrainian history was a part, has disintegrated.

In his essay Von Hagen writes about the two competing imperial views on the history of Eastern Europe, the German and the Russian. Although that approach was probably correct for Eastern Europe as a whole, in the case of Ukraine it was Russian and Polish historiography that dominated the scene. And in North America only Russian historiography had the opportunity to present its view of the Ukrainian past. The views of Russian émigré historians were shared for decades by the American scholarly community, and it took the entire lifetime of a generation of Ukrainian 'professional ethnic' scholars, as well as the emergence of an independent Ukrainian state, to challenge those beliefs.

Ironically, the rise of an independent Ukraine also brought a major negative change in the status of 'ethnic' Ukrainian historians in their diaspora communities in the United States and Canada. If before independence they enjoyed the high prestige and full support of the communities that funded Ukrainian studies chairs in North American universities, including the most prestigious ones, after the achievement of independence historians found themselves effectively overshadowed by other diaspora professionals. With the rise of new political and economic opportunities in Ukraine, it was not the historian Omeljan Pritsak, the founder of Ukrainian studies at Harvard, but the economist Bohdan Hawrylyshyn, an acquaintance of George Soros and advisor to the Ukrainian government, who came to be considered a hero of the diaspora community. This list of negative changes in the status of 'ethnic' historians within their community could be extended. There is little doubt that the emergence of an independent Ukraine attracted the attention of the Western political and scholarly community more than ever before to the field of Ukrainian studies, but the status that this specialty enjoyed as part of the huge government-supported Sovietology establishment was gone forever. During the USSR's last years of existence the Ukrainian question was considered vital for the life or death of the Soviet empire. In the mid-1980s Alexander Motyl of Columbia University wrote an entire book, *Will the Non-Russians Rebel?* exclusively on the basis of Ukrainian material. His major assumption was that the USSR would survive if the Ukrainians did not rebel. Indeed, the USSR did not survive the 1991 Ukrainian referendum, but the collapse of the USSR meant the end of Sovietology as a discipline and of the special place of Ukrainian studies in that field.

Once Ukraine freed itself in the mid-1990s of the third-largest nuclear arsenal in the world, it became one of a number of Eastern European countries located between Russia and Germany. Von Hagen tends to explain the absence of separate fields of study devoted to the 'non-historical' nations of Eastern Europe by the fact that, at the beginning of the nineteenth century – the formative years of European historiography – those nations did not exist on the political map of Europe. One can counter this suggestion with the argument that Sweden, along with other countries of northern Europe, existed on the map at that time, but Swedish history has not become established as a discipline in North American universities. What counts in this respect, apart from historiographic tradition, is the economic and political importance of a given nation for the rest of the world. Just as the history of Finland is studied as part of northern European history, so the history of Ukraine is on its way to occupying a place of its own among the histories of the Eastern European lands. Although chairs of East European history do exist in major North American universities, in most of them there is a growing tendency to replace the history of the former Soviet bloc with the history of Russia and Eastern Europe. In such courses, a place should be reserved for the history of Ukraine. Given the disappearance of the Soviet threat and the new tendencies in American foreign policy, it is doubtful that any new chairs of Ukrainian history will be established in the West, except those endowed by Ukrainians.

Von Hagen concludes his essay with the remark that 'Ukrainian history can serve as a wonderful vehicle to challenge the national state's conceptual hegemony and to explore some of the most contested issues of identity formation.' This statement would seem to deserve agreement, with only one caveat. Not only Ukrainian history but also Ukraine's present *will* be such a 'wonderful vehicle' if the experiment that is now going on within the boundaries of Ukraine – the creation of a non-ethnic state surrounded by 'normal' ethnically based nation-states of Eastern Europe – *actually* succeeds.

14 Imagining Early Modern Ukraine

It would appear that present-day Ukrainian historiography remains a battleground between different political and scholarly agendas and approaches.[1] In the 1990s, communist historiography in Ukraine (unlike in Belarus) withdrew from the battlefield without accepting actual battle. The immediate victor was the national paradigm, whose most important elements were either reimported into Ukraine from the West (mostly through reprints of the works of diaspora historians) or rediscovered in the writings of Ukrainian authors of the interwar period, many of whom subscribed to the statist paradigm of Ukrainian history. One of the outcomes of such swift victory was that while Soviet-era ideas yielded without major resistance to the set of political and cultural postulates associated with the national paradigm, the actual bearers of the old ideas never left the historiographic field. They merely changed their colours (from red to blue and yellow) and replaced Marx and Lenin with Mykhailo Hrushevsky and Viacheslav Lypynsky as their new classics.

Today, after more than a decade of positioning and repositioning themselves on the battlefield, the practitioners of the historical profession in Ukraine have split into four major groups. Most of them carry the banner of the national paradigm, which they constantly adjust and readjust to meet the demands of the changing political environment. Thus they slowly shifted from the promotion of Ukrainian state- and nation-building in the 1990s to the commemoration of the Pereiaslav Agreement with Muscovy (1654) in the early 2000s. A second, relatively small group of Soviet-era historians who remained active in the field protested the 'excessive' nationalization of the Ukrainian historical narrative or tried to promote ideas of East Slavic commonality and unity. A third, much larger group criticized the professional establishment from the viewpoint of Ukrainian statist historiography of the interwar period. The 1990s also saw the emergence in Ukraine of a fourth, small but very prominent group of practitioners – especially influential among the younger generation of historians – who rejected not only Soviet-era postulates but also the dogmatism with which the national paradigm was accepted and applied by many historians of the Soviet school. They promote an ethos of professionalism, dissociate themselves from the servility towards the state characteristic of the historiographic mainstream, and turn to the West (in the broad sense of the term, also including Poland) in search of new methods and approaches to historical research.[2]

Natalia Yakovenko emerged as one of the leaders of the latter group,[3] and she had no peer among nonconformists in the profession who study early modern Ukrainian history – the 'golden age' of the Ukrainian national narrative and a highly competitive field in which the majority of Ukraine's most famous historians made their names. She came as close to playing the role of public intellectual as any of her professional colleagues in present-day Ukraine. Yakovenko emerged on the Ukrainian historiographic scene in the early 1990s after years of relative obscurity, when she was largely involved in archival work and the publication of documentary sources. Her first monograph, *The Ukrainian Nobility from the Late Fourteenth to the Mid-Seventeenth Century (Volhynia and Central Ukraine)* (1993), impressed the Ukrainian reader with the novelty of its subject, focusing as it did on the nobiliary elite as opposed to those Soviet-era favourites, peasants and burghers, or the Cossack heroes of the national narrative.[4] It also demonstrated the author's deep knowledge of the sources (Yakovenko began as a student of classical philology and, in addition to researching Latin sources on Ukrainian history, she has co-authored a Latin textbook). The book also indicated that its author was at home in the vast, mostly pre- or non-Soviet, literature on the subject. By concentrating on the history of elites, Yakovenko positioned herself as a continuator of the tradition established in Ukrainian historiography by Viacheslav Lypynsky. In her next major work, *An Outline History of Ukraine: From Ancient Times to the End of the Eighteenth Century* (1997),[5] Yakovenko declared her desire to go beyond not only the populist paradigm, which she associated with the name of Mykhailo Hrushevsky, but also the 'statist' one, closely associated with Lypynsky. As Yakovenko wrote in her introduction to the book, she proposed to focus on the individual and the way in which he/she functioned in society. Her ultimate goal was to free Ukrainian history from old stereotypes and purge the 'virus' of modern agendas from the historian's interpretation of the past. She also expressed interest in examining stereotypes of human behaviour and the mechanisms of their change, attitudes towards the 'other,' and the ways in which individuals perceived power and viewed their moral duties and obligations. It was difficult to accomplish all these tasks in a historical survey covering more than eight hundred years, especially given that there was very little to synthesize when it came to studies of medieval and early modern Ukrainian mentality, the history of stereotypes, or even intellectual history. Substantial groundwork had to be done first. Hence the publication of *The Parallel World* (2002) – another contribution of this prolific author to the field of early modern Ukrainian history.[6]

Natalia Yakovenko considers this book a continuation of the research undertaken in her monograph on the Ukrainian nobility. In it she moves on from examining the hard data on the history of the nobility as a social stratum to studying the elusive world of its mental stereotypes, perceptions, opinions, and ideological paradigms. Most of *The Parallel World* deals with the nobility in the broad sense of the term, from princes and magnates to petty nobles, including the Cossacks (with their 'knightly' discourse, self-identification, and ethos), who aspired to gentry status. Certainly this collection of essays represents a return to Yakovenko's established subject at a new stage of her career in which she has developed different historiographic interests. The book could not have appeared or, more precisely, would have differed in character, were it not for Yakovenko's earlier work on the *Outline History* and her many years of co-editing (with Oleksii Tolochko and Lesia Dovha) the pioneering journal *Mediaevalia Ucrainica*. Despite its title, the journal was devoted mainly to early modern Ukraine and focused on the history of mental stereotypes and ideas.

What are the 'hard facts' about Yakovenko's new book? First of all, it was attractively produced by the Krytyka publishing house in Kyiv and won a number of prestigious publishers' awards in Ukraine in 2002. *The Parallel World* consists of eleven essays, most of them issued earlier but revised for the 2002 publication. Nine of these essays deal with Ukrainian history of the early modern period (from the second half of the sixteenth century to the mid-seventeenth), while the remaining two discuss the interpretation of some aspects of that period in twentieth-century Ukrainian historiography. In explaining the structure of her book, whose constituent essays differ widely in individual focus and scope, Yakovenko draws on the arsenal of postmodern historiography. She claims, for example, that the nature of the subject under investigation (things 'subjective, personal, and latent in the individual') precludes systematic description, which would only amount to oversimplification. The same applies, in her opinion, to the nature of the sources under study, which, as she puts it, are neither 'systemic' nor connected with one another.

Yakovenko certainly does not go so far as to proclaim the death of narrative. The object of her challenge is what she calls 'national history,' meaning the national paradigm of Ukrainian history. There can be little doubt, however, that Yakovenko challenges certain elements of the national paradigm from within 'the system,' remaining faithful to the idea of Ukrainian history as such. Indeed, her book concentrates so exclusively on Ukraine that the other component of the early modern 'Ruthenian nation,' Belarus, is all but absent – this despite the fact that one can hardly separate early modern Belarus from Ukraine of the same period, especially when it comes to the history of ideas and perceptions. If it is not the national narrative of Ukrainian history that Yakovenko rejects when she speaks of 'national history,' what is it? It is safe to assume that what she really wants to do is to cleanse Ukrainian historiography of its old myths and stereotypes, update its methodological repertoire, and place Ukrainian history into a broader historiographic context. Given the period under consideration, that broader context consists of the intellectual trends and social and cultural identities of the Polish-Lithuanian Commonwealth, which encompassed most of the Ukrainian lands until the late eighteenth century.

The trouble with updating the methodological repertoire of national history at the beginning of the third millennium is that the latest and trendiest revisionist approaches were constructed in the West in opposition to or in defiance of national history and the methods used to narrate it. Adopting them for the purpose of renewing a national narrative presents a challenge and creates a tension that is often felt in Yakovenko's book. Declaring her method to be that of historical and anthropological research, Yakovenko lists a number of questions that informed her writing, among them the motivations of social behaviour, the hierarchy of values, and the structure of cultural meanings. To deal with these questions, Yakovenko marshals an impressive array of sources, much more varied in character than those used by her predecessors. Most of her narrative sources come from outside the canon of Ukrainian 'polemical literature' of the sixteenth and seventeenth centuries and are written more often in Polish and Latin than in the literary Ruthenian of the time. Bringing into her discussion sources written not only in non-Ruthenian languages but also by non-Ruthenians makes Yakovenko's vision fresh and provocative. That is certainly true of her interpretation of Polish and Latin panegyrics, largely ignored by Ukrainian and, to some degree, also by Polish students of early modern literature. She also exploits diaries and correspondence to the fullest as sources of information, without limiting her discussion to an analysis of the discourse created by those narratives. Her intimate knowledge of archival sources, especially the court materials of Volhynia and the Kyiv region, shields her very reliably against the temptation to treat the literary discourse of that day as a direct reflection of actual social practices and behaviours.

As one would expect, Yakovenko's generally critical attitude towards the paradigm of 'national history,' her use of new sources and careful rereading of old ones results in the slaughter of quite a few sacred cows of the Ukrainian national narrative and in the presentation of a fragmented but also new and credible image of early modern Ukraine as seen through the eyes of its nobiliary elite. One of those sacred cows is the image of the Poles and Polish culture as the ultimate 'other' of early modern Ukrainian culture and identity. By situating the Ukrainian nobility's political, social, and cultural ideas and values in the broader context of the political and cultural perceptions and practices of the Polish-Lithuanian Commonwealth, Yakovenko makes it possible to provide new explanations of a number of important phenomena of Ukrainian social and cultural life of the period. Those phenomena were defined by the political beliefs and conventions of pedagogical practice and the warrior ethos shared by all the noble elites of the Commonwealth irrespective of their religious and national traditions. This new approach certainly does not sit well with supporters of the traditional version of the Ukrainian historical narrative (built from its very inception on the 'othering' of the Poles), which degenerated in Soviet times into the depiction of the Polish nobility as the ultimate colonizer of Ukraine and exploiter of the Ukrainian popular masses.

The methods of 'othering,' if not actually demonizing, the Polish nobility and its state in twentieth-century Ukrainian history textbooks are discussed in the last essay of the collection, entitled 'Poland and Poles in History Schoolbooks.' On the one hand, Yakovenko registers certain improvements in the treatment of Poland and the Poles in post-1991

Ukrainian historical surveys. These include a fairly objective assessment of the historical significance of the Union of Lublin between the Kingdom of Poland and the Grand Duchy of Lithuania (1569), the inclusion of Polish-language literature written by Ukrainians or on Ukrainian territory in the discussion, the presentation of historical Poland as a cultural 'bridge' between Ukraine and the West, and the reevaluation of the role of the church union in Ukrainian history. On the other hand, she points to the survival in textbooks of many anti-Polish stereotypes derived from Soviet and old Ukrainian historiography. One of them is the presentation of the Poles as an occupying force in Ukraine and of Poland as a state that consciously conducted a policy of subjugating and denationalizing Ukrainians. Another 'hiccup' of the previous approach is the treatment of early modern Poland and Ukraine as two absolutely separate entities whose relations consisted entirely of mutual animosity and perpetual conflict.

Why is it wrong to treat Poland as imperial power in the region and Polish policy in early modern Ukraine as colonial?[7] Yakovenko believes that this anachronistic approach does not fit the historical reality 'on the ground.' She shows very convincingly how the stereotypes of Soviet historiography survive in post-Soviet textbooks, pointing out the Soviet-style depiction of the Jewish massacres during the Koliivshchyna Uprising (1768) as a war against leaseholders and tavernkeepers (368). Yakovenko is also highly effective in uncovering the roots of the demonizing of Poland and Poles in the Ukrainian national narrative of the nineteenth century. Her main argument appears sound and well presented. In essence, she argues that the two early modern peoples, the Poles and the Ukrainians/Ruthenians, had quite a few features in common. After decades of coexistence in a single state, the Polish and Ruthenian elites shared a common educational background and political culture; they also subscribed to the same 'knightly' ethos. Moreover, they often dealt with similar problems, cooperated in the defence of the steppe frontier against Tatar incursions, and adhered to common social forms in town and country. Still, adopting an overtly polemical tone from time to time, Yakovenko herself does not avoid occasional oversimplification. She implies, for example, that Hrushevsky's focus on ethnos and territory in Ukrainian history led to the treatment of all non-Ukrainian elements on that territory as aggressors (369), and she claims without further explanation or qualification that at the time of the Khmelnytsky Uprising, the term 'Pole' was used not as an ethnonym but as a political designation (373).

Despite her offhand remark that 'Poles' in mid-seventeenth-century Ukraine meant 'nobles,' irrespective of ethnic background, while Polish identity was not ascribed to Polish commoners, Yakovenko is careful not to throw her support behind the belief, popular in present-day Polish historiography and often accepted in the West, in the existence of one Polish civic nation that allegedly crossed ethnocultural boundaries and amalgamated the Polish, Lithuanian, and Ruthenian (Ukrainian-Belarusian) nobility.[8] For Yakovenko, however close the Ukrainian nobility was or could have been in political culture and practices to the Polish nobility, it remained Ukrainian (not even Ruthenian), and as such constitutes the subject of her research. In general, Yakovenko demonstrates exemplary knowledge of the Polish historiography of the subject. It is here that she feels historiographically at home, and it is Polish historiography that often serves as her window on the West. It is also from Polish historical works that she borrows some of the ideas and approaches that irritate her critics in Ukraine.[9] Her work shows how much Ukrainian historians could benefit from working together with, not in opposition to, their colleagues in Ukraine's 'near West.' As for Western scholarship, Yakovenko's research demonstrates how much more productive and accurate results can be obtained by comparing Ukrainian political and cultural realities with those of early modern Poland and Lithuania rather than with Western Europe of the period.

It would be hard to find a better example of interaction between Polish and Ukrainian historical and political ideas in early modern times than the panegyrics devoted to Ukrainian princely families and analysed in Yakovenko's essay 'The Topos of "United Peoples" in Panegyrics to the Princes Ostrozky and Zaslavsky (At the Sources of Ukrainian Identity).' The closely related princely families of the Ostrozkys and Zaslavskys (the latter took over the possessions of the former once the Ostrozkys' male line died out) began their 'public career' in the mid-sixteenth century as pillars of Orthodoxy but converted to Roman Catholicism in the course of the seventeenth century. As Yakovenko shows, conversion did not change their role as protectors of the interests and privileges, including religious rights, of the Ukrainian Orthodox nobility. Nor did it change the princes' image of themselves as heirs of the Rurikid dynasty of Kyivan Rus' and as leaders of the Rus' community in general. How do we know that? Partly on the basis of ideas presented in panegyrics written in honour of the Ostrozkys and Zaslavskys in the late sixteenth and early seventeenth centuries. Of all the panegyrics analysed by Yakovenko, only six were written by Ruthenian authors, while thirty-nine were the work of Poles, most of whom were clients or servants of the princely families. By tracing the genealogy of the Ruthenian princes back to legendary times, those authors also tried to associate their family stories with Polish founding myths. On the other hand, it was the same non-Orthodox and non-Ruthenian authors who tried to please their masters by articulating the latter's Rus' identity in writing. These same Polish panegyrists created for their patrons the virtual space of Rus' – a territory rooted in the historical tradition of the thirteenth-century Galician-Volhynian state of Danylo of Halych and encompassing the Ukrainian lands annexed to the Kingdom of Poland.

It is in these writings of the Polish-educated and non-Orthodox panegyrists of culturally Polonized Rus' princes that Yakovenko finds the early modern origins of Ukrainian identity. Despite the somewhat paradoxical nature of her argument, it makes a good deal of sense. No social group in Ukraine came closer than the princes to imagining their homeland within boundaries approximating the ethnic Ukrainian territories of the time. The Orthodox literati, by contrast, were promoting the concept of the unity of the Ukrainian-Belarusian Orthodox population throughout the Commonwealth (including the Grand Duchy of Lithuania), while in the 1640s the nobility, if one judges by the statements of its leader, Adam Kysil, was insisting on the commonality of four eastern palatinates of the Kingdom of Poland, with the notable exception of Galicia.[10] The princes, on the other hand, could not imagine their Rus' without Galicia, for the medieval state of Danylo of Halych was the only link they could establish between themselves and the Rurikid glory of Kyivan times.

A historian operating within the parameters of the traditional Ukrainian narrative could hardly imagine these Polonized princes, to say nothing of their Polish panegyrists, as early promoters of proto-Ukrainian identity. Yakovenko tackles another important mythologem of that narrative head-on in her essay 'Religious Conversions: An Attempt at a View from Within.' There she deals with the conversion of the Ukrainian elites to Roman Catholicism, which was treated in traditional Ukrainian historiography of the nineteenth and early twentieth centuries as a betrayal of the masses by the elites. In this view, religious conversion was equated with the abandonment of Ruthenian identity. Yakovenko's main targets here are Mykola Kostomarov and Mykhailo

Hrushevsky. (The latter did indeed write about the 'betrayal of the elites,' but, contrary to Yakovenko's suggestion, never believed in the nobility's 'almost complete abandonment of Orthodoxy as early as on the eve of the Khmelnytsky Uprising' [13].) Yakovenko pledges to avoid such 'reflexive history,' claiming that there were no mass conversions of Ukrainian nobles to Catholicism. Most of her essay is concerned, nevertheless, not with the nobility in general but with conversions and intermarriages among its upper ranks – the Rus' princes and magnates. And here Yakovenko proves (significantly extending our knowledge of the subject in the process) that an absolute majority of the traditional leaders of Rus' was indeed abandoning the traditional religion of Rus'. Certainly that did not mean the automatic loss of Rus' identity, but it shows that Kostomarov was at least partly right in his interpretation. Where he went wrong was in generalizing his view to encompass the nobility as a whole. As has been shown by Henryk Litwin's research, which Yakovenko substantiates with her own calculations of the rate of intermarriage between Orthodox and non-Orthodox nobles, an absolute majority of the Ruthenian nobility (up to 90 per cent) remained faithful to Eastern Christianity.[11]

Not trusting (and for good reason) the claims of the competing religious parties regarding the numbers of actual conversions, Yakovenko also seems to reject those cases when the conversions in question involved a transfer from one Rus' church, the Orthodox, to another – the Uniate, created at the Council of Brest (1596) by the subordination of part of the Orthodox Metropolitanate of Kyiv to Rome. This approach cannot be accepted without further discussion. For Yakovenko, who seemingly regards the Orthodox and Uniate churches as two branches of one confession, divided by mere jurisdictional boundaries, these were not real conversions. Nevertheless, they were treated as such by Ruthenian contemporaries on both sides of the religious divide. The confessional border in Ukraine split the communities of the formerly united Metropolitanate of Kyiv, with the Uniates ending up on the Catholic side. The Uniate hierarchy accepted the dogmas of the Roman Catholic Church and, in an era of advancing confessionalization, ceased to be Orthodox in the eyes of the guardians of both the Catholic and the Orthodox religious traditions. That development was reflected in statements of Jesuit proselytizers and Orthodox intellectuals alike.

Where Yakovenko seems perfectly right, however – and this would appear to be her main contribution to the study of early modern Ukrainian religiosity – is in claiming that the Rus' princes were highly tolerant in religious affairs, if not actually indifferent to the confessional quarrels going on around them. They readily married outside their religion, allowed their wives and children to belong to different churches, and tolerated monks of different traditions at their courts. Although it would be hard to treat that phenomenon as 'ritual belief' (for the princes easily abandoned their own rite), the picture that Yakovenko presents with unprecedented clarity exposes the superficial nature of the religiosity of the Rus' princely elites, whose economic and political interests encouraged them to be flexible on the issue. This is especially true for the second half of the sixteenth century, when confessional borders were not clearly demarcated or guarded and the catechization of nominal Christians had yet to occur. The situation clearly changed with the advance of confessionalization in the first half of the seventeenth century. The extent of change is well illustrated by the data on interconfessional marriages among the Rus' princes and nobility, carefully assembled by Yakovenko. It appears that among the princes, marriages outside their confession diminished from approximately 50 per cent in the period 1540–1615 to 29 per cent in the years 1616–50. One explanation of that phenomenon could be the established fact that by 1616 most of the princely families had already abandoned Orthodoxy and proceeded to marry within their new confession (predominantly Roman Catholicism). But the same phenomenon can also be explained in other ways. Between the 1620s and the 1640s, the conflict over the church union among the Rus' elites clearly defined the boundaries between the two confessions in Rus' society and forced the elites to make a choice. At the same time, the confessionalization of religious life in the Commonwealth reached new heights, making interconfessional marriages and families an exception to the general rule. These developments should also be held responsible for the decline in the number of interconfessional marriages not only among the princes but also among the Ruthenian nobility in general. According to Yakovenko's calculations, they declined from 16 per cent in the years 1581–1615 to 12 per cent between 1616 and 1650 (36).

Do these low figures, as well as the virtual absence of Ruthenian nobiliary marriages outside the Orthodox Church prior to 1581, indicate that the nobility at large was religiously and culturally more traditional than the princes? Apparently they do, even allowing for the possibility that marriages between Orthodox and Uniates (whom Yakovenko treats as parts of the same 'Orthodox rite' [p. 38]) did not make it into her statistics. But were the nobles more religious in general and less 'superficial' in their faith than the princes? Yakovenko shows quite convincingly that they were not. She also argues that the Ukrainian nobility's religiosity was not so different from that of their Polish and Lithuanian counterparts. Although the Ukrainian nobles were much less integrated into Commonwealth society and culture than the princes and the magnates, Yakovenko demonstrates that they all shared a common knightly ethos, which she calls 'the soldier's faith' (*zhovnirs'ka vira*).

What was that 'faith'? Yakovenko offers a reply to this and a number of other war-related questions in her pioneering essay 'How Many Faces Has War? The Khmelnytsky Uprising through the Eyes of Contemporaries.' She draws the reader's attention to episodes usually overlooked by historians who write Ukrainian or Polish national history. These include examples of Commonwealth troops looting Roman Catholic churches and monasteries, as well as Khmelnytsky's army going after the possessions of Orthodox churches and Ruthenian burghers. Indeed, the cases discussed by Yakovenko complicate or seriously undermine the traditional narratives of the Khmelnytsky Uprising. She rightly argues that in the seventeenth century church property was considered legitimate war booty regardless of the denomination to which it belonged, and that professional soldiers on all sides of the conflict shared that 'knightly' attitude towards it. All of them, whether Polish soldiers or Ukrainian Cossacks, took part in the same 'functionally specialized subculture.' This is a highly valid observation, and Yakovenko should be complimented on applying it to the study of the Khmelnytsky Uprising. But can we go on to assert, as she does, that 'professional self-identification prevailed over ethnic or confessional identity' of the combatants (208)?

This statement raises a number of important questions about the hierarchy of identities in early modern Ukraine. Joint banquets organized after or between battles by soldiers fighting on opposite sides and their occasional fraternization with the enemy, instances of which Yakovenko cites in her essay, are of course not limited to early modern times. It can also be said that throughout history, professional solidarity among warriors has rarely overridden their political, national, and institutional loyalties, to say nothing of cultural ones. Otherwise, why would they fight one another in armies divided along ethno-religious lines, as was often the case in the Khmelnytsky Uprising? If indeed the 'soldier's faith' prevailed over 'ethnic or confessional identity,' then why were there no Roman Catholic or Protestant colonels and officers among the rebel elite? Why did Stanisław Michał Krzyczewski have to change his name to Mykhailo Krychevsky and convert from Roman Catholicism to Orthodoxy in order to become a colonel in Khmelnytsky's army? Why did Jews have to accept Orthodoxy to avoid being slaughtered by the rebels? Yakovenko recognizes that the religious purification of the land or, in other words, the creation of a monoconfessional Orthodox polity was one of the goals of the Ukrainian side in the uprising. Nevertheless, she seems to ascribe that program to the leadership of the uprising, the hierarchy of the Orthodox Church, and the peasant masses, which, in her opinion, were more susceptible to religious propaganda than were the Cossacks. The 'old' pre-1648 Cossacks, for their part, allegedly subscribed to the denominationally indifferent 'soldiers' subculture. What this interpretation does not take into account is that the leaders of the uprising were recruited from the same Cossack stratum; the pillaging of Orthodox churches and monasteries was more often the work of peasant rebels than of the 'old' Cossacks; and that the Cossacks showed their readiness to use religious slogans in politics as early as the 1620s.[12] But Yakovenko is certainly right to argue that the professional soldiers (including nobles and Cossacks) were far removed from the image of fighters for religion and nationality presented in traditional historical accounts of the Khmelnytsky Uprising.

Yakovenko's reinterpretation of the sources opens new vistas in the study of the largest Cossack uprising in Ukrainian history. Hers is probably the first attempt by a Ukrainian historian to discuss the human costs of the war. This approach challenges many of the traditional Ukrainian interpretations of the uprising as a struggle for national and social liberation, as well as Polish attempts to depict the war as the heroic epic of their forefathers. It also undermines the interpretation of the uprising as a struggle for the preservation of the Orthodox faith or for the reunification of Ukraine with Russia – paradigms characteristic of imperial Russian and Soviet historiography. Furthermore, Yakovenko's research shows how careful one should be in taking contemporary narratives of the revolt at face value. Telling in that regard is her discussion of an episode in Wawrzyniec Rudawski's seventeenth-century chronicle account of the uprising. As Yakovenko demonstrates, Rudawski's comments on the Polish hero and Ukrainian villain, Prince Jeremi Wiśniowiecki (Yarema Vyshnevetsky, the scion of a Ruthenian princely family who converted from Orthodoxy to Roman Catholicism), were based not on the chronicler's acquaintance with contemporary sources but on his reading of Roman authors. The phrase attributed by Rudawski to Wiśniowiecki, who allegedly encouraged his soldiers to torture the captured rebels with the injunction 'Torment them so that they feel they are dying,' was in fact based on words attributed to Emperor Caligula by Suetonius. Rudawski's description of the attack of the rebel army led by Maksym Kryvonis on the town of Polonne, with its considerable Jewish population, was based on Tacitus's description of the fall of Cremona. Polish historians clearly followed ancient models in their descriptions of the war, as did Jewish writers, who modelled their stories on instances of martyrdom for the faith borrowed from the rich Jewish tradition – a practice recently documented by Edward Fram.[13] In their turn, the Orthodox authors of the period (including Paul of Aleppo and the author of the Eyewitness Chronicle) stressed the religious motives of the Cossacks in their struggle with the non-Orthodox.[14]

The reality on the ground was considerably more complex than the picture presented by confessionally minded authors on all sides of the conflict. A telling indication of this is the archival data cited by Yakovenko about the losses inflicted on the Volhynian town of Kyselyn by a joint rebel and Tatar attack in the autumn of 1648. As Yakovenko notes, of thirty-five Christian dwellings in Kyselyn, only fifteen survived; out of thirty-seven Jewish dwellings, twenty survived. The rest were burned. What lies behind these figures and this strange selection of victims, which challenges every traditional narrative of the Khmelnytsky Uprising? Was it the religious indifference of the rebels, as Yakovenko claims, the unpredictable Tatar factor, or the direction of the wind on a given day? We do not know, but the tragedy of Kyselyn obliges us to pose new questions, seek new answers, and challenge existing interpretations of the war. Indeed, it is Yakovenko's analysis of the sources, pioneering and provocative in many ways, that has placed these questions on the agenda of historians of early modern Ukraine.

Not all the essays collected in Natalia Yakovenko's latest book have been considered here, and even those discussed in some detail contain important points omitted in my survey, partly for reasons of space. But the incomplete and fragmented character of the 'parallel world' of early modern Ukraine, skilfully reconstructed by Yakovenko, also could not but influence the nature of this review. One cannot help thinking how fortunate it was that Yakovenko wrote a 'systematic' survey of Ukrainian medieval and early modern history before she decided that many of the topics and phenomena discussed there precluded such an enterprise by their very nature, to say nothing of the incompleteness of the sources. Yakovenko is rightly sceptical of the prospect that her book might win over opponents in the ranks of the Ukrainian historiographic establishment or persuade them to eradicate the 'virus of contemporaneity.' Her hopes lie with the younger generation of Ukrainian scholars, whom she encourages to study the 'second reality' or 'parallel world' of human views and ideas. Here, the prospects are clearly more favourable.

15 Crossing National Boundaries

The Historiographic Tradition

Among Mykhailo Hrushevsky's manuscripts in the Volodymyr Vernadsky National Library of Ukraine in Kyiv there is a copy of his unpublished review of Osyp Hermaize's *Ukraïne and the Don in the Seventeenth Century,* which appeared as an article and a separate offprint in 1928.[1] The review was written for the journal *Ukraïna,* of which Hrushevsky himself was the editor, but that particular issue failed to appear because of Hrushevsky's arrest in the early spring of 1931.[2] At the time the review was written, Hermaize was also under arrest, accused by Stalin's secret police of having participated in the bogus Union for the Liberation of Ukraine. The themes underlying Hermaize's book and Hrushevsky's comments on it were the history of Russo-Ukrainian relations and prospects for the comparative study of Ukrainian and Russian Cossackdom. To be sure, it was not the interest of the two Ukrainian historians in those topics (or not such interest alone) that led to their arrest. Nevertheless, the ideas they expressed on the subject compel attention, not least because they were put forward under such dramatic circumstances. The Soviet regime was then involved in the 'liquidation of Cossackdom as a class' (to repeat the overused Stalinist euphemism) in the course of forced collectivization in the Kuban and Don regions, as well as in the suppression of historical scholarship.

What were those ideas? Hermaize argued that future research on Ukrainian Cossackdom depended on a comparative approach and advocated a search for analogues in the history of the Russian Cossacks. Hrushevsky gave particular attention to that argument of Hermaize's but maintained that it was too early to undertake comparative research. He argued that one could compare only equally well researched subjects, noting that the Russian Cossacks had not been studied nearly so thoroughly as the Cossacks of Ukraine. He also stressed the differences between them, which were related to the special role of the Dnipro Cossacks in Ukrainian history. Hrushevsky wrote: 'Ukrainian Cossackdom, becoming a state-building, socially organizational element, taking on the role of a national representation and the obligations of defending national interests, rose immeasurably above the primitive analogues of the Cossack company or the Cossack Host.' The latter, in Hrushevsky's opinion, denoted those elements of social organization that were common to the Ukrainian and Russian Cossacks. Still, Hrushevsky did not brush off the notion of a comparative approach to the history of Cossackdom: in the conclusion of his review, he stated that in order to acquire a better understanding of their own Cossackdom, Ukrainian historians would have to study Russian Cossackdom as well.[3]

Hrushevsky's hopes that Ukrainian scholars would lend their Russian colleagues a hand did not materialize, partly because the whole subject was about to fall under the rubric of completely or predominantly prohibited topics of research. In the Ukraine of the 1930s, historical textbooks turned the Cossack uprisings into peasant wars and revolts, marginalizing the Cossacks in historiography and turning them into the villains of the Marxist historical narrative. Contributing to that development was the takeover of the anti-elitist theories of populist historiography by Soviet Marxist historiography, as well as the discrediting of the Cossack tradition on the grounds that it had been widely invoked by Ukrainian opponents of the Bolshevik regime during the revolution. In Ukraine, the revival of research on Cossackdom in the 1960s was followed by the anti-Cossack campaign of the 1970s, waged under the slogans of proletarian internationalism and the struggle against Ukrainian bourgeois nationalism, which hindered scholarly activity in that area until the last years of the USSR. In Russia, Cossack support for the tsarist regime during the Revolution of 1917 and opposition to collectivization in the late 1920s and early 1930s only aggravated the traditional marginalization of Cossack history. If in Ukrainian national historiography the Cossacks were traditionally considered (with a few notable exceptions) a positive element that had played an important role in the history of Ukrainian statehood and nation building – features outlined by Hrushevsky in his review of Hermaize's work – in Russia they were slighted by many historians, including such patriarchs of Russian historiography as Sergei Soloviev, as a destructive element that complicated the building and consolidation of Russian nationhood instead of facilitating it.[4]

It was only outside the USSR that research on Cossackdom could develop without interference from the Soviet authorities. Not surprisingly, then, during the 1980s more research was published on the history of the Ukrainian Cossacks in Poland and the United States than in Ukraine.[5] In the West, research on the subject continued for most of the twentieth century. It was spearheaded by Ukrainian émigré authors and Western-educated historians of Ukrainian background, who continued to regard the Cossack past as one of the most glorious eras of their history – one that had contributed significantly to the making of the Ukrainian nation.[6] Russian historians, writers, and publicists associated with the postrevolutionary and post–Second World War Cossack emigrations to the West continued to write about Russian (Don, Terek, etc.) Cossackdom, contributing mostly to the recent (late nineteenth- and early twentieth-century) annals of that social group. One of the most influential books of the era on the history of the Cossacks was written by a non-Russian scholar, Günther Stökl, and published in West Germany in 1953.[7]

In the United States, the image of Cossackdom was tarnished, especially in the last decades of the twentieth century, by the close association of their history with that of anti-Semitism in Eastern Europe – an association reinforced by their participation in the pogroms that followed the Revolution of 1917. Still, the general public continued to buy books on the subject, fascinated with the romantic image of the Cossack emanating from the works of Nikolai Gogol (Mykola Hohol) and Leo Tolstoy, as well as by the history of Cossack involvement in the Napoleonic wars and the Crimean campaign. Most of the books about Cossacks that appeared in the English-speaking world in the second half of the twentieth century treated all of them, Russian and Ukrainian alike, as a homogeneous group. These works were overwhelmingly popular in nature, written not by professional historians specializing in the field but by amateurs. Far from promoting a comparative approach, they oversimplified the historical texture, doing more to distort interpretation than to refine it.[8]

This was true even of the more intelligent and thoroughly researched works on Cossack history that appeared at the time, including Philip Longworth's *The Cossacks* (1970). Assessing the work in the *Slavic Review*, the Ukrainian émigré scholar Ivan L. Rudnytsky, while indicating its merits, also lamented the author's failure to identify the specific features of Ukrainian Cossackdom and its differences from the Russian variety. As an example of Longworth's lack of attention to the national specificities of the Ukrainian Cossacks and his tendency to observe Ukrainian history through the prism of the Russian historical paradigm, Rudnytsky quoted from Longworth's description of Ukrainian Cossack festivities after one of their victories over the Poles, where the former were portrayed as playing Russian balalaikas. Rudnytsky also challenged Longworth's refusal to treat the Hetmanate – a polity that emerged from the victories of 1648 – as a Cossack state, as well as his assertion that the Ukrainian Cossacks had little in the way of national identity.[9] In the exchange of letters that followed, Longworth accused Rudnytsky of denying the importance of the comparative approach to the history of Cossackdom. Rudnytsky, for his part, expressed support for comparative studies, while further developing his ideas about the leading role of the Cossacks in early modern Ukraine and their contribution to the growth of national identity in the Hetmanate.[10] Thus, not unlike Hrushevsky forty years earlier, Rudnytsky affirmed the commitment of Ukrainian historians to comparative research but insisted on the uniqueness of the Ukrainian Cossacks, stressing their distinct national identity and nation-building role.

Pros and Cons of the National Paradigm

Today, the task of comparative research on the history of Cossackdom should be formulated as an appeal to cross the boundaries of national historiography and go beyond the parameters designated by the national paradigm. As that national paradigm came to be applied to East European history in the nineteenth century, the romanticized Cossack past was quickly appropriated by national historians. How useful was the paradigm to the study of Cossack history? Was it a stimulus or a setback to research? Let us begin by enumerating the positive effects of the national idea on historiography. First of all, it should be pointed out that most of what we know about Cossackdom today has been collected, evaluated, and interpreted by historians working within the parameters of national historiography. It was the national paradigm that shifted historians' attention from dynasties and empires to social groups and the popular masses – a development that benefited the study of the Cossacks. The disintegration of the all-Russian historical narrative in the nineteenth and early twentieth centuries and the emergence on its ruins of Russian and Ukrainian national historiographies revealed the importance of a number of differences between Ukrainian and Russian Cossackdom that had earlier been overlooked or underestimated. The new national paradigm applied by Ukrainian and Russian historians drew the boundary between Cossack hosts and polities exactly where it had been from the sixteenth century to the late eighteenth century – along the Polish-Muscovite border – and helped clarify differences caused by centuries of existence within politically, religiously, and culturally distinct polities. It also directed scholarly attention to questions of the national identity of the Cossacks that either had not been raised before or had been discussed only in terms of the all-Russian supranational approach.

At the same time, the national paradigm brought some major distortions into the field. In Russia, as mentioned previously, the Cossacks were marginalized as a subject of research, since it was believed that Russian nation building had originated and proceeded in the capitals and central regions of the country and not on its periphery, which was settled and guarded by the Cossacks. In Ukraine, on the contrary, too much attention was paid to the nation-building activities of Cossackdom (or activities susceptible to such interpretation) at the expense of research on their social and cultural history. This approach also tended to marginalize the history of the non-Cossack parts of Ukraine and exaggerate the role of Cossackdom in the Ukrainian past. Furthermore, the lumping together of the Hetmanate, Cossack formations on the Right Bank of the Dnipro, and the Zaporozhian Host under the rubric of Ukrainian Cossackdom obscured differences between them, made it 'unpatriotic' to study tensions and conflicts between the Hetmanate and the Zaporozhians, and deflected attention from parallels between the development of the Zaporozhian Host and, for example, the Don Cossacks. Significantly narrowed under Soviet rule, the concept of Ukrainian Cossackdom usually excluded the Kuban Cossacks, as they ended up on the Russian side of the Soviet-era border. Conversely, the category of Russian Cossackdom left virtually no room for recognition of the national specificity of the Kuban Cossacks. Western scholars tended to question the Cossack character of the Hetmanate, while their Soviet colleagues, studying Cossack participation in the so-called peasant wars of the seventeenth and eighteenth centuries, continued to claim that none of the Cossack-led revolts had achieved its goals, as the rebels were invariably defeated. Thus the study of Cossack statehood remained outside the purview of specialists in the history of Russian Cossackdom.

Is there an effective way to utilize the potential of national historiographies that distinguish for good reason between Russian and Ukrainian (Muscovite and Polish-Lithuanian) Cossacks, while avoiding their pitfalls? It is one of the goals of this chapter to suggest that there is indeed such a way, and that it is directly related to comparative research in the field – an idea often suggested earlier but not carried out because of unfavourable circumstances: Soviet scholars had to work under political constraints, while Western researchers were denied access to East European archives and libraries.[11] The recent (post-1991) resurgence of Cossack studies in Ukraine,[12] Russia,[13] and the West (where in the course of the last decade there has emerged a younger generation of scholars combining Western historical methodologies with newly acquired access to archival sources)[14] has put this task back on the scholarly agenda. Research recently undertaken in both East and West not only attests to new interest in the history of Cossackdom on the part of scholarly communities in those countries but also indicates the new potential for comparative research in the field.[15] What are the most promising directions for such research? In this chapter I shall try to provide at least a partial answer by putting some of the themes pertaining to seventeenth-century Cossackdom into a broader, 'all-Cossack' context. I shall do so by discussing three papers on the history of the Don and Siberian Cossacks delivered by Christopher Witzenrath, Brian Boeck, and Nikolai Mininkov at the conference 'The History of Muscovite Russia from the Perspective of the Regions' organized at the University of Vienna in June 2003 by Andreas Kappeler.

Governments and Cossacks

One of the themes discussed on the basis of extensive archival research by Christoph Witzenrath[16] is the relationship between the state authorities and the Cossacks in the early stages of their development as a social body. For scholars familiar with the early history of the Dnipro Cossacks, the picture drawn by Witzenrath presents many parallels with the early history of Ukrainian Cossackdom and suggests a number of research topics that could contribute to a better understanding of Cossack history on both sides of the Russo-Ukrainian historiographic divide. These topics include the social origins of the Cossacks, the organization of early Cossack bands, the functioning of institutions of military democracy in militarized border societies, the role of leaders (otamans/atamans) in Cossack communities, and the level of contacts between the Cossack settlements and the metropole. No less important is the comparative study of relations between the Cossacks and the state authorities – a topic for the study of which (especially in the earlier periods) we have many more sources than for research on the social history of Cossackdom. Relations between Muscovite voevodas (military governors) and Cossack bands in Siberia in the sixteenth and seventeenth centuries can be compared with those between the border starostas of the Grand Duchy of Lithuania and the Dnipro Cossacks in the early and mid-sixteenth century. Imposing taxes on products of Cossack trade (furs in Siberia and fish, honey, etc. in Ukraine) was one way in which both states exploited Cossack economic activity for their benefit. Equally important in government-Cossack relations were the attempts of border administrators based in fortified settlements (*zamky* in Ukraine and *ostrogi* in Siberia) to control the Cossacks' military activities. These and other parallels, which would become more obvious in the course of further research, can establish similarities in early Cossack social organization and economic and military activity throughout the Eurasian borderland, while revealing similar methods applied by governments (Lithuanian, Polish, and Russian) to control Cossack activities.

A comparison of government-Cossack relations in Siberia and the Dnipro region reveals not only parallels but also major differences in the status of the Russian and Ukrainian Cossacks and the policies of their home states. Like the above-mentioned parallels, these differences suggest questions of great importance for the better understanding of Cossackdom. I shall mention only three of them here – in my opinion, the most obvious ones. The first major difference concerns the government stipend or wages paid to the Cossacks and the extent of control exercised by government officials over their actions. It appears from the Russian sources (and is confirmed in all three papers discussed here) that the Russian Cossacks were much more heavily dependent on the tsar's stipend and supplies from the state than were the Ukrainian Cossacks under Lithuanian, Polish, or Russian rule. True, the Ukrainian Cossacks occasionally received a stipend and supplies from the tsar before 1648, but those payments were infrequent and directly related to specific military expeditions. They were also much less dependent on payments from the Lithuanian and Polish treasuries. First, it was only the registered Cossacks who received wages; second, wages were tied to participation in government-sponsored military campaigns and were often delayed or not paid at all. The conditions put forward by the Cossacks at the start of the Khmelnytsky Uprising show that by the mid-seventeenth century the salary demands of the registered Cossacks had receded into the background and lost most, if not all, of the importance ascribed to them in the late sixteenth century. It is worth examining to what degree, as Cossackdom matured and the Cossacks turned from steppe trade and warfare to a more settled way of life and membership in a distinct social order, the role of government payments diminished in Poland-Lithuania and Muscovy.

Another important difference in state-Cossack relations on both sides of the Russo-Ukrainian divide is related to the goals of government policy with regard to the Cossacks. In Muscovy, the stipend was paid almost exclusively for services rendered by the Cossacks in their places of settlement and encouraged them to fight the enemies of the state and protect its borders. The history of the first Cossack register (and, consequently, the first Cossack wages) in Ukraine is profoundly different. There, during the 1570s, the Cossacks were organized and paid their wages by the Polish kings Zygmunt August and Stefan Batory not in order to fight the Crimean Tatars and Turks but to remove the aggressive Cossack element from the steppe borderland and deploy it far from home, on the battlefields of the Livonian War with Russia. The actual initiative to do so came from the Ottoman sultan, and up to the mid-seventeenth century the Polish-Lithuanian authorities spent more time preventing the Cossacks from attacking the Ottomans and their vassals (the Crimea and Moldavia) than organizing them for battle against those southern adversaries. Muscovy, on the other hand, was much less intrusive when it came to actions of the Don Cossacks against the Ottomans and the Crimea. In the late 1630s and early 1640s Muscovy refused to accept the 'gift' of the captured Ottoman fortress of Azov from Cossack hands, and in its relations with Istanbul until the 1670s it denied any responsibility for the actions of the Cossacks. Once Muscovy admitted responsibility, it attempted to make use of the Cossacks in its military confrontation with the Ottomans in the North Azov region. Only much later were the Don Cossacks employed by the government to fight its enemies beyond the Don.

One more important difference in relations between the Russian and Ukrainian Cossacks and their respective governments is that Muscovy and Lithuania, and later Poland-Lithuania, were represented in their dealings with the Cossacks by very different types of servitors. In the case of Muscovy they were voevodas (military governors), often rotated by the central government and entirely dependent on the will and whim of the tsar and his courtiers. In Poland-Lithuania, the border administrators were often scions of Rus' princely families – rich, semi-autonomous of the central government, and often intent on their own military, economic, and even political agendas. Although certain parallels can be drawn between the private Cossack armies of Prince Kostiantyn Ostrozky in Ukraine and the Stroganov family in Siberia, the crucial difference between them was that Ostrozky, as palatine of Kyiv and administrator of a number of starosta districts in Ukraine, was part of the state apparatus and represented not only his own economic power but also the power of the state. This was not the case with the Stroganovs, who cooperated closely with the state but did not replace it in Siberia. The weakness of the central authorities and the variety of political actors with their own agendas in the borderlands of the Polish-Lithuanian Commonwealth undoubtedly contributed to the development of Ukrainian Cossackdom as a much more powerful and independent force than Russian Cossackdom. Both states regarded the Cossacks as a cheap substitute for standing armies and expensive fortifications in the borderlands, but there was a great difference in the degree of autonomy that the Polish and Russian governments were prepared (or forced) to grant the Cossack hosts under their control.

The Politics of the Tsars

The papers by Boeck[17] and Mininkov[18] offer a number of important insights into the history of relations between the Don Cossacks and the Muscovite authorities, as they reveal the strategies applied by both sides in the long process of negotiating their respective rights and obligations. Bringing the Ukrainian Cossacks' relations with Warsaw and Moscow into the picture helps define those strategies even better. Let us begin with the policy of the Muscovite authorities vis-à-vis Cossackdom. Boeck demonstrates very convincingly how flexible that policy was and how the authorities were prepared to retreat upon encountering Cossack resistance, only to reintroduce their agenda once conditions improved. The history of Muscovite involvement in Ukraine in the second half of the seventeenth century offers numerous examples of the same tendency. In 1667, for example, Moscow was prepared to soften its position regarding the deployment of voevodas in Ukraine, but in 1672 it orchestrated the election of a new hetman with powers significantly reduced in comparison to those of his predecessors. It might be argued that this was not so different from (and probably originated with) the policy of Moscow's rulers towards their eastern neighbours and vassals. The latter, as Andreas Kappeler has shown, entailed the establishment of 'a loose protectorate, which was concluded by means of an oath, by installing a loyal ruler. From the Russian point of view that established a client status to which it could always refer in the future, whereas the other side saw it at the most as a personal and temporary act of submission.'[19] The fact that the Moscow and Don Cossacks had different interpretations of the oath of 1671, or that the Ukrainian Cossacks and the Muscovite authorities took different views of their respective obligations under the conditions brokered at Pereiaslav in 1654, did not affect the readiness of the Muscovite authorities to use those treaties as an instrument of subordination, as they had done in their relations with nomads. In the Ukrainian case, the Muscovite authorities even resorted to falsifying treaties, as was the case with the 'Articles of Bohdan Khmelnytsky,' which Prince Aleksei Trubetskoi prevailed upon Yurii Khmelnytsky to sign in 1659.

Kappeler's research indicates another parallel between Moscow's policy towards the Cossacks and its approach to the steppe nomads – the pitting of one group of new subjects against another. Still, there were important differences between the implementation of that policy in the Don and other Russian areas and in Ukraine. In the first instance, the Russian government often tried to use the Cossack officer stratum to curtail Cossack unrest. Examples of the 'betrayal' of the interests of the Cossack masses by well-to-do Cossacks in the uprisings led by Stepan Razin and Emelian Pugachev and the handing over of their leaders to the authorities (much lamented in Soviet historiography) attest to the success of that policy. In the Ukrainian case, we also see examples of Cossack officers handing over their hetmans to Moscow (the fate that befell Demian Mnohohrishny and Ivan Samoilovych), but those were cases of conflict within elite ranks, not of elites being used to curtail the antigovernment activities of the masses. There are almost no instances of the latter in the 'Muscovite' history of Ukrainian Cossackdom, but they abound in its pre-1648, 'Polish-Lithuanian' period. Petro Konashevych-Sahaidachny, who led the Host in the late 1610s and early 1620s, stands out as a hetman who was able to steer clear of a direct Cossack confrontation with officialdom, but a number of his less fortunate followers, such as Hryhorii Chorny, paid with their lives for choosing loyalty to the government over loyalty to the Host. These episodes in the history of Ukrainian Cossackdom's relations with the Commonwealth authorities find clear parallels in the history of the Don and other Russian Cossack hosts and their dealings with Muscovy.

The situation seems less clear when it comes to the history of the Ukrainian Cossacks' relations with Muscovy. There we encounter much more frequent attempts on the part of the tsarist authorities to make use of the Cossack officers not to control the rank-and-file Cossacks but to curtail the power of the hetmans or provoke intra-elite conflicts. It was the Cossack 'rabble' that the tsarist government exploited to split the common front of the hetmans and Cossack officers against Moscow. The place where that rabble concentrated and where opposition to the Cossack officer stratum of the Hetmanate ran especially high was Zaporizhia on the lower Dnipro, the cradle of Dnipro Cossackdom. Very early on, the Muscovite authorities learned to encourage and support Zaporozhian opposition to the Hetmanate elites. That was the case with the uprising led in 1658 by the Zaporozhian otaman Yakiv Barabash and the Poltava colonel Martyn Pushkar against Hetman Ivan Vyhovsky, who considered his allegiance to Moscow conditional on the tsar's non-interference in the internal politics of the Hetmanate. The Moscow authorities were also behind the election to the hetmancy of Ivan Briukhovetsky (1663–8), the candidate of the Zaporozhians and rank-and-file Cossacks, who dramatically expanded Moscow's influence in Ukraine.

Playing masses against elites turned out successfully in Ukraine but was a tactic rarely applied by Moscow in its relations with other Cossack hosts. Why was that so? There is more than one answer to the question, but what seems certain is that Moscow approached the Hetmanate with tactics normally reserved for enemy states, not for its own subjects or Cossack hosts under its jurisdiction. In the former instance, the exploitation of social tensions as a means of destabilization was viewed as a legitimate way to make the elites more accommodating towards Russian demands. In the second instance, such destabilization was evidently regarded as unacceptable, for the Moscow government itself would have to deal with the consequences of social upheaval in the 'no-man's-land' on its borders. Thus Moscow's policy towards the Hetmanate in the second half of the seventeenth century more closely resembled its policy towards the Polish-Lithuanian Commonwealth a century later (during the Koliivshchyna Uprising of 1768) than towards the Cossack hosts under its jurisdiction.

This brings us to the all-important issue of the Cossack state. The Hetmanate offers students of Cossackdom the sole instance of a successful Cossack uprising followed by the transformation of the political, social, and economic institutions created by Cossackdom into an apparatus of state power and control of a large territory with a long tradition of existence under conditions different from those prevailing among the Cossacks. The history of the Hetmanate provides rich material for the comparative study of Cossackdom and for informed speculation in the genre of virtual history concerning what might have been expected of Russian Cossackdom if one of the uprisings led by Razin, Kondrat Bulavin, or Pugachev had been successful. The creation of the Hetmanate may be seen as a logical result of the evolution of the Cossacks from steppe bandits and tradesmen into a military force in the service of magnates and the state, and then into a distinct social order cognizant of the need for a polity of its own in order to protect its interests effectively. It might also be regarded as the Cossacks' ultimate response to the pressure applied to them by the dominant powers of the region.

What strategies did the Cossacks employ in their negotiations with the state? One was to use their military service to the state as a lever to maintain and extend their social, economic, and political prerogatives. In the Ukrainian case, that strategy led to the spectacular growth of the Cossack register and its concomitant rights and privileges in the first decades of the seventeenth century. In the Russian case, it ensured the growth and continuing existence of some of the Cossack hosts well into the twentieth century. Another strategy was associated with military expeditions abroad, which allowed the Cossacks not only to enrich themselves through robbery but also to collect additional payments from neighbouring powers for participation in such campaigns. The Zaporozhians, for example, were occasionally paid by the Habsburgs and Muscovites for their campaigns against the Ottomans and their vassals. Foreign expeditions thus helped the Cossacks offset the political and economic restrictions imposed on them by their home states. Yet another strategy was exemplified by military revolts that would usually start within Cossack ranks but then spread to the populace and spark major uprisings.

The history of Cossackdom is punctuated by revolts that were eventually suppressed by the authorities, with the notable exception of the Khmelnytsky Uprising. While such revolts often brought immediate setbacks, in the long run they generally helped the Cossacks maintain their autonomy vis-à-vis the state. Last but not least in the repertoire of Cossack dealings with the authorities was the tactic of fleeing state jurisdiction. On the level of small Cossack bands and individuals, that strategy ensured the longevity of Cossackdom and its continuing penetration into ever more remote parts of the Eurasian steppe. On the level of organized Cossack hosts, that 'ultimate' argument was often used as a threat by the Don Cossacks and actually implemented by the 'Nekrasovites,' who fled to the Crimean jurisdiction in 1709. The Ukrainian Cossacks, for their part, often fled to Muscovy after the failed uprisings of the first half of the seventeenth century, foreshadowing Khmelnytsky's decision to accept the Muscovite protectorate in 1654. Khmelnytsky's failed attempt to enlist the Ottomans as his political sponsors in the mid-seventeenth century inspired later attempts by Hetman Petro Doroshenko (1665–76) and the Zaporozhians after the Battle of Poltava (1709), who became subjects of the Crimean khan after Aleksandr Menshikov destroyed the Sich on the orders of Peter I.

One more question that the comparative approach to the history of Cossackdom helps pose, and can be helpful in answering, is why Cossack institutions survived longest under Muscovy, while succumbing much earlier under Ottoman, Crimean, and Polish rule. This question cannot be answered merely by indicating the vastness of Russia and the long existence of an open frontier in the East. One should also take account of the various policies adopted towards the Cossacks by their home states and the ways in which the Cossacks responded to them. A comparative approach to the history of the Cossack hosts exposes the flaws of Cossack-centred historiography in both its Ukrainian and Russian incarnations, for that historiography regards the curtailment of Cossack freedoms as the main goal of Moscow's policy. In reality, the ruling elite in Moscow was often more than reluctant to extend the power of the tsar over the tumultuous Cossack hosts. It is safe to suggest that foreign-policy considerations, and not the urge to restrict Cossack freedoms, were paramount in the formulation of Moscow's policy towards the Cossacks for most of the seventeenth century. The desire not to provoke powerful enemies such as the Ottomans and the Polish-Lithuanian Commonwealth, as well as reluctance to become involved in 'unruly' Cossack politics, dictated caution in Moscow's relations with the Cossacks, as evidenced by the policy pursued towards Ukraine in the late 1660s by the Ambassadorial Office under Afanasii Ordin-Nashchokin.

Christians and Muslims

The conventional treatment of the role played by the Cossack hosts in international relations also seems to be dogged by misconceptions. In today's historical imagination, both the Russian and the Ukrainian Cossacks appear as fighters against the Tatars and the Ottomans. It is quite true that both groups were involved in that military, political, and civilizational conflict on the borders of the Christian and Muslim worlds, and both Catholic Poland-Lithuania and Orthodox Russia enlisted the Cossacks in their conflicts with Istanbul and Bakhchesarai. But were the Cossacks mere pawns in a game played by the great powers of the region? The history of both Ukrainian and Russian Cossackdom shows otherwise, even though both entities were able to extract numerous privileges from their Christian sovereigns and protectors for their defence of what was considered to be the Christian cause. What is often overlooked in that regard is that the Cossacks adopted many elements of the culture and traditions of their non-Christian adversaries and spent more time living in peace with them than in conflict. Indeed, they sometimes preferred to ally themselves with the 'infidels' rather than with Christian monarchs. These elements in the history of Cossackdom are easy to pass over, given the prevailing historiographic tradition that portrays the Cossacks as warriors for the faith. This is particularly easy to do in today's Russia, where the modern national myth tends to exclude the infidel Tatars from the Russian historical narrative, but somewhat more difficult in Ukraine, where the newly constructed national mythology stresses the tradition of cooperation between Cossacks and Crimean Tatars against Polish oppression.

That tradition includes a number of episodes in seventeenth-century Ukrainian history. As early as the 1620s, the Ukrainian Cossacks became involved in Crimean affairs on the side of one of the pretenders to the Crimean throne. Khmelnytsky's spectacular victories over Polish forces in 1648–9 would have been all but impossible without the help of the Tatar cavalry. After Ivan Mazepa's defeat at Poltava, the hetman in exile, Pylyp Orlyk, linked his plans for a return to power to joint military action with the Crimean Khanate, and, as noted above, the Zaporozhians moved their Sich to Tatar territory at the time. Moreover, there were several Cossack hetmans (besides Khmelnytsky and Doroshenko) who favoured the Ottoman orientation at one time or another or accepted the protectorate of the sultans or khans. In a comparative context, these and other examples of cooperation between

Ukrainian Cossackdom and the southern Muslim powers pose the question of why, despite the fact that a number of Russian Cossack leaders contemplated alliances with the Muslims or intended to seek their protection, those plans succeeded only in the case of the Nekrasovites. Clearly, a discussion of the issue should take account of numerous factors – political, economic, social, international, and geographic. Ethnocultural and religious factors, which played an important role in the history of Cossackdom, should also be considered. Both Russian and Ukrainian Cossacks had a cultural boundary with their Muslim neighbours but differed considerably when it came to boundaries with the governments of their home states. In Russia there was no such boundary, but in Ukraine it was all-important, as it divided the Orthodox Ruthenian Cossacks from the Polish Catholic authorities. Under these circumstances, an alliance of Ukrainian Cossacks with ethnically distinct Muslims against ethnically distinct Catholics was apparently far less problematic than an alliance of Russian Cossacks with Muslim Tatars against the Orthodox Russian state. To be sure, this is a hypothesis that should be tested by further research. It brings us, however, to the highly contested question of Cossack national and religious identity – a problem that cannot be adequately addressed without employing the comparative method.

The question of Cossack identity in general and distinctions between the ethnic consciousness of Ukrainian and Russian Cossacks, while extremely important for the national historiographies of Russia, Ukraine, and Poland, remains much less studied than other aspects of Cossack history. Far more has been written about Cossack involvement in religious life, especially the major religious conflicts of the epoch – the struggle for and against the church union in Ukraine and Belarus and the Old Believers in Russia. Here, as in other areas of Cossack history, the comparative approach helps formulate a number of new questions and opens fresh perspectives on the history of the Cossacks themselves and the religious and cultural history of the region. Certain parallels can be drawn between the support offered by the Russian and Ukrainian Cossacks to the persecuted churches in their home states: Orthodoxy in the Polish-Lithuanian Commonwealth and the Old Belief in Muscovy. In both cases, the Cossacks and the persecuted churches found themselves in similar circumstances, living side by side in remote areas of the country. Under pressure from the authorities, to whom they were opposed, they needed each other's support: the Cossacks, especially when involved in acute conflicts with the government, needed religious legitimation of their actions, while the church required the military and economic muscle of the Cossacks to oppose officialdom and survive. In Ukraine and Russia alike, close relations were established between the Cossacks and the persecuted churches, but the intensity of that cooperation and its outcome were quite different. In Ukraine, Cossacks helped save the persecuted church from destruction by the state, and under the banner of Orthodoxy they later created a monoconfessional state. In Russia, after a brief flirtation with the Old Belief and acute internal conflict, discussed by Mininkov and touched upon by Boeck, the Cossack elites preferred to remain under the jurisdiction of the state church, never fully raising the banner of the 'old faith' in their struggle with the authorities.

Why did the Russian Cossacks behave differently from the Ukrainian Cossacks and not give their full support to the dissident priests and monks against their reform-minded hierarchs, who were backed by the power of the state? Why did they not fully utilize the potential of such cooperation and declare 'holy war' on the state? Again, there is no clear and simple answer to this question, but there are several possible explanations, one of which I shall discuss. It might be argued that the major difference between the Russian and Ukrainian cases was the attitude of the Cossack officer stratum towards the persecuted religion. The Zaporozhians sided with the oppressed church, while the Don Cossacks, as shown once again in the papers by Mininkov and Boeck, aligned themselves with the government. The Zaporozhian and Don Cossack officers were clearly focused on different tasks and subordinated the religious issue to the achievement of those tasks. The Ukrainian Cossack officers, as exemplified by Konashevych-Sahaidachny, who ensured the restoration of the Orthodox hierarchy in 1620, were struggling for the recognition of particular rights within the Polish-Lithuanian Commonwealth. To obtain those rights they needed powerful allies, whom they could find among the Orthodox nobility of the Commonwealth. Their ethnic origin also inclined them to side with other members of the Orthodox coalition, the Ruthenian princes, nobles, and burghers, in the ethnocultural and religious conflict. All these factors were absent in the case of the Don Cossacks. The alliance of their officers with the persecuted church could not possibly help them acquire important allies and improve their standing vis-à-vis the state. Positioned on the Orthodox-Muslim border, they chose loyalty to the powerful Orthodox state and its church over allegiance to the spiritually strong but resource-poor Old Believer movement.

While the attitude of the Cossack officer stratum was an important factor in determining the strategies adopted by the Ukrainian and Russian Cossacks in religious conflicts with the state, it does not explain all the differences between them in that regard. Rather, this brief examination of the positions taken by the Ukrainian and Russian Cossack elites demonstrates the potential of the comparative approach to the study of Cossackdom. This is equally true of the other problems in the history of Cossackdom discussed in this chapter, which generally offers more questions than answers – not inappropriate at this stage in the study of such a multifaceted phenomenon as Cossackdom. Making a case for the comparative study of anything, including Cossackdom, may be seen today as old-fashioned, attesting among other things to the methodological backwardness of anyone advocating such an 'innovation' in an era of advancing postmodern scholarship. Yet there is no way to recognize the uniqueness of the voices of the past without comparing them one to another. Nor can we skip the comparative stage in the historiography of Cossackdom and pretend that the goals set by historians before Stalin's suppression of historical scholarship in the 1930s have already been achieved or are irrelevant to today's scholarly agenda. In order to move forward, present-day historiography must go back and pick up the thread of research where our predecessors were obliged to abandon it for reasons beyond their control.

16 Beyond Nationality

'Getting history wrong is an essential factor in the formation of a nation,' wrote Ernest Renan, basing this observation on his analysis of the nation-building experience in nineteenth-century Europe.[1] Many historians today tend to agree with Renan's statement and are doing their best to 'get history right' as they search for alternatives to national history. More often than not they face an uphill battle in that regard, both within and outside their profession.

On the one hand, the influence of globalization in North America and European integration on the other side of the Atlantic have certainly shaken the old belief in nationality as the only legitimate principle for organizing the history of humankind. The retreat of primordialism in nationality studies and the demonstration of the temporal and constructed nature of national identities, as well as the interpretation of nationalities as imagined communities, further undermined the legitimacy of the nationality principle in historical writing. On the other hand, most historians continue to practise national history, and the governments of nation-states continue to encourage the use of history for purposes of patriotic education. An international group of scholars currently working on a five-year program of the European Science Foundation entitled 'Representations of the Past: The Writing of National Histories in Europe' observed that the rise of radical right-wing and separatist movements in many West European states 'has put national history center stage.' They also pointed out that, 'if anything, the proliferation of new nation states in eastern Europe after 1989 brought about a renewed interest in national histories in many of the former Communist states.'[2]

Asking historians in Eastern Europe to abandon the national approach to history after decades of suppression of national narratives by the communist authorities may be rather like asking Leopold von Ranke to tone down his nationalist and statist rhetoric after the unification of Germany. Still, one can approach East European historians with much more hope today than could have been mustered in dealing with German and Italian historians in the second half of the nineteenth century. For one thing, writing traditional national history today means contributing to the isolationism and provincialism of East European historiography imposed by decades of existence behind the Iron Curtain. The new nations of Eastern Europe want to be part of a united Europe, while their younger historians want to be part of the larger European and world community of historians.

But how is one to overcome the deficiencies of present-day writing on the history of Eastern Europe – deficiencies often caused by decades of totalitarian rule in that part of the world and general indifference on the part of Western historians to the history of nations without a state of their own? Here I shall discuss the possibilities of rewriting, reshaping, and restructuring East European historical narratives, focusing on the history of Ukraine – an entity defined for the purposes of this essay primarily in territorial terms. I shall start by discussing the formation of the national paradigm of Ukrainian history and considering its pluses and minuses. I shall then look at alternatives to national history. They include rewriting the Ukrainian historical narrative along the lines of multiethnic and local history, as well as applying methods employed in transnational, regional, and international history. Finally, I shall discuss the prospects for treating Ukrainian history in the context of broader supranational areas, including East Central Europe and Eurasia. By analysing recent developments in the field, I hope to indicate the direction of future research on the history of the region.

National History

If one were to choose a specific date for the beginning of modern Ukrainian historiography, the year 1895 would probably fit the bill. In December of that year the editorial board of the Ukrainophile journal *Kievskaia starina* (Kyivan Antiquity) published the prospectus of a survey of Ukrainian history and announced a competition for writers willing to produce such a work. The most recent survey of 'Little Russian' history had been published more than fifty years earlier, in 1843.[3]

The winner was Aleksandra Efimenko, who subsequently published a *History of the Ukrainian People* (1906). There are several interesting observations to be made about the competition and its winner. First, the date of the competition indicates how late Ukrainian intellectuals turned their attention to the need for a national historical narrative. The Polish Society of Friends of Scholarship came up with such an initiative for Polish history as early as 1808, while the Russian Empire created the position of official historiographer even earlier, in 1803 – it was taken by Nikolai Karamzin. It was a sign of new times that a woman became the 'official historiographer' of Ukraine as a result of the 1895 competition. The Ukrainian women's movement was taking shape at this time, and the symbol of Mother Ukraine was becoming increasingly popular in Ukrainian national discourse.[4] A sign of the tolerance of the Ukrainian movement at the time was Efimenko's ethnic origin: she was a Russian, born and raised in northern Russia, where she met and married her Ukrainophile husband, who had been exiled to Arkhangelsk gubernia from Ukraine. A sign of the weakness of the Ukrainian movement was that Efimenko did not hold a doctorate in history and had no university position.[5]

Intellectual inspiration for writing a survey of Ukrainian history came from Mykhailo Drahomanov, a former professor of ancient (Roman) history at Kyiv University. He was dismissed from his position in 1875 for allegedly conspiring to bring about Ukraine's secession from Russia and left for Switzerland to avoid imminent arrest. Inspired by the ideas of Giuseppe Mazzini, Drahomanov imagined Ukraine as part of a future European federation and called for a synthesis of Ukrainian history presented in a European context. He further maintained that the new narrative should go beyond national and confessional paradigms – a reference to the dominant interpretation of Ukrainian history as a struggle between Orthodox Rus' and Catholic Poland. Drahomanov wrote in 1891: 'Our history must be examined as a whole in all its eras … and in each of these eras we must pay attention to the growth or decline of population, the economy, mores and ideas in the community and the state, education, and the direct or indirect participation of Ukrainians of all classes and cultures in European history and culture.'[6]

Drahomanov's ideas were taken to heart by Mykhailo Hrushevsky, who, according to David Saunders, was the 'Macaulay, Michelet, and von Ranke of Ukraine (or in East European terms, its Palacky, Lelewel, and Kliuchevskii).'[7] Hrushevsky was the first historian to hold a university chair of Ukrainian history.[8] The chair was established in 1894 at

Lviv (Lemberg, Lwów) University in Austria-Hungary and officially designated as a chair of world history with special emphasis on the history of Eastern Europe. Hrushevsky published the first volume of his academic *History of Ukraine-Rus'* in 1898. In 1904 he not only presented a general outline of Ukrainian history as a national narrative in his article on the 'traditional' scheme of 'Russian' history but also convinced the Russian authorities of the need to publish his *Survey History of the Ukrainian People*, which presented a coherent narrative of the Ukrainian national past. Hrushevsky and his students at Lviv University responded very seriously to Drahomanov's idea of creating a Ukrainian historical narrative that would deal not only with politics and religion but also with economic, demographic, intellectual, and cultural history. But their main concern was to establish Ukrainian history as a distinct field of study on a par with the history of Russia, Austria-Hungary, and Poland.[9]

In carrying out that task, they faced challenges from all these historiographic traditions. One kind of challenge came from statist historiographies on both sides of the Russo-Austrian border. In 1853, once the shock of the Revolution of 1848 and the 'spring of the nations' had receded in the Habsburg Empire, the Austrian historian and advisor to the imperial minister of education Josef Alexander Helfert undertook to formulate an official view of the meaning, role, and tasks of national history (*Nationalgeschichte*). In a pamphlet entitled 'On National History and Its Current State of Cultivation in Austria,' he wrote: 'It is true that mankind is divided into a great number of tribes that differ as to language and color. But according to our ideas, national history is not the history of any such group defined by its racial origin. We think that national history is the history of the population of a territory that is politically united, subordinate to the same authority and living under the protection of the same law. For us, Austrian national history is the history of the Austrian state and people as a whole.'[10] For the vast majority of nineteenth-century Russian historians, from Nikolai Karamzin to Sergei Soloviev, their national history was also defined not as the annals of a particular ethnonational group but of the state and those who had settled its territory.[11]

Another type of challenge came from Russian and Polish authors who subscribed to the ethnonational principle. Russian historians such as Vasilii Kliuchevsky employed a notion of Russianness in their writings that was quite broad in scope and included the three 'Russian' tribes – the Great Russians, Little Russians (Ukrainians), and Belarusians. Ukraine was a special case in the changing imperial narrative of Russian history. The Russian dynastic historical narrative, which was constructed in course of the fifteenth and sixteenth centuries, had always been based on the foundations of Kyivan history. So was the Russian national narrative. In dealing with the all-Russian historical paradigm, Ukrainian historians tried to delimit the past and establish a Ukrainian claim to many significant episodes of the imperial historical narrative, including the history of Kyivan Rus'. The problem that Ukrainian historians faced in relating their historical paradigm to the Polish one was different from the challenge posed by Russian historiography. In dealing with Poland, the task was not so much one of presenting Ukrainian history as a distinct process, separate from the Polish grand narrative (this had already been achieved by the turn of the twentieth century), as of giving the Ukrainian nation a sense of equality in relations with its historically dominant and culturally much more Westernized counterpart, which was also far more advanced in terms of nation building.[12]

What were the main characteristics of the Ukrainian historical narrative? In defining the time frame of Ukrainian history, the new narrative presented the Ukrainian nation as more ancient than the Russian, and thus deserving of full support in its quest for sovereign cultural and political development, unhindered by interference from its younger sibling. In order to achieve that goal, the starting point of the narrative had to be moved as far back as possible. Consequently, the new narrative, worked out according to prevailing scholarly standards, established the Ukrainian claim to Kyivan Rus'. That approach put the Ukrainian narrative on a collision course with traditional Russian historiography, creating a conflict akin to the one between Swedish and Norwegian historians over the ethnic origins of the Varangians. In territorial terms, the new Ukrainian narrative linked the history of Orthodox Russian Ukraine with that of Greek Catholic Austrian Ukraine. Hrushevsky, who managed this feat, could also be called the Henri Pirenne of Ukrainian history.[13]

The new narrative of Ukrainian history followed the development of the Ukrainian people through a sequence of rises, declines, and revivals. Like Heinrich von Sybel and other German historians of his era, who created a myth of a German nation as a sleeping beauty awakened by the 'kiss' of the wars of liberation, Ukrainian historians believed in and worked towards the 'awakening' of their own nation.[14] Not unlike the Russian narrative, the Ukrainian one was teleological, although its final destination was not the reunification of the Russian people but the emancipation of one of its parts from the oppression of another.

After the Revolution of 1917, the main competition for the Ukrainian national narrative came from various Marxist narratives of Ukrainian history. All of them were products of class-based discourse that focused mainly on the theme of social antagonism. In Marxist narratives, class figured as the main agent of history, as opposed to the state or the all-Russian nation, which had played that role in the old Russian historiography. During the 1930s, the class-based discourse of Soviet Marxist historiography was adjusted to serve the purposes of the imperial project, which meant keeping the non-Russian nations of the USSR under Russian control. Hence it was the gradual rehabilitation of the old imperial Russocentric paradigm that led the way to the creation of a new supranational Soviet narrative – the history of the peoples of the USSR. Was the emergence of the Ukrainian national narrative of any consequence for the construction of the official Soviet paradigm? Yes, it was. In Soviet historiography, the traditional Russian narrative was now divested of its Ukrainian component (except for the history of Kyivan Rus'), and a parallel Ukrainian narrative was permitted to exist within the framework of the obligatory 'History of the USSR.'[15]

Multiethnic History

As the national paradigm took centre stage in Ukrainian historiography after 1991, the Ukrainian nation finally emerged victorious in its historiographic competition with dynasties, states, and the dominant Russian and Polish nations.[16] While that change in perspective corrected numerous wrongs done to Ukrainians in Russocentric and Polonocentric narratives, did it do justice to the history of Ukraine as a country and territory?

This question should be answered in the negative. Not only were significant portions of Ukrainian territorial and cultural history sidelined in the process, but large numbers of ethnic Ukrainians were allotted little space in the Ukrainian national narrative. Hrushevsky, for example, was criticized in his lifetime for replacing the early modern history of Ukraine with that of Cossackdom – an important but still a minority element of the Ukrainian population in its day. Hrushevsky also reduced the history of the nineteenth century to that of the Ukrainian liberation movement. Intellectual and cultural currents that were not part of the Ukrainian national project were left out of his narrative, which followed the rise, fall, and resurgence of the nation.[17] Thus, neither Nikolai Gogol nor Ilia Repin, both ethnic Ukrainians born in Ukraine, made it into the mainstream of Ukrainian national history. Those who opposed the Ukrainian national movement – the so-called Little Russians such as Mikhail Yuzefovich, the instigator of the Ems Ukase (1876), which prohibited Ukrainian-language publications in the Russian Empire – became part of the story, but only as traitors and villains. The Russophiles of Galicia and the Ruthenians of Transcarpathia fared no better. On the other hand, there is a tendency to Ukrainize groups and institutions that never possessed an identity that might be called Ukrainian. Recent research on the formation of political, cultural, and national identities in the lands now known as Russia, Ukraine, and Belarus points to the danger of assigning to the masses of the population national identities that did not exist at the time and did not become 'majority faiths' at least until the twentieth century.[18]

If not all Ukrainians made it into the national narrative of Ukrainian history, that is even more true of representatives of other ethnic groups. As Andreas Kappeler has recently noted, one cannot write the history of state institutions in Ukraine, its trade and economy, or its urban centres by focusing on Ukrainians alone.[19] They certainly dominated the countryside but were a minority in the cities, which were dominated by Russians, Jews, Poles, and Germans. It would be unfair to state that minorities are completely absent from the Ukrainian national narrative, but as a rule they have been portrayed as aggressors, oppressors, and exploiters in the struggle with whom the Ukrainian nation was born. There is little doubt that the minorities must be included in the new narrative of Ukrainian history, not just as 'others' but as part of the collective 'we' – an all-important element of Ukrainian history that differentiated it from the history of other lands. Today there are positive developments to be noted in the research and writing of a multiethnic history of Ukraine.

The first attempt to write such a history was made by Paul Robert Magocsi of the University of Toronto. His *History of Ukraine*, almost 800 pages in length, was published in 1996 and became a multiethnic alternative to Orest Subtelny's more traditional narrative *Ukraine: A History*, which first appeared in 1988 and went on to sweep Ukraine in numerous editions of its Ukrainian translation.[20] Magocsi managed to produce a much more complete history of Ukraine as a territory than did

Subtelny, but there is certainly room for improvement. As often happens when new horizons are opened for historical research, the initiative comes from outside the profession. That is certainly the case with Anna Reid's *Borderland: A Journey through the History of Ukraine*, first published in 1997. Reid, a Kyiv-based correspondent for the *Economist* and the *Daily Telegraph* in the mid-1990s, tells the dramatic history of Ukraine through stories of individual cities and regions. She begins in Kyiv and ends in Chornobyl, using a chapter on the western city of Kamianets-Podilskyi to tell the story of the Poles and their history in Ukraine, a chapter on Donetsk and Odesa to tell the story of the Russians, and chapters on Ivano-Frankivsk and Chernivtsi to tell the story of the Jews and the Holocaust. Her chapter on the villages of Matusiv and Lukovytsia in the Ukrainian heartland tells the story of the Ukrainian famine of 1932–3. Reid does not attempt to reach a compromise or find a middle ground between the often conflicting stories told by her acquaintances. Instead, she tries to present different perspectives on the history of the land that all her acquaintances consider to be their home. What emerges from her book is a mosaic that represents the multiethnic character of today's Ukrainian nation as much as it represents its history, conceptualized in territorial terms.

The mental mapping of Ukraine was impossible in the past and is hardly possible today without taking into account the diversity of Ukraine's regions. Historically speaking, Ukraine took shape as territories traditionally belonging to different political, economic, and cultural zones were brought together under the banner of ethnonational unity. Understanding a particular region means not only studying it in isolation but also comparing it with other regions of a given state. It also means going beyond existing national borders to take account of the historical connections that formed its unique character and identity. Among Ukraine's historical regions, the best-studied is Galicia in western Ukraine – the object of attention not only of Ukrainian but also Austrian, German, Polish, and American historians. One of the latest additions to the field is a book by Alison Frank, *Oil Empire: Visions of Prosperity in Austrian Galicia*. This is the kind of work that combines elements of economic, social, and political history. Yaroslav Hrytsak's recent treatment of the formative years of Ivan Franko presents a fresh look at political and cultural developments in Galicia and undermines many postulates of traditional Ukrainian historiography with regard to the national awakening of the nineteenth century.[21] The innovative character of both books becomes more apparent if one considers that

Galicia – a region that both Poles and Ukrainians have called their Piedmont – has been treated in both historiographic traditions almost exclusively within the context of the national paradigm.

The political and social history of Ukraine's Donbas region in Eastern Ukraine has been another attractive subject for Western historians. It was treated in a number of studies, including Charters Wynn's *Workers, Strikes and Pogroms,* and a superb monograph by Hiroaki Kuromiya, *Freedom and Terror in the Donbass.* What is lacking so far is work on the comparative history of historical regions that cross national boundaries. For one thing, Ukrainian historiography would certainly benefit from a work comparing industrialization and its impact on political, social, and cultural aspects of everyday life in, for example, Ukrainian Galicia and the Baku region of Azerbaijan.

The main challenge in writing a multiethnic and multiregional history of Ukraine is to see another ethnic group or region not as an enemy but as a neighbour – not always an easy task when the history in question is as tragic as that of Ukraine. Anna Reid writes in *Borderland* that the Ukrainians inherited a legacy of violence. Back in 1917, Volodymyr Vynnychenko, a renowned Ukrainian novelist and at that time premier of the Ukrainian government, observed that one cannot read Ukrainian history without taking a bromide.[22] The time has come to change that situation, not by prescribing a different medication but by treating the problem – the nature of the Ukrainian narrative.

New approaches to the history of the violent conflicts that have punctuated Ukrainian history over the centuries have yielded some very encouraging results, which are apparent in the work of scholars both in Ukraine and abroad. Natalia Yakovenko, now the leading Ukrainian historian of the early modern era, recently challenged one of the most powerful myths of the Ukrainian national narrative, that of the Khmelnytsky Uprising. She approached it not from the perspective of Ukrainian state or nation building but from that of its human cost, discussing the ruinous consequences of the uprising not only for its main victims, the Poles and the Jews, but also for its alleged beneficiaries, the Ukrainians. Yakovenko's new account of the Khmelnytsky Uprising, presented in an article entitled 'How Many Faces Has War?' was met with criticism in the Ukrainian scholarly press. She was accused of promoting the Polish viewpoint on the history of the revolt. Nevertheless, there are signs that Yakovenko's reinterpretation of the uprising, which cost hundreds of thousands of lives and left deep scars in the historical memories not only of Jews and Poles but of Ukrainians as well, will make its way into the new master narrative of Ukrainian history. After all, the second edition of her survey of Ukrainian history up to 1800 was recently issued in Kyiv and nominated as a major book of the year 2005.[23]

The construction of a new multiethnic and multicultural narrative of Ukrainian history requires the intensification of research on ethnic and religious minorities. The situation in the field of the history of Ukrainian Jewry, the second largest of Ukraine's minorities before the Second World War and one of its smallest today, is indicative of the challenges facing Ukrainian historiography with regard to the history of the country's minorities. When it comes to the Jewish role in the Ukrainian historical tradition, it has been depicted almost exclusively in negative terms. Only in the first decades of the twentieth century did the situation begin to change. Mykhailo Hrushevsky went out of his way to discuss the plight of the Jews during the Khmelnytsky Uprising, producing one of the most sympathetic twentieth-century accounts of Jewish history in Ukraine. He also supported the work of the Jewish department of the Academy of Sciences of Ukraine in the 1920s. But with the advance of the Soviet class-based paradigm, Jews were cleansed from the pages of Soviet textbooks. As a group they were replaced by the socially defined category of leaseholders and tavernkeepers in the early modern era and figured only as 'Soviet citizens' when it came to the discussion of Nazi atrocities against the Jewish population of the USSR.

Since 1991, Jews have remained largely absent from the Ukrainian historical narrative, but they are now being included in some aspects of it, such as the study of the Second World War.[24] Ukrainian historians like Zhanna Kovba have been exploring the history of the Jewish community during the war, while such authors as John-Paul Himka, Marco Carynnyk, and Sofiia Grachova have placed the question of Ukrainian complicity in the Holocaust on the scholarly agenda.[25] At this point there are three centres of Jewish studies in Ukraine. Nevertheless, research on Jewish history in Ukraine remains in its initial phase, as compared with the achievements of Moscow-based scholars. There is a clear need for the translation into Ukrainian of major Western works dealing with the history of Jewish communities in Ukraine.[26]

Writing a multiethnic history of Ukraine is of course an important way of dealing with the deficiencies of the dominant narrative of Ukrainian history. This exercise is useful from the political and the scholarly point of view. It helps present a much richer mosaic of

Ukrainian history and replaces the confrontation of competing ethnic narratives with their coexistence. Nevertheless, writing multiethnic history does not mean moving 'beyond ethnicity.' It means, rather, diversifying the approach instead of abandoning the paradigm altogether. As Kappeler has noted recently, the multiethnic approach shares the same set of weaknesses as the ethnonational one, since it is liable to lapse into primordialism, a teleological approach, and the marginalization of non-ethnic groups and institutions. These problems can be overcome by means of transnational approaches to the history of Ukraine.[27]

Transnational History

Over the course of its history, Ukraine has been a borderland not only of different state formations but, much more importantly, of different civilizational and cultural zones. Ukraine was always a border zone between the Eurasian steppe lands controlled by nomads and the settled forest regions. Kyiv, the future capital of Ukraine, was founded as a border post between these two worlds. The struggle for survival against the steppe nomads and the later colonization of the steppe lands constitute one of the most important themes of Ukrainian history, although the history of Ukraine's 'moving frontier' – the scene of interaction between governments, settlers, and nomads – has never found its Frederick Jackson Turner or Herbert Eugene Bolton. The Crimea and the northern Black Sea region, settled by Greek colonists in ancient times, was a peripheral but lasting part of the Mediterranean world – the territories defined by the Roman *limes*, which coincide, at least in the case of Ukraine, with the northern borders of Mediterranean powers, including the Ottoman Empire, and with the northern boundary of present-day Islam. Having accepted Christianity from Byzantium in 988, the Kyivan princes found themselves on the border between Eastern and Western Christendom – another all-important dividing line in Ukrainian history that the early modern Ukrainian elites tried to erase by promoting union between Christian churches.[28]

Centuries of borderland existence contributed to the fuzziness and fragmentation of Ukrainian identity. Borders were created and policed to divide people, but the borderlands served as contact zones where economic transactions (legal and illegal) took place, loyalties were traded, and identities negotiated.[29] Ukraine's steppe borderland called into existence a special category of steppe dwellers, known as the

Cossacks, and a special type of identity. They are usually presented as ferocious fighters against Islam and the nomads of the steppe. But what remains largely unexplained within the national narrative of Ukrainian history is why they gave themselves a Turkic name, why they dressed in baggy pantaloons like their enemies the Ottomans, why they shaved their heads like their enemies the Crimean Tatars, and why the most popular visual image of them is preserved in the Buddha-like paintings called 'Cossack Mamai.' The answer to these questions is quite simple. Not only did the Cossacks flout state frontiers, giving constant headaches to their nominal superiors in Warsaw and Moscow, but they also crossed the cultural boundaries dividing the steppe and the settled area, Christianity and Islam, Polish nobiliary democracy and Muscovite autocracy.[30]

The cultural history of the Cossacks, and indeed of Ukraine as a cultural borderland, has not yet been written. Recent research on the iconography of the Feast of the Protection of the Mother of God indicates the importance of Ukraine as an area of multiple cultural transfers.[31] Ideas emanating from the West were received, reshaped, or misinterpreted to fit local religious and cultural traditions and passed on farther east and south to the Orthodox lands of Muscovy and the Balkans. That was certainly the case with the set of ideas and models associated with the confessionalization of religious, social, and political life in Western and Central Europe of the Reformation era. First it was the creation of the Uniate Church. Then Kyivan intellectuals under the leadership of Metropolitan Peter Mohyla produced the first Orthodox *Confession of Faith* and exported models of Orthodox confessionalization developed under the influence of their relations with Catholics, Protestants, and Uniates to the rest of the Eastern Christian world.[32] As Ihor Ševčenko has shown, Metropolitan Mohyla was a man of many cultural words, and one might add that in this respect he was representative of the Ukrainian elite culture of his time.[33] The transfer of cultural models from Kyiv to the east continued in the second half of the seventeenth century and for the better part of the eighteenth. After the extension of the Muscovite protectorate to eastern Ukraine in 1654, Kyivan chroniclers first introduced the idea of the ethnocultural nation into Muscovite historiography. It was a new idea to the Muscovite elites. As Edward Keenan has convincingly shown, prior to 1654 the Muscovites did not think of their relations with other Eastern Slavs in ethnic or ethnonational terms.[34] In the first decades of the eighteenth century, Kyivan clergymen led by Teofan Prokopovych helped Peter I Westernize the Russian Empire.[35]

The new interest in the history of empires in the West, as well as in the former USSR (apparent, for example, in the articles published over the last few years in the Kazan journal *Ab Imperio*), allows historians of Ukraine to present their research in a new comparative framework. The history of Ukraine offers unique opportunities for research on relations between centres and peripheries, as well as on interrelations between imperial peripheries, bypassing decision makers in the imperial capitals. Andreas Kappeler's seminal book on the multiethnic history of the Russian Empire sets one to thinking of ways in which the Ukrainian experience under Moscow and St Petersburg can be discussed and better understood against the background of the history of other non-Russian ethnic groups in the Russian Empire.[36] Terry Martin's *Affirmative Action Empire* helps explain the role of Ukraine in the formulation of Soviet nationality policy. Roman Szporluk's articles encourage scholars to take a close look at the legacy of the Habsburg, Romanov, and Ottoman Empires in Ukrainian history.[37] Andreas Kappeler's project on the comparative history of cities along the Austro-Russian border exemplifies the comparative study of Ukraine's economic, political, cultural, and religious institutions in the Russian and Habsburg Empires. Another interesting comparative project, directed by Guido Hausmann, studies academic life in East Central European universities, including those of Cracow, Warsaw, Vilnius, Lviv, and Kharkiv. This is one of a number of research initiatives undertaken in the last few years by German and Austrian historians with the cooperation of their colleagues in Ukraine, but so far there have been very few initiatives from Ukraine itself. Certainly, Ukrainian history would benefit from a cross-national study of the Carpathian Mountains or the Dnipro Basin. Research on Ukrainian regions that constituted parts of different empires can contribute to the ongoing discussion on the typology of empires, their relation to the notion of progress, the importance of violence in their history, etc.

A number of American and West European historians are now involved in very productive research that is reconceptualizing the history of the Second World War in Ukraine – the site of some of its major battles and worst atrocities, including the Holocaust. New research is introducing elements of multiethnic and local history, as well as the history of everyday life, into the study of Ukrainian history. In his book *Making Sense of War*, Amir Weiner has presented a new image of the war as experienced and interpreted by the multiethnic population of Vinnytsia oblast in central Ukraine. Karel C. Berkhoff made use of rich

Soviet and German archives to reconstruct everyday life in German-occupied eastern and central Ukraine in his book *Harvest of Despair*, while Kate Brown, in *A Biography of No Place*, considers the multiethnic history of Eastern Volhynia between 1923 and 1953, with the war serving as the focal point of her multilayered study. Brown's work is especially interesting for its close attention to forced migrations from the region; for example, it follows Polish exiles to their new places of settlement in Kazakhstan. Another example of research dealing with the history of the war is Timothy Snyder's book *The Reconstruction of Nations*. It discusses, among other things, the Volhynian massacres of 1943–4 as an example of ethnic cleansing and an outcome of the brutalization of society initiated by the Holocaust.

Most Western works on the history of the Second World War challenge the dominant national narrative of Ukrainian history, but, even more importantly, they supersede the traditional debate shaped by the confrontation between the Soviet-era narrative of the Great Patriotic War and the national narrative of the liberation struggle against the Nazis and communists. This is an achievement that most Ukrainian historians and Ukrainian society at large cannot claim as their own. The public debate of the spring of 2005 about Ukraine's role in the Second World War yielded no results, as society remained sharply divided. Attempts to reconcile organizations representing Red Army veterans and fighters of the Ukrainian Insurgent Army failed and resulted in street fights between supporters of the two sides. Today, Ukrainian historians have not yet managed to create a master narrative of Ukraine's Second World War.[38] There is also a long way to go before the Ukrainian experience is fully incorporated into the global historical narrative, whether we consider such events as the two world wars, the Revolution of 1917, the history of communism, or ecological history, of which Chornobyl is and will remain an important part.

Area Studies

The question about the role area studies should play on university campuses is contested by a variety of academic forces and open for discussion today. But as long as politicians and political commentators, and not only academic administrators, continue to perceive today's world in terms of the Middle East, Central Asia, or Eastern Europe, the question of the broader identity of individual nations and their histories remains highly important when it comes to encounters and negotiations with the outside world.

Mark von Hagen began his recent article on Eurasia as an antiparadigm for the post-Soviet era with the statement that the fall of the USSR 'has provoked several crises of identity for historians of the region, as they try to relocate their subject in the broader intellectual contexts of a changing academic culture of historical writing.'[39] Von Hagen suggested that one way to overcome these multiple crises is to reinvent the field as Eurasian studies. He claimed for the Eurasian paradigm most of the new research published in the West and in the region after the dissolution of the USSR. That research is characterized by a desire to move away from state- and nation-based narratives towards the history of territory. Its salient characteristics include an interest in studying the history of empires and interconnections between them, as well as the history of borderlands and diasporas.

What are the borders of the newly emerging field of Eurasian studies, and should Ukraine or East Central Europe be considered part of that field? The research reviewed by von Hagen indicates quite clearly that the Eurasian 'renaissance' is largely limited to the area previously covered by specialists hired to teach Russian/Soviet history at their universities. Few historians of the former Eastern Europe are rallying to the banner of the new Eurasianism. Also controversial are the attempts of such Japanese historians as Kimitaka Matsuzato to formulate the concept of a 'Slavic Eurasia.'[40] In the eyes of many Ukrainian historians, Eurasia is little more than a new name for the territory of the USSR, manifesting an attempt by specialists trained in Russian and Soviet area studies to stake out their pre-1991 territory under a more up-to-date and politically correct designation. That goal of the new Eurasianism harks back to its intellectual sources of the interwar era. Back then, Eurasianism emerged as a trend in Russian political thought, which was searching for a way to preserve the integrity of the Russian Empire without resorting to the Bolsheviks' supranational class ideology.[41]

Many East European historians envision their countries as part of East Central Europe. That term replaced *Mitteleuropa*, coined during the First World War by the German strategist Friedrich Naumann to define the lands 'between Germany and Russia,' which he expected to constitute a post-war German sphere of influence. The war in fact resulted in the disintegration of the empires that had controlled those territories, creating a zone that became known as Eastern Europe. Among those who promoted the concept of Eastern Europe was the Polish historian Oscar Halecki. After emigrating to the United States in the aftermath of the Second World War, he published a book entitled

The Limits and Divisions of European History (1950). There he revised and developed some of his earlier ideas on the history of Eastern Europe and suggested a new name that stressed its close relation to the West. The name he proposed was 'East Central Europe.' While politicians and the media continued to speak and write about the countries of the Soviet bloc as parts of Eastern Europe, academics were more willing to adopt the new name for the region. It was promoted mainly by historians of Poland, including Halecki himself, Piotr Wandycz, and others. The University of Washington Press published a multivolume series on the history of East Central Europe, and a number of chairs in history departments of North American universities used the term in their courses.[42] The term broke into official discourse in the countries of the region, notably in Poland, after the velvet revolutions of 1989. In the academic sphere, the strongest promoter of the East Central European concept has been the Institute of East Central Europe in Lublin. Over the last fifteen years, under the leadership of Professor Jerzy Kłoczowski, the institute has organized scores of conferences and published dozens of volumes dealing with the history of the region.[43]

Kłoczowski and the concept of East Central Europe have been perceived as principal targets by some participants in the 'East Slavic Round Tables' organized by the Institute of Slavic Studies of the Russian Academy of Sciences in the years 2001–3. According to the organizer of the round tables, Leonid Gorizontov, in Russia the main alternative to the concept of East Central Europe has been the idea of all-Russian culture, which brings together Russians, Ukrainians, and Belarusians not on a regional basis but on linguistic, cultural, and ultimately national grounds.[44] That concept was given scholarly formulation during the interwar period in the works of the renowned Russian linguist Nikolai Trubetskoi, one of the founders of the original Eurasian school. Although some participants in the round tables have criticized Trubetskoi's concept, others continue to support the view that Russia and Ukraine were 'reunited' in the mid-seventeenth century – an indication of the continuing belief of some Russian scholars in the primordial unity of an 'all-Russian' nation.[45] Moreover, the treatment of problems of Ukrainian history under the auspices of the Institute of Slavic Studies, within the framework established by the round tables devoted to the history and culture of the Eastern Slavs, indicates that Eurasianist ideas and concepts of all-Russian unity continue to inform present-day Russian discussions on the history of Ukraine and Eastern Europe in general.

It would appear that Ukrainian historians are generally most comfortable with a view of their country not as part of a Russian-dominated Eurasia but as part of East Central Europe. The latter concept gained popularity in Ukraine after 1991. A Society of Historians of East Central Europe, chaired by Professor Natalia Yakovenko, was formed in the early 1990s, and in 2001 a *History of East Central Europe* was published in Lviv under the editorship of Leonid Zashkilniak.[46] The new Ukrainian president, Viktor Yushchenko, also sees the future and, indeed, the mission of his country as bound up with East Central Europe. In his address to the Ukrainian parliament in February 2006, Yushchenko expressed his confidence that it was 'Ukraine's historical destiny to serve as the basis for integration processes in the central and east European region.'[47] Whether Ukraine establishes itself as part of East Central Europe will depend mostly on political developments in the region, but one should not underestimate the role of historians in shaping a sense of broader 'belonging,' especially in new nations whose identity is still in the formative stage.

In assessing the development of the national interpretation of Ukrainian history, it should be admitted that the introduction of the national paradigm approximately one hundred years ago had both positive and negative consequences. In Ukraine, as in other nations, the deconstruction of an imperial narrative and the promotion of a national one helped change the field in qualitative terms. The advent of national historiographies in a region dominated by imperial paradigms helped shift the attention of historians and citizens alike from dynasties and states to peoples; from elites to masses; from ruling nations to submerged ones, thereby contributing to the development of the kind of historical vision that we share today. On the other hand, the insistence of twentieth-century Ukrainian historians on the national paradigm sidelined important elements of their subject, marginalizing the history of ethnic minorities, neglecting the history of social classes and groups not central to the nation-building process, and distorting the history of regions and border areas.

The post-1991 Ukrainian historical narrative is still distant from Drahomanov's ideal of Ukrainian history as he formulated it back in 1891. It is not fully integrated into the European historical narrative, and while it now covers all periods of the Ukrainian past, it does not always pay 'attention to the growth or decline of population, the economy, mores and ideas in the community and the state, education, and the direct or indirect participation of Ukrainians of all classes and cultures in European history and culture.'[48] The current state of research on Ukrainian history may be explained by several factors. The years of Soviet control and the dominance of a Russocentric historiography could not but hinder attempts to imagine Ukraine in any other context than the history of the Ukrainian nation. The country's lack of sovereignty turned statehood into an obsession for many Ukrainian historians in the West, leaving little time or energy for the exploration of other avenues of the Ukrainian past. Still, there are signs that the situation is changing for the better. The major positive development of the last fifteen years in the West has been what one might call the deghettoization of Ukrainian history and the appearance of young scholars not burdened by the legacy of Cold War-era historiography. Most of the new directions in research on Ukrainian history are associated with the work done by Western scholars and the new generation of scholars in Ukraine.

The history of Ukraine should be rethought in order to overcome the limitations imposed on it by the centuries-old national paradigm. This would help integrate the Ukrainian past into the history of Eastern and Central Europe. One would like to believe that the future of Ukraine lies in the European Union, but its past should stay where it belongs, in the multiplicity of worlds created by civilizational and imperial boundaries throughout the history of the territory known today as Ukraine. There is little doubt that Ukrainian history can only benefit from being imagined outside the limits imposed on historical thinking by the national paradigm. Methods applied today in micro- and macrohistorical study will certainly make Ukrainian history richer, more complete, and more true to the life experience of people of various nationalities, cultures, and political persuasions who settled that territory in the past and those who live there today. This new Ukrainian history will also enrich and help reshape the history of Eastern Europe, as well as of the whole European continent.

Probably the most promising approach to the history of Ukraine is to think of it as a civilizational and cultural borderland; a dividing line, but also a bridge between Central and Eastern Europe. That approach has been applied successfully to the history of other East European countries, including Poland and Hungary. But Ukraine fits that paradigm better than any other country of the region, given its centuries-old situation as a crossroads not only between Eastern and Central Europe but also between Eastern Europe and the Balkans, the Mediterranean world, and the Eurasian steppelands. In the Ukrainian historiographic tradition, the East-West approach has been associated with the work of Ivan L. Rudnytsky and Ihor Ševčenko. Although the history of Ukraine as a multiethnic country and a cultural borderland has not yet been written, compared with representatives of other national historiographies, historians of Ukraine have a head start in that undertaking. They are uniquely positioned to study the history of their country in its full scope, whether it be the history of Polish-, Russian- or Ottoman-dominated lands and territories, at different stages in its development.

Notes

Note on Transliteration

1 Cf. editorial prefaces and glossary in Mykhailo Hrushevsky, *History of Ukraine-Rus'*, 7: xix–xxvi, liii–lvi.

Introduction

1 See Plokhy, *Unmaking Imperial Russia: Mykhailo Hrushevsky and the Writing of Ukrainian History.*

1 Empire or Nation?

1 Kliuchevskii, *Sochineniia*, 1:34.
2 See Velychenko, 'Rival Grand Narratives of National History.'
3 Rogger, *National Consciousness*, 3.
4 See Greenfeld, *Nationalism*, 238–9.
5 Tolz, *Russia*, 16.
6 For a survey of the history of the Russian Empire during the rule of Anna Ioannovna and Elizabeth, see Dukes, *The Making of Russian Absolutism*, 112–44; and Anisimov, *Rossiia v seredine XVIII veka*, and *Elizaveta Petrovna*.
7 Quoted in Rogger, *National Consciousness*, 30–1. Cf. Wortman, *Scenarios of Power*, abridged ed., 44–51.
8 See Vlasovs'kyi, *Narys istoriï Ukraïns'koï pravoslavnoï tserkvy*, 2:129–30.
9 At some point Peter allegedly stated that 'we need Europe for a few decades before we turn our backside to it.' See Cross, '"Them": Russians on Foreigners,' 79.

10 On the development of the cult of Peter I during Elizabeth's reign, see Riasanovsky, *The Image of Peter the Great*, 23–34. On its anti-Western overtones, see Rogger, *National Consciousness*, 32–3.

11 For biographies of Catherine II, see Madariaga, *Russia in the Age of Catherine the Great*, and Alexander, *Catherine the Great*.

12 Quoted in Dukes, *The Making of Russian Absolutism*, 155. On the discourse associated with Catherine's ascension to the Russian throne, see Wortman, *Scenarios of Power*, 52–8.

13 Rogger, *National Consciousness*, 35–9.

14 Ibid. Continuing the tradition established by Peter I, Catherine's supporters offered her the official title 'Mother of the Fatherland,' but she declined the honour. On the development of the cult of Peter I under Catherine II, see Riasanovsky, *The Image of Peter the Great*, 34–45.

15 Quoted in Cross, '"Them": Russians on Foreigners,' 79.

16 Ibid., 84–5. Criticism was directed primarily at foreign tutors, who often had no qualifications to teach Russian youth.

17 On the incorporation of the Cossack polity into the empire, see Kohut, *Russian Centralism and Ukrainian Autonomy*.

18 On Shcherbatov and his writings, see Artem'eva, *Mikhail Shcherbatov*.

19 See Vinogradov, *Ocherki po istorii russkogo literaturnogo iazyka XVII–XIX vekov*, 213.

20 On the *Synopsis*, see Plokhy, *The Origins of the Slavic Nations*, 258–66.

21 On the Rozumovskys, see Vasil'chikov, *Semeistvo Razumovskikh*.

22 In the Russian historiographic tradition, Lomonosov has often been considered an embodiment of Russian genius – an essentially non-Western and anti-Western force for good in Russian science, literature, and culture. See the most recent publication on Lomonosov issued under the auspices of the Russian Academy of Sciences: Fomin, *Lomonosov*. On Trediakovsky, who enjoys popularity among literary scholars but never matched Lomonosov's stature in the popular imagination, see Reyfman, *Vasilii Trediakovsky*.

23 For a detailed biography of Müller and an extensive analysis of politics within the academy, see J.L. Black, *G.-F. Müller and the Imperial Russian Academy*.

24 On Teplov, see Daniel, *A Statesman at the Court of Catherine the Great*.

25 On the attempts of eighteenth-century Russian rulers to prevent the Western publication of works deemed harmful to Russia, see Cross, '"Them": Russians on Foreigners,' 82–3.

26 On the Müller debate, see Black, *G.-F. Müller and the Imperial Russian Academy*, 109–22. Cf. Shanskii, 'Zapal'chivaia polemika.' For a general survey of the development of polemics on the Varangian issue in the eighteenth

century, see Khlevov, *Normanskaia problema v otechestvennoi istoricheskoi nauke*, 4–17.

27 On Lomonosov and his participation in the debate, apart from the above-mentioned works by Black and Shanskii, see Rogger, *National Consciousness*, 209–16; and Peshtich, *Russkaia istoriografiia XVIII veka*, pt 2, 164–209.

28 On A.I. Mankiev, see Peshtich, *Russkaia istoriografiia*, pt 1, 103–9.

29 On Tatishchev, see Peshtich, *Russkaia istoriografiia XVIII veka*, pt 1, 222–75; pt 2, 124–63; and Iukht, 'Pobornik novoi Rossii.' For Tatishchev's invention of sources and events, see Tolochko, *'Istoriia Rossiiskaia' Vasiliia Tatishcheva.*

30 For an English-language summary of Tatishchev's views on the origins of Rus', see Rogger, *National Consciousness*, 196–9.

31 For a brief discussion of Schlözer's and LeClerc's views on Russian history and reactions to them in Russian historiography, see ibid., 186–8, 219–22, 227–38.

32 On the historical views of Catherine II, see Peshtich, *Russkaia istoriografiia XVIII veka*, pt 2, 252–64. On Boltin, see Shanskii, *Iz istorii russkoi istoricheskoi mysli. I. N. Boltin*. On Shcherbatov, see idem, 'Chto dolzhno istoriku.'

33 On the multiethnic approach to the early history of Rus' in the works of Catherine II and Boltin, see Elena Pogosian, 'Rus' i Rossiia v istoricheskikh sochineniiakh 1730–80–kh godov,' 16–19.

34 Quoted in Zorin, *Kormia dvuglavogo orla*, 106. At one point the Crimea was considered a potential place of settlement for the British convicts who eventually ended up in Australia. See Cross, '"Them": Russians on Foreigners,' 80.

2 Incorporated Identity

1 Despite these changes in the numbers of ethnic Russians, Ukrainians, and Belarusians between the census of 1718–19 and that of 1795, the proportion of Eastern Slavs in the empire remained almost the same, amounting to 86 per cent in the first case and 83 per cent in the second. See Kappeler, *The Russian Empire*, 115–17.

2 Raeff, 'Ukraine and Imperial Russia,' 70.

3 See Saunders, *The Ukrainian Impact on Russian Culture, 1750–1850*, 55–8. On Ukrainian medical doctors in the Russian Empire, see S.P. Ruda, 'Medytsyna,' in *Istoriia ukraïns'koï kul'tury*, 737–9.

4 See Greenfeld, *Nationalism*, 238–9.

5 The dominance of Ukrainians among church hierarchs was so complete that in 1754 Empress Elizabeth found herself obliged to order the Synod to include Great Russians among those appointed as bishops and archimandrites. The

order was largely ignored until the accession of Catherine II. See Kharlampovich, *Malorossiiskoe vliianie na velikorusskuiu tserkovnuiu zhizn'*; and Vlasovs'kyi, *Narys istorii Ukrains'koï pravoslavnoï tserkvy*, 2: 134–6.

6 See Kohut, 'Ukraine: From Autonomy to Integration (1654–1830s),' 188.

7 On the absorption of the Hetmanate, see Kohut, *Russian Centralism and Ukrainian Autonomy*.

8 Kappeler, *'Great Russians' and 'Little Russians,'* 8.

9 On Divovych, see Oleksander Ohloblyn, 'Semen ta Oleksa Divovychi,' in idem, *Liudy staroï Ukraïny*, 14–23. For the text of the 'Conversation,' see Divovych, 'Razgovor Velikorossii s Malorossiieiu.' For a Ukrainian translation of the poem, see *Tysiacha rokiv*, vol. 4, bk 2, 115–44. On the 'Brief Description of Little Russia,' see Apanovich, *Rukopisnaia svetskaia kniga XVIII v. na Ukraine*, 187–201; and Bovhyria, '*Korotkyi opys Malorosiï* (1340–1734) u rukopysnykh spyskakh XVIII st.'

10 See Divovych, 'Razgovor Velikorossii s Malorossiieiu,' 414.

11 Ibid., 394.

12 On the political ideas of the Cossack officers in the Mazepa era, see Plokhy, *The Origins of the Slavic Nations*, 277–83, 333–42. On Khazar mythology, see Lutsenko, Introduction to *Hryhorij Hrabjanka's 'The Great War of Bohdan Xmel'nyc'kyj,'* lii–lvi. On the concept of fatherland in Cossack political thought of the Mazepa era, see Sysyn, 'Fatherland in Early Eighteenth-Century Political Thought.' On Cossack rights, see Kohut, 'In Search of Perpetual Rights and Liberties.'

13 These texts have been reissued most recently in *Tysiacha rokiv*, vol. 4, bk 2, 99–103, 147–66. The speech is not dated, but the petition bears the year 1764. On the relation of both documents to the Hlukhiv council, see Kohut, *Russian Centralism*, 86–90, nn. 75, 76.

14 *Tysiacha rokiv*, vol. 4, bk 2, 99–103.

15 Ibid., 147–66.

16 The participants in the council were clearly less optimistic on the issue of the Hetmanate's power and the strength of its Cossack army than was Divovych, who claimed that Little Russia had ten battle-ready regiments. In fact, those taking part in the council came together to find a solution to the political, social, and economic decline that was fully apparent by the mid-eighteenth century.

17 On court politics and their impact on the decision to abolish the office of hetman, see Kohut, *Russian Centralism*, 78–86, 95–101. On the Myrovych affair, see Bil'basov, *Ioann Antonovich i Mirovich*.

18 Quoted in Kohut, *Russian Centralism*, 104. Cf. idem, 'Ukraine: From Autonomy to Integration (1654–1830s),' 188. In referring to wolves looking to the

forest, Catherine had in mind the Russian proverb 'No matter how much you feed a wolf, he still looks to the forest [in order to escape].'

19 For the text of Teplov's memorandum, see Vasylenko, 'H.N. Teplov i ioho "Zapiska o neporiadkakh v Malorossii."'

20 For the texts of the instructions to Ukrainian delegates to the Legislative Commission, see *Nakazy malorossiiskim deputatam 1767 goda i akty o vyborakh deputatov v Komissiiu sochineniia ulozheniia*. Cf. the Ukrainian translation of select instructions in *Tysiacha rokiv,* vol. 4, bk 2, 188–279. For excerpts from Poletyka's works, see ibid., 270–4. On the Poletykas, see Oleksander Ohloblyn, 'Andrii Poletyka,' in his *Liudy staroï Ukraïny,* 193–98. For a discussion of the Ukrainian elections to the Legislative Commission and the participation of Ukrainian deputies in its work, see Kohut, *Russian Centralism,* 125–90.

21 On the incorporation of the Ukrainian gentry into the social structure of the empire, see Miller, 'Ocherki iz istorii i iuridicheskogo byta staroi Malorossii.'

22 Quoted in Saunders, *The Ukrainian Impact,* 41–2.

23 Quoted in Saunders, *The Ukrainian Impact,* 69. For a biography of Bezborodko, see Grigorovich, *Kantsler kniaz' Aleksandr Andreevich Bezborod'ko v sviazi s sobytiiami ego vremeni*. For a discussion of Bezborodko's career and his Ukrainian identity or lack thereof, see Saunders, *The Ukrainian Impact,* 69–81; and Kohut, *Russian Centralism,* 259–63.

24 See 'Nakaz Chernihivs'koho shliakhetstva,' in *Tysiacha rokiv,* vol. 4, bk 2, 192–201, here 194.

25 Kohut, *Russian Centralism,* 261.

26 See Ruban, *Kratkaia letopis' Malyia Rossii s 1506 po 1776 god.*

27 Quoted ibid., 260.

28 See Saunders, *The Ukrainian Impact,* 76–7.

29 On Ruban and his writings and publications, see ibid., 119–26.

30 On Tumansky and his family, see Oleksander Ohloblyn, 'Tumans'ki,' in idem, *Liudy staroï Ukraïny,* 238–61. See also Zhurba, *Stanovlennia ukraïns'koï arkheohrafiï,* 44–93.

31 Quoted in Saunders, *The Ukrainian Impact,* 132.

32 Greenfeld, *Nationalism,* 238.

33 On Kapnist, see Oleksander Ohloblyn, 'Vasyl' Kapnist,' in idem, *Liudy staroï Ukraïny,* 49–114. His mission is discussed in Edgerton, 'Laying a Legend to Rest'; and Dashkevych, 'Berlin, kviten' 1791 r.'

3 Ukraine or Little Russia?

1 On the role of historical myth in the process of modern nation building, see Smith, *The Ethnic Origins of Nations,* 174–208.

2 See Berger, Donovan, and Passmore, 'Apologias for the Nation-State in Western Europe since 1800.'

3 On the connection between literary and criminal forgery in the Age of Enlightenment, see Baines, *The House of Forgery in Eighteenth-Century Britain*. On the function of historical forgeries in East Central Europe and Ukraine, see Hrabovych, 'Slidamy natsional'nykh mistyfikatsii.'

4 See Trevor-Roper, 'The Invention of Tradition,' 17–18. For the impact of Macpherson's poetry on the rise of the romantic movement, see Gaskill, *Reception of Ossian in Europe*. On the reception of Ossian in the Russian Empire, see Levin, *Ossian v russkoi literature*. On the invention of historical sources in eighteenth-century Russia, see Tolochko, *'Istoriia Rossiiskaia' Vasiliia Tatishcheva*, especially 504–23.

5 On the *Igor Tale* as a late eighteenth-century text, see Keenan, *Josef Dobrovský and the Origins of the* Igor' Tale.

6 See *Istoriia Rusov ili Maloi Rossii*. For a brief summary of the unknown author's historical argument, see Velychenko, *National History as Cultural Process*, 156–8.

7 Although Shevchenko was an admirer of the 'History of the Rus'' and popularized its heroic version of the Cossack past, he did not share the anonymous author's anti-Polish attitudes or his nobiliary bias against the popular masses.

8 See Ohloblyn, 'Where Was *Istoriya Rusov* Written?' Hryhorii Poletyka has been regarded as the author of the 'History' by Vladimir Ikonnikov, Oleksander Lazarevsky, Mykola Vasylenko, Dmytro Doroshenko, Yaroslav Dzyra, and Hanna Shvydko. Mykhailo Hrushevsky advanced the hypothesis of the co-authorship of Hryhorii and Vasyl Poletyka. The latter was considered the sole author by Vasyl Horlenko, Anatolii Yershov, and Illia Borshchak. The hypothesis about Bezborodko's authorship was first suggested by Mykhailo Slabchenko and further developed by Pavlo Klepatsky, Andrii Yakovliv, and Mykhailo Vozniak. See Oleksander Ohloblyn, 'Istoriia Rusov,' in *Encyclopedia of Ukraine*, 2:360.

9 Ohloblyn, who was by far the most productive and influential student of the monument, also pushed the 'nationalization' of the 'History' to the limit, claiming that it was 'a declaration of the rights of the Ukrainian nation' inspired by the 'idea of Ukrainian political sovereignty,' as well as 'an act of indictment against Muscovy.' See his introduction to a Ukrainian translation of the work, *Istoriia Rusiv*, v–xxix. For a survey of the nineteenth- and early twentieth-century reception of the 'History of the Rus'' and research on the monument, see Vozniak, *Psevdo-Konys'kyi i psevdo-Poletyka*, 5–96. Cf. Kravchenko, *Narysy z ukraïns'koï istoriohrafiï*, 101–16.

10 Shevchuk, 'Nerozhadani taiemnytsi "Istorii Rusiv,"' in *Istoriia Rusiv*, trans. into modern Ukrainian by Ivan Drach (Kyiv, 1991), 28.

11 For a critical assessment of the latest Ukrainian publications on the topic, see Kravchenko, 'Istoriia Rusiv u suchasnykh interpretatsiiakh.'

12 See the entry 'Little Russian Mentality' by Bohdan Kravtsiv in *Encyclopedia of Ukraine*, 3:166.

13 *Istoriia Rusov ili Maloi Rossii*, iii–iv.

14 See Storozhenko, 'Malaia Rossiia ili Ukraina?' 287–8.

15 See Czacki, 'O nazwisku Ukrainy i początku Kozaków.' On Czacki and his activities, see Dybiec, *Nie tylko szablą. Nauka i kultura polska w walce o utrzymanie tożsamości narodowej, 1795–1918*, 75–80, 112–13.

16 On the secular school and gymnasium in Novhorod-Siverskyi, see Oleksander Ohloblyn's essay on the founding director of both schools, Ivan Khalansky, in Ohloblyn, *Liudy staroï Ukraïny*, 262–9.

17 On Markov, see Zhurba, *Stanovlennia ukraïns'koï arkheohrafiï*, 94–119.

18 See *Kratkaia rossiiskaia istoriia dlia upotrebleniia iunoshestvu, nachinaiushchemu obuchat'sia istorii, prodolzhennaia do iskhoda XVIII stoletiia, sochinennaia v Kieve uchitelem Maksimom Berlinskim* (Moscow, 1800). The 'Short History,' adopted as a textbook in the Kyiv Theological Academy, was used there in that capacity in 1804. See Tsentral'nyi derzhavnyi istorychnyi arkhiv Ukraïny u misti Kyievi, fond 1711, op. 1, no. 120, fols 84, 90.

19 See Berlinskii, *Kratkaia rossiiskaia istoriia*, 93–106. On Berlynsky and his writings, see David Saunders, *The Ukrainian Impact*, 209–12; Braichevs'kyi, 'Maksym Berlyns'kyi ta ioho "Istoriia mista Kyieva"'; and Kravchenko, *Narysy z ukraïns'koï istoriohrafiï*, 80–4.

20 Berlinskii, *Kratkaia rossiiskaia istoriia*, 93, 96–7, 98–9.

21 See Ohloblyn's introduction to *Istoriia Rusiv*, viii; and Shevel'ov, '*Istoriia Rusov* ochyma movoznavtsia.'

22 Berlinskii, *Kratkaia rossiiskaia istoriia*, 100.

23 Ibid., 101.

24 On Berlynsky's attempts to publish the manuscript, see Saunders, *The Ukrainian Impact*, 211. In citing this work, Volodymyr Kravchenko (*Narysy z istoriï ukraïns'koï istoriohrafiï*, 81) gives a somewhat different title: 'Istoricheskoe obozrenie Malorossii.'

25 On Anastasevych, see Saunders, *The Ukrainian Impact*, 140–4. The translation of Czacki's article appeared in pt 1, no. 1 of *Ulei* for 1811. Two of Berlynsky's contributions, 'Razdelenie Malorossii na polki' and 'O gorode Kieve,' appeared in the same year, in pt 1, no. 3, and pt 2, no. 8 of the journal respectively. Anastasevych visited Berlynsky in Kyiv in 1811, and afterwards they stayed in touch by correspondence. See excerpts from

Berlynsky's private diary in the Volodymyr Vernadsky Library, National Academy of Sciences of Ukraine (Kyiv), Manuscript Institute, fond 175, no. 1057, section 2, fols 1–55.

26 On the debate over the language of instruction at the Kyiv gymnasium, see Saunders, *The Ukrainian Impact*, 31–2. At some point before the spring of 1817, Berlynsky came into conflict with the then director of the Kyiv gymnasium and petitioned the St Petersburg authorities in that regard. See a letter to Berlynsky from his brother Matvii, dated 2 March 1817 in St Petersburg, in the Volodymyr Vernadsky Library, National Academy of Sciences of Ukraine (Kyiv), Manuscript Institute, fond 175, no. 1057, section 1, fols 7–8.

27 See Saunders, *The Ukrainian Impact*, 211. On Symonovsky and his writings, see Ohloblyn, *Liudy staroï Ukraïny*, 219–36.

28 On the use of these terms in Cossack historiography of the early eighteenth century, see Sysyn, 'The Image of Russia and Russian-Ukrainian Relations in Ukrainian Historiography of the Late Seventeenth and Early Eighteenth Centuries.'

29 On Markovych's attitude to the issue of the Cossacks and Ukraine, see Tolochko, 'Kyievo-Rus'ka spadshchyna v istorychnii dumtsi Ukraïny pochatku XIX st.,' 303.

30 See *Istoriia Rusov*, 68–74.

31 Ibid., 208.

32 Ibid., 236, 253.

33 Ibid., 161, 167, 172, 179.

34 Ibid., 242, 253.

35 On the 'Ukrainian line' and the names of the gubernias in question, see the *Encyclopedia of Ukraine*, 2:451; 3:165; 5:398.

36 See Skovoroda, *Tvory u dvokh tomakh*, 2:316.

37 On Czartoryski's activities and efforts to restore Polish statehood in the first decade of the nineteenth century, see Wandycz, *The Lands of Partitioned Poland, 1795–1918*, 33–42. On Polish plans for Right-Bank Ukraine in connection with Napoleon's policies in Eastern Europe, see Borshchak, *Napoleon i Ukraïna*. Cf. Vadym Adadurov, 'Narodzhennia odnoho istorychnoho mitu,' 227, 233.

38 On the growth of anti-Polish sentiment in Russian society during that period, see Zorin, *Kormia dvuglavogo orla ... Literatura i gosudarstvennaia ideologiia v Rossii v poslednei treti XVIII–pervoi treti XIX veka*, 157–86.

39 On the struggle for the recognition of Cossack ranks and historical writings produced in order to establish the nobiliary status of the Hetmanate's elite, see Kohut, *Russian Centralism and Ukrainian Autonomy*, 248–84.

40 *Istoriia Rusov,* iv.
41 Quoted in Kravchenko, *Narysy z ukraïns'koï istoriohrafiï*, 83. The article 'O gorode Kieve,' published in *Ulei* in 1811, was an excerpt from Berlynsky's larger study, 'History of the City of Kyiv.' This particular assessment, which would probably have infuriated the author of the 'History of the Rus',' was also apparently less than pleasing to the publishers of Berlynsky's work. According to Kravchenko, it was not included in the 1991 edition of *Istoriia mista Kyieva*.
42 See Kravchenko, *Narysy z ukraïns'koï istoriohrafiï*, 83–4.
43 See Tsarinnyi, 'Ukrainskoe dvizhenie,' 142–3.
44 On Berlynsky's interpretation of the Ukrainian past in his unpublished 'History of Little Russia,' see Kravchenko, *Narysy z ukraïns'koï istoriohrafiï*, 84.
45 On Russian interpretations of Ukrainian history in the first decades of the nineteenth century, including the tendency to claim the history of Kyivan Rus' for Russia alone, see Tolochko, 'Kyievo-Rus'ka spadshchyna,' 266–309.
46 Smith, *The Ethnic Origins of Nations*, 3.
47 Hobsbawm, 'Identity History Is Not Enough,' in idem, *On History*, 276.
48 For a discussion of the impact of Mickiewicz's poetry on the Polish, Lithuanian, and Belarusian national revivals, see Snyder, *The Reconstruction of Nations*, 29–43, 281–3.

4 The Missing Mazepa

1 On the anathematization of Mazepa and the ritual performed on his effigy on the orders of Aleksandr Menshikov, see Subtelny, *The Mazepists*, 39–40. Cf. Rigel'man, *Litopysna opovid' pro Malu Rosiiu ta ïï narod i kozakiv uzahali*, 547.
2 For a discussion of the incident, see Sapozhnikov, 'Zagadochnye portrety.' Cf. Zholtovs'kyi, *Ukraïns'kyi zhyvopys XVII-XVIII st.*, 225.
3 See Subtelny, *The Mazepists*, 1. On the anathematization of Mazepa, see Brogi, 'Mazepa, lo zar e il diavolo.' A church service commemorating the victory over the Swedes at the Battle of Poltava also featured a condemnation of Mazepa, who was identified with Judas. See Pogosian, *Petr I – arkhitektor rossiiskoi istorii*, 177.
4 See Babinski, *The Mazeppa Legend in European Romanticism*.
5 The picture, originally known as a portrait of a 'Little Russian,' was later retitled 'Field Hetman.' The new name (*napol'nyi getman* in Russian) derived from a misunderstanding of the catalogue description of the picture, which stated that it was a not fully (*napolno* in eighteenth-century Russian) completed portrait of a hetman. Later it was taken to be a portrait of Mazepa. See Bilets'kyi, *Ukraïns'kyi portretnyi zhyvopys*, 124.

6 As in the case of Mazepa, the portraits of Polubotok that circulated in Ukraine during the nineteenth century had nothing to do with the true image of the acting hetman. In real life, he was rather stocky and did not fit the requirements of a romantic hero. As a result, portraits of his father, Leontii, which fit those requirements much better, were disseminated as portraits of Pavlo Polubotok, popularizing the idea of Ukraine's struggle for its autonomous rights (ibid., 124, 219–21).

7 See the English translation of the poem 'Irzhavets'' in *The Poetical Works of Taras Shevchenko: The Kobzar*, 325–6.

8 For a reproduction of the 1845 watercolour, see *Shevchenkivs'kyi slovnyk*, 2:333.

9 For a comprehensive discussion of the origins of the iconographic composition of the *Pokrova*, see Gębarowicz, *Mater Misericordiae – Pokrow – Pokrowa w sztuce i legendzie Środkowo-Wschodniej Europy.*

10 Shevchenko, *Bliznetsy*, in idem, *Povne zibrannia tvoriv*, 4:26–7.

11 For a discussion of the circumstances in which the icon was painted and its ideological message, see my *Tsars and Cossacks*, 55–62. Cf. the reproduction of the Sulymivka *Pokrova*, ibid., plate XI.

12 On the importance of the Cossack myth for the Ukrainian nation-building project, see Armstrong, 'Myth and History in the Evolution of Ukrainian Consciousness.'

13 See Hrushevs'kyi, *Iliustrovana istoriia Ukraïny.* The book appeared in numerous editions in Ukraine between 1912 and 1918 and was later repeatedly reprinted in the West.

14 Despite its title, the essay also covered Ukrainian painting of the eighteenth century. See Kuz'min, 'Ukrainskaia zhivopis' XVII veka.'

15 Ibid., 458–9.

16 Kuzmin's high opinion of Mazepa's role in the development of Ukrainian art was apparently influenced by Hrushevsky's treatment of the hetman. In his essay, Kuzmin made reference to one of the Cossack-era portraits in Hrushevsky's survey (ibid., 462, 170–6). In turn, Kuzmin's essay influenced quite a few Ukrainian scholars, including Mykola Holubets, the author of a survey of Ukrainian art (1922). There, Holubets repeated almost verbatim some of Kuzmin's basic assessments. He noted the influence on Ukrainian art of 'Ukraine's unification with Russia' and the profound impact of Ivan Mazepa's activities on the Westernization of Ukrainian art forms. See Holubets', *Nacherk istoriï ukraïns'koho mystetstva*, 234, 240–1.

17 See Zholtovs'kyi, *Vyzvol'na viina ukraïns'koho narodu v pam'iatkakh mystetstva XVI-XVIII st.*, 53–4.

18 See *Narysy z istoriï ukraïns'koho mystetstva*, 94–5, plate VI, illustrations nos 159, 160.

19 See Lohvyn, *Po Ukraïni*, 71.

20 See Bilets'kyi, *Ukraïns'kyi portretnyi zhyvopys*, 82.

21 Ibid., 191–2. Biletsky's critique of the social egoism of the Cossack officer stratum was directly applied to the sponsors of the *Pokrova* icons by Zholtovsky, who wrote: 'The "Cossack *Pokrovas*" present a profoundly conceived image of the contemporary Hetmanate, its elite, the colonels, captains, and Cossack officers, who based themselves on the power of the tsarist Russian regime and gradually entered the ranks of the "well-born nobiliary stratum"' (Zholtovs'kyi, *Ukraïns'kyi zhyvopys XVII–XVIII st.*, 231–4).

22 See Bilets'kyi, *Ukraïns'ke mystetstvo druhoï polovyny XVII–XVIII stolit'*, 6–7, 98, 100.

23 Although he stayed away from the 'Mazepa problem,' Biletsky questioned Shevchenko's suggestion that the author of the icon was a foreigner, noting that an artist of such qualifications could have been trained in the Kyivan Cave Monastery as easily as in the West (ibid., 36–7).

24 See Sichyns'kyi, *Ivan Mazepa.*

25 See Hordyns'kyi, *Ukraïns'ka ikona XII–XVIII storich*, 22–3.

26 See, for example, the album of reproductions published for Western consumption in 1996 by Liudmyla Miliaieva. It includes three Cossack *Pokrovas* – those from Deshky (with the portrait of Bohdan Khmelnytsky), Sulymivka, and Novhorod-Siverskyi (see *The Ukrainian Icon*, 68–74). As in her earlier publications, Miliaieva avoids any comment on the ideological meaning of the icons, focusing instead on their characteristics as works of art.

27 See Umantsev, *Mystetstvo davn'oï Ukraïny*, 242.

28 See Stepovyk, *Istoriia ukraïns'koï ikony X–XX stolit'*, 66.

5 The Historian as Nation Builder

1 Nevill Forbes, one of the leading twentieth-century Western experts on the languages, history, and culture of the Slavs, was a reader in Russian at Oxford when he wrote this letter. For the text, see Tsentral'nyi derzhavnyi istorychnyi arkhiv Ukraïny u Kyievi (henceforth TsDIAK), fond 1235, no. 303, pp. 107–10.

2 On Mykhailo Hrushevsky's academic career, see Prymak, *Mykhailo Hrushevsky*; Vynar, *Mykhailo Hrushevs'kyi i Naukove Tovarystvo im. Tarasa Shevchenka, 1892–1930*; and Plokhy, *Unmaking Imperial Russia.*

3 One of his followers at the time, the future Ukrainian political leader and historian Dmytro Doroshenko, left the following words in his memoirs concerning Hrushevsky's arrival in St Petersburg in the spring of 1906: 'His great scholarly and public services; his extraordinary organizational talent created great authority and deep respect for him. In our eyes he was a

symbol of pan-Ukrainian unification; in those days his word was law for us.' See Doroshenko, *Moï spomyny pro davnie-mynule (1901–1914 roky)*, 83; cf. Prymak, *Mykhailo Hrushevsky*, 76.

4 See, for example, reviews of Hrushevsky's works by Ludwik Kolankowski in *Kwartalnik Historyczny* 27 (1913): 348–65, and Czesław Frankiewicz, ibid., 31 (1917): 174–7.

5 See a comment to that effect in Andrei Storozhenko's pamphlet on the history of the Ukrainian movement, published under the pseudonym A. Tsarinnyi, *Ukrainskoe dvizhenie. Kratkii istoricheskii ocherk preimushchestvenno po lichnym vospominaniiam* (Berlin, 1925), repr. in *Ukrainskii separatizm v Rossii*, 161.

6 See Volkonskii, *Istoricheskaia pravda i ukrainofil'skaia propaganda.*

7 On Hrushevsky's appointment to the Lviv University position, see Zashkil'niak, 'M. Hrushevs'kyi i Halychyna (Do pryïzdu do L'vova 1894 r.).' On the Polish-Ukrainian political agreement in Galicia, see Ihor Chornovol, *Pol's'ko-ukraïns'ka uhoda, 1890–94.*

8 See Bahalii, 'Akad. M.S. Hrushevs'kyi i ioho mistse v ukraïns'kii istoriohrafiï (Istorychno-krytychnyi narys),' 174–5.

9 See Hrushevs'kyi, 'Sprava ukraïns'kykh katedr i nashi naukovi potreby.' For a Russian translation, see 'Vopros ob ukrainskikh kafedrakh i nuzhdy ukrainskoi nauki,' in idem, *Osvobozhdenie Rossii i ukrainskii vopros*, 149–94.

10 Prymak, *Mykhailo Hrushevsky*, 82.

11 See Plokhy, *Unmaking Imperial Russia*, 54–5.

12 See a draft of Hrushevsky's letter to Sviatopolk-Mirsky in TsDIAK, fond 1235, op. 1, no. 275, fol. 161[v]. Hrushevsky apparently did not know or preferred to ignore the fact that in Russian bureaucratic and nationalist circles Sviatopolk-Mirsky was perceived as a promoter of Polish interests.

13 On the Ukrainian campaign to lift the ban on Ukrainian-language publications in 1904–6, see Andriewsky, 'The Politics of National Identity,' 42–78, 114–19.

14 See Plokhy, *Unmaking Imperial Russia*, 56–61. On the Ukrainian deputies in the First Duma and their activities, see Andriewsky, 'The Politics of National Identity,' 163–99. Cf. Gerus, 'The Ukrainian Question in the Russian Duma, 1906–17.'

15 Grushevskii, 'Edinstvo ili raspadenie?' *Ukrainskii vestnik*, no. 3 (4 June 1906): 39–51, repr. in idem, *Osvobozhdenie Rossii i ukrainskii vopros*, 55–67, here 61.

16 See Hrushevs'kyi, 'Konstytutsiine pytannia i ukraïnstvo v Rosiï,' *Literaturno-naukovyi vistnyk* 8, no. 6 (1905): 245–58; also separately: Lviv, 1905. An abridged version of the article appeared in Russian translation in idem, *Osvobozhdenie Rossii i ukrainskii vopros*, 121–31.

17 Hrushevsky also indicated the deep federalist traditions of the Ukrainian movement, although he refused to support his claim for Ukrainian autonomy with reference to the historical rights of Ukraine. See Grushevskii, 'Natsional'nyi vopros i avtonomiia,' *Ukrainskii vestnik*, no. 1 (21 May 1906): 8–17, repr. in idem, *Osvobozhdenie Rossii i ukrainskii vopros*, 68–80; idem, 'Nashi trebovaniia,' *Ukrainskii vestnik*, no. 5 (18 June 1906): 267–73, repr. in *Osvobozhdenie Rossii i ukrainskii vopros*, 86–92; idem, 'O zrelosti i nezrelosti,' *Ukrainskii vestnik*, no. 4 (11 July 1906): 203–8, repr. in idem, *Osvobozhdenie Rossii i ukrainskii vopros*, 81–5.

18 See Grushevskii, 'Iz pol'sko-ukrainskikh otnoshenii Galitsii. Neskol'ko illiustratsii k voprosu: avtonomiia oblastnaia i natsional'no-territorial'naia,' in idem, *Osvobozhdenie Rossii i ukrainskii vopros*, 195–264.

19 See Grushevskii, 'Na drugoi den',' *Ukrainskii vestnik*, no. 11 (2 August 1906): 743–8, repr. in idem, *Osvobozhdenie Rossii i ukrainskii vopros*, 6–11.

20 See Grushevskii, 'Protiv techeniia,' in *Osvobozhdenie Rossii i ukrainskii vopros*, 1–5.

21 In this Hrushevsky was quite close to the position taken by Bohdan Kistiakovsky, an ethnic Ukrainian and a leader of the 'liberation of Russia' movement who opposed Ukrainian nationalism but believed that Ukrainians could become equal members of the liberation movement if they organized on an ethnic basis. See Susan Heuman, *Kistiakovsky*, 114–15.

22 On the Polish political action that led to the issuing of the edict, see Gervais-Francelle, 'La grève scolaire dans le royaume de Pologne.' On Ukrainian reaction to the edict, see Andriewsky, 'The Politics of National Identity,' 75–88.

23 See Grushevskii, 'Ravnoiu meroiu,' *Syn otechestva*, no. 73 (12 May 1905), repr. in idem, *Osvobozhdenie Rossii i ukrainskii vopros*, 101–3.

24 Hrushevs'kyi, 'Bezhluzda natsional'na polityka Rosiï,' *Dilo*, no. 100 (18 May 1905), quoted in Prymak, *Mykhailo Hrushevsky*, 73. In August 1905, Hrushevsky noted in his diary: 'It looks as if there will be reaction and somnolence in Russia, and the Ukrainians are again prepared to lie down on the stove, having obtained nothing, while the Poles are gaining power over them as well. Sorrow overcomes me for our people and foreigners alike' ('Shchodennyky M.S. Hrushevs'koho [1904–1910 rr.],' 15).

25 See Grushevskii, 'Vstrevozhennyi muraveinik,' *Ukrainskii vestnik*, no. 6 (25 June 1906): 331–41, repr. in idem, *Osvobozhdenie Rosii i ukrainskii vopros*, 149–94.

26 See Hrushevs'kyi, 'Za ukraïns'kyi maslak (v spravi Kholmshchyny),' *Rada*, 1907, nos. 2–4; also separately: *Za ukraïns'kyi maslak (v spravi Kholmshchyny)* (Kyiv, 1907). Russian translation: 'Za ukrainskuiu kost' (vopros o Kholmshchine),' in *Osvobozhdenie Rossii i ukrainskii vopros*, 278–91.

27 On the formation of the Kholm province, see Weeks, *Nation and State in Late Imperial Russia*, 172–92; and Chmielewski, *The Polish Question in the Russian State Duma*, 117–20.

6 Renegotiating the Pereiaslav Agreement

1 See excerpts from Lypyns'kyi, *Ukraïna na perelomi*, 56–7.
2 See Kohut, 'In Search of Perpetual Rights and Liberties.'
3 See Mikhnovs'kyi, 'Samostiina Ukraïna,' 128–30.
4 *Radians'ka entsyklopediia istoriï Ukraïny*, 1:336.
5 See Hrushevs'kyi, 'Khmel'nyts'kyi i Khmel'nychchyna.'
6 Ibid., 17, 20. In an essay on the 250th anniversary of the Pereiaslav Agreement, Hrushevsky attributed this defect of Khmelnytsky's to his education in the Oriental school of diplomacy. See Hrushevs'kyi, '250 lit,' 2.
7 Ibid., 16–19, 22–4.
8 See Drahomanov, 'The Lost Epoch,' 156–7.
9 See Antonovych, *Pro chasy kozats'ki na Ukraïni*. On the parallels in Antonovych's and Hrushevsky's interpretations of Pereiaslav, see Kravchenko, 'Kontseptsiï Pereiaslava v ukraïns'kii istoriohrafiï,' 492–3; and Ias', 'Obrazy Pereiaslava v ukraïns'kii istoriohrafiï,' 548–50.
10 See Hrushevs'kyi, *Iliustrovana istoriia Ukraïny*, 312–16.
11 On the evolution of Hrushevsky's political views and their impact on his interpretation of the Khmelnytsky Uprising, see Plokhy, *Unmaking Imperial Russia*, 281–345.
12 Hrushevs'kyi, *Istoriia Ukraïny-Rusy*, 9:868.
13 On Soloviev's interpretation of Pereiaslav, see Velychenko, *National History as Cultural Process*, 102–3; and Brekhunenko, 'Pereiaslavs'ka rada 1654 roku v rosiis'kii istoriohrafiï,' 615–19.
14 See Kostomarov, *Bogdan Khmel'nitskii*, 549–65. On the interpretation of Pereiaslav in the Ukrainian chronicles and Kostomarov's position on the issue, see Basarab, *Pereiaslav 1654*, 59–80, 103–9.
15 See Hrushevs'kyi, *Istoriia Ukraïny-Rusy*, 9:755.
16 For Karpov's critique of Kostomarov, see his *Gospodin Kostomarov kak istorik Malorossii*.
17 Hrushevs'kyi, *Istoriia Ukraïny-Rusy*, 9:752.
18 See Hrushevs'kyi, 'Khmel'nyts'kyi i Khmel'nychchyna,' 19–20. The documents on the Pereiaslav negotiations that Kostomarov did not include in vol. 3 of *Akty, otnosiashchiesia k istorii Iugo-Zapadnoi Rossii* were published by Karpov in vol. 10 of the series.
19 See Hrushevs'kyi, *Pereiaslavs'ka umova Ukraïny z Moskvoiu 1654 roku. Statti i teksty* (Kyiv, 1917–18), reprinted in *Pereiaslavs'ka rada 1654 roku*, 5–54.

20 See Nol'de, *Ocherki russkogo gosudarstvennogo prava*; and Rozenfel'd, *Prisoedinenie Malorossii k Rossii (1654–1793)*. On Hrushevsky's reviews of both works, see Ias', 'Obrazy Pereiaslava,' 556–9.

21 See Hrushevs'kyi, *Istoriia Ukraïny-Rusy*, 9:755.

22 Ibid. Cf. Miakotin, *Ocherki sotsial'noi istorii Ukrainy v XVII–XVIII vv.*

23 See Hrushevs'kyi, *Pereiaslavs'ka umova*, 17.

24 See Hrushevs'kyi, *Istoriia Ukraïny-Rusy*, 9:754.

25 Ibid., 758–60.

26 Ibid., 757.

27 Ibid., 866–9.

28 See Hrushevs'kyi, 'Khmel'nyts'kyi i Khmel'nychchyna,' 23.

29 See Hrushevs'kyi, '250 lit,' 1, 5.

30 See Hrushevs'kyi, 'Bohdanovi rokovyny,' 209, 211–12.

31 See Ias', 'Obrazy Pereiaslava,' 555–7.

32 See Hrushevs'kyi, *Pereiaslavs'ka umova*, 22–7. Cf. Kravchenko, 'Kontseptsiï Pereiaslava,' 497.

33 See Hrushevs'kyi, *Istoriia Ukraïny-Rusy*, 9:955.

34 Ibid., 1051–60.

35 Ibid., 1035.

36 Ibid., 969.

37 See Okinshevych, 'Natsional'no-demokratychna kontseptsiia istoriï prava Ukraïny v pratsiakh akad. M. Hrushevs'koho.'

38 Ibid., 106.

39 See Iastrebov, 'Natsional'no-fashysts'ka kontseptsiia selians'koï viiny 1648 roku na Ukraïni.'

40 On the interpretation of the Khmelnytsky Uprising in the works of Pokrovsky, Yavorsky, and their followers, see chapter 7 of the present work.

41 Hrushevsky's uncritical treatment of the diary of Paul of Aleppo was also harshly criticized in early 1934 by Volodymyr Zatonsky, a senior party official in charge of education. See Plokhy, *Unmaking Imperial Russia*, 408–9.

42 Iastrebov, 'Natsional'no-fashysts'ka kontseptsiia,' 77.

43 Ibid., 76.

44 See M.H., 'Die Ukraine, Glanz and Niedergang.'

45 See Narizhnyi, review of Mykhailo Hrushevs'kyi, *Istoriia Ukraïny-Rusy*.

46 See Lypyns'kyi, 'Ukraïna na perelomi,' in *Pereiaslavs'ka rada*, 55–66.

47 See Hrushevs'kyi, *Istoriia Ukraïny-Rusy*, 9:1491, 1497–8.

48 Harasymchuk, 'Z nahody poiavy IX tomu "Istoriï Ukraïny-Rusy" M. Hrushevs'koho,' 537–8.

49 Ibid., 540.

50 In his *Kozaczyzna ukrainna w Rzeczypospolitej Polskiej do końca XVIII wieku*, Franciszek Rawita-Gawroński, who had been known for his attacks on the

Ukrainian national movement since the early 1900s, not only ascribed the very existence of Ukraine to political intrigue but also held Hrushevsky personally responsible for the creation of Ukraine as a historical entity. Moreover, he criticized Hrushevsky for his allegedly pro-Russian and anti-Polish historical opinions and for treating the Cossacks as Ukrainian national heroes. For Rawita-Gawroński, the Cossacks represented first and foremost the forces of anarchy; he singled out Petro Konashevych-Sahaidachny as the only positive figure among the early Ukrainian Cossack hetmans because of his conciliatory policies towards the Polish government. Apart from its rabid anti-Ukrainianism, Rawita-Gawroński's book failed to introduce any new ideas into the study of early Cossack history. In his general treatment of the historical developments of that period, he relied on the works of earlier Polish authors, most notably on the studies and ideas of Aleksander Jabłonowski.

51 On the 'lesser evil' theory in Soviet historiography, see Brekhunenko, 'Pereiaslavs'ka rada 1654 roku,' 640–3.

52 For the text of the theses, see Basarab, *Pereiaslav 1654*, app. 8, 271–88.

53 Ibid., 275.

54 *Radians'ka entsyklopediia istoriï Ukraïny*, 1:336.

55 For the text of Braichevsky's brochure 'Annexation or Reunification?' the minutes of the discussion about it at the Institute of History in the summer of 1974, and Braichevsky's written response to the accusations against him in that discussion, see Braichevs'kyi, 'Pryiednannia chy vozz'iednannia? Tryptykh.' On Hrushevsky, see the abstract of Rem Symonenko's presentation at the 1974 discussion in *Pereiaslavs'ka rada*, 346.

56 For a survey of post-1991 trends in Ukrainian historiography on the Khmelnytsky Uprising and the Pereiaslav Agreement, see chapter 11 in this volume; and Kravchenko, 'Kontseptsiï Pereiaslava v ukraïns'kii istoriohrafiï,' 512–21.

57 See Lypyns'kyi, excerpts from *Ukraïna na perelomi* in *Pereiaslavs'ka rada*, 55–66; Lashchenko, 'Pereiaslavs'kyi dohovir 1654 r. mizh Ukraïnoiu i tsarem moskovs'kym'; Iakovliv, 'Dohovir het'mana Bohdana Khmel'nyts'koho z moskovs'kym tsarem Oleksiiem Mykhailovychem 1654 r.'; and Ohloblyn, 'Ukraïns'ko-moskovs'ka uhoda 1654.'

58 See the articles by Viktor Brekhunenko, Viktor Holubets', and Taras Chukhlib in *Pereiaslavs'ka rada*, 605–52, 747–74.

59 See Zaborovskii, 'Pereiaslavskaia rada i moskovskie soglasheniia 1654 g.' On major trends in the development of contemporary Russian historiography on Pereiaslav, see Brekhunenko, 'Pereiaslavs'ka rada 1654 roku,' 646–50.

60 See Yakovliv, 'The Judicial Character of the Pereyaslav Treaty'; and Ohloblyn, 'The Pereyaslav Treaty and Eastern Europe.' On the interpretation of Pereiaslav in English-language historiography, see Frank Sysyn, 'Anhlomovna istoriohrafiia Pereiaslavs'koï uhody u XX storichchi.'

61 See references to the 'Pereiaslav Agreement' in the titles of appropriate sections in Subtelny, *Ukraine: A History*, 134–6; and Magocsi, *A History of Ukraine*, 207–16.

62 See Nagel's'kyi, 'Pereiaslavs'ka uhoda 1654 roku v pol's'kii istoriohrafiï.'

63 Various aspects of diplomatic and military developments in the region have been discussed in the extensive literature that has appeared since the publication of volume 9 of the *History*, but none of these works can match Hrushevsky's narrative in scope and attention to detail. For general works on diplomatic relations in 1654–5, see Fedoruk, *Mizhnarodna dyplomatiia i polityka Ukraïny, 1654–57*; and *Russkaia i ukrainskaia diplomatiia v Evrazii*; and Zaborovskii, *Rossiia, Rech Pospolitaia i Shvetsiia v seredine XV veka*. On specific issues of Russian foreign policy at the time, see Zaborovskii, 'Poslednii shans umirotvoreniia,' and 'Bor'ba russkoi i pol'skoi diplomatii i pozitsiia Osmanskoi imperii v 1653–54 gg.' On Russian policy towards the Crimea, see Sanin, *Otnosheniia Rossii i Ukrainy s Krymskim khanstvom v seredine XVII veka*. For documents on Muscovy's relations with the Eastern patriarchs after Pereiaslav, see Chentsova, *Vostochnaia tserkov' i Rossiia posle Pereiaslavskoi rady, 1654–1658*. On Russo-Ukrainian relations, see Fedoruk, 'Perehovory Rechi Pospolytoï z Moskvoiu i ukladannia Vilens'koho myru (1654–1656).' On the Muscovite-Cossack contest for Belarus, see Horobets', 'Ukraïns'ko-rosiis'ki zmahannia za Bilorus' (1654–1659).' On the political consequences of the Battle of Zhvanets, see Stepankov, 'Kam'ianets'ka uhoda i Pereiaslavs'ka rada.' On the Polish-Lithuanian Commonwealth on the eve of the Zhvanets campaign, see Ciesielski, *Sejm brzeski 1653 r. Studium z dziejów Rzeczypospolitej w latach 1652–1653*. On Polish expeditions in Ukraine in 1654–5, see Kersten, *Stefan Czarniecki, 1599–1665*. Cf. *Stefan Czarniecki: żołnierz, obywatel, polityk*.

64 On the public debate about the commemorations, see Kuzio, 'Ukraine's "Pereiaslav Complex" and Relations with Russia'; and Kohut, 'Facing Ukraine's Russian Legacy.'

7 Bourgeois Revolution or Peasant War?

1 Pokrovskii, *Russkaia istoriia v samom szhatom ocherke*; see the reprint of the tenth edition of the book. On Pokrovsky, see Enteen, *The Soviet Scholar-Bureaucrat*; and Szporluk, Introduction to Pokrovskii, *Russia in World History*.

2 For the text of Lenin's letter to Pokrovsky welcoming the publication *of Russkaia istoriia v samom szhatom ocherke*, see Pokrovskii, *Izbrannye proizvedeniia*, 3:3–4.

3 Comparing Russian and Ukrainian history of the early modern period, Pokrovsky claimed that the major difference between the Russian and Ukrainian (Dnipro) Cossacks lay in the latter's ability to find allies among the local burghers. The burghers, organized in confraternities, fought against the church union introduced at the Council of Brest in 1596. In Pokrovsky's opinion, the union was little more than a tool of the Polish government to oppress the petty Ukrainian burghers in the interests of the rich merchants. See Pokrovskii, *Izbrannye proizvedeniia*, 3:80–1.

4 The fourth edition of the book appeared in 1917, while the fifth edition was published and reprinted three times in 1918 and once in 1919. See Vynar, *Mykhailo Hrushevs'kyi, 1866–1934*, 29–35.

For some future Ukrainian activists, the 'awakening' of their Ukrainian identity began with the reading of Hrushevsky's *Iliustrovana istoriia Ukraïny.* That was the case with the prominent Ukrainian linguist and cultural activist Yurii Sheveliov (George Y. Shevelov), who read Hrushevsky's work in Kharkiv in 1923–4. See his memoirs, *V Ukraïni*, in *Ia–meni–mene ... (i dovkruhy)*, 1:74–5. Apparently realizing the danger posed by Hrushevsky's writings, the secret police instructed its local branches in Ukraine to collect information on those who showed an interest in Hrushevsky's *Istoriia Ukraïny-Rusy.* See a secret police circular of August 1925 in *Mykhailo Hrushevs'kyi*, ed. P.S. Sokhan', nos 41, 64.

5 During the First World War Yavorsky served as an officer in the Austro-Hungarian army. In 1918 he was on the staff of an Austro-Hungarian military mission, first to the Central Rada and then to Hetman Pavlo Skoropadsky. Yavorsky's conversion to communism took place in 1919, when he prepared the defection of units of the Ukrainian Galician Army to the Bolsheviks. When the Galician Sich Riflemen abandoned the Bolsheviks in 1920, Yavorsky remained true to his communist convictions and stayed with his Bolshevik comrades. For a short biography of Yavorsky, see Santsevych, *M.I. Iavors'kyi*, 5–27.

6 See Hrushevsky's letter of 4 September 1934 to Viacheslav Molotov in Nikitin, 'Pis'mo istorika M.S. Grushevskogo V.M. Molotovu,' 95–7.

7 Pokrovskii, with the assistance of Nikol'skii and Storozhev, *Russkaia istoriia s drevneishikh vremen*; see the reprint, based on the seventh edition, which appeared in 1924–5.

8 For a brief summary of Pokrovsky's views on 'Russian' history, see Szporluk, Introduction to Pokrovskii, *Russia in World History*, 16–19; and Barber, *Soviet Historians in Crisis*, 58–67.

9 Pokrovskii, *Izbrannye proizvedeniia*, 1:461–7.

10 For Pokrovsky's views on the Cossack revolts and the Khmelnytsky Uprising, see chapter 9, 'The Struggle for Ukraine,' in vol. 2 of *Russkaia istoriia s drevneishikh vremen*, 1:450–517. The chapter is divided into the following sections: 'Western Rus' in the Sixteenth and Seventeenth Centuries,' 'The Cossack Revolution,' and 'Ukraine under Muscovite Dominion.'

11 The editors of the 1966 edition tried to 'correct' Pokrovsky's harsh characterization of Khmelnytsky. They claimed that despite his 'class limitations' Khmelnytsky understood that the best option for the further development of the Ukrainian people lay in reunification with the Russian people. These remarks, informed by the 'Theses on the Reunification of Ukraine with Russia' (1954), reflected a new paradigm of Soviet historiography. It placed less emphasis on the class factor, which was paramount for Pokrovsky, and stressed the importance of nationality, as well as reintroducing the cult and veneration of heroes in history. Both features were characteristic of Russian imperial historiography and were strongly rejected by Pokrovsky. (For editorial comments, see Pokrovskii, *Izbrannye proizvedeniia*, 1:495–6.)

12 Ironically, many of Pokrovsky's assertions amounted to little more than a further development of the young Hrushevsky's populist views, first expressed in his essay of 1898 on Bohdan Khmelnytsky and his period. See Hrushevs'kyi, 'Khmel'nyts'kyi i Khmel'nychchyna.'

13 See Shums'kyi, 'Stara i nova Ukraïna,' 96.

14 For Yavorsky's views on the Khmelnytsky revolt, see 'The Cossack Revolution,' chap. 2 of Iavors'kyi, *Istoriia Ukraïny v styslomu narysi* (Kharkiv, 1928), 39–56. Cf. his *Korotka istoriia Ukraïny* (Kharkiv, 1927), 51–8.

15 See the introduction to Sukhyno-Khomenko, *Odminy i bankrutstvo ukraïns'koho natsionalizmu*.

16 On Sukhyno-Khomenko, see Mace, *Communism and the Dilemmas of National Liberation*, 158, 245, 254, 256, 262, 298. On Sukhyno-Khomenko's polemics of 1930 with Mykola Khvyliovy, see Ilnytzkyj, *Ukrainian Futurism, 1914–1930*, 160–1.

17 For Rozhkov's application of the materialist method to the history of Russia, see his *Obzor russkoi istorii s sotsiologicheskoi tochki zreniia*.

18 See Sukhyno-Khomenko, *Odminy i bankrutstvo ukraïns'koho natsionalizmu*, 7–94.

19 For Sukhyno-Khomenko's 'friendly criticism' of Yavorsky, whom in the autumn of 1929 he still tried to save from further attacks by Yavorsky's opponents, see his article 'Na marksysts'komu istorychnomu fronti,' *Bil'shovyk Ukraïny*, nos 17–18 (September 1929): 47–52; no. 19 (15 October 1929): 54.

20 See Sukhyno-Khomenko's comment in 'Dyskusiia z pryvodu skhemy istoriï Ukraïny M. Iavors'koho,' *Litopys revoliutsiï*, 1930, no. 5: 322–3.

21 For Hrushevsky's application of the term 'first revival' to the Ukrainian history of the late sixteenth and early seventeenth centuries, see his *Istoriia ukraïns'koï literatury*, vol. 5, *Kul'turni i literaturni techiï na Ukraïni v XV–XVI vv. i pershe vidrodzhennia (1580–1610 rr).* See also Plokhy, 'Revisiting the Golden Age,' xlii–xlvii.

22 See, for example, the remarks of Horodetska during the Yavorsky discussion of May 1929, *Litopys revoliutsiï*, 1930, no. 5: 297 (see note 20 above).

23 Karpenko also criticized those who tended to explain everything with the help of Pokrovsky's theory of commercial capitalism. Although that line of argument implied a critique of Pokrovsky himself, Karpenko managed to present it in a way that looked like a defence of Pokrovsky and an attack on Yavorsky. In Ukraine Karpenko developed into an expert on Pokrovsky. He wrote an article on Pokrovsky's historical views that was published in December 1928, on the occasion of Pokrovsky's sixtieth birthday. See Karpenko, 'Mistse M.M. Pokrovs'koho v istoriohrafiï.' In the early 1930s Karpenko, who by then had replaced the well-known Ukrainian historian Dmytro Yavornytsky as director of the historical museum in Dnipropetrovsk, was attacked in *Pravda* for opportunism and nationalism. See Chentsov, 'Ideoloh ukraïns'koho natsionalizmu,' 118; and Tereshchenko, 'V chomu ïï vyna,' 125.

24 See Karpenko's original presentation, Horodetska's critique of him, and his response to that critique and restatement of his previous position in 'Dyskusiia z pryvodu skhemy istoriï Ukraïny M. Iavors'koho,' *Litopys revoliutsiï*, 1930, no. 5: 214–18, 295–7, 316–19 (see note 20 above).

25 See Sokolov, 'Razvitie istoricheskikh vzgliadov M.N. Pokrovskogo,' 66.

26 On the debates over Pokrovsky's scheme of Russian history in Moscow, see Barber, *Soviet Historians in Crisis*, 58–67.

27 Iastrebov, 'Tomu dev'iatoho persha polovyna,' 148.

28 Ibid., 147.

29 Ibid.

30 Ibid., 148.

31 Iastrebov, 'Natsional-fashysts'ka kontseptsiia selians'koï viiny 1648 roku na Ukraïni,' 60.

32 See *Narys istoriï Ukraïny*, 67–72. The first edition was published in Ufa in 1942. On the changing image of Khmelnytsky in Soviet historiography of the Second World War period, see Yekelchyk, 'Stalinist Patriotism as Imperial Discourse.'

33 See Iastrebov, 'Natsional-fashysts'ka kontseptsiia selians'koï viiny 1648 roku na Ukraïni,' 82.

34 Ibid., 73.

35 Ibid., 72. For more on Yastrebov's interpretation of the Pereiaslav Agreement, see chapter 6 of this volume.

8 The People's History

1 See *Dzherela z istoriï pivdennoï Ukraïny.* Two additional volumes were published later; their contents are not discussed in the present chapter.
2 Zelnik, 'Russian Bebels'; *Cultures in Flux*; *Voices of Revolution, 1917*; Halfin, *Terror in My Soul*; Hellbeck, *Revolution on My Mind*; Fitzpatrick, 'Lives Under Fire'; and Coleman, 'Becoming a Russian Baptist.'
3 Grigorenko, *V podpol'e mozhno vstretit' tol'ko krys.*
4 Hrushevs'kyi, *Shchodennyk, 1883–1894*. Cf. also the published diaries of other leading activists of the period: Kistiakovs'kyi, *Shchodennyk*; Chykalenko, *Shchodennyk, 1861–1929*; Vernadskii, *Dnevniki, 1917–21*; Vynnychenko, *Shchodennyk.*
5 Miller, *'Ukrainskii vopros' v politike vlastei i russkom obshchestvennom mnenii*, 31–41.
6 Ibid., 96–196. Cf. Savchenko, *Zaborona ukraïnstva 1876 r.*
7 Arguments in favour of just such a 'solution' to the Ukrainian question were summarized in works by supporters of the pan-Russian project during the years of revolution. See Linnichenko, 'Malorusskaia kul'tura'; and Liapunov, 'Edinstvo russkogo iazyka v ego narechiiakh.'
8 Vasyl' Rubel', 'Istoriia ...,' in *Dzherela z istoriï pivdennoï Ukraïny*, bk 1, 102.
9 Ibid., 132, 134, 141.
10 Mikhail Alekseev, 'Memuary,' in *Dzherela z istoriï pivdennoï Ukraïny*, bk 2, 498.
11 Rubel', 'Istoriia ...,' 130.
12 Alekseev, 'Memuary,' 490–1.
13 Rubel', 'Istoriia ...,' 102.
14 Alekseev, 'Memuary,' 508, 521.
15 Rubel', 'Istoriia ...,' 160.
16 Oleksandr Onysymovych Zamrii, 'Zapovit svoiemu pokolinniu,' in *Dzherela z istoriï pivdennoï Ukraïny*, bk 1, 215–16, 225–6, 234–5, 236–7; Iaroshenko, 'Shchodennyk,' 272.
17 Rubel', 'Istoriia ...,' 164. Andrii referred to this compatriot, Volodymyr Moiseiovych Bohuslavsky, as a brave man and a good companion.
18 Alekseev, 'Memuary,' 517–18, 522, 533; Zamrii, 'Zapovit,' 238, 242.
19 Rubel', 'Istoriia ...,' 159, 165–6, 175–6, 178. Of Andrii's three closest comrades who informed his family of his death, one, Timofei Skarzhinsky (Tymofii Srazhynsky), was illiterate, and his origin was not indicated in the letter written by Sergei Kharkov on his behalf. Andrii's second comrade,

Volodymyr Chirka, came from the Kobryn region near the Ukrainian-Belarusian border, while the third, Nikolai Kozlov, who also appears to have been illiterate, came from Russia (the village of Znamenka; Rubel', 'Istoriia,' 180).

20 On the Ukrainization of the army, see von Hagen, 'The Russian Imperial Army and the Ukrainian National Movement in 1917.'
21 Iaroshenko, 'Shchodennyk,' 268.
22 Alekseev, 'Memuary,' 549.
23 Zamrii, 'Zapovit,' 237.
24 Ibid., 229.
25 The Provisional Government's instruction of 4 August 1917 recognized the authority of the General Secretariat of the Central Rada over the Kyiv, Volhynia, Podilia, and Poltava gubernias and part of the Chernihiv gubernia. See Verstiuk, *Ukraïns'ka Tsentral'na Rada*, 180; text of instruction in appendix 11, 304–6. On the attitude of Russian democrats to the problem of 'New Russia,' see Vynnychenko, *Vidrodzhennia natsiï*, 1:167–8, 319.
26 Text of the Third Universal in Verstiuk, *Ukraïns'ka Tsentral'na Rada*, appendix 14, 315–18.
27 Alekseev, 'Memuary,' 549.
28 Ibid.
29 Mykola Vasyl'ovych Molodyk, 'Spohady,' in *Dzherela z istoriï pivdennoï Ukraïny*, vol. 5, bk 1, pt 1, 333–5.
30 Alekseev, 'Memuary,' 549; Iaroshenko, 'Shchodennyk,' 275–80.
31 Iaroshenko, 'Shchodennyk,' 281–2.
32 Ibid., 286–7.
33 Molodyk, 'Spohady,' 337.
34 The most complete account of the Ukrainization policy is to be found in Martin, *The Affirmative Action Empire*, 75–124, 209–72, 325–8, 344–72.
35 Molodyk, 'Spohady,' 333.
36 Ibid.
37 Zamrii, 'Zapovit,' 245.
38 Iaroshenko, 'Shchodennyk,' 277.
39 Molodyk, 'Spohady,' 337–8.
40 Iaroshenko, 'Shchodennyk,' 277.
41 Ibid., 473. What remained unchanged in these records were the Russian names of the months of the year.
42 Ibid., 306.
43 Serhii Tsipko, 'Moï spomyny pro mynule ...,' in *Dzherela z istoriï pivdennoï Ukraïny*, bk 2, 783.
44 Ibid., 784.

45 Ibid., 783.
46 Komov, 'Rubel' Vasyl' Dmytrovych,' 37–9.
47 Hrushevs'kyi, *Iliustrovana istoriia Ukraïny*. Further references are to the Winnipeg reprint of this work issued in 1918. The editions of 1917–19 are cited in *Mykhailo Hrushevs'kyi, 1866–1934: Bibliographic Sources*, 28, 32, 35.
48 Rubel', 'Istoriia …,' 107–10.
49 See, for example, the exposition of Ukrainian history in Matvii Yavorsky's popular *Korotka istoriia Ukraïny*. The book was used as a text in 'institutions of socialist upbringing.' In 1927 the State Publishing House of Ukraine issued its fifth stereotype edition.
50 On the role of the Cossack myth in Hryshevsky's work, as well as his treatment of the social factor in Ukrainian history, see Plokhy, *Unmaking Imperial Russia*, 193–207.
51 Rubel', 'Istoriia …,' 104–5. Cf. Hrushevs'kyi, *Iliustrovana istoriia Ukraïny*, 362–7, 428.
52 Rubel', 'Istoriia …,' 119.
53 Ibid., 102–3.
54 Ibid., 182.
55 Komov, 'Rubel' Vasyl' Dmytrovych,' 37–9.
56 Alekseev, 'Memuary,' 617.
57 On living conditions of peasant migrants and dekulakized peasants in another giant industrial centre of the first five-year plan, Magnitogorsk, see Kotkin, *Magnetic Mountain*, especially the chapter 'Living Space and the Stranger's Gaze,' 157–97.
58 Molodyk, 'Spohady,' 340.
59 Ibid., 341.
60 Ibid., 353.
61 Ibid., 322.
62 For a survey of interwar western Ukrainian historiography and the work of émigré historians, see Ohloblyn's appendix to Doroshenko and Ohloblyn, *A Survey of Ukrainian Historiography*, 372–436.
63 Tsipko, 'Moï spomyny,' 783.
64 On the identity-building project in the DP camps, see Kulyk, 'The Role of Discourse in the Construction of an Émigré Community.'
65 Tsipko, 'Moï spomyny,' 792–3, 803.
66 Ibid., 797–803.
67 Alekseev, 'Memuary,' 490.
68 Ibid., 765, 769.
69 Zamrii, 'Zapovit,' 257.
70 See Alekseev, 'Memuary,' 507.

9 History and Territory

1 On imperial disintegration, national self-determination, and border conflicts, see Cobban, *The Nation State and National Self-Determination*, 295–9; Prescott, *The Geography of Frontiers and Boundaries*, 109–78; and Coakley, 'National Territories and Cultural Frontiers.'
2 See Voshchanov's statement in *Izvestiia*, 29 August 1991.
3 See quotations from an internal memorandum on the Crimea prepared by Vladimir Lukin, then chairman of the Committee on International Affairs of the Russian parliament and later ambassador to the United States (*Komsomol'skaia pravda*, 22 January 1991); an interview with S. Baburin and N. Pavlov, members of the Russian parliamentary group that visited the Crimea in December 1991 (*Literaturnaia Rossiia*, 31 January 1992); and Ukrainian protests against the creation and activities of the Russian Supreme Soviet ad hoc committee on the status of Sevastopol, called into existence at the Seventh Congress of People's Deputies of Russia in December 1992 (*Uriadovyi kur'ier*, 11 December 1992; *Pravda Ukraïny*, 23 January 1993; and *UKRAINFORM Reports*, 20 February 1993).
4 *Pravda Ukraïny*, 7 April 1992, quoted in Solchanyk, 'Ukraine and Russia,' 3.
5 Ibid.
6 On the myth of Sevastopol, see chapter 10 of this volume.
7 *Literaturnaia Rossiia*, 8 January 1993. On the development of the Sevastopol mythology and its uses and abuses in the early 1990s, see chapter 10 of this volume.
8 *Robitnycha hazeta*, 23 January 1993.
9 There is a significant literature on Mykhailo Hrushevsky and his writings. See part 2 of this volume.
10 Armstrong, 'Myth and History in the Evolution of Ukrainian Consciousness,' 133.
11 Ibid., 128.
12 On the development of Cossack mythology, see Sysyn, 'The Reemergence of the Ukrainian Nation and Cossack Mythology'; and Gerus, 'Manifestations of the Cossack Idea in Modern History.'
13 For an outline of the Cossack period of Ukrainian history, see Subtelny, *Ukraine: A History*, 105–98; and Subtelny and Vytanovych, 'Cossacks.'
14 On the history of the Chernihiv region, see the following works: Backus, *Motives of West Russian Nobles in Deserting Lithuania for Moscow, 1377–1514*; and M.T. Iatsura, 'Chernihivs'ka oblast',' in *Istoriia mist i sil Ukraïns'koï RSR*, 15–17.
15 For an account of these events, see Subtelny, *Ukraine: A History*, 143–73.

16 See Druzhinina, *Kiuchuk-Kainardzhiiskii mir 1774 goda*, and *Severnoe Prichernomor'e v 1775–1800 gg.* The imperial absorption of the Crimea is discussed by Fisher, *The Russian Annexation of the Crimea*, and *The Crimean Tatars*.

17 On the partitions of Poland, see Halecki, *Borderlands of Western Civilization*, 258–75.

18 For Bezborodko's views on the main goals of Russian foreign policy, see Kohut, *Russian Centralism and Ukrainian Autonomy*, 261–2.

19 On Ukrainian settlement of the new territories in the eighteenth and nineteenth centuries, see Polons'ka-Vasylenko, *The Settlement of Southern Ukraine (1750–1775)*; Golobutskii (Holobuts'kyi), *Chernomorskoe kazachestvo*, *Zaporozhskoe kazachestvo*, and *Zaporiz'ka Sich v ostanni roky svoho isnuvannia 1734–1775*; Kabuzan, *Zaselenie Novorossii*; and Bruk and Kabuzan, 'Migratsii naseleniia v Rossii v 18 – nachale 19 veka.'

20 Kohut, *Russian Centralism and Ukrainian Autonomy*, 7, 29–32.

21 Ibid., 59–63, 258–76.

22 On the reemergence of the Khmelnytsky cult after the defeat at Poltava, see Plokhy, 'The Symbol of Little Russia.'

23 On the gentry's struggle for the recognition of its rights, see Kohut, *Russian Centralism and Ukrainian Autonomy*, 248–57. On Ukrainian historiography of the period, see Doroshenko, *A Survey of Ukrainian Historiography*. On the 'Conversation' and the 'History of the Rus',' see chapters 2 and 3 of this volume.

24 There is an extensive literature on Shevchenko's life and writings. On his interpretation of Cossack history, see Grabowicz, 'Three Perspectives on the Cossack Past.'

25 On the national revival in Galicia, see Kozik, *The Ukrainian National Movement in Galicia, 1819–1849*; Rudnytsky, 'The Ukrainians in Galicia under Austrian Rule'; and Himka, 'Priests and Peasants,' and 'The Greek Catholic Church and Nation-Building in Galicia, 1772–1918.'

26 See Subtelny, *Ukraine: A History*, 255–79; *Radians'ka entsyklopediia istoriï Ukraïny*, 4:461.

27 For a general survey of Soviet interpretations of Ukrainian and Belarusian history, see Szporluk, 'National History as a Political Battleground.' On changes in the Soviet interpretation of the Ukrainian past in the late 1920s and early 1930s, see chapter 7 of this volume.

28 On the national 'awakening' among the Soviet Ukrainian intelligentsia of the period, see Mykhailo Koval', 'Pid "kovpakom" beriïvs'koï derzhbezpeky,' *Ukraïns'kyi istorychnyi zhurnal*, 1992, nos 10–11: 111–22.

29 On the political purge of the 1970s in Ukraine, see Solchanyk, 'Politics in Ukraine in the Post-Shelest Period.' On the fate of one of the persecuted,

Mykola Kytsenko, a writer and senior Soviet official in the Zaporizhia region, see Olena Apanovych, 'Nam bronzy ne treba!' *Ukraïns'ka kul'tura,* 1993, no. 1: 8–9.

30 On the celebrations of the five-hundredth anniversary of the Zaporozhian Cossacks in 1990, see Sysyn, 'The Reemergence of the Ukrainian Nation and Cossack Mythology,' 858–9.

31 This information is based on the author's interviews with Communist Party officials in the Cherkasy and Dnipropetrovsk regions (summer 1990–spring 1991).

32 On the participation of communist officials in the celebrations of the 340th anniversary of the Battle of Berestechko in Volhynia, see the joint statement issued on that occasion by the Lviv, Volhynia, and Rivne regional committees of the Communist Party of Ukraine (*Radians'ka Ukraïna,* 13 February 1991).

33 Solzhenitsyn, 'Kak nam obustroit' Rossiiu?' See also Solzhenitsyn's 'Appeal on the December 1991 Referendum,' in which he proposed to calculate the referendum results in Ukraine separately for each region (*Christian Democracy,* 1992, no. 17: 9–10).

34 On separatist tendencies in eastern and southern Ukraine, see M. Khudan, 'Daiosh Respubliku Novorosiia,' *Literaturna Ukraïna,* 22 November 1990; O. Oliinykiv, 'Nashchadky Chepihy i Holovatoho,' *Kul'tura i zhyttia,* 5 August 1990; and Sysyn, 'The Reemergence of the Ukrainian Nation and Cossack Mythology,' 861.

35 See Leonid Zalizniak, 'Vid kozats'koï vol'nosti – do Novorosiï,' *Pam'iatky Ukraïny,* 1991, no. 2: 21; Volodymyr Kravtsevych, 'Berezan' i Izmail vziali Zaporozhtsy,' *Narodna armiia,* 28 October 1992.

36 See Volodymyr Kravtsevych, 'Kto zhe stroil "Russkuiu slavu"?' *Narodna armiia,* 6 November 1992.

37 See the articles on Cossack history in *Radians'ka entsyklopediia istoriï Ukraïny,* 4 vols (Kyiv, 1969–72), 2:406–14.

38 See Roman Ivanychuk's memoirs in *Berezil',* 1992, nos 11–12: 125. The novel *Mal'vy* (first edition: *Mal'vy: Roman* [Kyiv, 1968]) was not included in bibliographies of Ivanychuk's works until the beginning of glasnost.

39 See Ivan Storozhenko's essay on the Battle of Zhovti Vody (1648) in Mytsyk, Storozhenko, Plokhii, and Koval'ov, *Tiï slavy kozats'koï povik ne zabudem,* and the list of Yurii Mytsyk's publications in *Bibliohrafiia prats' vchenykh Dnipropetrovs'koho universytetu.*

40 See the article by V. Butkevych, 'Pravo na Krym,' *Narodna armiia,* 8 July 1992. Noting the first abolition of the Sich by Peter I in 1709 and the resettlement of the Cossacks to territories controlled by the Crimean Tatars, Butkevych

claimed that from 1709 to 1734 Zaporizhia and the Crimea constituted one body politic that gained international recognition as a result of the Treaty of Prut between Russia and Turkey (1711). He also stressed the special relations between the Crimea and Zaporizhia on the eve of the imperial abolition of the Zaporozhian Sich in 1775.

41 *Literaturna Ukraïna*, 10 January 1991. This information was drawn from the memoirs of a Turkish traveller, Evlia Chelebi, who visited the Crimea in 1666.

42 For a report on a visit to Sevastopol by the 'Cossacks-Zaporozhians' folk ensemble from the city of Zaporizhia, see *Molod' Ukraïny*, 14 January 1993.

43 See the article on the history of Ukrainian settlement in the Kuban by V. Ivanys, V. Kubijovyč, and M. Miller in *Encyclopedia of Ukraine*, 2:687–95. For the interpretation of Kuban history in Ukraine in the early 1990s, see Petro Lavriv, 'Kubans'ki kozaky,' *Narodna hazeta*, 1993, no. 8.

44 *Biuleten' Ukraïns'koï respublikans'koi partiï*, 1993, no. 10. On the collaboration of the Ukrainian and Kuban Cossacks, see the statement of Hetman Volodymyr Muliava on the meeting of delegations of Ukrainian and Kuban Cossacks in Kyiv on 2 March 1993 (*Molod' Ukraïny*, 19 March 1993).

45 See the article on this march in the newspaper of the Ukrainian Armed Forces, *Narodna armiia*, 21 October 1992: Anatolii Zaborovs'kyi, 'Kozaky v kinnomu pokhodi.'

46 N. Narochnitskaia, *Literaturnaia Rossiia*, 21 August 1992.

47 See Coakley, 'National Territories and Cultural Frontiers,' 41.

10 The City of Glory

1 See Smith, *The Ethnic Revival*, 165–7.

2 Dunlop, *The Rise of Russia and the Fall of the Soviet Empire*, and 'Russia: Confronting Loss of Empire.'

3 Dunlop, 'Russia: Confronting Loss of Empire,' 45–6.

4 Pipes, 'Weight of the Past,' 5–6.

5 For the peculiarities of Russian imperialism, see *The End of Empire?*

6 See chapters 2 and 3 of this volume.

7 Breuilly, *Nationalism and the State*, 350.

8 On the results of the referendum on independence in Ukraine, see Potichnyj, 'The Referendum and Presidential Elections in Ukraine.'

9 In the autumn of 1996, Georgii Tikhonov, chairman of the Duma Committee on Commonwealth of Independent States Affairs, echoing numerous declarations of the presidential hopeful, Moscow mayor Yurii Luzhkov, publicly stated that Sevastopol 'was, is and will be Russian' (see 'Ukraine-Russia Differences Continue,' *Ukrainian News*, 9–27 October 1996, 5; 'Duma Passes Law

Barring Division of Black Sea Fleet,' *OMRI Daily Digest*, 24 October 1996; and 'Russian Duma Enacts Black Sea Fleet Bill,' *Monitor Report*, 24 October 1996). Even the Russian premier, Viktor Chernomyrdin, who was usually much more responsible in his public statements, went on record as saying at the summit of the Organization for Security and Cooperation in Europe in Lisbon at the end of 1996 that 'Sevastopol is a Russian city; all the soil there is covered with the bones of Russian sailors.' See *Den'*, 10 December 1996.

10 See *Literaturnaia Rossiia*, 8 January 1993.

11 See 'Obrashchenie potomkov geroev Sevastopolia k Prezidentu, pravitel'stvu i Federal'nomu Sobraniiu Rossii,' *Krymskoe vremia*, 1996, no. 116. One of the many ironies of the appeal lies in the fact that Admiral Nakhimov was never married and had no children. See his biography, Davydov, *Nakhimov*.

12 Smith, 'Culture, Community and Territory.'

13 Armstrong, 'Myth and History in the Evolution of Ukrainian Consciousness,' 133.

14 On the theory of official nationality, see Riasanovsky, *Nicholas I and Official Nationality in Russia, 1825–1855*.

15 Smith, 'Culture, Community and Territory,' 454.

16 See the account of the Battle of Borodino in the standard Soviet history of the USSR: *Istoriia SSSR s drevneishikh vremen do nashikh dnei*, 4:125–32.

17 There is a rich literature in both English and Russian on the history of the Crimean War. For an account of the events of the war, see Goldfrank, *The Origins of the Crimean War*; and Barker, *The Vainglorious War, 1854–56*. On the diplomatic consequences of the war for Russia, see Narochnitskaia, *Rossiia i otmena neitralizatsii Chernogo moria, 1856–1871*.

18 See Riasanovsky, *Nicholas I and Official Nationality in Russia*, 165–7.

19 This approach to the history of the Crimean War was inherited by Soviet historiography and can be found in almost all Soviet publications on the history of the war. See, for example, *Istoriia SSSR s drevneishikh vremen do nashikh dnei*, 4:517–68.

20 See Wortman, *Scenarios of Power*, 2:174–5.

21 On the eve of the Russo-Turkish war of 1877–8 there appeared a number of publications in Russia devoted to the history of the Crimean War and the defence of Sevastopol. See *Opisanie oborony goroda Sevastopolia*; *Sbornik rukopisei, predstavlennykh E.I.V. gosudariu nasledniku tsesarevichu o Sevastopol'skoi oborone sevastopol'tsami*; and *Materialy dlia istorii Krymskoi voiny i oborony Sevastopolia*. See also publications that came out at the time of the war: Bogdanovich, *Vostochnaia voina*; and Dubrovin, *Vostochnaia voina 1853–1856 godov*.

22 Anderson, *Imagined Communities*, 86–7.
23 See Davydov, *Nakhimov*, 141, 162–6.
24 Ibid., 51–2, 83–7.
25 See Tolstoy, *The Sevastopol Sketches*.
26 See *Istoriia mist i sil Ukraïns'koï RSR. Kryms'ka oblast'*, 163–4.
27 The Soviet interpretation of the defence of Port Arthur included many elements of the Port Arthur mythology. See *Istoriia SSSR s drevneishikh vremen do nashikh dnei*, 6:100–10.
28 On Mikhail Pokrovsky, see Szporluk's introduction to Pokrovskii, *Russia in World History*.
29 See Berkov, *Krymskaia kampaniia*; and Lagovskii, *Oborona Sevastopolia*.
30 On the defence of Sevastopol in 1941–2, see *Istoriia mist i sil Ukraïns'koï RSR*, 178–86; and *Istoriia goroda-geroia Sevastopolia, 1917–1957*, 199–257.
31 See *Radians'ka entsyklopediia istoriï Ukraïny*, 3:214.
32 See Tarle, *Gorod russkoi slavy*. In 1955 the same publishing house released a book by Gorev, *Voina 1853–1856 gg. i oborona Sevastopolia*.
33 See N. Druzhinin, 'Ot redaktora,' in Tarle, *Krymskaia voina*, 5–8. In the late 1940s Evgenii Tarle also wrote a book about Admiral Nakhimov: *Nakhimov*.
34 Tarle, *Gorod russkoi slavy*, 3.
35 Ibid., 16.
36 Ibid., 15.
37 Ibid.
38 See Tarle, *Gorod russkoi slavy*. On Nikolai Pirogov's participation in the defence of Sevastopol, see the publication of his letters and memoirs in Pirogov, *Sevastopol'skie pis'ma i vospominaniia*.
39 See Tarle, *Gorod russkoi slavy*, 114–15.
40 Ibid., 75–167. Nakhimov was presented in the same way in the numerous Soviet publications on his life and activities. Compare Aslanbegov, *Admiral P.S. Nakhimov*; Belavenets, *Admiral Pavel Stepanovich Nakhimov*; Novikov, *Admiral Nakhimov*; Tarle, *Nakhimov*; *Admiral Nakhimov. Stat'i i ocherki*; *P.S. Nakhimov. Dokumenty i materialy*; Polikarpov, *Pavel Stepanovich Nakhimov*; and Davydov, *Nakhimov*.
41 See, for example, the chapter on the history of Sevastopol in *Istoriia mist i sil Ukraïns'koï RSR. Kryms'ka oblast*, 142–205; and *Istoriia goroda-geroia Sevastopolia*. The latter book is identified as the second volume of a two-volume history of Sevastopol. The first volume never appeared.
42 See *Istoriia mist i sil Ukraïns'koï RSR. Kryms'ka oblast*, 151; and *Radians'ka entsyklopediia istoriï Ukraïny*, 2:391.
43 See Blizniuk, *Na bastionakh Sevastopolia*.

44 See *Literaturnaia Rossiia*, 8 January 1993:
На осколках нашей сверхдержавы
Величайший парадокс истории
Севастополь – город русской славы,
Но … не на российской территории.
45 Solzhenitsyn, *'The Russian Question' at the End of the Twentieth Century*, 30.
46 Ibid., 48–50.
47 Ibid., 96.

11 The Ghosts of Pereiaslav

1 On the treatment of the Pereiaslav Agreement in pre-Soviet and early Soviet Ukrainian historiography, see chapters 6 and 7 of this volume. For an account of events leading up to and following the Pereiaslav Agreement, see Torke, 'The Unloved Alliance,' 42–8.
2 For the audio record of the BBC program on Bohdan Khmelnytsky, see 'Nash vybir' at www.bbc.co.uk/ukrainian. For the treatment of Khmelnytsky's image in modern historiography, see Sysyn, 'The Changing Image of the Hetman.'
3 See 'Nash vybir' at www.bbc.co.uk/ukrainian. Cf. the following statement by the Ukrainian journalist and historian Serhii Makhun: 'They now talk about the Pereiaslav Council in somewhat subdued tones. But under whose "hand" was Bohdan Khmelnytsky supposed to go in that complex political situation, and under pressure from the absolute majority of the population of Ukraine? Perhaps [under the 'hand'] of the Turkish sultans and the Crimean khan, who had caused great distress to Khmelnytsky himself?' ('Iak rozirvaty kolo vzaiemnoho rakhunku obraz?' *Den'*, 25 December 1999).
4 For one of the first attempts to reevaluate the legacy of Soviet historiography, see *Sovetskaia istoriografiia*. On the interrelation of national identity and historical memory in Ukraine, see Kuzio, *Ukraine*, 198–229; and Wanner, *Burden of Dreams*.
5 See the text of the declaration in *Slava ukraïns'koho kozatstva*, 306.
6 Ibid. On the activities of the Ukrainian Cossacks and their links to political parties and the armed forces in Ukraine, see Hryb, 'New Ukrainian Cossacks – Revival or Building New Armed Forces?' For the role of the Cossack heritage in the Ukrainian national revival in the late 1980s and early 1990s, see Sysyn, 'The Reemergence of the Ukrainian Nation and Cossack Mythology'; and chapter 9 of this volume.
7 On the historiographic debates over the significance of the Pereiaslav Agreement, see Basarab, *Pereiaslav 1654*. On differences between Russian and Ukrainian historians in the interpretation of Ukrainian history, see

Velychenko, *National History as Cultural Process*, and *Shaping Identity in Eastern Europe and Russia*.

8 On the peculiarities of the nation-building project in Ukraine, see Arel, 'Ukraine – The Temptation of the Nationalizing State'; Szporluk, 'Nation-Building in Ukraine'; and the relevant chapters in Motyl, *Dilemmas of Independence*; Kuzio, *Ukraine: State and Nation Building*.

9 See the English translation of the *Theses on the Three-Hundredth Anniversary of the Reunion of the Ukraine with Russia (1654–1954)* in Basarab, *Pereiaslav 1654*, 270–88.

10 In 1998, a suggestion to name the university after Oles Honchar, a graduate of the university, was rejected.

11 For Sanin's remarks, see the recording of the BBC program on Bohdan Khmelnytsky, 'Nash vybir,' at www.bbc.co.uk/ukrainian.

12 See Zaborovskii, 'Pereiaslavskaia rada i moskovskie soglasheniia 1654 goda': 39.

13 Ibid., 39, 45.

14 See Samuilov, 'O nekotorykh amerikanskikh stereotipakh v otnoshenii Ukrainy,' 1997, no. 3:84. For a Ukrainian response to Samuilov's article, see Oleksii Haran', 'Pro "rasyzm Hrushevs'koho" ta "pol's'ku intryhu." Rosiis'ka nauka dolaie "amerykans'ki stereotypy shchodo Ukrainy,"' *Den'*, 5 August 1997.

15 Ironically, Kostomarov's views on Khmelnytsky and the Pereiaslav Agreement were considered anti-Russian by nineteenth-century Russian historians. For Kostomarov's treatment of the Pereiaslav Agreement and a critique of Kostomarov by Gennadii Karpov, a student of Sergei Soloviev's, see Basarab, *Pereiaslav 1654*, 103–9. On Kostomarov's life, see Prymak, *Mykola Kostomarov: A Biography*.

16 For a political biography of Hrushevsky, see Prymak, *Mykhailo Hrushevsky: The Politics of National Culture*. On his historiographic views, see Sysyn, 'Introduction to the *History of Ukraine-Rus'*.' For Hrushevsky's views on the history of the Ukrainian Cossacks, see Plokhy, 'Revisiting the Golden Age.'

17 Samuilov, 'O nekotorykh amerikanskikh stereotipakh v otnoshenii Ukrainy,' 1997, no. 3:93.

18 Ibid., 1997, no. 4:93.

19 Ibid., 1997, no. 3:95.

20 See the English translation of the *Theses* in Basarab, *Pereiaslav 1654*, 275.

21 Samuilov, 'O nekotorykh amerikanskikh stereotipakh v otnoshenii Ukrainy,' 1997, 4:90.

22 On developments in Ukrainian historiography since independence, see Subtelny, 'The Current State of Ukrainian Historiography'; von Hagen, 'Does Ukraine Have a History?' and Kohut, 'Vidchytuvannia

Het'manshchyny.' On the historical factor in Russo-Ukrainian disputes, see Wilson, 'The Donbas between Ukraine and Russia.'

23 See Mytsyk, 'Natsional'no-vyzvol'na viina ukraïns'koho narodu 1648–1658 rr.,' 34–5. Mytsyk also mentions the case of 'Kornilovshchina,' but one could add to this list the official names given to all sorts of 'nationalist' deviations in the ranks of the Ukrainian Communist Party, such as 'Volobuievshchyna,' 'Skrypnykivshchyna,' 'Iavorshchyna,' and 'Shelestivshchyna.' In contemporary Ukraine, all these terms have a strong negative connotation.

24 See chapter 7 of this volume.

25 See the English translation of the *Theses* in Basarab, *Pereiaslav 1654*, 273. Cf. chapter 6 of this volume.

26 Reprinted in Tolochko, *Vid Rusi do Ukraïny*, 296.

27 Smolii, 'Het'man Bohdan Khmel'nyts'kyi i ioho doba,' 15. Among Khmelnytsky's mistakes, Smolii listed the withdrawal of Cossack forces from western Ukraine in late 1648 and the deterioration of Cossack relations with Moldavia, Wallachia, and Transylvania in 1654–5.

28 Instead, making reference to the writings of a Ukrainian nationalist ideologue, the interwar publicist Dmytro Dontsov, Smolii claims that Ukraine did not unite with Russia into a single state but instead joined a Russo-Ukrainian confederation. See ibid., 21–2; and Smolii, 'Natsional'no-vyzvol'na viina v konteksti ukraïns'koho derzhavotvorennia,' 18–19.

29 See Solchanyk, 'Politics and the National Question in the Post-Shelest Period,' 12. For a summary and analysis of Braichevsky's views on the 'reunification' issue, see Basarab, *Pereiaslav 1654*, 202–13. For the Ukrainian and English texts of Braichevsky's essay, see Braichevs'kyi, *Pryiednannia chy vozz'iednannia?*; and *Annexation or Reunification: Critical Notes on One Conception*.

30 The term was not officially accepted at that time but clearly remained attractive in the eyes of leading Ukrainian historians. For the 1960s discussion, see Apanovych, 'Natsional'no-vyzvol'ni viiny v epokhu feodalizmu'; and Boiko, 'Shche raz pro kharakter natsional'no-vyzvolnykh voien v epokhu feodalizmu.'

31 See Smolii and Stepankov, *Ukraïns'ka natsional'na revoliutsiia XVII st. (1648–1676)*. On the use of outdated Soviet terminology and concepts by Smolii and Stepankov, see Natalia Yakovenko's review of the book, 'V kol'orakh proletars'koï revoliutsiï,' in *Ukraïns'kyi humanitarnyi ohliad*, 2000, no. 3: 58–78. For a discussion of the term 'revolution' in relation to the Khmelnytsky Uprising, see Sysyn, 'War der Chmel'nyćkyj-Aufstand eine Revolution?' Ukrainian version: 'Chy bulo povstannia Bohdana Khmel'nyts'koho revoliutsiieiu? Zauvahy do typolohiï Khmel'nychchyny.'

32 For the latest version of Stepankov's argument on issues of terminology and chronology in the 'Ukrainian national revolution,' see his 'Ukraïns'ka natsional'na revoliutsiia XVII st.' See Sukhyno-Khomenko's remarks in the discussion of 1929 with Yavorsky in *Litopys revoliutsiï*, 1930, no. 5: 322–3, and the chapter on 'The Great Ukrainian Bourgeois Revolution' in Sukhyno-Khomenko, *Odminy i bankrutstvo ukraïns'koho natsionalizmu*, 28–51.

33 See Mytsyk, 'Natsional'no-vyzvol'na viina ukraïns'koho narodu 1648–1658 rr.,' 30–1.

34 For the use of the term 'war of national liberation' in Tolochko's writings, see his 'Pid mistechkom Berestechkom' (1991) and 'Bohdan Khmel'nyts'kyi' (1995) in his *Vid Rusi do Ukraïny*, 147–50. A prominent historian of Kyivan Rus' and a well-known political figure, Tolochko remains a strong supporter of independent Ukrainian statehood but was 'lost' by the dominant Ukrainian elites at the 'nationalization' stage of the Ukrainian state-building project. Since 1995, he has challenged many aspects of the 'nationalization' of Ukrainian cultural life and historiography, becoming a villain in the eyes of the Ukrainian historical establishment. For his 'rebellious' ideas, see his articles and interviews of 1995–7, including 'Imeet li Ukraina natsional'nuiu ideiu?' 'Shche raz pro ukraïns'ku natsional'nu ideiu,' and 'Inakomysliashchii Tolochko,' ibid., 334–95.

35 See Smolii, 'Natsional'no-vyzvol'na viina v konteksti ukraïns'koho derzhavotvorennia,' 10.

36 For a portrayal of Khmelnytsky as a state builder first and foremost, see, apart from works by Smolii, Stepankov, and Mytsyk, the text of a speech delivered by Petro Tolochko at one of the events commemorating the four-hundredth anniversary of Khmelnytsky's birth, 'Bohdan Khmel'nyts'kyi,' in Tolochko, *Vid Rusi do Ukraïny*, 147–50.

37 See Smolii, 'Natsional'no-vyzvolna viina v konteksti ukraïns'koho derzhavotvorennia,' 10.

38 The statist approach to the definition of the main goals of the Khmelnytsky Uprising in Ukrainian historiography was criticized by Russian historians at a scholarly conference held in Moscow in January 1995 to commemorate the 340th anniversary of the Pereiaslav Council. See Zaborovskii, 'Rossiisko-ukrainskaia konferentsiia, posviashchennaia 340–letiiu Pereiaslavskoi rady.'

39 For the use of this term in Ukrainian historiography, see Mytsyk, 'Natsional'no-vyzvol'na viina ukraïns'koho narodu 1648–1658 rr.,' 30. Cf. Smolii and Stepankov, *Ukraïns'ka derzhavna ideia*, 84.

40 Apparently, the same logic underlay the views of Ukrainian autonomists in the second half of the eighteenth century. One of them, the Cossack secretary Semen Divovych, represented the Russo-Ukrainian arrangement as a

union of two equal partners, Great and Little Russia, under a common tsar. For a discussion of Divovych's views on the Pereiaslav Agreement, see chapter 2 of this volume. For a critique of the view of the Pereiaslav Agreement as an act of confederation, see Longworth, 'Ukraine: History and Nationality,' 117.

41 See the BBC monitoring service transcript of Russian TV news for 23 January 2004. On the political ramifications of Kuchma's decree, see Kuzio, 'Ukraine's "Pereiaslav Complex" and Relations with Russia'; and Kohut, 'Facing Ukraine's Russian Legacy.'

12 Remembering Yalta

1 On the symposium organized by the Crimean authorities to mark the sixtieth anniversary of the Yalta Conference, see Liudmila Obukhovskaia, 'Imet' uvazhenie k proshlomu,' *Krymskaia pravda*, 9 February 2005. There is an extensive literature on the conference, most of it published during the Cold War. For a post-Cold War assessment of the decisions made at Yalta, see Gardner, *Spheres of Influence*.

2 See Jedlicki, 'Historical Memory as a Source of Conflicts in Eastern Europe,' 226.

3 On the origins of the concept of *Mitteleuropa* and its transformation into the notion of Eastern and, later, East-Central Europe, see Busek and Brix, *Projekt Mitteleuropa*; and Łaszkiewicz, 'A Quest for Identity.'

4 See Suny, *The Revenge of the Past*.

5 On the role of history in postcommunist Eastern Europe, see Rosenberg, *The Haunted Land*; Borneman, *Settling Accounts*; and Kaplan, *Balkan Ghosts*.

6 For a Russian commentary on the outcome of discussions between Powell and Lavrov during a conference of foreign ministers of OSCE member nations in Sofia, see Artur Blinov and Artem Terekhov, 'Krakh mifa o zonakh vliianiia,' *Nezavisimaia gazeta*, 9 December 2004.

7 See Evgenii Grigor'ev, 'MID RF otstoial Kaliningrad,' *Nezavisimaia gazeta*, 16 November 2004.

8 See Artem Blinov, 'Tokio daiut trubu, no ne ostrova,' *Nezavisimaia gazeta*, 17 January 2005, and 'Ul'timatum proigravshego,' *Nezavisimaia gazeta*, 10 March 2005.

9 On the history of the Baltic states after the Soviet takeover, see Misiunas and Taagepera, *The Baltic States*.

10 On the controversy accompanying the Moscow launch of the book presented by Vike-Freiberga to Putin, see Ivan Gorshkov, 'Ėto prosto tochka zreniia latyshei,' *Nezavisimaia gazeta*, 4 February 2005.

11 See Vaira Vike-Freiberga, 'Was Rußland von Deutschland lernen kann,' *Der Tagesspiegel*, 6 May 2005. For Russian reaction to Vike-Freiberga's decision to come to Moscow for the VE Day celebrations, see Kirill Reznik-Martov, 'Bush priglasil prezidenta Latvii v Moskvu,' *Nezavisimaia gazeta*, 8 February 2005.

12 See the commentary of the Information and Press Department of the Russian Ministry of Foreign Affairs, http://www.mid.ru/brp_4.nsf/sps/314872473059B3E2C3256FA60050BAC4.

13 For the Polish discussion of the consequences of the Yalta Conference in response to the statement issued by the Russian Ministry of Foreign Affairs, see Tadeusz M. Płużański, 'Jałta – zwycięstwo Stalina, zdrada Zachodu,' 26 February 2005, mazowsze.k-raj.com.pl/pluzanski.shtml; Marek Ostrowski, 'Druz'iam moskovitam,' http://www.pravda.ru/world/2005/5/14/38/19148_Polska.html; and the transcript of the discussion on Radio Swoboda on 16 March 2005, with the participation of Polina Oldenburg and Aleksei Dzikovitsky, http://www.svoboda.org/archive/.

14 There is an extensive literature on the Katyn massacre. At the time of writing, the latest monograph on the subject is Sanford, *Katyn and the Soviet Massacre of 1940*.

15 See Wojciech Jaruzelski, 'Ich empfand den 8. Mai als riesige Erleichterung,' *Die Welt*, 3 May 2005.

16 See Jacek Lepiarz's summary of Kwaśniewski's interview with *Die Welt* in the online version of *Polityka*, 27 February 2005. On Kwaśniewski's participation in the Wrocław commemorations, see Trybuna.com.pl, http://www.trybuna.com.pl/n_show.php?code=2005050903.

17 See Artem Mal'gin, 'Nad imidzhem pridetsia rabotat',' *Nezavisimaia gazeta*, 16 May 2005.

18 See the interview with Sergei Lavrov in *Izvestiia*, 17 May 2005. Cf. the text of the interview on the website of the Information and Press Department of the Russian Ministry of Foreign Affairs, http://www.mid.ru/brp_4.nsf/sps/1B0BC3CE4ACCA28EC32570040020C546.

19 For the text of Bush's Riga speech, see http://www.whitehouse.gov/news/releases/2005/05/20050507–8.html.

20 For a survey of the American debate prompted by Bush's Riga speech, see Elisabeth Bumiller, 'In Row over Yalta, Bush Pokes at Baltic Politics,' *International Herald Tribune*, 16 May 2005.

21 Quoted in Matt Welch, 'When Men Were Men and Continents Were Divided,' Reason on Line, 10 May 2005, www.reason.com/hitandrun/2005/05/when_men_were_m.shtml.

22 See Chamberlin, 'The Munich Called Yalta,' in *The Yalta Conference*.

23 See Bumiller, 'In Row over Yalta, Bush Pokes at Baltic Politics.'

24 See Arthur Schlesinger, Jr., 'Yalta Delusions,' *The Huffington Post*, 9 May 2005, www.huffingtonpost.com/theblog/archive/2005/05/yalta-delusions.html. Here Schlesinger summarized some of his arguments presented in the October 1967 issue of *Foreign Affairs*. For a reprint of the article, see 'Origins of the Cold War' in *The Yalta Conference*, 152–83.

25 See Jacob Heilbrunn, 'Once Again, the Big Yalta Lie,' *Los Angeles Times*, 10 May 2005.

26 See Pat Buchanan, 'Was WWII Worth It? For Stalin, Yes,' AntiWar.com, 11 May 2005, http://www.antiwar.com/pat/?articleid=5899. Cf. Chester Wilmot, 'Stalin's Greatest Victory,' in *The Yalta Conference*, 59–84.

27 See 'Yalta Regrets,' *National Review* online, 11 May 2005, www.nationalreview.com/editorial/editorial2200505110923.asp.

28 Anne Applebaum, 'Saying Sorry,' *Washington Post*, 11 May 2005, A17.

29 See Iuliia Petrovskaia, 'Troinaia diplomatiia Busha,' *Nezavisimaia gazeta*, 11 May 2005; and Artur Blinov, 'Ia sidel riadom s drugom,' *Nezavisimaia gazeta*, 13 May 2005.

30 See 'Ialta – shans, kotorym ne sumeli vospol'zovat'sia,' RIA 'Novosti,' 1 March 2005.

31 See Trukhachev's translation of Ostrowski's article and his commentary on it in Pravda.ru for 21 February 2005, http://www.pravda.ru/world/2005/5/14/38/19148_Polska.html.

32 On the rise of Stalin's popularity in Putin's Russia, see Mendelson and Gerber, 'Failing the Stalin Test.'

33 On the Russian politics of remembrance, as reflected in the composition of the memorial during the Yeltsin period, see Schleifman, 'Moscow's Victory Park.'

34 For the text of the appeal, see 'Oskvernenie Dnia Pobedy,' *Grani*, 12 April 2005, http://grani.ru/Society/m.87674.html.

35 See Iu. Krupnov, 'Kto vyigral voinu? Narod ili Stalin?' *Internet protiv teleėkrana*, 10 October 2005.

36 See Fedor Lukianov, 'Den' Pobedy: mezhdunarodnyi aspekt,' *Izvestiia*, 29 April 2005, http://www.globalaffairs.ru/articles/3986.html. Cf. Lukianov's much less critical article about Yalta in the 8 February 2005 issue of *Vremia novostei*, 'Global'nyi disbalans: mir posle Ialty,' http://www.vremya.ru/.

37 See Viktor Sheinis, 'Ten' vozhdia narodov,' *Nezavisimaia gazeta*, 20 May 2005.

38 See Mykola Semena, 'U tsentri uvahy chy na zadvorkakh? Ukraina vtrachaie mizhnarodnyi prestyzh, zabuvaiuchy pro svoiu rol' u mizhnarodnii istorii,' *Dzerkalo tyzhnia*, 15–22 January 2005.

39 See 'Ukraina i Vtoraia mirovaia voina,' *Krymskoe obozrenie*, 1 February 2005; and 'V Krymu otmechaiut 60–iu godovshchinu Ialtinskoi konferentsii,' *Krymskoe obozrenie*, 6 February 2005.

40 See Liudmila Obukhovskaia, 'Ialta 1945–2005: ot bipoliarnogo mira k geopolitike budushchego,' *Krymskaia pravda*, 1 February 2005, and 'Imet' uvazhenie k proshlomu,' *Krymskaia pravda*, 9 February 2005.

41 For reaction to Hrach's statement by the leaders of the Tatar Mejlis, see Tsentr informatsiï ta dokumentatsiï kryms'kykh tatar, http://www.cidct.org.ua/press/2005/20050104.html#33.

42 See Iurii Shapoval, 'Ukraïns'ka Druha Svitova,' *Dzerkalo tyzhnia*, no. 15 (543), 23 April–6 May 2005; Serhii Makhun, '"Zolotyi veresen'"abo "vyrishennia pytannia shliakhom druzhn'oï zhody,"' *Dzerkalo tyzhnia*, no. 36 (564), 17–23 September 2005; and Vladyslav Hrynevych, 'Iak Ukraïnu do vstupu v OON hotuvala stalins'ka "konstytutsiina reforma" voiennoï doby,' *Dzerkalo tyzhnia*, no. 41 (569), 22–8 October 2005.

43 See Serhii Hrabovs'kyi and Ihor Losiev, 'Ialta 1945: triumf svobody, chy peremoha zla?' *Svoboda*, no. 5, 2005.

44 See Viacheslav Anisimov, 'Radist' zi sl'ozamy na ochakh, abo pro polityku, istoriiu i moral' na zori XXI stolittia,' *Dzerkalo tyzhnia*, no. 11 (539), 26 March–1 April 2005.

45 See Vitalii Radchuk, 'Velyka Vitchyzniana chy Druha Svitova?' *Dzerkalo tyzhnia*, no. 26 (554), 9–15 July 2005. For diametrically opposing views on the issue, see the articles in Ukraine's leading Internet newspaper, *Ukraïns'ka pravda*, by Serhii Hrabovs'kyi, 'Chas povertatysia z viiny,' *Ukraïns'ka pravda*, 6 May 2006, and Dmytro Krapyvenko and Pavlo Slobod'ko, 'Tvir do Dnia Peremohy,' *Ukraïns'ka pravda*, 8 May 2006, http://www.pravda.com.ua.

46 On the actions of the communists and the leadership of the Soviet Army veterans' association relating to the failure of the planned reconciliation, see Hrabovs'kyi, 'Chas povertatysia z viiny'; Mykola Velychko, 'NKVD ne prostylo UPA,' *Ukraïns'ka pravda*, 10 May 2005, http://www.pravda.com.ua; Volodymyr Danyliuk, 'Prymyrennia veteraniv. Misiia nezdiisnenna,' *Dzerkalo tyzhnia*, no. 11 (539), 26 March–1 April 2005; and Iryna Mahdysh, 'Nasha porazka u Druhii Svitovii viini,' *Dzerkalo tyzhnia*, no. 21 (549), 4–10 June 2005.

47 Ron Popeski, 'Leftists, Nationalists Scuffle in Ukraine over WW2,' Reuters, Kiev, Ukraine, 15 October 2005.

13 The History of a Non-Historical Nation

1 See Rudnytsky, 'The Role of the Ukraine in Modern History'; and Pritsak and Reshetar, Jr., 'The Ukraine and the Dialectics of Nation-Building.'

2 Von Hagen, 'Does Ukraine Have a History?' 658.

3 Kohn, *The Idea of Nationalism*, 330.

4 On Hrushevsky, see chapters 5 and 6 of this volume.

14 Imagining Early Modern Ukraine

1 On the political uses and abuses of Ukrainian and Belarusian history during the Soviet era, see Szporluk, 'National History as a Political Battleground.'

2 For an assessment of post-1991 Ukrainian historiography, see Subtelny, 'The Current State of Ukrainian Historiography'; Kohut, 'History as a Battleground'; Kasianov, 'Rewriting and Rethinking'; and Kuzio, 'Historiography and National Identity among the Eastern Slavs,' and 'Post-Soviet Ukrainian Historiography and School Textbooks in Ukraine.'

3 Yakovenko currently chairs the Department of History at the Kyiv Mohyla Academy National University and is editor-in-chief of *Ukraïns'kyi humanitarnyi ohliad*, which reviews works on Ukrainian history and studies in the humanities. She is also president of the Ukrainian Society for the Study of East Central Europe and chairs a highly successful seminar for young historians at the Kyiv Mohyla Academy.

4 Iakovenko, *Ukraïns'ka shliakhta z kintsia XIV do seredyny XVII stolittia*.

5 Iakovenko, *Narys istoriï Ukraïny z naidavnishykh chasiv do kintsia XVIII stolittia*.

6 Iakovenko, *Paralel'nyi svit*.

7 For a recent discussion of the applicability of the imperial paradigm to the Polish-Lithuanian Commonwealth, see Roman Szporluk's dialogue with Andrzej Nowak, 'Czy Polska była imperium?'

8 For examples of the acceptance of that paradigm in the West, see Walicki, *Poland between East and West*, 10; and Snyder, *The Reconstruction of Nations*, 3.

9 Yakovenko has been accused of attempting to introduce old Polish historiographic myths into Ukrainian historiography under the guise of postmodernism. See Valerii Stepankov's critique of Yakovenko's views (partly based on her *Paralel'nyi svit*) in his '1648 rik.'

10 On the model of identity advanced by the Orthodox intellectuals, see Plokhy, *The Cossacks and Religion*, 145–75. On Adam Kysil's regionalism, see Sysyn, 'Regionalism and Political Thought in Seventeenth-Century Ukraine.' Cf. Sysyn, *Between Poland and the Ukraine*, 20–36, 104–14.

11 See Litwin, 'Catholicization among the Ruthenian Nobility and Assimilation Processes in the Ukraine during the Years 1569–1648.'

12 For a discussion of Cossack attitudes towards religion and their involvement in religious conflict during the decades preceding the Khmelnytsky Uprising, as well as the role of the religious factor in the war itself, see Plokhy, *The Cossacks and Religion*, 100–44.

13 See Fram, 'Creating a Tale of Martyrdom in Tulczyn, 1648.'

14 Cf. my treatment of Polish, Jewish, and Ukrainian accounts of the Khmelnytsky Uprising in *The Cossacks and Religion*, 176–206.

15 Crossing National Boundaries

1 See Hermaize, 'Ukraïna ta Din u XVII st.'
2 For the text of the review, see Volodymyr Vernadsky National Library of Ukraine (Kyiv), Manuscript Institute, fond X, no. 2913.
3 Ibid.
4 For a brief survey of the development of Cossack studies in Ukraine, see Plokhy, *The Cossacks and Religion*, 6–10, and chapter 9 of this book. The most important works on Cossack history published in Ukraine in the 1950s and 1960s include Kryp'iakevych, *Bohdan Khmel'nyts'kyi*; Golobutskii, *Zaporozhskoe kazachestvo*; and Apanovych, *Zbroini syly Ukraïny pershoï polovyny XVIII stolittia*.

On the development of the Russian historiography of Cossackdom, see Barrett, *At the Edge of Empire*, 1–11; and O'Rourke, *Warriors and Peasants*, 13–15.

5 The Polish historiography of Ukrainian Cossackdom made a dramatic turn towards an unbiased interpretation of the subject with the publication of Wójcik's *Dzikie Pola w ogniu*. Among Polish authors who contributed to the field in the 1980s were Teresa Chynczewska-Hennel (*Świadomość narodowa kozaczyzny i szlachty ukraińskiej w XVII wieku*), and Władysław Serczyk (*Na dalekiej Ukrainie. Dzieje Kozaczyzny do 1648 r.*). The second volume of Serczyk's work appeared under the title *Na płonącej Ukrainie. Dzieje Kozaczyzny, 1648–51*.
6 The most important contributions to the history of the Ukrainian Cossacks published outside Soviet Ukraine include Krupnyckyj, *Hetman Mazepa und seine Zeit (1687–1709)*, and *Het'man Danylo Apostol i ioho doba*; Doroshenko, *Het'man Petro Doroshenko*; Ohloblyn, *Het'man Ivan Mazepa i ioho doba*; Okinshevich, *Ukrainian Society and Government, 1648–1781*; Gajecky, *The Cossack Administration of the Hetmanate*; Subtelny, *The Mazepists*; and Kohut, *Russian Centralism and Ukrainian Autonomy*.
7 Stökl, *Die Entstehung des Kosakentums*. Among the works of Russian émigré authors of the interwar period, a study by Svatikov, *Rossiia i Don*, deserves special attention.
8 For examples of popular books on the history of Cossackdom, see Hindus, *The Cossacks*; Seaton, *The Horsemen of the Steppes*; Groushko, *Cossack: Warrior Riders of the Steppes*; and Ure, *The Cossacks*.
9 See Rudnytsky, 'A Study of Cossack History.'

10 See Longworth, 'Letter to the Editor,' *Slavic Review* 33, no. 2 (June 1974): 413; 'Professor Rudnytsky Replies,' ibid., 414–16.

11 Among the authors who sought to apply a comparative approach to the history of Cossackdom was McNeill (*Europe's Steppe Frontier, 1500–1800*). His work nevertheless demonstrated the weakness of an attempt to synthesize findings in a field that still required a good deal of source-based research.

12 In Ukraine there has been a real explosion of research on Cossackdom, which always symbolized the spirit of Ukrainian independence and historical distinctiveness. Since 1991, it has become a central concern of historians in Ukraine. Among recent additions to the field are Shcherbak, *Formuvannia kozats'koho stanu v Ukraïni*; Lep'iavko, *Kozats'ki viiny kintsia XVI st. v Ukraïni*, and *Ukraïns'ke kozatstvo v mizhnarodnykh vidnosynakh*; Smolii and Stepankov, *Bohdan Khmel'nyts'kyi*; Storozhenko, *Bohdan Khmel'nyts'kyi i voienne mystetstvo u vyzvol'nii viini ukraïns'koho narodu seredyny XVII stolittia*; Fedoruk, *Mizhnarodna dyplomatiia i polityka Ukraïny, 1654–1657*; Iakovleva, *Het'manshchyna v druhii polovyni 50–kh rokiv XVII stolittia*; Horobets', *Vid soiuzu do inkorporatsiï*, *Prysmerk Het'manshchyny*, and *Elita kozats'koï Ukraïny v poshukakh politychnoï lehitymatsiï*; Chukhlib, *Kozats'kyi ustrii pravoberezhnoï Ukraïny*; Lyman, *Tserkovnyi ustrii Zaporoz'kykh Vol'nostei*; Shyian, *Kozatstvo Pivdennoï Ukraïny ostann'oï chverti XVII st.*; and Bachyns'ka, *Dunais'ke kozats'ke viis'ko, 1828–1868*. On contacts between Ukrainian and Don Cossackdom, see Brekhunenko, *Stosunky ukraïns'koho kozatstva z Donom u XVI – seredyni XVII st.*

For more literature on the subject, see the bibliographies in Plokhy, *The Cossacks and Religion* and *Tsars and Cossacks*. See also the bibliographic additions in Mykhailo Hrushevsky, *History of Ukraine-Rus'*, vols 7 and 8, and bibliographies appended to individual articles in *Ukraïns'ke kozatstvo*.

13 For examples of recent research on the Russian Cossacks, see Stanislavskii, *Grazhdanskaia voina v Rossii XVII veka*; Mininkov, *Donskoe kazachestvo na zare svoei istorii*, and *Donskoe kazachestvo v ėpokhu pozdnego srednevekov'ia*; Zuev, *Russkoe kazachestvo Zabaikal'ia vo vtoroi chetverti XVIII – pervoi polovine XIX vv.*; Sen', '*Voisko Kubanskoe Ignatovo Kavkazskoe*.'

14 For recent Western works on the history of the Cossacks, see Kumke, *Führer und Geführte bei den Zaporoger Kosaken*; Barrett, *At the Edge of Empire*; O'Rourke, *Warriors and Peasants*; Boeck, 'Shifting Boundaries on the Don Steppe Frontier.'

15 For an application of such an approach, see Brian Boeck's review of recent works on Don, Kuban, and Ukrainian Cossacks in *Kritika: Explorations in Russian and Eurasian History* 4, no. 3 (summer 2003): 735–46.

16 See Witzenrath, 'Die sibirischen Kosaken im institutionellen Wandel der Handels-Frontier.'
17 Boeck, 'Capitulation or Negotiation.'
18 Mininkov, 'Donskie atamany vtoroi poloviny XVII veka.'
19 Kappeler, *The Russian Empire*, 52.

16 Beyond Nationality

1 Quoted in Hobsbawm, *On History*, 270. For a different translation of the same statement, see Renan, 'What is a Nation?' 50.
2 See Berger, 'Representations of the Past,' 74.
3 See Markevich, *Istoriia Malorossii*.
4 On the development of the Ukrainian women's movement in the late nineteenth and early twentieth centuries, see Bohachevsky-Chomiak, *Feminists despite Themselves*.
5 See Efimenko, *Istoriia ukrainskogo naroda*. On Efimenko, see Markov, *A. Ia. Efimenko – istorik Ukrainy*.
6 See Drahomanov, 'Chudats'ki dumky pro ukraïns'ku natsionalnu spravu,' 490; quoted in Plokhy, *Unmaking Imperial Russia*, 156.
7 David Saunders, review of Plokhy, *Unmaking Imperial Russia*, *English Historical Review* 221, no. 490 (2006): 253.
8 See ibid., 253–5.
9 On Hrushevsky, see chapters 5 and 6 of this volume.
10 Quoted in Leitsch, 'East Europeans Studying History in Vienna (1855–1918),' 140.
11 See Kappeler, *The Russian Empire*, 8.
12 On the challenges faced by the Ukrainian national narrative vis-à-vis its Russian and Polish counterparts, see Plokhy, *Unmaking Imperial Russia*, 92–212.
13 On Henri Pirrene and his construction of the Belgian historical narrative, see Koninckx, 'Historiography and Nationalism in Belgium.'
14 On German national historiography, see Iggers, 'Nationalism and Historiography, 1789–1996.'
15 See Plokhy, *Unmaking Imperial Russia*, 419–22.
16 On the current state of historical research in Ukraine, see Kasianov, 'Rewriting and Rethinking'; and Kuzio, 'Historiography and National Identity among the Eastern Slavs.'
17 Some of the shortcomings of Hrushevsky's scheme were pointed out by his colleague Dmytro Bahalii in the 1920s. See his 'Akad. M.S. Hrushevs'kyi i ioho mistse v ukraïns'kii istoriohrafiï (Istoryko-krytychnyi narys).'

18 The dangers of that approach are spelled out in Plokhy, *The Origins of the Slavic Nations*.

19 See Kappeler, 'From an Ethnonational to a Multiethnic to a Transnational Ukrainian History.'

20 In Ukraine this work was translated into both Ukrainian and Russian and served as a textbook for university students through the first years of independence.

21 See Hrytsak, *Prorok u svoïi vitchyzni.*

22 On Vynnychenko, see Rudnytsky, 'Volodymyr Vynnychenko's Ideas in the Light of His Political Writings.'

23 See Iakovenko, *Narys istoriï seredn'ovichnoï ta rann'omodernoï Ukraïny* (Kyiv, 2005). For the first edition, see idem, *Narys istoriï Ukraïny z naidavnishykh chasiv do kintsia XVIII stolittia* (Kyiv, 1997). On Yakovenko and her interpretation of Ukrainian history, see chapter 14 of this volume.

24 On the absence of Jews in the standard narratives of Ukrainian history, see Petrovsky-Shtern, 'In Search of a Lost People,' and 'Jews in Ukrainian Thought.'

25 See Kovba, *Liudianist' u bezodni pekla*; Himka, 'War Criminality,' http://www.univie.ac.at/spacesofidentity/_Vol_5_1/_HTML/Himka.html; Berkhoff and Carynnyk, 'The Organization of Ukrainian Nationalists'; and Grachova, 'Vony zhyly sered nas?'; and Tsarynnyk, 'Zolochiv movchyt'.'

26 See, for example, Redlich, *Together and Apart in Berezhany*; or Dean, *Collaboration in the Holocaust.*

27 See Kappeler, 'From an Ethnonational to a Multiethnic to a Transnational Ukrainian History.'

28 On Ukraine as a cultural borderland between the Christian East and West, see Rudnytsky, 'Ukraine between East and West'; and Ševčenko, *Ukraine between East and West*. On the Ukrainian steppe frontier, see the recent publications by Chornovol, '"Dyke pole" i "dykyi zakhid,"' and idem, 'Seredn'ovichni frontyry ta moderni kordony.'

29 Mark von Hagen has recently made a strong case for the application of the borderland paradigm to the history of Eastern Europe in general and Ukrainian history in particular. See his 'Empires, Borderlands and Diasporas,' and 'Povertaiuchysia do istorii Ukraïny.'

30 On the strategies applied by the Cossack officers, who had to operate simultaneously in a number of worlds, see Frick, 'The Circulation of Information about Ivan Vyhovs'kyj.'

31 See Plokhy, *Tsars and Cossacks*.

32 See Plokhy, *The Cossacks and Religion*, 65–99.

33 See Ševčenko, *Ukraine between East and West*, 164–86.

34 Keenan, 'Muscovite Perceptions of Other East Slavs before 1654 – An Agenda for Historians.'
35 On Prokopovych and his role in the formation of Russian imperial identity, see Plokhy, 'The Two Russias of Teofan Prokopovyč.'
36 See Kappeler, *The Russian Empire*. Cf. his *'Great Russians' and 'Little Russians,'* 8.
37 See Szporluk, *Russia, Ukraine, and the Breakup of the Soviet Union*.
38 See chapter 12 of this volume.
39 Von Hagen, 'Empires, Borderlands and Diasporas,' 445.
40 See Matsuzato, Preface to *Emerging Meso-Areas in the Former Socialist Countries*; cf. Hrystak, 'On Sails and Gales, and Ships Driving in Various Directions.'
41 On the interplay of national and imperial elements in the thought of one of the leading Eurasianists, Nikolai Trubetskoi, see Mark Bassin, 'Classical Eurasianism and the Geopolitics of Russian Identity,' http://www.dartmouth.edu/~crn/crn_papers/Bassin.pdf.
42 See Wandycz, *The Lands of Partitioned Poland, 1795–1918*.
43 For a list of publications edited by Kłoczowski and conferences organized by the institute, see the institute's website, http://www.iesw.lublin.pl/dzialalnosc.php http://www.iesw.lublin.pl/wyd_listalph.php.
44 See Gorizontov, 'Istoricheskie puti i pereput'ia vostochnykh slavian glazami rossiiskikh uchenykh.'
45 See M.A. Robinson's and B.N. Floria's contributions to the discussion in *Na putiakh stanovleniia ukrainskoi i belorusskoi natsii*, 24–32.
46 *Istoriia Tsentral'no-Skhidnoï Ievropy*.
47 See the English translation of Viktor Yushchenko's State of the Nation address of 9 February 2006, http://orangeukraine.squarespace.com/long-articles/2006/2/16/yushchenkos-state-of-the-nation-address.html.
48 Cf. note 6 above.

Bibliography

Adadurov, Vadym. 'Narodzhennia odnoho istorychnoho mitu: problema "Napoleon i Ukraïna" u vysvitlenni Il'ka Borshchaka.' *Ukraina moderna* (Kyiv and Lviv) 9 (2005): 212–36.

Admiral Nakhimov. Stat'i i ocherki. Moscow, 1954.

Akty, otnosiashchiesia k istorii Iuzhnoi i Zapadnoi Rossii, sobrannye i izdannye Arkheograficheskoi komissiei. 15 vols. St Petersburg, 1861–92.

Alexander, John T. *Catherine the Great: Life and Legend*. New York and Oxford, 1989.

Althoen, David. 'Natione Polonus and the Naród Szlachecki: Two Myths of National Identity and Noble Solidarity.' *Zeitschrift für Ostmitteleuropa-Forschung* 52, no. 4 (2003): 475–508.

Anderson, Benedict. *Imagined Communities: Reflections on the Origin and Spread of Nationalism*. London and New York, 1995.

Andriewsky, Olga. 'The Politics of National Identity: The Ukrainian Question in Russia, 1904–1912.' PhD diss., Harvard University, 1991.

– 'The Russian-Ukrainian Discourse and the Failure of the "Little Russian Solution," 1782–1917.' In *Culture, Nation, and Identity: The Ukrainian-Russian Encounter (1600–1945)*, ed. Andreas Kappeler, Zenon E. Kohut, Frank E. Sysyn, and Mark von Hagen, 182–214. Edmonton and Toronto, 2003.

Anisimov, Evgenii. *Elizaveta Petrovna*. Moscow, 2002.

– *Rossiia v seredine XVIII veka*. Moscow, 1986.

Antonovych, Volodymyr. *Pro chasy kozats'ki na Ukraïni*. Chernivtsi, 1896; repr. Kyiv, 1991.

Apanovich, Elena. *Rukopisnaia svetskaia kniga XVIII veka na Ukraine. Istoricheskie sborniki*. Kyiv, 1983.

Apanovych, Olena. 'Nam bronzy ne treba!' *Ukraïns'ka kul'tura*, 1993, no. 1: 8–9.

– 'Natsional'no-vyzvol'ni viiny v epokhu feodalizmu.' *Ukraïns'kyi istorychnyi zhurnal*, 1965, no. 12: 29–38.

– *Zbroini syly Ukraïny pershoï polovyny XVIII stolittia*. Kyiv, 1968.
Arel, Dominique. 'Ukraine – The Temptation of the Nationalizing State.' In *Political Culture and Civil Society in Russia and the New States of Eurasia*. Vol. 7 of The International Politics of Eurasia, ed. Vladimir Tismaneanu, 157–88. Armonk, NY, and London, 1995.
Armstrong, John A. 'Myth and History in the Evolution of Ukrainian Consciousness.' In *Ukraine and Russia in Their Historical Encounter*, 125–39.
Artem'eva, T.V. *Mikhail Shcherbatov*. St Petersburg, 1994.
Aslanbegov, A.B. *Admiral P.S. Nakhimov*. St Petersburg, 1898.
Babinski, Hubert F. *The Mazeppa Legend in European Romanticism*. New York, 1974.
Bachyns'ka, Olena. *Dunais'ke kozats'ke viis'ko, 1828–1868*. Odesa, 1998.
Backus, Oswald P. *Motives of West Russian Nobles in Deserting Lithuania for Moscow, 1377–1514*. Lawrence, KS, 1957.
Bahalii, Dmytro. 'Akad. M.S. Hrushevs'kyi i ioho mistse v ukraïns'kii istoriohrafiï (Istorychno-krytychnyi narys).' *Chervonyi shliakh*, no. 1 (46) (January 1927): 160–217.
Baines, Paul. *The House of Forgery in Eighteenth-Century Britain*. Burlington, 1999.
Barber, John. *Soviet Historians in Crisis, 1928–1932*. London, 1981.
Barker, A.J. *The Vainglorious War, 1854–56*. London, 1970.
Barrett, Thomas M. *At the Edge of Empire: The Terek Cossacks and the North Caucasus Frontier, 1700–1860*. Boulder, CO, 1999.
Basarab, John. *Pereiaslav 1654: A Historiographical Study*. Edmonton, 1982.
Belavenets, P.I. *Admiral Pavel Stepanovich Nakhimov*. Sevastopol, 1902.
Bem, Ewa. 'Termin "ojczyzna" w literaturze XVI i XVII wieku. Refleksje o języku.' *Odrodzenie i Reformacja w Polsce* 34 (1989): 131–57.
Bercoff, Giovanna Brogi. *Królestwo Słowian. Historiografia Renesansu i Baroku w krajach słowiańskich*. Izabelin, 1998.
– 'Ruś, Ukraina, Ruthenia, Wielkie Księstwo Litewskie, Rzeczpospolita, Moskwa, Rosja, Europa środkowo-wschodnia: o wielowarstwowości i polifunkcjonalizmie kulturowym.' In *Contributi italiani al XIII congresso internazionale degli slavisti*, ed. Alberto Alberti et al., 325–87. Pisa, 2003.
Berger, Stefan. 'Representations of the Past: The Writing of National Histories in Europe.' *Debatte* 12, no. 1 (2004): 73–96.
Berger, Stefan, Mark Donovan, and Kevin Passmore. 'Apologias for the Nation-State in Western Europe since 1800.' In idem, *Writing National Histories: Western Europe since 1800*, 3–14. London and New York, 1999.
Berkhoff, Karel C. *Harvest of Despair: Life and Death in Ukraine under Nazi Rule*. Cambridge, MA, 2004.

Berkhoff, Karel C., and Marco Carynnyk, 'The Organization of Ukrainian Nationalists and Its Attitude toward Germans and Jews: Iaroslav Stets'ko's 1941 *Zhyttiepys*.' *Harvard Ukrainian Studies* 23, nos 3–4 (December 1999): 147–84.

Berkov, E. *Krymskaia kampaniia*. Moscow, 1939.

[Berlinskii, Maksim]. *Kratkaia rossiiskaia istoriia dlia upotrebleniia iunoshestvu, nachinaiushchemu obuchat'sia istorii, prodolzhennaia do iskhoda XVIII stoletiia, sochinennaia v Kieve uchitelem Maksimom Berlinskim*. Moscow, 1800.

Berlyns'kyi, Maksym. *Istoriia mista Kyieva*. Kyiv, 1991.

Bibliohrafiia prats' vchenykh Dnipropetrovs'koho universytetu. Istoriia Ukraïny XV–XVIII stolit', 1918–90. Dnipropetrovsk, 1992.

Bil'basov, V.A. *Ioann Antonovich i Mirovich*. Moscow, 1908.

Bilets'kyi, Platon. *Ukraïns'ke mystetstvo druhoï polovyny XVII-XVIII stolit'*. Kyiv, 1981.

– *Ukraïns'kyi portretnyi zhyvopys XVII–XVII st. Problemy stanovlennia i rozvytku*. Kyiv, 1969.

Black, J.L. *G.-F. Müller and the Imperial Russian Academy*. Kingston and Montreal, 1986.

Blizniuk, A.M. *Na bastionakh Sevastopolia*. Minsk, 1989.

Boeck, Brian. 'Capitulation or Negotiation: Relations between the Don Host and Moscow in the Aftermath of the Razin Uprising.' In *Die Geschichte Rußlands im 16. und 17. Jahrhundert*, 382–94.

– 'Shifting Boundaries on the Don Steppe Frontier: Cossacks, Empires and Nomads to 1739.' PhD diss., Harvard University, 2002.

Bogdanovich, M.I. *Vostochnaia voina*. Pts 3–4. St Petersburg, 1877.

Bohachevsky-Chomiak, Martha. *Feminists despite Themselves: Women in Ukrainian Community Life, 1884–1939*. Edmonton, 1988.

Boiko, Ivan. 'Shche raz pro kharakter natsional'no-vyzvol'nykh voien v epokhu feodalizmu.' *Ukrains'kyi istorychnyi zhurnal*, 1966, no. 2: 84–7.

Borneman, John. *Settling Accounts: Violence, Justice, and Accountability in Postsocialist Europe*. Princeton, 1997.

Borshschak, Il'ko. *Napoleon i Ukraïna*. Lviv, 1937.

Bovhyria, Andrii. '*Korotkyi opys Malorosiï* (1340–1734) u rukopysnykh spyskakh XVIII st.' *Istoriohrafichni doslidzhennia v Ukraïni*, vyp. 14, 340–63. Kyiv, 2004.

Braichevs'kyi, Mykhailo. 'Maksym Berlyns'kyi ta ioho "Istoriia mista Kyieva."' In Maksym Berlyns'kyi, *Istoriia mista Kyieva*, 5–20.

– *Pryiednannia chy vozz'iednannia?* Toronto, 1972. English translation: *Annexation or Reunification: Critical Notes on One Conception*, trans. and ed. George P. Kulchycky. Munich, 1974.

– 'Pryiednannia chy vozz'iednannia? Tryptykh.' In *Pereiaslavs'ka rada*, 294–418.

Brekhunenko, Viktor. 'Pereiaslavs'ka rada 1654 roku v rosiis'kii istoriohrafiï.' In *Pereiaslavs'ka rada*, 605–52.

– *Stosunky ukraïns'koho kozatstva z Donom u XVI – seredyni XVII st*. Kyiv and Zaporizhia, 1998.

Breuilly, John. *Nationalism and the State*. 2d ed. Chicago, 1993.

Brogi, Giovanna. 'Mazepa, lo zar e il diavolo. Un inedito di Stefan Javorskij.' *Russica Romana* 7 (2000): 167–88.

Brown, Kate. *A Biography of No Place: From Ethnic Borderland to Soviet Heartland*. Cambridge, MA, 2004.

Brudny, Yitzhak M. *Reinventing Russia: Russian Nationalism and the Soviet State, 1953–91*. Cambridge, MA, and London, 2000.

Bruk, S.I., and V.M. Kabuzan. 'Migratsiia naseleniia v Rossii v 18 – nachale 19 veka. (Chislennost', struktura, geografiia).' *Istoriia SSSR*, 1984, no. 4: 41–59.

Busek, Erhardt, and Emil Brix. *Projekt Mitteleuropa*. Vienna, 1986.

Chamberlin, William Henry. 'The Munich Called Yalta.' In *The Yalta Conference*, ed. Richard F. Fenno, 84–98. 2nd ed. Lexington, MA, Toronto, and London, 1972.

Chentsov, Viktor. 'Ideoloh ukraïns'koho natsionalizmu.' In *Vidrodzhena pam'iat'*, ed. Valentyn Ivanenko [=*Reabilitovani istoriieiu. Dnipropetrovs'ka oblast'*, no. 1], 106–21. Dnipropetrovsk, 1999.

Chentsova, Vera. *Vostochnaia tserkov' i Rossiia posle Pereiaslavskoi rady, 1654–1658*. Moscow, 2004.

Chmielewski, Edward. *The Polish Question in the Russian State Duma*. Knoxville, TN, 1970.

Chornovol, Ihor. '"Dyke pole" i "dykyi zakhid."' *Krytyka*, 2006, no. 4.

– *Pol's'ko-ukraïns'ka uhoda, 1890–94*. Lviv, 2000.

– 'Seredn'ovichni frontyry ta moderni kordony.' *Krytyka*, 2006, no. 10.

Chukhlib, Taras. *Kozats'kyi ustrii pravoberezhnoï Ukraïny. Ostannia chvert' XVII st*. Kyiv, 1996.

Chykalenko, Ievhen. *Shchodennyk, 1861–1929*. Vol. 1. Kyiv, 1993.

Chynczewska-Hennel, Teresa. *Świadomość narodowa kozaczyzny i szlachty ukraińskiej w XVII wieku*. Warsaw, 1985.

Ciesielski, Tomasz. *Sejm brzeski 1653 r. Studium z dziejów Rzeczypospolitej w latach 1652–1653*. Toruń, 2003.

Coakley, John. 'National Territories and Cultural Frontiers: Conflicts of Principle in the Formation of States in Europe.' In *Frontier Regions in Western Europe*, ed. Malcolm Anderson, 34–49. London, 1983.

Cobban, Alfred. *The Nation State and National Self-Determination*. London, 1969.

Coleman, Heather J. 'Becoming a Russian Baptist: Conversion Narratives and Social Experience.' *Russian Review* 61 (January 2002): 94–112.

Cracraft, James. 'Empire versus Nation: Russian Political Theory under Peter I.' *Harvard Ukrainian Studies* 10, nos 3–4 (December 1986): 524–41.

Cross, Anthony. '"Them": Russians on Foreigners.' In *National Identity in Russian Culture: An Introduction*, ed. Simon Franklin and Emma Widdis, 74–92. Cambridge, 2004.

Cultures in Flux: Lower-Class Values, Practices, and Resistance in Late Imperial Russia, ed. Stephen P. Frank and Mark D. Steinberg. Princeton, 1994.

Czacki, Tadeusz. 'O nazwisku Ukrainy i początku Kozaków.' *Nowy Pamiętnik Warszawski* (October-December 1801), bk 4, 32–40.

Daniel, Wallace L. *A Statesman at the Court of Catherine the Great*. Newtonville, MA, 1991.

Dashkevych, Iaroslav. 'Berlin, kviten' 1791 r.: misiia V.V. Kapnista. Ïi peredistoriia ta istoriia.' *Ukraïns'kyi arkheohrafichnyi shchorichnyk* (Kyiv) 1 (1992): 220–60.

Davydov, Iu. *Nakhimov*. Moscow, 1970.

Dean, Martin. *Collaboration in the Holocaust: Crimes of the Local Police in Belorussia and Ukraine, 1941–44*. New York, 2000.

Divovych, Semen. 'Razgovor Velikorossii s Malorossiieiu.' In *Ukraïns'ka literatura XVIII stolittia*, ed. V.I. Krekoten', 384–415. Kyiv, 1983.

Doroshenko, Dmytro. *Het'man Petro Doroshenko. Ohliad ioho zhyttia i politychnoï diial'nosty*. New York, 1985.

– *Moï spomyny pro davnie-mynule (1901–1914 roky)*. Winnipeg, 1954.

Doroshenko, Dmytro, and Olexander Ohloblyn. *A Survey of Ukrainian Historiography*. New York, 1957.

Drahomanov, Mykhailo. 'The Lost Epoch: Ukrainians under the Muscovite Tsardom, 1654–1876' (ca. 1878). In *Towards an Intellectual History of Ukraine: An Anthology of Ukrainian Thought from 1710 to 1995*, ed. Ralph Lindheim and George S.N. Luckyj, 152–61. Toronto, 1996.

– *Vybrane*. Kyiv, 1991.

Druzhinina, Elena. *Kiuchuk-Kainardzhiiskii mir 1774 goda (ego podgotovka i zakliuchenie)*. Moscow, 1955.

– *Severnoe Prichernomor'e v 1775–1800 gg*. Moscow, 1959.

Dubrovin, N. *Vostochnaia voina 1853–1856 godov. Obzor sobytii po povodu sochineniia M.I. Bogdanovicha*. St Petersburg, 1878.

Dukes, Paul. *The Making of Russian Absolutism, 1613–1801*. London and New York, 1982.

Dunlop, John B. *The Rise of Russia and the Fall of the Soviet Empire*. Princeton, 1993.

– 'Russia: Confronting Loss of Empire.' In *Nations and Politics in the Soviet Successor States*, ed. Ian Bremmer and Ray Taras, 43–72. Cambridge, 1993.

Dybiec, Julian. *Nie tylko szablą. Nauka i kultura polska w walce o utrzymanie tożsamości narodowej, 1795–1918*. Cracow, 2004.

'Dyskusiia z pryvodu skhemy istorii Ukraïny M. Iavors'koho.' *Litopys revoliutsiï*, 1930, nos 2, 3–4, 5.

Dzherela z istoriï pivdennoï Ukraïny. Vol. 5, pt. 1. *Memuary ta shchodennyky.* 2 bks, ed. Anatolii Boiko. Zaporizhia, 2005.

Edgerton, W.B. 'Laying a Legend to Rest: The Poet Kapnist and Ukrainian-German Intrigue.' *Slavic Review* 30, no. 3 (1971): 551–60.

Efimenko, Aleksandra. *Istoriia ukrainskogo naroda.* 2 pts. St Petersburg, 1906.

Emerging Meso-Areas in the Former Socialist Countries: Histories Revived or Improvised? Ed. Kimitaka Matsuzato. Sapporo, 2005.

Encyclopedia of Ukraine. Ed. Volodymyr Kubijovyč and Danylo Husar Struk. 6 vols. Toronto, 1984–2001.

The End of Empire? The Transformation of the USSR in Comparative Perspective. Vol. 9 of The International Politics of Eurasia, ed. Karen Dawisha and Bruce Parrott. Armonk, NY, and London, 1997.

Enteen, George M. *The Soviet Scholar-Bureaucrat: M.N. Pokrovskii and the Society of Marxist Historians.* University Park, PA, and London, 1978.

Fedoruk, Iaroslav. *Mizhnarodna dyplomatiia i polityka Ukraïny, 1654–57.* Vol. 1, *1654.* Lviv, 1996.

– 'Perehovory Rechi Pospolytoï z Moskvoiu i ukladannia Vilens'koho myru (1654–1656).' In *Pereiaslavs'ka rada*, 796–862.

Fisher, Alan W. *The Crimean Tatars.* Stanford, 1978.

– *The Russian Annexation of the Crimea.* Cambridge, 1970.

Fitzpatrick, Sheila. 'Lives Under Fire: Autobiographical Narratives and Their Challenges in Stalin's Russia.' In *De Russie et d'aillleurs: Feux croisés sur l'histoire,* ed. Martine Godet, 225–32. Paris, 1995.

Fomin, Viacheslav. *Lomonosov: genii russkoi istorii.* Moscow, 2006.

Fram, Edward. 'Creating a Tale of Martyrdom in Tulczyn, 1648.' In *Jewish History and Jewish Memory: Essays in Honor of Yosef Hayim Yerushalmi*, ed. Elisheva Carlebach et al., 89–109. Hanover and London, 1998.

Frank, Alison. *Oil Empire: Visions of Prosperity in Austrian Galicia.* Cambridge, MA, 2005.

Frick, David. 'The Circulation of Information about Ivan Vyhovs'kyj.' *Harvard Ukrainian Studies* 17, nos 3–4 (December 1993): 251–78.

Gajecky, George. *The Cossack Administration of the Hetmanate.* 2 vols. Cambridge, MA, 1978.

Gardner, Lloyd C. *Spheres of Influence: The Great Powers Partition Europe, from Munich to Yalta.* Chicago, 1993.

Gaskill, Howard, ed. *Reception of Ossian in Europe.* Cardiff, 2004.

Gębarowicz, Mieczysław. *Mater Misericordiae – Pokrow – Pokrowa w sztuce i legendzie Środkowo-Wschodniej Europy.* Wrocław, 1986.

Gerus, Oleh. 'Manifestations of the Cossack Idea in Modern History: The Cossack Legacy and Its Impact.' *Ukraïns'kyi istoryk*, 1986, nos 1–2: 22–39.
– 'The Ukrainian Question in the Russian Duma, 1906–17: An Overview,' *Studia Ucrainica* 4 (Ottawa, 1984): 157–73.
Gervais-Francelle, Céline. 'La grève scolaire dans le royaume de Pologne.' In *La première révolution russe*, ed. François-Xavier Coquin and Céline Gervais-Francelle, 261–98. Paris, 1986.
Die Geschichte Rußlands im 16. und 17. Jahrhundert aus der Perspektive seiner Regionen. Ed. Andreas Kappeler. Wiesbaden, 2004.
Goldfrank, David M. *The Origins of the Crimean War*. London, 1994.
Golobutskii, V. [Volodymyr Holobuts'kyi]. *Chernomorskoe kazachestvo*. Kyiv, 1956.
– *Zaporozhskoe kazachestvo*. Kyiv, 1957.
Gorev, L. *Voina 1853–1856 gg. i oborona Sevastopolia*. Moscow, 1955.
Gorizontov, L.E. 'Istoricheskie puti i pereput'ia vostochnykh slavian glazami rossiiskikh uchenykh.' In *Na putiakh stanovleniia ukrainskoi i belorusskoi natsii: faktory, mekhanizmy, sootneseniia*, ed. Leonid Gorizontov, 3–18. Moscow, 2004.
Grabowicz, George. 'Three Perspectives on the Cossack Past: Gogol', Ševčenko and Kuliš.' *Harvard Ukrainian Studies* 5 (1981): 179–94.
Grachova, Sofiia. 'Vony zhyly sered nas?' *Krytyka*, 2005, no. 4.
Greenfeld, Liah. *Nationalism: Five Roads to Modernity*. Cambridge, MA, 1992.
Grigorenko, Petr. *V podpol'e mozhno vstretit' tol'ko krys*. Moscow, 1997.
Grigorovich, N.I. *Kantsler kniaz' Aleksandr Andreevich Bezborod'ko v sviazi s sobytiiami ego vremeni*. 2 vols. St Petersburg, 1879–81.
Groushko, Mike. *Cossack: Warrior Riders of the Steppes*. New York, 1993.
Halecki, Oscar. *Borderlands of Western Civilization: A History of East Central Europe*. New York, 1952.
– *The Limits and Divisions of European History*. New York, 1950.
Halfin, Igal. 'From Darkness to Light: Student Communist Autobiography during NEP.' *Jahrbücher für Geschichte Osteuropas* 45, no. 2 (1997): 210–36.
– *Terror in My Soul: Communist Autobiographies on Trial*. Cambridge, MA, 2003.
Harasymchuk, Vasyl'. 'Z nahody poiavy IX tomu "Istoriï Ukraïny-Rusy" M. Hrushevs'koho.' In Ia. O. Fedoruk, 'Vidhuk Vasylia Harasymchuka na IX tom "Istoriï Ukraïny-Rusy" M. Hrushevs'koho,' *Ukraïns'kyi arkheohrafichnyi shchorichnyk*, new series, vyp. 3–4, 534–41. Kyiv, 1999.
Hastings, Adrian. *The Construction of Nationhood: Ethnicity, Religion and Nationalism*. Cambridge, 1997.
Hellbeck, Jochen. 'Fashioning the Stalinist Soul: The Diary of Stepan Podlubnyi.' *Jahrbücher für Geschichte Osteuropas* 44, no. 3 (1996): 344–73.
– *Revolution on My Mind: Writing a Diary under Stalin*. Cambridge, MA, 2006.

Hermaize, Osyp. 'Ukraïna ta Din u XVII st.' *Zapysky Kyïvs'koho Instytuta narodnoï osvity*, 1928, no. 3: 106–96; also separately, Kyiv, 1928.
Heuman, Susan. *Kistiakovsky: The Struggle for National and Constitutional Rights in the Last Years of Tsarism*. Cambridge, MA, 1998.
Himka, John-Paul. 'The Greek Catholic Church and Nation-Building in Galicia, 1772–1918.' *Harvard Ukrainian Studies* 8 (1984): 426–52.
– 'Priests and Peasants: The Greek Catholic Pastor and the Ukrainian National Movement in Austria, 1867–1900.' *Canadian Slavonic Papers* 21 (1979): 1–14.
– 'War Criminality: A Blank Spot in the Collective Memory of the Ukrainian Diaspora.' *Spaces of Identity* 5, no. 1 (2005): 9–24.
Hindus, Maurice Gerschon. *The Cossacks: The Story of a Warrior People*. Garden City, NY, 1945; repr. Westport, CT, 1970.
Hobsbawm, Eric. *Nations and Nationalism since 1780: Programme, Myth, Reality*. 2d ed. Cambridge, 1992.
– *On History*. New York, 1997.
Holobuts'kyi, Volodymyr. *Zaporiz'ka Sich v ostanni roky svoho isnuvannia 1734–1775*. Kyiv, 1961.
Holubets', Mykola. *Nacherk istoriï ukraïns'koho mystetstva*. Lviv, 1922. Repr. New York, 1973.
Hordyns'kyi, Sviatoslav. *Ukraïns'ka ikona XII-XVIII storich*. Philadelphia, 1973.
Horobets', Viktor. *Elita kozats'koï Ukraïny v poshukakh politychnoï lehitymatsiï: stosunky z Moskvoiu ta Varshavoiu, 1654–1665*. Kyiv, 2001.
– *Prysmerk Het'manshchyny. Ukraïna v roky reform Petra I*. Kyiv, 1998.
– 'Ukraïns'ko-rosiis'ki zmahannia za Bilorus' (1654–1659).' In *Natsional'no-vyzvol'na viina ukraïns'koho narodu seredyny XVII stolittia: polityka, ideolohiia, viis'kove mystetstvo*, ed. Valerii Smolii, 112–30. Kyiv, 1998.
– *Vid soiuzu do inkorporatsiï: ukraïns'ko-rosiis'ki vidnosyny druhoï polovyny XVII–pershoï chverti XVIII st*. Kyiv, 1995.
Hosking, Geoffrey. 'The Freudian Frontier.' *Times Literary Supplement*, 10 March 1995, 27.
– *Russia: People and Empire, 1552–1917*. London, 1998.
– 'The Russian National Myth Repudiated.' In *Myths and Nationhood*, ed. Geoffrey Hosking and George Schöpflin, 198–210. London, 1997.
Hrabovych, Hryhorii [Grabowicz, George]. 'Slidamy natsional'nykh mistyfikatsii.' *Krytyka* 5, no. 6 (June 2001): 14–23.
Hrushevsky, Mykhailo. *History of Ukraine-Rus'*. Ed. Frank E. Sysyn et al. Vols. 1, 7, 8, 9.1. Edmonton and Toronto, 1997–2005.
Hrushevs'kyi, Mykhailo. '250 lit.' *Literaturno-naukovyi vistnyk* 7, no. 1 (1904): 1–6.
– 'Bohdanovi rokovyny.' *Literaturno-naukovyi vistnyk* 10, nos. 8–9 (July-September 1907): 207–12.

– *Iliustrovana istoriia Ukraïny*. Kyiv, 1911, 1912, 1913, 1915, 1917. Repr. of 1913 edition: Kyiv, 1990, 1992.
– *Istoriia ukraïns'koï literatury*. 5 vols. Kyiv and Lviv, 1923–7. Repr. New York, 1959–60. Vol. 6. Kyiv, 1995.
– *Istoriia Ukraïny–Rusy*. 10 vols. 1st ed. Lviv and Kyiv, 1898–1937. Vols 1–4. 2d ed. Lviv and Kyiv, 1904–7. Vol. 1. 3d ed. Kyiv, 1913. Repr. New York, 1954–8; Kyiv, 1991–2000.
– 'Khmel'nyts'kyi i Khmel'nychchyna. Istorychnyi eskiz.' *Zapysky Naukovoho tovarystva imeny Shevchenka* 23–4 (1898): 1–30.
– [Mikhail Grushevskii]. *Osvobozhdenie Rossii i ukrainskii vopros. Stat'i i zametki*. St Petersburg, 1907.
– *Pereiaslavs'ka umova Ukraïny z Moskvoiu 1654 roku. Statti i teksty*. Kyiv, 1917–18.
– *Shchodennyk, 1883–1894*. Ed. Leonid Zashkil'niak. Kyiv, 1997.
– 'Shchodennyky M.S. Hrushevs'koho [1904–1910 rr.].' Ed. Ihor Hyrych. *Kyïvs'ka starovyna*, 1995, no. 1: 10–30.
– 'Sprava ukraïns'kykh katedr i nashi naukovi potreby.' *Literaturno-naukovyi vistnyk* 10, no. 1 (1907): 42–57; no. 2: 213–20; no. 3: 408–18; also separately: Lviv, 1907.
– *Tvory u 50 tomakh*. Ed. Pavlo Sokhan' et al. Vols 1, 5, 7. Lviv, 2002–5.
Hryb, Olexander. 'New Ukrainian Cossacks – Revival or Building New Armed Forces?' *Ukrainian Review* 46, no. 1 (spring 1999): 44–53.
Hryhorij Hrabjanka's 'The Great War of Bohdan Xmel'nyc'kyj.' Cambridge, MA, 1990.
Hrytsak, Iaroslav. *Prorok u svoïi vitchyzni. Franko ta ioho spil'nota (1856–86)*. Kyiv, 2006.
Hrytsak, Yaroslav. 'On Sails and Gales, and Ships Driving in Various Directions: Post-Soviet Ukraine as a Test-Case for the Meso-Area Concept.' In *Emerging Meso-Areas in the Former Socialist Countries*, 42–68.
Iakovenko, Natalia. *Narys istoriï Ukraïny z naidavnishykh chasiv do kintsia XVIII stolittia*. Kyiv, 1997; 2d rev. ed. Kyiv, 2005.
– *Paralel'nyi svit. Doslidzhennia z istoriï uiavlen' ta idei v Ukraïni XVI-XVII st.* Kyiv, 2002.
– *Ukraïns'ka shliakhta z kintsia XIV do seredyny XVII stolittia (Volyn' i Tsentral'na Ukraïna)*. Kyiv, 1993.
– 'V kol'orakh proletars'koï revoliutsiï.' *Ukraïns'kyi humanitarnyi ohliad* 3 (2000): 58–78.
Iakovleva, Tetiana. *Het'manshchyna v druhii polovyni 50–kh rokiv XVII stolittia. Prychyny i pochatok Ruïny*. Kyiv, 1998.
Iakovliv, Andrii. 'Dohovir het'mana Bohdana Khmel'nyts'koho z moskovs'kym tsarem Oleksiiem Mykhailovychem 1654 r.' (1954). In *Pereiaslavs'ka rada*, 91–155.

Ias', Oleksii. 'Obrazy Pereiaslava v ukraïns'kii istoriohrafiï.' In *Pereiaslavs'ka rada*, 524–604.

Iastrebov, Fedir. 'Natsional-fashysts'ka kontseptsiia selians'koï viiny 1648 roku na Ukraïni (Z pryvodu 2 polovyny IX t. 'Istoriï Ukraïny-Rusy' akad. M. Hrushevs'koho).' *Zapysky Istorychno-arkheohrafichnoho instytutu*, 1934, no. 1: 55–120.

– 'Tomu dev'iatoho persha polovyna.' *Prapor marksyzmu*, 1930, no. 1: 133–48.

Iavors'kyi, Matvii. *Istoriia Ukraïny v styslomu narysi*. Kharkiv, 1928.

– *Korotka istoriia Ukraïny*. Kharkiv, 1927.

Iggers, Georg G. 'Nationalism and Historiography, 1789–1996: The German Example in Historical Perspective.' In *Writing National Histories: Western Europe since 1800*, ed. Stefan Berger, Mark Donovan, and Kevin Passmore, 15–29. London and New York, 1999.

Ilnytzkyj, Oleh S. *Ukrainian Futurism, 1914–1930: A Historical and Critical Study*. Cambridge, MA, 1997.

Istoriia goroda-geroia Sevastopolia, 1917–1957. Kyiv, 1958.

Istoriia mist i sil Ukraïns'koï RSR. Kryms'ka oblast'. Kyiv, 1974.

Istoriia Rusiv. Trans. Viacheslav Davydenko. New York, 1956.

Istoriia Rusiv. Introduction by Valerii Shevchuk, trans. into modern Ukrainian by Ivan Drach. Kyiv, 1991. Repr. Kyiv, 2001, 2003.

Istoriia Rusov ili Maloi Rossii. Sochinenie Georgiia Konisskogo, Arkhiepiskopa Belorusskogo. Moscow, 1846. Repr. Kyiv, 1991.

Istoriia SSSR s drevneishikh vremen do nashikh dnei. 12 vols. Moscow, 1966–80.

Istoriia Tsentral'no-Skhidnoï Ievropy. Ed. Leonid Zashkilniak. Lviv, 2001.

Istoriia ukraïns'koï kul'tury. Vol. 3. Kyiv, 2003.

Iukht, A.I. 'Pobornik novoi Rossii.' In *Istoriki Rossii XVIII – nachalo XX veka*, ed. A.N. Sakharov, 8–27. Moscow, 1996.

Iusova, Nataliia. '"Problema davn'orus'koi narodnosti" v pratsi V.V. Mavrodina "Obrazovanie drevnerusskogo gosudarstva" (1945 r.).' *Ruthenica* (Kyiv), 1 (2002): 152–63.

Jedlicki, Jerzy. 'Historical Memory as a Source of Conflicts in Eastern Europe.' *Communist and Post-Communist Studies* 32, no. 3 (September 1999): 225–32.

Kabuzan, V.M. *Zaselenie Novorosii (Ekaterinoslavskoi i Khersonskoi gubernii) v 18 – pervoi polovine 19 veka (1719–1859)*. Moscow, 1976.

Kaplan, Robert D. *Balkan Ghosts: A Journey through History*. New York, 1993.

Kappeler, Andreas. 'From an Ethnonational to a Multiethnic to a Transnational Ukrainian History.' In *A Laboratory of Transnational History: Ukrainian History and Historiography since 1991* (forthcoming).

– *'Great Russians' and 'Little Russians': Russian-Ukrainian Relations and Perceptions in Historical Perspective*. The Donald W. Treadgold Papers in Russian, East European and Central Asian Studies, no. 39. Seattle, WA, 2003.

– *The Russian Empire: A Multiethnic History*. Harlow, 2001.

Karpenko, H. 'Mistse M.M. Pokrovs'koho v istoriohrafiï.' *Chervonyi shliakh*, 1928, no. 12: 167–79.

Karpov, Gennadii. *Gospodin Kostomarov kak istorik Malorossii*. Moscow, 1871.

Kasianov, Georgii. 'Rewriting and Rethinking: Contemporary Historiography and Nation Building in Ukraine.' In *Dilemmas of State-Led Nation Building in Ukraine*, ed. Taras Kuzio and Paul D'Anieri, 29–46. Westport, CT, 2002.

Keenan, Edward L. *Josef Dobrovský and the Origins of the* Igor' Tale. Cambridge, MA, 2003.

– 'Muscovite Perceptions of Other East Slavs before 1654 – An Agenda for Historians.' In *Ukraine and Russia in Their Historical Encounter*, 20–38.

Kersten, Adam. *Stefan Czarniecki, 1599–1665*. Warsaw, 1965.

Kharlampovich, Konstantin. *Malorossiiskoe vliianie na velikorusskuiu tserkovnuiu zhizn'*. Kazan, 1914.

Khlevov, A.A. *Normanskaia problema v otechestvennoi istoricheskoi nauke*. St Petersburg, 1997.

Kistiakovs'kyi, Oleksandr. *Shchodennyk*. 2 vols. Kyiv, 1994–5.

Kliuchevskii, V.O. *Sochineniia*. Vol. 1. Moscow, 1956.

Kohn, Hans. *The Idea of Nationalism: A Study of Its Origins and Background*. New York, 1944.

Kohut, Zenon E. 'Facing Ukraine's Russian Legacy: Politics and History in the Late Kuchma Era.' *The Harriman Review* 15, nos 2–3 (May 2005): 20–4.

– 'History as a Battleground: Russian-Ukrainian Relations and Historical Consciousness in Contemporary Ukraine.' In *The Legacy of History in Russia and the New States of Eurasia*, ed. Frederick S. Starr, 123–46. Armonk, NY, 1994.

– 'In Search of Perpetual Rights and Liberties: The Pereiaslav Agreement (1654) and the Construction of an Ideal Image of Cossack Ukraine (1650–1800s).' In *Festschrift for Iaroslav Isaievych* (forthcoming).

– *Russian Centralism and Ukrainian Autonomy: Imperial Absorption of the Hetmanate, 1760s–1830s*. Cambridge, MA, 1988.

– 'Ukraine: From Autonomy to Integration (1654–1830s).' In *Conquest and Coalescence: The Shaping of the State in Early Modern Europe*, ed. Mark Greengrass, 182–96. London, 1991.

– 'Vidchytuvannia Het'manshchyny: Derzhavotvorchi derzhavoshukannia.' *Krytyka*, 2000, no. 6.

Komov, V. 'Rubel' Vasyl' Dmytrovych.' In Vasyl Rubel', *Narysy z istoriï sela Mala Bilozerka*. Zaporizhia, 2003.

Koninckx, Christian. 'Historiography and Nationalism in Belgium.' In *Conceptions of National History: Proceedings of Nobel Symposium 78*, ed. Erik Lönnroth, Karl Molin, and Ragnar Björk, 34–86. Berlin and New York, 1994.

Kostomarov, Nikolai. *Bogdan Khmel'nitskii*. 5th ed. St Petersburg, 1904.

Kotkin, Stephen. *Magnetic Mountain: Stalinism as a Civilization*. Berkeley, Los Angeles, and London, 1995.

Kovba, Zhanna. *Liudianist' u bezodni pekla: povedinka mistsevoho naselennia Skhidnoï Halychyny v roky 'ostatochnoho rozv'iazannia ievreis'koho pytannia.'* Kyiv, 2000.

Kozik, Jan. *The Ukrainian National Movement in Galicia, 1819–1849*. Ed. Lawrence D. Orton. Edmonton, 1986.

Kravchenko, Volodymyr. 'Istoriia Rusiv u suchasnykh interpretatsiiakh.' In *Synopsis: Essays in Honor of Zenon E. Kohut*, ed. Serhii Plokhy and Frank E. Sysyn, 275–94. Edmonton, 2005.

– 'Kontseptsiï Pereiaslava v ukraïns'kii istoriohrafiï.' In *Pereiaslavs'ka rada*, 463–522.

– *Narysy z ukraïns'koï istoriohrafiï epokhy natsional'noho vidrodzhennia (druha polovyna XVIII – seredyna XIX st.)*. Kharkiv, 1996.

Krupnyckyj, Borys. *Hetman Mazepa und seine Zeit (1687–1709)*. Leipzig, 1942.

Krupnyts'kyi, Borys. *Het'man Danylo Apostol i ioho doba*. Augsburg, 1948.

Kryp'iakevych, Ivan. *Bohdan Khmel'nyts'kyi*. Kyiv, 1954.

Kulyk, Volodymyr. 'The Role of Discourse in the Construction of an Émigré Community: Ukrainian Displaced Persons in Germany and Austria after World War II.' In *European Encounters: Migrants, Migration and European Societies since 1945*, ed. Reiner Ohliger, Karen Schönwälder, and Phil Triadafilopoulos, 211–35. Aldershot, UK, 2002.

Kumke, Carsten. *Führer und Geführte bei den Zaporoger Kosaken: Struktur und Geschichte kosakischer Verbände im polnisch-litauischen Grenzland (1550–1648)*. Berlin, 1993.

Kuromiya, Hiroaki. *Freedom and Terror in the Donbass: A Ukrainian-Russian Borderland, 1870s–1990s*. Cambridge, 2003.

Kuzio, Taras. 'Historiography and National Identity among the Eastern Slavs: Towards a New Framework.' *National Identities* 3, no. 2 (July 2001): 109–32.

– 'Post-Soviet Ukrainian Historiography and School Textbooks in Ukraine.' *Internationale Schulbuchforschung* 23, no. 1 (January 2001): 27–42.

– *Ukraine: State and Nation Building*. London and New York, 1998.

– 'Ukraine's "Pereiaslav Complex" and Relations with Russia.' *RFE/RL Poland, Belarus and Ukraine Report* 4, no. 18 (7 May 2002); repr. in *Ukrainian Weekly* 50, no. 26 (26 May 2002).

Kuz'min, Evgenii. 'Ukrainskaia zhivopis' XVII veka.' In Igor' Grabar', *Istoriia russkago iskusstva*. Vol. 6 (=*Istoriia zhivopisi*. Vol. 1, *Dopetrovskaia ėpokha*), 455–80. Moscow, 1914.

Lagovskii, A. *Oborona Sevastopolia. Krymskaia voina 1854–1855 gg*. Moscow, 1939.

Lashchenko, Rostyslav. 'Pereiaslavs'kyi dohovir 1654 r. mizh Ukraïnoiu i tsarem moskovs'kym.' (1923). In *Pereiaslavs'ka rada*, 67–90.

Łaszkiewicz, Hubert. 'A Quest for Identity: East-Central Europe and Its Historians.' In *East-Central Europe's Position within Europe: Between East and West*, ed. Jerzy Kłoczowski, 60–74. Lublin, 2004.

LeDonne, John P. *The Russian Empire and the World, 1700–1917: The Geopolitics of Expansion and Containment*. New York and Oxford, 1997.

Leitsch, Walter. 'East Europeans Studying History in Vienna (1855–1918).' In *Historians as Nation-Builders: Central and South-East Europe*, ed. Dennis Deletant, Harry Hanak, and Hugh Seton-Watson, 139–56. London, 1988.

Lep'iavko, Serhii. *Kozats'ki viiny kintsia XVI st. v Ukraïni*. Chernihiv, 1996.

– *Ukraïns'ke kozatstvo v mizhnarodnykh vidnosynakh (1561–1591)*. Chernihiv, 1999.

Levin, Iurii. *Ossian v russkoi literature: konets XVIII-pervaia tret' XIX veka*. Leningrad, 1980.

Liapunov, B.M. 'Edinstvo russkogo iazyka v ego narechiiakh.' (1919). In *Ukrainskii separatizm v Rossii*, 385–98.

Lieven, Dominic. *Empire: The Russian Empire and Its Rivals*. New Haven and London, 2001.

Lindner, Rainer. *Historiker und Herrschaft: Nationsbildung und Geschichtspolitik in Weißrussland im 19. und 20. Jahrhundert*. Munich, 1999.

– *Historyki i ŭlada. Natsyiatvorchy ptratsės i histarychnaia palityka ŭ Belarusi XIX–XX st*. Minsk, 2003.

Linnichenko, Ivan. 'Malorusskaia kul'tura.' (1919). In *Ukrainskii separatizm v Rossii*, 315–29.

– *Malorusskii vopros i avtonomiia Malorossii. Otkrytoe pis'mo professoru M.S. Grushevskomu*. Petrograd and Odesa, 1917. Repr. in *Ukrainskii separatizm v Rossii*, 253–79.

Litwin, Henryk. 'Catholicization among the Ruthenian Nobility and Assimilation Processes in the Ukraine during the Years 1569–1648.' *Acta Poloniae Historica* 55 (1987): 57–83.

Lohvyn, Hryhorii. *Po Ukraïni. Starodavni mystets'ki pam'iatky*. Kyiv, 1968.

Lomonosov, Mikhail. *Drevniaia Rossiiskaia istoriia ot nachala rossiiskogo naroda*. St Petersburg, 1766.

Longworth, Philip. *The Cossacks*. New York, 1970.

– 'Ukraine: History and Nationality.' *Slavonic and East European Review* 78, no. 1 (January 2000): 115–24.

Łowmiański, Henryk. *Studia nad dziejami Wielkiego Księstwa Litewskiego*. Poznań, 1983.

Lutsenko, Yuri. Introduction to Hryhorij Hrabjanka, *Hryhorij Hrabjanka's 'The Great War of Bohdan Xmel'nyc'kyj.'* Cambridge, MA, 1990.

Lyman, Ihor. *Tserkovnyi ustrii Zaporoz'kykh Vol'nostei (1734–1775)*. Zaporizhia, 1998.

Lypyns'kyi, Viacheslav. *Ukraïna na perelomi*. (1920). Excerpts in *Pereiaslavs'ka rada*, 55–66.

M.H. 'Die Ukraine, Glanz and Niedergang (M. Hrushevs'kyj, *Geschichte der Ukraine*).' *Prager Presse* 11, no. 99, 11 April 1931.

Mace, James E. *Communism and the Dilemmas of National Liberation: National Communism in Soviet Ukraine, 1918–1933*. Cambridge, MA, 1983.

Madariaga, Isabel de. *Russia in the Age of Catherine the Great*. New Haven, CT, 1981.

Magocsi, Paul Robert. *A History of Ukraine*. Toronto, 1996.

Markevich, Nikolai. *Istoriia Malorossii*. 5 vols. Moscow, 1842–3.

Markov, P.G. *A. Ia. Efimenko – istorik Ukrainy*. Kyiv, 1966.

Martin, Terry. *The Affirmative Action Empire: Nations and Nationalism in the Soviet Union, 1923–1939*. Ithaca, NY, and London, 2001.

Marx, Anthony W. *Faith in Nation: Exclusionary Origins of Nationalism*. New York, 2003.

Materialy dlia istorii Krymskoi voiny i oborony Sevastopolia. Ed. N. Dubrovin. 5 vols. St Petersburg, 1871–5.

Matsuzato, Kimitaka. Preface to *Emerging Meso-Areas in the Former Socialist Countries*, 7–18.

Mazepa e il suo tempo. Storia, cultura, società / Mazepa and His Time: History, Culture, Society. Ed. Giovanna Siedina. Alessandria, 2004

McNeill, William H. *Europe's Steppe Frontier, 1500–1800*. Chicago, 1964.

Mediaevalia Ucrainica: Mental'nist' ta istoriia idei. 5 vols. Kyiv, 1992–8.

Mendelson, Sarah E., and Theodore P. Gerber. 'Failing the Stalin Test.' *Foreign Affairs* 85, no. 1 (January-February 2006): 2–8.

Miakotin, Veniamin. *Ocherki sotsial'noi istorii Ukrainy v XVII–XVIII vv.* Vol. 1, vyp. 1. Prague, 1926.

Mikhnovs'kyi, Mykola. 'Samostiina Ukraina.' Repr. in *Politolohiia. Kinets' XIX – persha polovyna XX st. Khrestomatiia*, ed. O.I. Semkiv, 126–35. Lviv, 1996.

Miller, A.I. *'Ukrainskii vopros' v politike vlastei i russkom obshchestvennom mnenii (vtoraia polovina XIX v.)*. St Petersburg, 2000. English translation: *The Ukrainian Question: The Russian Empire and Nationalism in the Nineteenth Century*. Budapest and New York, 2003.

Miller, D. 'Ocherki iz istorii i iuridicheskogo byta staroi Malorossii. Prevrashchenie kazatskoi starshiny v dvorianstvo.' *Kievskaia starina*, 1897, no. 1: 1–31; no. 2: 188–200; no. 3: 351–74; no. 4: 1–47.

Milner-Gulland, Robin. *The Russians*. Oxford, 1997.

Mininkov, N.A. 'Donskie atamany vtoroi poloviny XVII veka: smena pokolenii i politicheskikh orientirov.' In *Die Geschichte Rußlands im 16. und 17. Jahrhundert*, 375–81.

– *Donskoe kazachestvo na zare svoei istorii.* Rostov-na-Donu, 1992.
– *Donskoe kazachestvo v ėpokhu pozdnego srednevekov'ia (do 1671 g.).* Rostov-na-Donu, 1998.
Misiunas, Romuald J., and Rein Taagepera. *The Baltic States: Years of Dependence, 1940–1990.* Berkeley, 1990.
Motyl, Alexander J. *Dilemmas of Independence: Ukraine after Totalitarianism.* New York, 1993.
Mykhailo Hrushevs'kyi: Mizh istoriieiu ta politykoiu (1920–1930–ti roky): Zbirnyk dokumentiv i materialiv. Ed. P.S. Sokhan'. Kyiv, 1997.
Mytsyk, Iurii. 'Natsional'no-vyzvol'na viina ukraïns'koho narodu 1648–1658 rr. (Pidsumky, problemy i perspektyvy doslidzhennia).' In *Bytva pid Korsunem i natsional'no-vyzvol'na viina seredyny XVII stolittia,* 27–59. Korsun'-Shevchenkivs'kyi, 1998.
Mytsyk, Iu., I. Storozhenko, S. Plokhii, and A. Koval'ov. *Tiï slavy kozats'koï povik ne zabudem.* Dnipropetrovsk, 1989.
Nagel's'kyi, Myroslav. 'Pereiaslavs'ka uhoda 1654 roku v pol's'kii istoriohrafiï.' In *Pereiaslavs'ka rada,* 653–79.
Nakazy malorossiiskim deputatam 1767 goda i akty o vyborakh deputatov v Komissiiu sochineniia ulozheniia. Kyiv, 1889.
Narizhnyi, Semen. Review of Mykhailo Hrushevs'kyi, *Istoriia Ukraïny-Rusy,* vol. 9. *Literaturno-naukovyi vistnyk* 30, vol. 151 (1931): 1027–9.
Narochnitskaia, L.I. *Rossiia i otmena neitralizatsii Chernogo moria, 1856–1871.* Moscow, 1989.
Narys istoriï Ukraïny. Ed. Kost' Huslystyi, Lazar Slavin, and Fedir Iastrebov. Ufa, 1942; Toronto, 1944.
Narysy z istoriï ukraïns'koho mystetstva. Kyiv, 1966.
Natsional'no-vyzvol'na viina ukraïns'koho narodu seredyny XVII stolittia: polityka, ideolohiia, viis'kove mystetstvo. Ed. Valerii Smolii et al. Kyiv, 1998.
Naukovyi zbirnyk, prysviachenyi profesorovi Mykhailovi Hrushevs'komu uchenykamy i prykhyl'nykamy z nahody ioho desiatylitn'oï naukovoï pratsi v Halychyni (1894–1904). Lviv, 1906.
Nikitin, E.N. 'Pis'mo istorika M.S. Grushevskogo V.M. Molotovu.' *Otechestvennye arkhivy,* 1998, no. 3: 94–8.
Nol'de, Boris. *Ocherki russkogo gosudarstvennogo prava.* St Petersburg, 1911.
Novikov, N.V. *Admiral Nakhimov.* Moscow, 1944.
Ohloblyn, Oleksander. *Het'man Ivan Mazepa i ioho doba.* New York, 1960.
– Introduction to *Istoriia Rusiv.* New York, 1956.
– *Liudy staroï Ukraïny.* Munich, 1959.
– 'The Pereyaslav Treaty and Eastern Europe.' *Ukrainian Quarterly* 10, no. 1 (winter 1954): 41–50.

– 'Ukraïns'ko-moskovs'ka uhoda 1654.' 1954. In *Pereiaslavs'ka rada*, 156–220.

– 'Where Was *Istoriya Rusov* Written?' *Annals of the Ukrainian Academy of Arts and Sciences in the U.S.* 3, no. 2 (1953): 670–95.

Okinshevich, Leo. *Ukrainian Society and Government, 1648–1781*. Munich, 1978.

Okinshevych, Lev. 'Natsional'no-demokratychna kontseptsiia istoriï prava Ukraïny v pratsiakh akad. M. Hrushevs'koho.' *Ukraïna*, 1932, nos 1–2: 93–109.

Opisanie oborony goroda Sevastopolia. Ed. E. Totleben. 2 vols. St Petersburg, 1871.

O'Rourke, Shane. *Warriors and Peasants: The Don Cossacks in Late Imperial Russia*. Basingstoke, 2000.

P.S. Nakhimov. Dokumenty i materialy. Moscow, 1954.

Pereiaslavs'ka rada 1654 roku (istoriohrafiia ta doslidzhennia). Ed. P.S. Sokhan' et al. Kyiv, 2003.

Peshtich, S.L. *Russkaia istoriografiia XVIII veka.* 3 pts. Leningrad, 1961–71.

Petrovsky-Shtern, Yohanan. 'In Search of a Lost People: Jews in Present-Day Ukrainian Historiography,' *East European Jewish Affairs* 33, no. 1 (2003): 67–82.

– 'Jews in Ukrainian Thought: Between the 1940s and the 1990s,' *Ukrainian Quarterly* 60, nos 3–4 (2004): 231–70.

Pipes, Richard. 'Weight of the Past: Russian Foreign Policy in Historical Perspective,' *Harvard International Review* 19, no. 1 (winter 1996–7): 4–12.

Pirogov, N.I. *Sevastopol'skie pisma i vospominaniia*. Moscow and Leningrad, 1950.

Plokhy, Serhii [Plokhii, Serhii]. *The Cossacks and Religion in Early Modern Ukraine*. Oxford, 2001.

– *The Origins of the Slavic Nations: Premodern Identities in Russia, Ukraine and Belarus*. Cambridge, 2006.

– 'Revisiting the Golden Age: Mykhailo Hrushevsky and the Early History of the Ukrainian Cossacks.' In Mykhailo Hrushevsky, *The Cossack Age to 1625*. Vol. 7 of *History of Ukraine-Rus'*, xxvii–lii. Edmonton and Toronto, 1999.

– 'The Symbol of Little Russia: The Pokrova Icon and Early Modern Ukrainian Political Ideology.' *Journal of Ukrainian Studies* 17, nos 1–2 (summer-winter 1992): 171–88.

– *Tsars and Cossacks: A Study in Iconography.* Cambridge, MA, 2002.

– 'The Two Russias of Teofan Prokopovyč.' In *Mazepa e il suo tempo*, 334–66.

– *Unmaking Imperial Russia: Mykhailo Hrushevsky and the Writing of Ukrainian History.* Toronto, 2005.

– 'Zhyttieva misiia Mykoly Koval's'koho.' *Dzerkalo tyzhnia* (Kyiv) 43 (622) (11–17 November 2006).

Pogosian, Elena. 'I.S. Mazepa v russkoi ofitsial'noi kul'ture 1708–1725 gg.' In *Mazepa e il suo tempo*, 315–32.

– *Petr I – arkhitektor rossiiskoi istorii.* St Petersburg, 2001.

– 'Rus' i Rossiia v istoricheskikh sochineniiakh 1730–80–kh godov.' In *Rossiia/ Russia. Kul'turnye praktiki v ideologicheskoi perspektive. Rossiia XVIII – nachalo XX veka*, comp. N.N. Mazur. Vol. 3 (11): 7–19. Moscow and Venice, 1999.

Pokrovskii, Mikhail. *Izbrannye proizvedeniia.* 4 vols. Moscow, 1965–7.

– *Russkaia istoriia v samom szhatom ocherke.* Moscow, 1920. Repr. of 10th ed. (1931) in idem, *Izbrannye proizvedeniia.* Vol. 3. Moscow, 1967.

Pokrovskii, Mikhail, with the assistance of N.M. Nikol'skii and V.N. Storozhev. *Russkaia istoriia s drevneishikh vremen.* 5 vols. Moscow, 1910–13. Repr. in idem, *Izbrannye proizvedeniia.* Vols 1–2. Moscow, 1965–6.

Polikarpov, V.D. *Pavel Stepanovich Nakhimov.* Moscow, 1950.

Polons'ka-Vasylenko, Natalia. *The Settlement of Southern Ukraine (1750–1775).* New York, 1955 [a special issue of *Annals of the Ukrainian Academy of Arts and Sciences in the U.S.*, no. 4 (1955)].

Potichnyj, Peter J. 'The Referendum and Presidential Elections in Ukraine.' *Canadian Slavonic Papers* 32, no. 2 (June 1991): 122–38.

Prescott, J.R.V. *The Geography of Frontiers and Boundaries.* Chicago, 1965.

Pritsak, Omeljan, and John S. Reshetar, Jr. 'The Ukraine and the Dialectics of Nation-Building.' *Slavic Review* 22 (1963): 224–55.

Prymak, Thomas. *Mykhailo Hrushevsky: The Politics of National Culture.* Toronto, 1987.

– *Mykola Kostomarov: A Biography.* Toronto, 1996.

Radians'ka entsyklopediia istorii Ukraïny. 4 vols. Kyiv, 1969–72.

Raeff, Marc. 'Ukraine and Imperial Russia: Intellectual and Political Encounters from the Seventeenth to the Nineteenth Century.' In *Ukraine and Russia*, 69–85.

Rawita-Gawroński, Franciszek. *Kozaczyzna ukrainna w Rzeczypospolitej Polskiej do końca XVIII wieku.* Warsaw, 1922.

Redlich, Shimon. *Together and Apart in Berezhany: Poles, Jews, and Ukrainians, 1919–1945.* Bloomington, IN, 2002.

Reid, Anna. *Borderland: A Journey through the History of Ukraine.* Boulder, CO, 1997.

Renan, Ernest. 'What is a Nation?' In *Nationalism in Europe from 1815 to the Present: A Reader*, 48–60. London and New York, 1996.

Reyfman, Irina. *Vasilii Trediakovsky: The Fool of the New Russian Literature.* Stanford, 1991.

Riasanovsky, Nicholas V. *A History of Russia.* 6th ed. New York and Oxford, 2000.

– *The Image of Peter the Great in Russian History and Thought.* New York, 1985.

– *Nicholas I and Official Nationality in Russia, 1825–1855.* Berkeley and Los Angeles, 1969.

Rigel'man, Oleksandr. *Litopysna opovid' pro Malu Rosiiu ta ïï narod i kozakiv uzahali.* Reprint of the 1847 ed. of *Letopisnoe povestvovanie o Maloi Rossii.* Kyiv, 1994.

Rogger, Hans. *National Consciousness in Eighteenth-Century Russia.* Cambridge, MA, 1960.

Rosenberg, Tina. *The Haunted Land: Facing Europe's Ghosts after Communism.* New York, 1996.

Rozenfel'd, I. *Prisoedinenie Malorossii k Rossii (1654–1793).* St Petersburg, 1915.

Rozhkov, N.A. *Obzor russkoi istorii s sotsiologicheskoi tochki zreniia.* 2 vyps. Moscow, 1905.

Ruban, Vasilii. *Kratkaia letopis' Malyia Rossii s 1506 po 1776 god.* St Petersburg, 1777.

Rudnytsky, Ivan L. *Essays in Modern Ukrainian History.* Ed. Peter L. Rudnytsky. Edmonton, 1987.

– 'Pereiaslav: History and Myth.' Introduction to Basarab, *Pereiaslav 1654*, xi–xxiii.

– 'The Role of the Ukraine in Modern History.' *Slavic Review* 22 (1963): 199–216.

– 'A Study of Cossack History.' *Slavic Review* 31, no. 4 (December 1972): 870–5.

– 'Ukraine between East and West.' In his *Essays in Modern Ukrainian History*, 1–10.

– 'The Ukrainians in Galicia under Austrian Rule.' In his *Essays in Modern Ukrainian History*, 315–52.

– 'Volodymyr Vynnychenko's Ideas in the Light of his Political Writings.' In his *Essays in Modern Ukrainian History*, 417–36.

Russkaia i ukrainskaia diplomatiia v Evrazii: 50–e gody XVII veka. Ed. L.E. Semenova, B.N. Floria, and I. Shvarts. Moscow, 2000.

Samuilov, Sergei. 'O nekotorykh amerikanskikh stereotipakh v otnoshenii Ukrainy.' *SShA: ėkonomika, politika, ideologiia*, 1997, no. 3: 84–96; no. 4: 81–90.

Sanford, George. *Katyn and the Soviet Massacre of 1940: Truth, Justice and Memory.* London and New York, 2005.

Sanin, G.A. *Otnosheniia Rossii i Ukrainy s Krymskim khanstvom v seredine XVII veka.* Moscow, 1987.

Santsevych, Anatolii. *M.I. Iavors'kyi: Narys zhyttia ta tvorchosti.* Kyiv, 1995.

Sapozhnikov, D. 'Zagadochnye portrety.' *Kievskaia starina*, 1884, no. 9: 732–42.

Saunders, David. *The Ukrainian Impact on Russian Culture, 1750–1850.* Edmonton, 1985.

Savchenko, F. *Zaborona ukraïnstva 1876 r.* Kharkiv and Kyiv, 1930. Repr. Munich, 1970.

Sbornik rukopisei, predstavlennykh E.I.V. gosudariu nasledniku tsesarevichu o Sevastopol'skoi oborone sevastopol'tsami. 3 vols. St Petersburg, 1872–3.

Schleifman, Nurit. 'Moscow's Victory Park: A Monumental Change.' *History and Memory* 13, no. 2 (2001): 5–34.

Seaton, Albert. *The Horsemen of the Steppes: The Story of the Cossacks*. London, 1985.

Sen', D.V. *'Voisko Kubanskoe Ignatovo Kavkazskoe': Istoricheskie puti kazakov-nekrasovtsev (1708 g. – konets 1920–kh gg.)* Krasnodar, 2001.

Serczyk, Władysław. *Na dalekiej Ukrainie. Dzieje Kozaczyzny do 1648 r.* Cracow, 1984.

– *Na płonącej Ukrainie. Dzieje Kozaczyzny, 1648–51*. Warsaw, 1998.

Ševčenko, Ihor. *Ukraine between East and West: Essays on Cultural History to the Early Eighteenth Century.* Edmonton and Toronto, 1996.

Shanskii, D.N. 'Chto dolzhno istoriku: Mikhail Mikhailovich Shcherbatov i Ivan Nikitich Boltin.' In *Istoriki Rossii XVIII – nachalo XX veka,* ed. A.N. Sakharov, 39–60. Moscow, 1996.

– *Iz istorii russkoi istoricheskoi mysli. I.N. Boltin*. Moscow, 1983.

– 'Zapal'chivaia polemika: Gerard Fridrikh Miller, Gotlib Zigfrid Baier i Mikhail Vasil'evich Lomonosov.' In *Istoriki Rossii. XVIII – nachalo XX veka,* ed. A.N. Sakharov, 28–38. Moscow, 1996.

Shcherbak, Vitalii. *Formuvannia kozats'koho stanu v Ukraïni (druha polovyna XVI – seredyna XVII st.)* Kyiv, 1997.

Shelukhyn, Serhii. *Ukraïna – nazva nashoï zemli z naidavnishykh chasiv.* Prague, 1936. Repr. Drohobych, 1992.

Shevchenkivs'kyi slovnyk. 2 vols. Kyiv, 1977.

Shevchenko, Taras. *Bliznetsy.* In idem, *Povne zibrannia tvoriv,* vol. 4, 7–138. Kyiv, 1964.

[Shevchenko, Taras]. *The Poetical Works of Taras Shevchenko: The Kobzar.* Trans. C.H. Andrusyshen and Watson Kirkconnell. Toronto, 1977.

Shevel'ov, Iurii (George Y. Shevelov). *Ia – mene – meni … (i dovkruhy). Spohady.* 2 vols. Kharkiv and New York, 2001.

– '*Istoriia Rusov* ochyma movoznavtsia.' In *Zbirnyk na poshanu prof. d-ra Oleksandra Ohloblyna*, ed. Vasyl' Omel'chenko, 465–82. New York, 1977.

Shums'kyi, Oleksander. 'Stara i nova Ukraïna.' *Chervonyi shliakh*, 1923, no. 2: 91–129.

Shyian, Roman. *Kozatstvo Pivdennoï Ukraïny ostann'oï chverti XVII st.* Zaporizhia, 1998.

Sichyns'kyi, Volodymyr. *Ivan Mazepa. Liudyna i metsenat*. Philadelphia, 1951.

Skovoroda, Hryhorii. *Tvory u dvokh tomakh*. 2 vols. Kyiv, 1994.

Slava ukraïns'koho kozatstva. Melbourne and Kyiv, 1999.

Smith, Anthony D. 'Culture, Community and Territory: The Politics of Ethnicity and Nationalism.' *International Affairs* 72, no. 3 (July 1996): 445–58.

– *The Ethnic Origins of Nations*. Oxford, 1986.

– *The Ethnic Revival*. Cambridge, 1981.

Smolii, Valerii. 'Het'man Bohdan Khmel'nyts'kyi i ioho doba.' In *Doba Bohdana Khmel'nyts'koho (Do 400–richchia vid dnia narodzhennia velykoho het'mana): zbirnyk naukovykh prats'*, ed. Valerii Smolii, 7–25. Kyiv, 1995.

– 'Natsional'no-vyzvol'na viina v konteksti ukraïns'koho derzhavotvorennia.' In *Natsional'no-vyzvol'na viina ukraïns'koho narodu*, 9–25.

Smolii, Valerii, and Valerii Stepankov. *Bohdan Khmel'nyts'kyi. Sotsial'no-politychnyi portret*. Kyiv, 1995.

– *Ukraïns'ka derzhavna ideia: problemy formuvannia, evoliutsiï, realizatsiï*. Kyiv, 1997.

– *Ukraïns'ka natsional'na revoliutsiia XVII st. (1648–1676)*. Kyiv, 1999.

Smolin, Mikhail. 'Ukrainskii tuman dolzhen rasseiat'sia, i russkoe solntse vzoidet.' In *Ukrainskii separatizm v Rossii*, 5–22.

Snyder, Timothy. *The Reconstruction of Nations: Poland, Ukraine, Lithuania, Belarus, 1569–1999*. New Haven and London, 2003.

Sokolov, O.D. 'Razvitie istoricheskikh vzgliadov M.N. Pokrovskogo.' In Pokrovskii, *Izbrannye proizvedeniia*, 1:5–71.

Solchanyk, Roman. 'Politics and the National Question in the Post-Shelest Period.' In *Ukraine after Shelest*, ed. Bohdan Krawchenko, 1–29. Edmonton, 1983.

– 'Ukraine and Russia: The Politics of Independence.' *Radio Free Europe Daily Reports*, 14 May 1992.

Solzhenitsyn, Aleksandr. 'Appeal on the December 1991 Referendum.' *Christian Democracy*, 1992, no. 17:9–10.

– 'Kak nam obustroit' Rossiiu?' *Literaturnaia gazeta*, 18 September 1990.

– *'The Russian Question' at the End of the Twentieth Century*. New York, 1995.

Sovetskaia istoriografiia. Ed. Iurii Afanas'ev. Moscow, 1996.

Stanislavskii, A.L. *Grazhdanskaia voina v Rossii XVII veka: kazachestvo na perelome istorii*. Moscow, 1990.

Stefan Czarniecki: żołnierz, obywatel, polityk. Ed. J. Kapec and N. Widok. Kielce, 1999.

Stepankov, V.S. 'Kam'ianets'ka uhoda i Pereiaslavs'ka rada: sproba doslidzhennia politychnykh naslidkiv Zhvanets'koï kampaniï.' In *Ukraïns'ko-rosiis'kyi dohovir 1654 r.: novi pidkhody do istoriï mizhderzhavnykh stosunkiv*, ed. Valerii Smolii, 6–13. Kyiv, 1995.

– '1648 rik: pochatok Ukraïns'koï revoliutsiï chy "domovoï viiny" v Rechi Pospolytii?' In *Ukraïna v Tsentral'no-Skhidnii Ievropi (z naidavnishykh chasiv do kintsia XVIII stolittia)*, vyp. 3, 369–414. Kyiv, 2003.

– 'Ukraïns'ka natsional'na revoliutsiia XVII st.: prychyny, typolohiia, khronolohichni mezhi (dyskusiini notatky).' In *Natsional'no-vyzvol'na viina ukraïns'koho narodu*, 26–45.

Stepovyk, Dmytro. *Istoriia ukraïns'koï ikony X-XX stolit'*. Kyiv, 1996.

Stökl, Günther. *Die Entstehung des Kosakentums*. Munich, 1953.
Storozhenko, A.V. 'Malaia Rossiia ili Ukraina?' 1918. In *Ukrainskii separatizm v Rossii*, 280–90.
Storozhenko, Ivan. *Bohdan Khmel'nyts'kyi i voienne mystetstvo u vyzvol'nii viini ukraïns'koho narodu seredyny XVII stolittia*. Vol. 1. Dnipropetrovsk, 1996.
Subtelny, Orest. 'The Current State of Ukrainian Historiography.' *Journal of Ukrainian Studies* 18, nos 1–2 (summer-winter 1993): 33–54.
– *The Mazepists: Ukrainian Separatism in the Early Eighteenth Century*. Boulder, CO, 1981.
– *Ukraine: A History*. Toronto, 1988.
Subtelny, Orest, and Illia Vytanovych. 'Cossacks.' In *Encyclopedia of Ukraine*, 1:593–95. Toronto, 1984.
Sukhyno-Khomenko, Volodymyr. 'Na marksysts'komu istorychnomu fronti,' *Bil'shovyk Ukraïny*, nos 17–18 (September 1929): 42–55; no. 19 (15 October 1929): 40–56.
– *Odminy i bankrutstvo ukraïns'koho natsionalizmu. Istoryko-publitsystychni narysy*. Kharkiv, 1929.
Suny, Ronald Grigor. *The Revenge of the Past: Nationalism, Revolution and the Collapse of the Soviet Union*. Stanford, 1993.
Svatikov, S.G. *Rossiia i Don*. Belgrade, 1924.
Sysyn, Frank. 'Anhlomovna istoriohrafiia Pereiaslavs'koï uhody u XX storichchi.' In *Pereiaslavs'ka rada*, 680–97.
– *Between Poland and the Ukraine: The Dilemma of Adam Kysil, 1600–1653*. Cambridge, MA, 1985.
– 'The Changing Image of the Hetman.' *Jahrbücher für Geschichte Osteuropas* 46, no. 4 (1998): 531–45. Ukrainian version: 'Minlyvyi obraz het'mana.' *Krytyka* 2, no. 14 (14 December 1998): 4–8.
– 'Fatherland in Early Eighteenth-Century Political Thought.' In *Mazepa e il suo tempo*, 39–53.
– 'The Image of Russia and Russian-Ukrainian Relations in Ukrainian Historiography of the Late Seventeenth and Early Eighteenth Centuries.' In *Culture, Nation, and Identity: The Ukrainian-Russian Encounter, 1600–1945*, ed. Andreas Kappeler et al., 108–43. Edmonton and Toronto, 2003.
– 'Introduction to the *History of Ukraine-Rus'*.' In Mykhailo Hrushevsky, *History of Ukraine-Rus'*, vol. 1, *From Prehistory to the Eleventh Century*, xxi–xlii. Edmonton and Toronto, 1997.
– 'The Reemergence of the Ukrainian Nation and Cossack Mythology.' *Social Research* 58, no. 4 (winter 1991): 845–64.
– 'Regionalism and Political Thought in Seventeenth-Century Ukraine: The Nobility's Grievances at the Diet of 1641.' *Harvard Ukrainian Studies* 6, no. 2 (1982): 171–85.

– 'War der Chmel'nyćkyj-Aufstand eine Revolution? Eine Charakteristik der "grossen ukrainischen Revolte" und der Bildung des Kosakischen Het'man-staates.' *Jahrbücher für Geschichte Osteuropas* 43, no. 1 (1995): 1–18. Ukrainian version: 'Chy bulo povstannia Bohdana Khmel'nyts'koho revoliutsiieiu? Zauvahy do typolohiï Khmel'nychchyny.' In *Prosphonema: Istorychni ta filolohichni rozvidky, prysviacheni 60–richchiu akademika Iaroslava Isaievycha*, ed. Bohdan Iakymovych et al., 571–8. Lviv, 1998.

Szporluk, Roman. Introduction to M.N. Pokrovskii, *Russia in World History: Selected Essays*, ed. Roman Szporluk, trans. Roman Szporluk and Mary Ann Szporluk, 1–46. Ann Arbor, MI, 1970.

– 'Nation-Building in Ukraine: Problems and Prospects.' In *The Successor States to the USSR*, ed. J.W. Blaney, 173–83. Washington, DC, 1995.

– 'National History as a Political Battleground: The Case of Ukraine and Belorussia.' In *Russian Empire: Some Aspects of Tsarist and Soviet Colonial Practices*, ed. Michael S. Pap, 131–50. Cleveland, 1985.

– *Russia, Ukraine, and the Breakup of the Soviet Union*. Stanford, 2001.

Szporluk, Roman, and Andrzej Nowak. 'Czy Polska była imperium?' *Arcana* 55–6, nos 1–2 (2004): 24–37.

Tarle, E.V. *Gorod russkoi slavy. Sevastopol' v 1854–1855 gg*. Moscow, 1954.

– *Krymskaia voina* (=*Sochineniia*. Vol. 8). Moscow, 1959.

– *Nakhimov*. Moscow, 1948.

Tereshchenko, Rem. 'V chomu ïï vyna.' In *Vidrodzhena pam'iat'* (=*Reabilitovani istoriieiu. Dnipropetrovs'ka oblast'*, no. 1), 122–32. Dnipropetrovsk, 1999.

Tolochko, Aleksei. *'Istoriia Rossiiskaia' Vasiliia Tatishcheva: istochniki i izvestiia*. Moscow and Kyiv, 2005.

Tolochko, Oleksii. 'Kyievo-Rus'ka spadshchyna v istorychnii dumtsi Ukraïny pochatku XIX st.' In V.F. Verstiuk, V.M. Horobets', and O.P. Tolochko, *Ukraïna i Rosiia v istorychnii retrospektyvi*, vol. 1, *Ukraïns'ki proekty v Rosiis'kii imperiï*, 250–350. Kyiv, 2004.

Tolochko, Petro. *Vid Rusi do Ukraïny: vybrani naukovo-populiarni, krytychni ta publitsystychni pratsi*. Kyiv, 1997.

Tolstoy, Leo. *The Sevastopol Sketches*. New York, 1986.

Tolz, Vera. *Russia*. London and New York, 2001.

Torke, Hans-Joachim. 'The Unloved Alliance: Political Relations between Muscovy and Ukraine in the Seventeenth Century.' In *Ukraine and Russia*, 39–66.

Trevor-Roper, Hugh. 'The Invention of Tradition: The Highland Tradition in Scotland.' In *The Invention of Tradition*, ed. Eric Hobsbawm and Terence Ranger, 15–41. Cambridge, 1997.

Trubetzkoy, Nikolai. 'The Legacy of Genghis Khan: A Perspective on Russian History not from the West but from the East.' In idem, *The Legacy of Genghis*

Khan and Other Essays on Russian Identity, ed. Anatoly Liberman, 161–232. Ann Arbor, MI, 1991.

Tsarinnyi, A. (Storozhenko, A.V.) 'Ukrainskoe dvizhenie. Kratkii istoricheskii ocherk, preimushchestvenno po lichnym vospominaniiam.' In *Ukrainskii separatizm v Rossii*, 133–252.

Tsarynnyk, Marko. 'Zolochiv movchyt'.' *Krytyka*, 2005, no. 5.

Tysiacha rokiv ukraïns'koï suspil'no-politychnoï dumky. 9 vols. Ed. Taras Hunczak et al. Kyiv, 2001.

Ukraina i sosednie gosudarstva v XVII veke. Materialy mezhdunarodnoi konferentsii. Ed. Tat'iana Iakovleva. St Petersburg, 2004.

Ukraine and Russia in Their Historical Encounter. Ed. Peter J. Potichnyj et al. Edmonton, 1992.

The Ukrainian Icon. Text by Liudmila Miliayeva. Bournemouth and St Petersburg, 1996.

Ukraïns'ka literatura XVIII st. Poetychni tvory. Dramatychni tvory. Prozovi tvory. Kyiv, 1983.

Ukraïns'ke kozatstvo. Mala entsyklopediia. Kyiv and Zaporizhia, 2002.

Ukrainskii separatizm v Rossii. Ideologiia natsional'nogo raskola. Comp. M.B. Smolin. Moscow, 1998.

Umantsev, F.S. *Mystetstvo davn'oï Ukraïny. Istorychnyi narys.* Kyiv, 2002.

Universaly Ivana Mazepy, 1687–1709. Comp. Ivan Butych. Kyiv and Lviv, 2002.

Ure, John. *The Cossacks.* London, 1999.

Vasil'chikov, Aleksandr. *Semeistvo Razumovskikh.* Vol. 1. St Petersburg, 1880.

Vasylenko, Mykola. 'H.N. Teplov i ioho "Zapiska o neporiadkakh v Malorossii."' *Zapysky Ukraïns'koho naukovoho tovarystva v Kyievi* 9 (1912): 13–23.

Velichko, Samuil (Samiilo Velychko). *Letopis' sobytii v Iugo-Zapadnoi Rossii v XVII veke.* 4 vols. Kyiv, 1848–64.

Velychenko, Stephen. *National History as Cultural Process: A Survey of Interpretations of Ukraine's Past in Polish, Russian and Ukrainian Historical Writing from the Earliest Times to 1914.* Edmonton, 1992.

– 'Rival Grand Narratives of National History: Russian/Soviet, Polish and Ukrainian Accounts of Ukraine's Past (1772–1991).' *Österreichische Osthefte*, 2000, nos 3–4: 139–60.

– *Shaping Identity in Eastern Europe and Russia: Soviet-Russian and Polish Accounts of Ukrainian History, 1914–1991.* New York, 1993.

Velychko, Samiilo. *Litopys.* Trans. Valerii Shevchuk. 2 vols. Kyiv, 1991.

– *Samiila Velychka Skazaniie o voini kozatskoi z poliakamy.* Ed. Kateryna Lazarevs'ka. Kyiv, 1926.

Vernadskii, Vladimir. *Dnevniki, 1917–21.* Kyiv, 1994.

Verstiuk, Vladyslav. *Ukraïns'ka Tsentral'na Rada: navchal'nyi posibnyk.* Kyiv, 1997.

Vinogradov, Viktor. *Ocherki po istorii russkogo literaturnogo iazyka XVII–XIX vekov.* 3rd ed. Moscow, 1982.

Visnyk Soiuzu vyzvolennia Ukraïny 3, no. 67 (3 December 1916).

Vlasovs'kyi, Ivan. *Narys istoriï Ukraïns'koï pravoslavnoï tserkvy.* 4 vols. New York, 1955–66.

Voices of Revolution, 1917. Ed., with introduction and comments, by Mark D. Steinberg. New Haven and London, 2001.

Volkonskii, A.M. *Istoricheskaia pravda i ukrainofil'skaia propaganda*. Turin, 1920. Repr. in *Ukrainskii separatizm v Rossii*, 25–123.

Von Hagen, Mark. 'Does Ukraine Have a History?' *Slavic Review* 54, no. 3 (fall 1995): 658–73.

– 'Empires, Borderlands and Diasporas: Eurasia as Anti-Paradigm for the Post-Soviet Era.' *American Historical Review* 109, no. 2 (April 2004): 445–68.

– 'Povertaiuchysia do istorii Ukraïny,' *Krytyka* (Kyiv), 2007, no. 6:11–15.

– 'The Russian Imperial Army and the Ukrainian National Movement in 1917.' *Ukrainian Quarterly* 54, nos 3–4 (fall-winter 1998): 220–56.

Vozniak, Mykhailo. *Psevdo-Konys'kyi i psevdo-Poletyka ('Istoriia Rusov' u literaturi i nautsi)*. Lviv and Kyiv, 1938.

Vynar, Liubomyr (Lubomyr R. Wynar). *Mykhailo Hrushevs'kyi i Naukove Tovarystvo im. Tarasa Shevchenka, 1892–1930*. Munich, 1970.

– ed. *Mykhailo Hrushevs'kyi, 1866–1934: Bibliographic Sources*. New York, Munich, and Toronto, 1985.

Vynnychenko, Volodymyr. *Shchodennyk*. 2 vols. Edmonton, 1980–3.

– *Vidrodzhennia natsiï*. 3 vols. Vienna, 1920.

Walicki, Andrzej. *The Enlightenment and the Birth of Modern Nationhood: Polish Political Thought from Noble Republicanism to Tadeusz Kościuszko*. Trans. Emma Harris. Notre Dame, IN, 1989.

– *Poland between East and West: The Controversies over Self-Definition and Modernization in Partitioned Poland*. Harvard Papers in Ukrainian Studies. Cambridge, MA, 1994.

Wandycz, Piotr. *The Lands of Partitioned Poland, 1795–1918*. Vol. 7 of *A History of East Central Europe*. Seattle and London, 1974.

Wanner, Catherine. *Burden of Dreams: History and Identity in Post-Soviet Ukraine*. University Park, PA, 1998.

Weeks, Theodore E. *Nation and State in Late Imperial Russia: Nationalism and Russification on the Western Frontier, 1863–1914*. DeKalb, IL, 1996.

Weiner, Amir. *Making Sense of War: The Second World War and the Fate of the Bolshevik Revolution*. Princeton, 2002.

Wilson, Andrew. 'The Donbas between Ukraine and Russia: The Use of History in Political Disputes.' *Journal of Contemporary History* 30, no. 2 (April 1995): 265–89.

– *The Ukrainians: Unexpected Nation*. New Haven and London, 2000.

Witzenrath, Christoph. 'Die sibirischen Kosaken im institutionellen Wandel der Handels-Frontier.' In *Die Geschichte Rußlands im 16. und 17. Jahrhundert*, 395–415.

Wójcik, Zbigniew. *Dzikie Pola w ogniu. O Kozaczyźnie w dawnej Rzeczypospolitej*, 3rd ed. Warsaw, 1968.

Wortman, Richard S. *Scenarios of Power: Myth and Ceremony in Russian Monarchy*. Vol. 2, *From Alexander II to the Abdication of Nicholas II*. Princeton, 2000.

– *Scenarios of Power: Myth and Ceremony in Russian Monarchy from Peter the Great to the Abdication of Nicholas II*. Abridged ed. Princeton and Oxford, 2006.

Wynn, Charters. *Workers, Strikes and Pogroms: The Donbass-Dnepr Bend in Late Imperial Russia, 1870–1905*. Princeton, 1992.

Yakovliv, Andriy (Andrii Iakovliv). 'The Judicial Character of the Pereyaslav Treaty.' *Ukrainian Quarterly* 10, no. 1 (winter 1954): 51–60.

Yekelchyk, Serhy. 'Stalinist Patriotism as Imperial Discourse: Reconciling the Ukrainian and Russian "Heroic Pasts," 1939–45.' *Kritika: Explorations in Russian and Eurasian History* 3, no. 1 (winter 2002): 51–80.

– *Stalin's Empire of Memory: Russian-Ukrainian Relations in the Soviet Historical Imagination*. Toronto, 2004.

Zaborovskii, Lev. 'Bor'ba russkoi i pol'skoi diplomatii i pozitsiia Osmanskoi imperii v 1653–54 gg.' In *Osvoboditel'nye dvizheniia na Balkanakh*, ed. G.L. Arsh, 63–75. Moscow, 1978.

– 'Pereiaslavskaia rada i moskovskie soglasheniia 1654 goda: problemy issledovaniia.' In *Rossiia – Ukraina: istoriia vzaimootnoshenii*, ed. A.I. Miller, V.F. Reprintsev, and B.N. Floria, 39–49. Moscow, 1997.

– 'Poslednii shans umirotvoreniia: peregovory B.A. Repnina vo L'vove 1653 g.' In *Ukraïna v tsentral'no-skhidnii Ievropi. Studiï z istoriï XI–XVIII stolit'*, ed. Valerii Smolii, 238–44. Kyiv, 2000.

– *Rossiia, Rech Pospolitaia i Shvetsiia v seredine XV veka*. Moscow, 1981.

– 'Rossiisko-ukrainskaia konferentsiia, posviashchennaia 340–letiiu Pereiaslavskoi rady.' *Otechestvennaia istoriia*, 1996, no. 5: 217.

Zashkil'niak, Leonid. 'M. Hrushevs'kyi i Halychyna (Do pryïzdu do L'vova 1894 r.).' In *Mykhailo Hrushevs'kyi i l'vivs'ka istorychna shkola*, ed. Iroslav Hrytsak and Iaroslav Dashkevych, 114–37. New York and Lviv, 1995.

Zelnik, Reginald E. 'Russian Bebels: An Introduction to the Memoirs of the Russian Workers Semen Kanatchikov and Matvei Fisher.' *Russian Review* 35 (July 1976): 249–89; (October 1976): 417–47.

Zholtovs'kyi, Pavlo. *Ukraïns'kyi zhyvopys XVII-XVIII st*. Kyiv, 1978.

– *Vyzvol'na viina ukraïns'koho narodu v pam'iatkakh mystetstva XVI–XVIII st*. Kyiv, 1958.

Zhurba, Oleh. *Stanovlennia ukraïns'koï arkheohrafiï: liudy, ideï, instytutsiï*. Dnipropetrovsk, 2003.

Zorin, Andrei. *Kormia dvuglavogo orla ... Literatura i gosudarstvennaia ideologiia v Rossii v poslednei treti XVIII – pervoi treti XIX veka*. Moscow, 2001.

Zubkova, Elena, and Aleksandr Kupriianov, 'Vozvrashchenie k 'russkoi idee': krizis identichnosti i natsional'naia istoriia.' In *Natsional'naia istoriia v sovetskom i postsovetskikh gosudarstvakh*, ed. S.V. Kuleshov et al., 299–328. Moscow, 1999.

Zuev, A.S. *Russkoe kazachestvo Zabaikal'ia vo vtoroi chetverti XVIII – pervoi polovine XIX vv.* Novosibirsk, 1994.

Index